Latter-day Saint
Perspectives on
Atonement

Latter-day Saint Perspectives on Atonement

Edited by
DEIDRE NICOLE GREEN
AND ERIC D. HUNTSMAN

Urbana, Chicago, and Springfield

© 2024 by the Board of Trustees
of the University of Illinois
All rights reserved
1 2 3 4 5 C P 5 4 3 2 1
♾ This book is printed on acid-free paper.

Library of Congress Cataloging-in-Publication Data
Names: Green, Deidre Nicole, 1981– editor. | Huntsman,
  Eric D., 1965– editor.
Title: Latter-day Saint perspectives on atonement / edited by
  Deidre Nicole Green and Eric D. Huntsman.
Description: Urbana : University of Illinois Press, [2024] |
  Includes bibliographical references and index.
Identifiers: LCCN 2023029694 (print) | LCCN
  2023029695 (ebook) | ISBN 9780252045448
  (hardback) | ISBN 9780252087554 (paperback) | ISBN
  9780252055058 (ebook)
Subjects: LCSH: Church of Jesus Christ of Latter-day
  Saints—Doctrines. | Atonement—Church of Jesus Christ
  of Latter-day Saints.
Classification: LCC BX8643.A85 L38 2024 (print) |
  LCC BX8643.A85 (ebook) | DDC 230/.9332—dc23/
  eng/20230712
LC record available at https://lccn.loc.gov/2023029694
LC ebook record available at https://lccn.loc.gov/2023029695

Contents

Acknowledgments   vii

Abbreviations   ix

Introduction: Atonement in Latter-day Saint Scripture and Thought   1

PART I. SCRIPTURAL AND HISTORICAL FOUNDATIONS

1. Atonement in the Old Testament: Implications for Latter-day Saints   15
   T. BENJAMIN SPACKMAN

2. Latter-day Saints and the Atonement in the New Testament   31
   ERIC D. HUNTSMAN

3. "He Shall Find Satisfaction Through His Knowledge": Atonement in Early Christianity and the Middle Ages   68
   ARIEL BYBEE LAUGHTON

4. "Atonement" in the Book of Mormon   94
   NICHOLAS J. FREDERICK

5. Saving the House of Israel: Collective Atonement in the Book of Mormon   115
   SHARON J. HARRIS

6. "This Perfect Atonement": Agency, Law, Theosis, and Atonement Theology in the Doctrine and Covenants   131
   J.B. HAWS

7. "I have, to be sure, been called to drink deep of the bitter cup": Nineteenth-Century Latter-day Saint Women and Atonement   161
   JENNIFER REEDER

   PART II. THEOLOGICAL EXPLORATIONS

8. Notes on Life, Grace, and Atonement   179
   ADAM S. MILLER

9. Atonement and Retributive Justice   194
   FIONA GIVENS

10. Relational Atonement: Groundwork   213
    BENJAMIN KEOGH

11. One Prophet's Vision of a Nonviolent Atonement: The Book of Mormon as Theological Resource   235
    JOSEPH M. SPENCER

12. Enveloping Grace   251
    DEIDRE NICOLE GREEN

    Selected Bibliography   277

    Contributors   307

    General Index   311

    Scriptural Index   321

Acknowledgments

I am grateful to Brian Birch who years ago invited and encouraged me to edit a volume of essays on Latter-day Saint perspectives on atonement. It has been a long journey to bring this to fruition, and it never would have started without his vision. Thanks goes to him as well for introducing Eric Huntsman to me with the suggestion that we collaborate on this volume. It has been great to work with Eric, who is so knowledgeable and gracious, a rare enough combination. I am grateful to many friends and colleagues who have shaped my thinking about atonement and helped refine my reflections on this crucial topic.

—Deidre Nicole Green

I am thankful to Deidre Green for inviting me to join her on this project. She is a careful reader, a gifted writer, and a thoughtful theologian. This anthology would not have taken the form it has without her vision and guidance. As always, I am also grateful to my wife and family for their support. I would like to especially recognize my daughter, Rachel Olivia Huntsman-Petersen. Her questions, belief, and desire to better understand and live our faith have been great motivations to me.

—Eric D. Huntsman

We would both like to recognize the individual contributors to this collection for sharing their research and ideas with us and with our readers. We are especially indebted to the University of Illinois Press and its staff, especially acquisitions editor Alison Syring, for accepting this project and bringing it to publication. Finally, we thank the College of Religious Education at Brigham Young University, which supported this book with a generous subvention. Religious Education, together with the Neal A. Maxwell Institute for Religious Scholarship, further supported the book's indexing.

—DNG and EDH

Abbreviations

Biblical Books

Old Testament

Gen	Genesis
Exod	Exodus
Lev	Leviticus
Num	Numbers
Deut	Deuteronomy
Josh	Joshua
Judg	Judges
Ruth	Ruth
1–2 Sam	1–2 Samuel
1–2 Kgs	1–2 Kings
1–2 Chr	1–2 Chronicles
Ezra	Ezra
Neh	Nehemiah
Esth	Esther
Job	Job
Ps/Pss	Psalm/Psalms
Prov	Proverbs
Eccl	Ecclesiastes
Song	Song of Solomon
Isa	Isaiah
Jer	Jeremiah
Lam	Lamentations
Ezek	Ezekiel

New Testament

Matt	Matthew
Mark	Mark
Luke	Luke
John	John
Acts	Acts
Rom	Romans
1–2 Cor	1–2 Corinthians
Gal	Galatians
Eph	Ephesians
Phil	Philippians
Col	Colossians
1–2 Thess	1–2 Thessalonians
1–2 Tim	1–2 Timothy
Titus	Titus
Phlm	Philemon
Heb	Hebrews
Jas	James
1–2 Pet	1–2 Peter
1–2–3 John	1–2–3 John
Jude	Jude
Rev	Revelation

Old Testament (continued)

Dan	Daniel
Hos	Hosea
Joel	Joel
Amos	Amos
Obad	Obadiah
Jonah	Jonah
Mic	Micah
Nah	Nahum
Hab	Habakkuk
Zeph	Zephaniah
Hag	Haggai
Zech	Zechariah
Mal	Malachi

Early Christian and Medieval Sources

Abelard	Peter Abelard
Comm. Rom.	*Commentary on the Epistle to the Romans*
Anselm of Canterbury,	Anselm of Canterbury
Cur Deus Homo (*CDH*)	*Why God Became Man?*
Athanasius	Athanasius
c. Ar.	*Defense against the Arians*
Inc.	*On the Incarnation of the Word*
Augustine	Augustine of Hippo
Trin.	*On the Trinity*
Barn	*Epistle to Barnabas*
Gregory of Nyssa	Gregory of Nyssa
Or. Cat.	*Great Catechetical Oration*
Ign.	Ignatius of Antioch,
Magn.	*Letter to the Magnesians*
Smyrn.	*Letter to Smyrneans*
Irenaeus	Irenaeus
Haer.	*Against Heresies*
Justin	Justin Martyr
Dial.	*Dialogue with Trypho*
Tertullian	Tertullian
Marc.	*Against Marcion*
Thomas Aquinas	Thomas Aquinas
Sum.	*Summa Theologiae*

Restoration Scripture and Other Latter-day Saint Sources

Book of Mormon

1 Ne	1 Nephi
2 Ne	2 Nephi
Jacob	Jacob
Enos	Enos
Jarom	Jarom
Omni	Omni
W of M	Words of Mormon
Mos	Mosiah
Alma	Alma
Hel	Helaman
3 Ne	3 Nephi
4 Ne	4 Nephi
Morm	Mormon
Ether	Ether
Moro	Moroni

Doctrine and Covenants

D&C	Doctrine and Covenants
OD	Official Declaration

Pearl of Great Price

Moses	Moses
Abr	Abraham
JS—M	Joseph Smith—Matthew
JS—H	Joseph Smith—History
A of F	Articles of Faith
JST	Joseph Smith Translation
CHL	Church History Library, The Church of Jesus Christ of Latter-day Saints, Salt Lake City

Latter-day Saint Perspectives on Atonement

Introduction
Atonement in Latter-day Saint Scripture and Thought

DEIDRE NICOLE GREEN
AND ERIC D. HUNTSMAN

When asked about the fundamental tenets of his faith, Joseph Smith (1805–1844), the founding prophet of The Church of Jesus Christ of Latter-day Saints, wrote:

> The fundamental principles of our religion is the testimony of the apostles and prophets concerning Jesus Christ, "that he died, was buried, and rose again the third day, and ascended up into heaven"; and all other things, are only appendages to these, which pertain to our religion.[1]

Similarly, the Church's third article of faith, written originally in 1842 as an explanation to John Wentworth, editor of the *Chicago Democrat*, reads, "We believe that through the atonement of Christ all men may be saved by obedience to the laws and ordinances of the gospel."[2] Despite the uniqueness of their theology in other areas, from the beginning Latter-day Saints shared with other Christians a fundamental belief in the salvific nature of the suffering, death, and resurrection of Jesus Christ. Indeed, Smith and other early Latter-day Saint leaders and thinkers inherited from traditional Christianity some basic assumptions about what the atonement was, although the third article of faith's emphasis on obedience to the restored gospel's laws and ordinances had already begun to separate them from the *sola fide* position of many of their mainly Reformed forebears.

The seeds of this departure were present from the Church's inception. Within just a couple years of its publication, Alexander Campbell (1788–1866) criticized the Book of Mormon because, among other reasons, it articulated positions on theological issues such as the atonement, which had been under debate "in New York for the last ten years."[3] The Book of Mormon straddles and evinces tension around these debates, affording varied perspectives on atonement. Speaking of Christianity more generally, Sydney Ahlstrom notes that in nineteenth-century America, particularly among more progressive Christian groups, a moral theory of atonement "became so prevalent a feature of liberalism that Fundamentalists invariably made an affirmation of the 'substitutionary theory'—an essential criterion of orthodoxy."[4] Although the Book of Mormon arguably upholds penal substitution theology, it also leaves room to decenter that view in favor of a moral theory of atonement among other possibilities. The present volume highlights this potential within Latter-day Saint theology, demonstrating that its multivocal and expanded canon allows for centering theories of atonement that do not rely solely on penal substitution.

Amid the nineteenth-century American theological debates shaping the Latter-day Saint view of atonement, one especially notable influence espoused by Methodists was known as the governmental theory of atonement, which holds that the atonement honors and sustains the moral law. This theory, which originated with the Dutch thinker Hugo Grotius (1583–1645), began to be adopted by some American ministers in the eighteenth century. According to this view, Christ's death did not work to redeem a debt but instead to maintain the dignity of the divine government. Brooks Holifield explains, "Having promulgated a moral law, God could not permit its subversion without allowing the destruction of the moral order itself. When Christ died to vindicate the honor of the law, he made it possible for God to forgive sinful rebels without upsetting the moral order." Some Americans took this theory to mean that "Christ died so that God could preserve a moral order for the sake of the creature."[5] This view was not the sole perspective among American Methodists, whom Holifield depicts as going in "every direction" in their atonement theories, including the notions of the satisfying of a debt, either through its payment or without payment. Nevertheless, he highlights that "most gravitated toward governmental theories," and by the end of the nineteenth century, "governmental images pleased many Methodists because the idea of Christ's having died to preserve moral government suggested a universal effect for Christ's death. Their overriding aim was to argue that he died for all, not for the elect alone."[6] Both the diversity of theoretical frameworks and the ultimate tendency toward inclusivity—perhaps even universalism—of the Methodist view of atonement resonate with the Latter-day Saint tradition from the nineteenth century to the present.[7]

Notwithstanding the clear influence of nineteenth-century theological ideas on the understanding of atonement within the Latter-day Saint tradition, its atonement theology has stood apart from mainstream debates in American theology in its particular emphasis on Gethsemane, particularly in the mid-twentieth century.[8] Despite this emphasis, as Douglas Davies points out,

Latter-day Saint hymnody still made the crucifixion central.[9] American religious historians note that over time, other forms of speculative theology largely associated with figures like Brigham Young, as well as Parley and Orson Pratt, gave way to an increased emphasis on repentance and atonement.[10] This suggests that the Latter-day Saint tradition esteems reflection on the atonement of Christ as a crucial and indispensable task.

Two different streams of thought produce tension in current Latter-day Saint considerations of atonement. On the one hand, the first Latter-day Saints had as their starting point the scriptural inheritance of the Hebrew Bible and the Greek New Testament as they received them through the King James Version. These biblical propositions came to them filtered through almost eighteen hundred years of Christian thinking about biblical propositions on atonement, although early Latter-day Saints were probably largely unaware of how much the many centuries of Christian thought shaped their reading of the Bible. On the other hand, their unique Restoration scripture—the Book of Mormon, the revelations of Smith and other prophets in the Doctrine and Covenants, and three revelatory collections in the Pearl of Great Price—together with the teaching of subsequent church authorities have shaped Latter-day Saint understanding of this fundamental Christian doctrine, often taking it in new directions. Until recently, there has not always been careful parsing of what had been *inherited* and what represents significantly *new* trajectories in understanding Jesus's atoning work.

The English term "atonement" is a neologism, apparently first crafted in 1513 by Thomas More (1478–1535) in his histories of Richard III and Edward VI, where it described a state of harmony, concord, or agreement.[11] His rival William Tyndale (c. 1494–1536) first applied it in a religious context in his 1526 and 1534 editions of the New Testament in English, using it at 2 Corinthians 5:18 for the Greek *katallagē*, which the King James Version of 1611 rendered as "reconciliation." While the KJV only used "atonement" for *katallagē* once in its version of the New Testament, at Romans 5:11, it used the familiar English term extensively throughout the Old Testament, usually as a rendering for forms of the Hebrew stem *kpr*, which signify redemption, ransoming, expiation, and the covering of guilt in a sacrificial context. Because Restoration scripture, which was presented in a largely King James idiom, uses "atonement" so frequently, it has become a standard part of both Latter-day Saint sermons and their religious vernacular.[12] Nevertheless, whereas *kpr* in the Hebrew Bible primarily referred to acts of expiation and *katallagē* in the Greek New Testament represented reconciliation with God, the English "atonement" in Christian thought has been used with a much broader semantic range, and this is particularly the case in Latter-day Saint theology. Indeed, many Latter-day Saints are not aware of how frequently they use the term compared to many other Christians. Because its biblical usage is primarily found in the Old Testament, among many lay Christians of other denominations it is primarily found in the preserve of theological discussions about atonement theory rather than in prevalent conversations about individual salvation. Although the popular explanation of the English term, that it means "at-one-ment," is not unique to Latter-day Saints, this explanation has become common within their community. For instance, noted Latter-day Saint thinker and writer G. Eugene England (1933–2001) explicated this etymology most vividly in a 1966 lecture at Stanford that was published the next year. In it, England described how our various estrangements from God

> can uniquely be healed through the Atonement of Christ. Atonement—a word whose pronunciation disguises its meaning, which is literally *at one ment*, a bringing to unity, a reconciliation of that which is estranged: man and man, man and God, or man and himself.[13]

While atonement is sometimes used narrowly for Jesus's acts to redeem us from sin, it has come to refer broadly to everything Christ did to make us one with God and one with himself.

While the atonement of Christ has been a central theme in the teaching of Latter-day Saint leaders, educators, and a host of missionaries, until recent decades atonement has received little theoretical or conceptual analysis. Latter-day Saints have, in many instances, been unaware of the nuances presented by the different biblical authors, the contributions of patristic writers and Protestant reformers, and the theological propositions of classical atonement theories. For example, outside of specialists, few Latter-day Saints are familiar with the groundbreaking work of Gustaf Aulén (1879–1977), a bishop in the Church of Sweden and a Lutheran theologian, whose 1930 study *Den Kristna Försoningstanken*, which was first translated into English as *Christus Victor*, provided a rubric for discussing atonement theory that is still widely used today.[14] Aulén articulated three broad categories based upon how scriptural and later patristic and Protestant writers sought to understand the focus of Christ's atoning work. The first of these categories, which he saw articulated from the writings of Anselm (c. 1033–1099) through those of the Protestant reformers, consisted of *objective* atonement models that were directed toward satisfying God and his laws. The second, a *subjective* model, focused on humanity and the transformative power of Christ's work to change individuals and communities. Aulén felt that his third category, which consisted of models in which Christ triumphed over Satan and those elemental forces arrayed against both God and humankind, actually represented the earliest propositions in the New Testament, but these had largely been forgotten or ignored by subsequent theologians.

Although Aulén's rubric is not without criticism, in some ways his schema provides a good starting point for noting distinctive aspects of Latter-day Saint theology. For instance, although they do not generally use Aulén's terminology, many Latter-day Saints—shaped partially by both the Protestant theology familiar to their early leaders and especially by the clear propositions of much of their new, distinctive scripture—have largely understood the atonement of Christ through the objective rubric of satisfaction or penal substitution models. Yet beyond these assumptions, the Restoration's promise of humanity's divine potential and its understanding of the healing and transformative aspects of the atonement are consonant with many aspects of Aulén's subjective category. Likewise, Latter-day Saints have not yet systematically explored the potentials of the Christus Victor approach, which is in harmony with some of the imagery of their unique scripture. Beyond this, promising new models are being offered by developments in contemporary theology, some of which have also begun to call into question the traditional approaches systematized by Aulén. For instance, feminist and womanist critics, among others, have raised objections to some classical approaches to atonement as potentially legitimizing violence.[15] Their critiques might pose an important question for Latter-day Saints: Is there room in restoration theology for the contributions of nonviolent models of atonement? Some of the authors in this volume employ the Latter-day Saint canon to this end.

This volume endeavors to brings together multiple and diverse approaches to thinking about Latter-day Saint perspectives on the atonement of Jesus Christ in light of various books of scripture in the Latter-day Saint canon, outside perspectives from both Western and Eastern Christian traditions, classical atonement theories, and contemporary reformulations of atonement theory. These essays have been written and gathered over the course of several years, and they have been divided into two distinct sections. The first, Scriptural and Historical Foundations, begins with surveys of atonement in the Hebrew Bible by Benjamin Spackman and the Greek New Testament by Eric Huntsman. Latter-day Saints know the Hebrew Bible as they received it in the form of the Christian Old Testament, which predisposed them to read Christian soteriology into the Jewish scriptures. Without setting this Christian lens aside, after carefully examining the meaning of atonement, salvation, and redemption in their original contexts, Spackman's essay draws connections with Latter-day Saint understanding of atonement before concluding with some new implications. Huntsman's review of the New Testament material is organized both chronologically and by authors or groups of texts, revealing both the development of early Christian understanding of atonement and the variety of terms and models that these texts employed. While these certainly can be understood according to Aulén's three categories, they are actually more diverse, with some of the lesser discussed models providing important points of contact for important Latter-day Saint views. Ariel Bybee Laughton's overview of patristic and medieval theology likewise reveals the limitation of Aulén's categories. In the process of demonstrating the diversity of thought about atonement that existed between the second and thirteenth centuries, she not only shows why writers like Irenaeus, Augustine, and Aquinas are important to Latter-day Saint theology, she also reminds us that Latter-day Saint theology, too, need not be seen as homogenous.

This underscoring of diversity is a helpful key to use in the remaining essays of the first section as it proceeds with treatments of atonement in the Latter-day Saint tradition's distinctive Restoration scripture and discourse. Despite the prominence of objective satisfaction models in these texts and writings, these need not always be viewed in the form of penal atonement theology. For instance, the Book of Mormon's description of Christ's atonement delivering humanity from "that awful monster, death and hell" and delivering his saints from "the devil, and death, and hell" (2 Ne 9:10, 19) is a quintessential image of Christus Victor. Furthermore, Restoration scripture and teaching are rich with emphases on healing, resurrection, and other subjective models that build upon and even transcend their biblical parallels. Nicholas Frederick's study of atonement in the Book of Mormon shows that even as it is connected with overcoming sin through the objective acts of Christ, particularly through the shedding of his blood, it is also tightly connected with the resurrection. By equating atonement and salvation and then showing how the latter in the Book of Mormon is communal as well as individual, Sharon Harris lays out the distinctive Latter-day Saint theory of corporate salvation through covenants. J.B. Haws's discussion of atonement in the Doctrine and Covenants then provides some of the most uniquely Latter-day Saint approaches to atonement, tracing that book's expansive view extending back to a pre-earth life and forward into an almost universalistic future application that includes a uniquely Latter-day Saint view of *theosis* or deification. While sampling the vast amount of Latter-day Saint discourse—much of it patriarchal—over the past one hundred and ninety years is beyond the scope of this volume, we have chosen instead to conclude this first section by highlighting female voices with Jennifer Reeder's rich retrospective of teachings on the atonement by nineteenth-century Latter-day Saint women. Reeder's essay not only reveals such women's understanding of atonement, it also illustrates their lived experience of it.

Because the biblical models identified and discussed by Spackman and Huntsman are some of the same ones present in Restoration scripture and early Latter-day Saint discourse, they had served as the foundation for the understanding of atonement in the Church since its founding. Unaware of the breadth of the patristic and medieval discussions of atonement surveyed by Laughton, the earliest Latter-day Saints appear to have used the largely satisfaction-oriented models of atonement prevalent in the largely Reformed Protestant milieu from which they arose. This tendency seems to have been reinforced by the Latter-day Saint response to the crises of modernism in the first half of the twentieth century, which O. Kendall White has described as a neo-orthodoxy that paralleled to some extent what was occurring in Christian evangelicalism.[16] Within this context, Lorin Hansen has observed that by and large "the Mormon doctrine of the Atonement consists mostly of simple definitions and statements about general purpose, conditions of application, and eternal consequences. Attempts to explain the actual mechanism of the Atonement are limited mostly to the use of metaphors and parables."[17]

For instance, Boyd K. Packer (1924–2015), a member of the Church's Quorum of the Twelve Apostles from 1970 until his death who served as either acting president or president of that body the last seventeen years of his life, crafted a parable in a 1977 General Conference talk about a debtor who needed a mediator to pay off his debt. Packer then used this parable to teach a satisfaction model based upon the Book of Mormon's teaching that Christ paid the debt demanded of "justice" on behalf of humanity.[18] Likewise Gordon B. Hinckley (1910–2008), fifteenth president of the Church, popularized a penal substitution model with a story of young boy who was spared corporal punishment at school when a friend stepped in to take a beating for him.[19] Both of these models are fitting given the canon's numerous allusions to atonement theories that emphasize satisfaction and penal substitution, which can be found in every book comprising the Latter-day Saint canon. In the Book of Mormon, for example, atonement is described as an event in which "mercy satisfieth the demands of justice," emphasizing that human repentance is required to make this satisfaction efficacious, otherwise "he that exercises no faith unto repentance is exposed to the whole law of the demands of justice" (Alma 34:16). It is made plain here that the atonement is necessary, rather than supererogatory (v.13), and that only Jesus Christ can satisfy these demands on behalf of sinners (vv. 9–13).

However, as various authors in this volume are quick to point out, the Book of Mormon also advances participatory, moral influence, and healing atonement models. For example, in a way that evokes notions of solidarity in suffering over against satisfaction or substitution, Jesus Christ is described as taking "upon him the pains and sicknesses of his people," so that "he may know according to the flesh how to succor his people according to their infirmities" (Alma 7:11–12). This latter exposition on atonement has been cited many more times by General Authorities propounding doctrine in the Church's semiannual General Conference than any previous one; Alma 7:11–13 has been cited around one hundred times in the last forty years, with the bulk of these instances being after 1990; this is at least twice the number of references to Alma 34.[20] This shift may parallel a trend in broader Christian theology to emphasize the compassion and empathy afforded through Jesus Christ's suffering in atonement and the intimacy this shared suffering can effect with individual believers.

This focus has encouraged Latter-day Saint thinkers and writers to start systematically reexamining atonement in Restoration scripture and teaching, often in light of multiple atonement theories. The work of two early trail blazers in this effort illustrate both the potential and the possible pitfalls involved such theological work by Latter-day Saint thinkers. The first was Eugene England's "That They Might Not Suffer: The Gift of Atonement," originally published in 1966.[21] England's essay is a rich Mormon rendition of the subjective moral influence theory of Peter Abelard (c. 1079–1142), yet one that was also deeply rooted in Restoration scripture. On the other hand, it also reflected the difficulty of such exploration when it appears to stray too far from perceived orthodoxy. Perhaps because England presented his theory as *the* explanation of Latter-day Saint atonement rather than as an interesting and important *aspect* of it, his ideas aroused considerable opposition among some of his contemporaries, including a few leading Church authorities, because it seemed to discount the reality of objective satisfaction models.[22] As his biographer, Terryl Givens, puts it, "Had England offered his interpretation as a supplement to or a tempering of substitutionary atonement rather than a wholesale replacement, he probably would have raised no hackles."[23] In contrast, Hansen published a lengthy article in 1994 entitled "The 'Moral' Atonement as a Mormon Interpretation."[24] Hansen's essay was considerably more nuanced than England's, providing new insights that augmented established views without threatening them. For instance, Hansen concluded his essay by writing,

> I find that the Mormon concept of Atonement has a rich concept of subjective process and has an unequivocal concept of Atonement as objective event. In contrast to both Orthodoxy and Liberalism, Mormonism has a sense of the importance to the Atonement of Gethsemane as well as Calvary. Mormon sources do not establish objective Atonement or subjective Atonement, one at the expense of the other.[25]

It is with this expansive view of "both/and" that we present here the remaining essays in the second section of this volume, Theological Explorations, which provide new perspectives that illustrate the breadth of possibilities in the Latter-day Saint tradition, holding them in dynamic tension with prevailing, traditional substitutionary models. Adam Miller proposes that the Latter-day Saint practice of "sealing" families together as an eternal unit is a third component of the reconciliation effected by atonement. He further discusses the necessity of a nonsequential theology in order to properly understand the notion of grace operative in atonement. Benjamin Keogh reframes the theology of atonement through the reconfiguration of the relationships involved. Offering an understanding of collective atonement, Keogh draws on the uniquely Latter-day Saint concept of Zion, arguing that "all relations between all persons must be healed" in order for divine law to be fulfilled and that this is why atonement must be construed as "infinite" within Latter-day Saint thought. The problem of violence becomes the focal point of the remaining essays. Joseph Spencer looks to the figure of Abinadi in the Book of Mormon to explore the possibility of a nonviolent atonement and does so by comparing two competing atonement theologies read through the lens of their corollary political theologies. Fiona Givens argues that Latter-day Saint theology has the resources to circumvent the legalistic social and cultural values that she believes unduly influence traditional Christian theories of atonement and holds forth possibilities for doing so. Finally, Deidre Green looks at how underappreciated images of redemption in Latter-day Saint thought figure a new self-relation for women while countering the glorification of violence that remains a point of critique of traditional atonement theologies.

We hope that our efforts in assembling this anthology will prove valuable for two reasons. First, as noted above, the atonement of Christ remains fundamental to Latter-day Saint belief. For insiders, coming to have faith in the atonement of Christ and, most of all, *experiencing* it is the fundamental purpose of our religion. For outsiders, there is a need to understand better how Latter-day Saint formulations are both similar to and different from the broader Christian tradition. Second, as traditional understandings of atonement have been widely challenged in recent decades, this book hopes to help to evaluate what is efficacious and ethical about Latter-day Saint perspectives and how they might be reconceived to provide a more robust theological account that responds to contemporary criticisms about atonement. To that end, this book aims to suit different audiences. It should be of interest to scholars working in Mormon Studies, as well as to mainstream Latter-day Saints of an intellectual bent. We also hope that this volume will also appeal to religious scholars interested in atonement theory more broadly. While there are a number of popular, devotional Latter-day Saint books on atonement, there are few available that are of a more rigorous and scholarly nature. As a collection of academic approaches, this book strives to make a unique contribution while aiming to make each chapter accessible enough that those without academic training in religious studies can benefit.

One crucial Book of Mormon passage describes the saving work of Jesus as "infinite and eternal" (Alma 34:10). While this has conventionally been explicated as describing an atonement that is not limited in time, space, or effect, we suggest that since it also suggests a salvific act beyond complete human comprehension, multiple approaches and perspectives are necessary to understand it more fully.

Notes

1. "Questions and Answers, 8 May 1838," *Elders' Journal* (July 1838): 42–44; Mark Ashurst-McGee et al., eds. *Documents, Volume 6: February 1838–August 1839* (Salt Lake City: Church Historian's Press, 2017), 3.

2. *Times and Seasons* 3.9 (Mar. 1, 1842), 709; Karen Lynn Davidson, David J. Whittaker, Mark Ashurst-McGee, and Richard L. Jensen, eds., *Histories, Vol. 1: Joseph Smith Histories, 1832–1844* (Salt Lake City: Church Historian's Press, 2012), 4.

3. Alexander Campbell, *Delusions: An Analysis of the Book of Mormon* (Boston: Benjamin Greene, 1832), 13; also quoted in E. Brooks Holifield, *Theology in America: Christian Thought from the Age of the Puritans to the Civil War* (New Haven: Yale University Press, 2003), 333.

4. Sydney E. Ahlstrom, "Introduction," in *Theology in America: The Major Protestant Voices from Puritanism to Neo-Orthodoxy*, edited by Sydney E. Ahlstrom (Indianapolis: Hackett Publishing Company, 1967), 70.

5. Holifield, *Theology in America: Christian Thought*, 132–33.

6. Holifield, *Theology in America: Christian Thought*, 267.

7. Readers interested in the governmental theory of atonement and its relation to Latter-day Saint theology can read chapter 6 of this volume, J.B. Haws, "'This Perfect Atonement': Agency, Law, Theosis, and Atonement Theology in the Doctrine and Covenants."

8. See, for instance, John Hilton III and Joshua P. Barringer, "The Use of 'Gethsemane' by Church Leaders: 1859–2018," *BYU Studies Quarterly* 58.4 (2019): 49–50.

9. Douglas J. Davies, *Joseph Smith, Jesus, and Satanic Opposition* (Farnham, Surrey: Ashgate Publishing Group, 2010), 140–41.

10. Holifield, *Theology in America: Christian Thought*, 339.

11. Thomas More, *Hist. Edward V* in *Workes*, 40, and *Hist. Richard III* in *Workes* (London: London, John Cawood, John Walley, and Richard Tottle, 1557), 41. See "atonement, n.," Oxford Reference, accessed May 10, 2023, https://www.oxfordreference.com/display/10.1093/oi/authority.20110803095432363. More seems to have built upon the Middle English adverbial expression *at onen*, meaning "in one."

12. "Atonement" appears 79 times in the KJV Old Testament and only once in the KJV New Testament. On the other hand, it appears 28 times in the Book of Mormon, 3 times in the Doctrine and Covenants, and once in the much shorter Pearl of Great Price. While the verb "atone" does not appear at all in the KJV, it appears 8 times in the Book of Mormon and once each in the Doctrine and Covenants and the Pearl of Great Price. The participle "atoning," also not found in the KJV, appears 3 times in the Book of Mormon and once in the Doctrine and Covenants.

13. Eugene England, "That They Might Not Suffer: The Gift of Atonement," *Dialogue* 1.3 (1966): 142; republished, https://www.dialoguejournal.com/wp-content/uploads/sbi/articles/Dialogue_V01N03_143.pdf, accessed March 14, 2023.

14. Gustaf Aulén, *Den kristna försoningstanken* (Stockholm: Svenska Kyrkans Diakonistyrelses Bokförlag, 1930); *Christus Victor: An Historical Study of the Three Main Types of the Idea of Atonement*, translated by A. G. Herbert (New York: Macmillan, 1931; reprinted, Eugene, OR: WIPF & Stock, 2003).

15. See, for instance, Delores Williams, *Sisters in the Wilderness: The Challenge of Womanist God-Talk* (Maryknoll, NY: Orbis, 1993) and Rita Nakashima Brock and Rebecca Ann Parker, *Proverbs of Ashes: Violence, Redemptive Suffering, and the Search for What Saves Us* (Boston: Beacon Press, 2001), as well as the essays collected in Joanne Carlson Brown and Carole R. Bohn, eds., *Christianity, Patriarchy, and Abuse: A Feminist Critique* (New York: Pilgrim's Press, 1989); Brad Jersak and Michael Hardin, eds., *Stricken by God? Nonviolent Identification and the Victory of Christ* (Grand Rapids, MI: Eerdmans, 2007); and J. Denny Weaver, *The Nonviolent Atonement,* 2nd ed. (Grand Rapids, MI: Eerdmans, 2011).

16. O. Kendall White Jr., *Mormon Neo-Orthodoxy: A Crisis Theology* (Salt Lake City: Signature Books, 1987).

17. Lorin K. Hansen, "The 'Moral' Atonement as a Mormon Interpretation," *Dialogue* 27.1 (Spring 1994): 195, and available at https://www.dialoguejournal.com/articles/the-moral-atonement-as-a-mormon-interpretation/, accessed March 14, 2023.

18. Boyd K. Packer, "The Mediator," *Ensign* (May 1977): 54–56.

19. This story, sometimes referred to as "He Took a Lickin' for Me," appeared in Hinckley's holiday message, "The Wondrous and True Story of Christmas," *Ensign* (Dec. 2000), 2–6. For other Latter-day Saint comparisons, see J. Clair Batty, "The Atonement: Do Traditional Explanations Make Sense?" *Sunstone* 8 (Nov./Dec. 1983), 11–16; Stephen E. Robinson, "Believing Christ," *Ensign* (Apr. 1992), 5–9.

20. See Scripture Citation Index, https://scriptures.byu.edu/, accessed March 14, 2023.

21. England, "That They Might Not Suffer," 141–55.

22. Terryl Givens, *Stretching the Heavens: The Life of Eugene England and the Crisis of Modern Mormonism* (Chapel Hill: University of North Carolina Press, 2021), 126–32.

23. Givens, *Stretching the Heavens*, 129.

24. Hansen, "The 'Moral' Atonement," 195–227.

25. Hansen, "The 'Moral' Atonement," 227.

PART I

Scriptural and Historical Foundations

CHAPTER 1

Atonement in the Old Testament

Implications for Latter-day Saints

T. BENJAMIN SPACKMAN

Latter-day Saints speak of atonement using vocabulary like *atone*, *save*, and *redeem*, and the corresponding nouns *atonement*, *savior*, *salvation*, *redeemer*, and *redemption*. They not only inherited these terms from their general Christian background; Joseph Smith had a particular interest in the Old Testament.[1] As a result, considering three common English terms—"atonement," "salvation," and "redemption"—their usual Hebrew equivalents as translated in the King James Version (KJV), and associated concepts in the Hebrew Bible is an important step in understanding Latter-day Saint perceptions of atonement. This is not, then, a deep investigation into how Israelites[2] might have conceived of atonement[3] but an examination of the Old Testament roots of Latter-day Saint atonement terminology in terms of their meaning within an ancient context and some short comment on the history of their English translational equivalents. In brief, Israelites understood "redeem" primarily in terms of kinship and "family law," secondarily as a covenantal term. Similarly, "save" and "salvation" are often found in political or martial contexts, where "victory" or even "success" is a more appropriate translation. "Atonement" belonged to priestly vocabulary, involving ritual purity and pollution.

Not surprisingly, current Latter-day Saint usage of these English terms often represents a significant shift from their meaning in the sources they were drawn from. The semantic distinctions between these terms have been blurred, if not erased entirely; they have also become highly theological, eschatological, and heavenly, whereas their conceptual Israelite origins are often grounded in the practical, concrete, and this-worldly. In other words, Latter-day Saint usage has flattened what was a diverse inherited landscape of conceptions, reflected in the terminology.

Israelite Terminology

Atonement

Unlike many other theological words which have come from Latin or Greek, "atonement" was coined as an etymological neologism, built from the meaning of its English parts, literally "at-one-ment," the resulting state or condition (suffix -*ment*) of being or becoming "at one" or (re)united, reconciled. The verb "atone" represents a later backformation from the noun and would indicate the process or action which brings about this state of one-ness. Note that this verb does not exist in the KJV;[4] when required, the translators used the circumlocution "to make atonement" (e.g., Lev 4:20, 26, 31, 35.)[5]

In the KJV, atonement appears almost entirely in the Old Testament. With the exception of Romans 5:11 ("we also joy in God through our Lord Jesus Christ, by whom we have now received the atonement"), all the occurrences of "atonement" in the Bible are found in the Old Testament. Furthermore, examination of the Old Testament distribution of "atonement" reveals a high concentration in chapters pertaining to priests and ritual matters, with fully 60 percent of the appearances found in Leviticus. The Book of Numbers accounts for another 20 percent. Leviticus chapter 16 alone accounts for nearly 20 percent of all occurrences, which is no surprise when one realizes the chapter concerns the Day of Atonement, *yôm hakkippūrîm*[6] or Yom Kippur. This concentration suggests that the Hebrew verb *kippēr* was a technical, priestly term, relating to ritual purity, pollution, and purification. Indeed, its usage is very rare outside of priestly texts and authors.

Linguistically, *kippēr* began with a very concrete meaning, something like "to rub, wipe," which in a ritual setting led to "purge, purify," as well as spinning off an entirely different meaning of "ransom" in which "innocent life [is] spared by substituting for it the guilty parties or their ransom."[7] Technical analyses have often made comparisons with an Akkadian cognate which figures prominently in Babylonian purification rites, although no firm conclusions have been drawn.

What does the priestly status of *kippēr* imply for its conception? The lengthy study of Leviticus by Jacob Milgrom (1923–2010), emeritus professor of Near Eastern Studies at Berkeley, represents a deep but accessible source among the many studies that have investigated *kippēr*. According to Milgrom, *kippēr* underwent a gradual shift in meaning. Only in the final stage did it yield:

> the abstract figurative notion of "atone" or "expiate." . . . Having begun as an action that eliminates dangerous impurity by absorbing it through direct contact (rubbing off) or indirectly (as a ransom/substitute), *kipper* develops into the process of expiation in general. . . . [in which] the offerer is cleansed of his impurities/sins and becomes reconciled, "at one" with God.[8]

Thus the *JPS Torah Commentary* can write that the

> ancient view of Yom Kippur is somewhat different from that which came to predominate in later Judaism, especially in the centuries following the destruction of the Second Temple of Jerusalem in 70 c.e. Atonement for the sins of the people eventually replaced the purification of the sanctuary per se as the central theme of Yom Kippur. This shift of emphasis is already suggested in verse 30: "For on this day atonement shall be made for *you* to cleanse *you* of all your sins; *you* shall be clean before the Lord." The purification of the sanctuary was understood to extend to the people—to relieve them of their transgressions as well. However, no ritual of purification was actually performed over the people, as was the case on other occasions.[9]

At the earliest stage, then, Yom Kippur and *kippēr* were narrowly concerned with cleansing of ritual impurity and pollution, and secondarily, removal of sin from the sanctuary. Since the build-up of sin and pollution eventually resulted in the catastrophic departure of the temple's deity,[10] purging it of that sin and pollution had the effect of repairing or maintaining the deity's presence and blessing. In a sense, then, while the term was more limited, the roots of "atonement" as bringing two back together or healing a rift were already present. Indeed, says one lexicon, "On one level [English at-one-ment] is, in fact, a good definition of the basic effect that to atone, make atonement (the vb. [*kāpar*]) had in the relationship between God and human beings within the Israelite cultic sacrificial system."[11]

Salvation

While Latter-day Saints continue to use the noun "salvation" with some ambiguity,[12] usage of the verb "to save" has dropped out almost entirely, perhaps in reaction to perceptions of Protestant usage or to avoid importation of any Protestant connotations culturally attached to the term, such as "cheap grace."[13] In the Old Testament, "salvation" and "save" represent forms of *yāša'*.[14] This verb happens to be familiar to English speakers from "hosanna" (Heb. *hoša' na*), meaning "save please!" which later becomes an acclamation of praise (Matt 21:9).[15]

In the Old Testament, this salvation primarily represented a very practical need of the here-and-now, not a future promise of wiping away the effects of death or sin. (Sin, with its accompanying ritual pollution, would have likely fallen under "atonement.") The Book of Psalms, for example, contains the heaviest concentration, accounting for 30 percent of the usage of *yasha'* in the Bible. Scot McKnight, an Evangelical Bible scholar, writes,

> The focus of the various images for salvation and deliverance in the psalms is on personal deliverance from enemies and life's real troubles rather than, as is often the case in Christian theology, on images of salvation in the afterlife

for the individual . . . It is this focus on real-life problems, such as being surrounded by enemies intent on killing the psalmist, that gives to the psalms a potent vision not only of salvation but also of a life of faith, a life of prayer, and a life of petitioning God for deliverance from physical dangers.[16]

While *yāša'* had the general meaning of "save, help," this salvation often had martial contexts. When the Psalmist repeatedly pleas for "salvation," it is not a prayer for atonement and afterlife, but a plea for national victory in war or deliverance from other nations. In Psalm 21, for example, "The salvation which God gives the king is primarily the conquest of his enemies."[17] The book of Judges accounts for another 10 percent of usages of *yāša'*, the highest concentration in the historical books. Several judges there are called *môšîa'*[18] or "savior" (*mošia'* is a present participle of *yāša'*), but that salvation is military/political. "In all these cases [in Judges] the salvation in question clearly is political—that is, military victory. The terms *saved* and *savior*, understood in this sense, are at least as important for understanding the roles of Israel's judges as *judged* and *judge*."[19] This background may help the reader of the KJV (the official English Bible of The Church of Jesus Christ of Latter-day Saints) understand why other translations read as "victory" or "give victory" where the KJV says "salvation" or "save," e.g., Psalms 20:6ff (JPS Tanakh), 44:6–7 (NAB)[20], 118:15 (NRSV)[21], and particularly clearly, Psalm 144:10 (NRSV, NIV, JPS).

This martial usage extends beyond Psalms and Judges into most other books of the Hebrew Bible. Israel's founding emancipation from Egypt is repeatedly referred to using forms of *yāša'*. For example, Exodus 14:13 looks forward to "the deliverance (*yəšû'at*) Yahweh will bring" and after the drowning of the pursuing Egyptian army, it is said "thus Yahweh saved (*yāša'*) Israel that day from the power of the Egyptians" (Exod 14:30.) While other uses in the legal and prophetic realm echo this imminent kind of "salvation," it is God's deliverance from slavery and the power of Egypt that will later be spiritualized, providing a model of divine aid in saving from foes far too great for mortals, namely, sin and death. Thus was Jesus named *yēshua'* (a nominal form of *yāša'*), because he would "save his people from their sins" (Matt 1:21). This spiritualized usage then becomes dominant in Christian theology and thought.

Redemption

Outside of theological settings, Americans find "redeem" in only one place, namely, at the grocery store, where coupons are redeemed. The store distributes coupons and then buys them back, or redeems them, and indeed, "buying back" is one of the oldest English meanings of "redeem."[22] Some other languages make this meaning clear, for example, the French *racheter*.[23] Made of the common prefix *re-* "again, back" and *acheter* "to buy, purchase," *racheter* literally means "to buy back, repurchase." However the North American usage[24] of "redeeming coupons" came about, it accurately reflects one of the functions of redemption in Israel, which was not theological, but fiscal. In "the Bible [redemption] retains its literal, commercial sense, as in reclaiming a pawned item or mortgaged property."[25]

Hebrew proper names reveal some surprising insight into the Israelite family framework of redemption. Most American English names today have been borrowed from older languages; they have meaning in their *Ur*-language, but that meaning is not evident or significant to English speakers on a daily basis. By contrast, a number of Hebrew theophoric names illustrate a key Israelite concept related to redemption, namely, kinship. Better understanding these names and their otherwise puzzling meanings can lead an interested student to scholarship on redemption and the meaning of kinship.

For instance, the meaning of the name Abijah/Joab/Eliab is "God is (my) father."[26] This could lead to a Christian—and especially Latter-day Saints with their belief in the literal kinship of men and women with God—understanding this as a doctrinal reflection of the fatherhood of God. Somewhat similarly, because the names Ahijah/Joah mean "God is (my) brother," Latter-day Saint readers, with their distinctive belief that the spirits of humanity share the same parent-child relationship with deity as did the premortal Jesus, might make naive sense of this name by assuming an allusion to the premortal Jesus's status as "our elder brother,"[27] an unscriptural but popular description among some Latter-day Saints.[28] Yet another piece of data, the name "God is (my) uncle," Ammiel/Eliam,[29] might require Latter-day Saints to reshape their limited conceptions in order to make sense of this expression of Israelite worldview. In what possible way could God be one's uncle?[30]

"Father," "brother," and "uncle" are all kinship terms. Far from expressing various Latter-day Saint (or even more generally Christian) doctrines, each of these names expressed one very important Israelite concept: God as a divine kinsman in general without equating him with a specific human relationship. Without explanation, the force of this concept is generally lost upon our very different culture. What did kinship mean, how was it that Israel could claim God as a kinsman, and what did that relationship entail?

Kinship was the fundamental structure governing societal interaction and functionality, and kin had particular duties to each other within that structure, including mutual love, loyalty, and support (Lev 19:17–18), avenging wrongful death (Num 35:6ff),[31] buying back (i.e., redeeming) family land that had been sold due to poverty (Lev 25:25–34) and family members who had been sold into slavery (Lev 25:47–50). The Levirate law of marrying a brother's childless widow to raise children in his name may also have been a duty of kinship.[32]

The advantages and duties of biological kinship described above could be extended to those outside the tribe, clan, or family through covenant, which included legal/ethical aspects, cultic aspects, and juridical aspects. Scott Hahn, a Catholic Bible scholar and author of *Kinship by Covenant* explains. "The covenant bears all these aspects because it is an extension of familial relationship, and the extended family, the *bet 'ab* [or "father's house"], was the central framework for the legal, religious, and political aspects of ancient Semitic society."[33] Since kinship-through-covenant extended familial relationships, the respective kinship terms that we think of as strictly biological took on broader meaning. "The interaction between kinship and covenant creates differences between the meanings of terms like 'father,' 'mother,' 'son,' 'daughter,' 'brother,' 'sister,' 'uncle,' or 'nephew' in the Bible, and the way we use these titles in everyday speech. In the Bible, their connotations are often more legal than biological. They identify a variety of people besides blood relatives."[34] In other words, these terms often identify people who are kin through covenant.

Frank Moore Cross (1921–2012), a master of ancient Semitic languages and emeritus Hebrew Bible professor at Harvard, broke new ground on this long-studied topic. "Often it has been asserted that the language of 'brotherhood' and 'fatherhood,' 'love,' and 'loyalty' is 'covenant terminology.' This is to turn things upside down. *The language of covenant, kinship-in-law, is taken from the language of kinship, kinship-in-flesh.*"[35] Through covenant, those "outside" could be brought "inside" as if they were and had been family all along, with all the blessings and duties implied.

Along with their eastern neighbors the Amorites and the Moabites,[36] Israelites held that covenant could extend the bonds of kinship not just to biologically unrelated humans, but also to deity. Although Yahweh had already graciously acted as *de facto* kinsman in freeing Israel from slavery in Egypt (Exod 6:6), he formally becomes Israel's divine kinsman through covenant in Exodus 24.[37] Various metaphors express this relationship throughout the Old Testament, including the marriage[38] metaphor familiar from the prophets as well as Israel being God's "son" or the "kin of Yahweh" (Heb. *'am yhwh*, traditionally "people of Yahweh").

Regardless of the familial metaphor chosen in any given passage (and there are many), it is the duty implied by the kinship metaphor that is important. Cross elaborates:

> The Divine Kinsman, it is assumed, fulfilled the mutual obligations and receives the privileges of kinship. He leads in battle, redeems from slavery, loves his family, shares the land of his heritage, provides and protects. He blesses those who bless his kindred, curses those who curse his kindred. The family of the deity rallies to his call to holy war, "the wars of Yahweh," keeps his *cultus*,

obeys his patriarchal commands, maintains family loyalty, loves him with all their soul, calls on his name.[39]

Israelites and their neighbors may have viewed this covenantal kinship as the primary relationship by which they approached deity. When in need of help, they called on God and expected him to respond because they were kin. *The Jewish Study Bible* echoes Cross: "Since Israel is God's near kinsman, when Israel is in distress it is God's veritable obligation to come to its aid and make whatever efforts are necessary in order to extricate it from its predicament."[40] As a relatively small and weak nation, Israel's collective problems were often political or martial. God as Israel's divine kinsman implied not only eventual redemption from slavery or oppression, but also divine violence on their behalf.

To summarize the relevant points, the duty of a kinsman, whether human or divine, kin-by-flesh or kin-by-law, included redeeming or buying back family land and family members who had fallen into trouble. One word—*gāʾal*— and its derivatives appear repeatedly throughout, which "primarily represent technical legal terminology of Israelite family law."[41] The Hebrew *gāʾal* may well mean something like "to act as kinsman" or "to carry out the duty of a kinsman" though it will never appear that way in translational glosses. Because English lacks a parallel term, translation varies based on the context of what duty is being carried out.[42] When *gāʾal* appears without such context, its various forms are simply translated as "redeem" or "redeemer." To indicate some of the cultural background, a few translations have opted for the neologism of "kinsman-redeemer" or "redeeming-kinsman." Thus, to claim God as "redeemer," to call upon him for redemption, was to claim kinship through a covenant relationship with him.[43]

Modern Latter-day Saint Applications of These Three Israelite Conceptions

Not being aware of Hebrew linguistics, many Latter-day Saints often use "atone," "redeem," and "save" without knowing the broader and distinct Israelite contexts behind these terms. Moreover, Latter-day Saint discourse tends to use the word *atonement* primarily in eschatological and theological contexts, focused on the obstacles of sin and death. While it makes sense that this would be of ultimate concern of a believing and practicing Latter-day Saint community, it should not exclude other aspects of atonement that can help them progress toward that goal. Latter-day Saints have also frequently relied on many types of extended metaphors to explain the complexities of the atonement, often financial and often extra-scriptural.[44] While these models are certainly useful, every metaphor or abstraction breaks down or is incomplete and can be misleading at some point. Latter-day Saint understandings can be enriched through careful use of atonement metaphors in pastoral care, personal discipleship, and scriptural exegesis. How, then, can the three Israelite concepts from the scriptures introduced above profitably broaden Latter-day Saint understanding of atonement?

Atonement

While the Latter-day Saint movement has neither a system for the expiation of ritual pollution or of defilement of the holy land (as did ancient Israel) nor a yearly ritual in which the temple(s) or land are ritually cleansed (as would correspond to the priestly notion of atonement), one can well imagine some Latter-day Saints drawing on the Hebrew concept to include cleansing the land, taking "pollution" as concrete instead of ritual, thus making an environmental application. BYU Professor George Handley's book *Home Waters*, subtitled *A Year of Recompenses on the Provo River,* gestures toward just such an understanding: "Ecological restoration is neither technophilia nor antihumanist escapism. It is repentance, plain and simple."[45]

Another, more personal, pastoral adaptation is possible. Thinking of atonement in financial or transactional terms has led some Latter-day Saints to struggle with perfectionism and an easy conflation of *worthiness* or *worthy* with *(self-)worth,* the idea or feeling that a person is loved, valued, or "worth" less because of mistakes, imperfections, and sins. Several productive ways of dealing with this have been suggested in the past, but more integration with the idea of ritual rather than just moral pollution might better fit the broader Latter-day Saint understanding of atonement.

Ritual uncleanness[46] was incurred regularly through a variety of means, including regular biological processes of both men and women as well as sin, and had little necessary bearing on one's righteousness or standing before God. Some encounters with uncleanness were an unavoidable part of creation and being alive; certainly, Jesus himself incurred ritual uncleanness in his life under Jewish law, even deliberately at times,[47] but this fact in no way undermined his sinlessness, divinity, goodness, or self-worth. He would have simply undergone the proper cleansing rituals like everyone else and regained his ritual state of "cleanliness." Nonetheless, like some other Christians, many Latter-day Saints continue to see such uncleanness in terms of sin and unworthiness, an idea that is perhaps encouraged by the Book of Mormon's use of Israelite language of ritual impurity in expressions such as "no unclean thing can dwell with God" (1 Ne 10:21; see also 1 Ne 15:34; Alma 7:21; 11:37; 40:26).

Salvation

On the one hand, the generic usage of *yāšaʿ* as "save, help" does not have much to add to Latter-day Saint conceptions, and its frequent specific martial context in the Hebrew Bible renders it the most difficult of these three terms to apply to a Latter-day Saint setting. The challenge lies in a stark cultural and moral difference between modern Western culture and the world of the Old Testament, namely, that they have become much more uncomfortable with (divine?) violence than they appear to have been. This martial usage of "save" depends on and elevates the aspect of God as "divine warrior" and "a man of war" (Exod 15:3). While the Old Testament is often caricatured as being a locus of violence,[48] this aspect of the ancient world is not limited to the Old Testament but is found in the New Testament in the apocalyptic depictions in the book of Revelation, as well as in the Book of Mormon in 3 Nephi 8–10. Divine violence in scripture is a complex issue; recognizing that Jesus establishes the two great laws as loving God and loving your neighbor as yourself by quoting directly from Deuteronomy 6:4 and Leviticus 19:18 is a first step in complicating simplistic contrasts between the Old Testament and other scripture.[49]

The depiction of God as engaging in violence, even in order to defend or protect his people from their enemies, nevertheless discomfits many modern readers, particularly as scriptural rhetoric sometimes glories in it. It is difficult to find aspects of divine violence in an atonement by a god who is motivated exclusively by infinite love, complete self-sacrifice, and altruistic concern. This conundrum is well worth puzzling over, and others may yet posit a good Christian application of this Hebraic concept of salvation.

Redemption

While concepts of divine kinship and kinship-by-covenant certainly resonate with family-focused contemporary Latter-day Saints, modern Western European and North American cultures lack the social structures that anciently enabled the theological ramifications of divine kinship. I suspect Israelites encountered kin-based redemptive interactions with some regularity, which rendered those aspects of divine kinship immanent and concrete instead of merely theoretical.

There is a kind of quasi-kinship among Latter-day Saints, however. Latter-day Saints moving almost anywhere in the world find an almost immediate extended "family" in their new congregation. Latter-day Saint networking provides some advantages similar to Israelite kinship. The formal duties of membership are often summed up by a Book of Mormon passage regarding the requirements for baptism, describing the duties members owe to each other as including being "willing to bear one another's burdens, that they may be light; Yea, and are [being] willing to mourn with those that mourn; yea, and comfort those that stand in need of comfort" (Mos 18:8–10). Accordingly, Latter-day Saints commonly perform the duties of community or even kinship for fellow Saints whom they know only remotely, if at all.

The cultural/legal institutions like debt-slavery or levirate marriage of the biblical period are no longer present, but fundamentally both Latter-day Saint and Israelite ideas of kinship and mutual responsibilities are concerned with relationships. On such a basic level, we can perhaps apply some of God-as-divine-kinsman to our ideas of atonement. If our relationship with God is not characterized primarily as debtor-creditor, but as kinsman-kinsman (whether kin by covenant or kin by nature), then perhaps we can do as the Israelites and call on him for help *in terms* of that relationship. That is, thinking of God as a family member we turn to for help instead of as a banker concerned primarily with having his debt repaid means that we are more likely to seek that help. Thus, Hebrews 4:15–16 recasts how we approach God on the basis of how we conceive of him: "We do not have a high priest who is unable to sympathize with our weaknesses, but we have one who in every respect has been tested as we are, yet without sin. Let us therefore approach the throne of grace with boldness, so that we may receive mercy and find grace to help in time of need" (NRSV).

In particular, the redemptive duties of kinship have direct application to Latter-day Saint family history and temple work. In this, Joseph Smith was inspired by Malachi's reference to the eschatological mission of Elijah: "I will send you the prophet Elijah before the great and terrible day of the LORD comes. He will turn the hearts of parents to their children and the hearts of children to their parents, so that I will not come and strike the land with a curse" (Mal 4:6 [NRSV]; cf. D&C 2:1–3). Subsequent revelations and teachings that grew from this passage established the Latter-day Saint doctrine of the redemption of the dead, whereby those who died without a knowledge of the restored gospel or an opportunity to receive its ordinances are believed to have the opportunity to be taught and then either accept or reject the gospel in the spirit world after death (see D&C 138:29–35). Then through practices such as "baptism for the dead" and other proxy ordinances in Latter-day Saint temples, living members of the Church serve as proxies for their ancestors to provide them saving ordinances. Not only do Latter-day Saints actively seek out their ancestors through genealogical research in order to provide them these necessary ordinances, members themselves are in some sense redeemed by the effort. As an 1842 revelation to Joseph Smith explained:

For we without them cannot be made perfect; neither can they without us be made perfect. Neither can they nor we be made perfect without those who have died in the gospel also; for it is necessary in the ushering in of the dispensation of the fulness of times, which dispensation is now beginning to usher in, that a whole and complete and perfect union, and welding together of dispensations, and keys, and powers, and glories should take place, and be revealed from the days of Adam even to the present time. (D&C 128:18).

Implications for Latter-day Saint Understandings of Atonement

Joseph Smith was very influenced by the Old Testament; as reflected through the King James Version, it provided him a rich repertoire of potential doctrines and practices, and often served as a catalyst for his own revelations. However, the concept of atonement was not as monolithic as either Joseph and the first Latter-day Saints might have seen it or certainly as many today commonly understand it. Rather, Israelites had a variety of cultural concepts and metaphors around atonement, not all of which have been explored here. Few Latter-day Saints are aware of these roots, but the implications of these concepts *for* Latter-day Saints are numerous. For example, the idea of kinship by covenant finds strong resonance among Latter-day Saints in their communal relations. One enters the Latter-day Saint community through a covenant ritual of baptism, and once integrated into the community, an individual both contributes to and benefits from strong mutual aid within the community. The Latter-day Saint social network functions much like kinship by covenant, though without the explicit socio-cultural term or conscious recognition of such. In my experience, Latter-day Saints who become aware of the Israelite concept of kinship by covenant express great enthusiasm for the idea, as it strengthens communal bonds and provides a feeling of "living scripturally." The extension of this idea into God as divine kinsman and the implications of atonement similarly tends to evoke appreciation and enthusiasm. Similarly, for Latter-day Saints who are uncomfortable with "save," learning about its Israelite semantics can help sever the term from perceived Protestant theological "ownership" of it. Thus, looking to scriptural usage and context to recover semantic roots can, at minimum, deepen theological understandings, ground Latter-day Saint usage deeper in scripture, and provide new trajectories to explore theology and texts both inherited from the Old Testament, shared with other Christians, or unique to Latter-day Saint teaching.

Notes

This paper was originally published as "The Israelite Roots of Atonement Terminology," *BYU Studies Quarterly* 55.1 (2016): 39–64. Written for a nonspecialist Latter-day Saints audience, it cited a number of popular sources to increase accessibility. I thank the editors of *BYU Studies* for allowing a revision for the audience of this anthology.

1. As Latter-day Saints use "Old Testament" as the standard description, I use the term here over "Hebrew Bible."

2. I use this term in the broadest possible way to mean the covenant people of the Old Testament, whether before or after Jacob/Israel, or north/south geographically.

3. See, e.g., Max Botner, Justin Duff, and Simon Dürr, eds., *Atonement: Jewish and Christian Origins* (Grand Rapids, MI: William B. Eerdmans, 2020).

4. Latter-day Saints in the English-speaking world have tended to use the King James Version as their common Bible, which has influenced perceptions of the text. See Philip Barlow, "Why the King James Version? From the Common to the Official Bible of Mormonism," *Dialogue* 22:2 (Summer 1986): 19–41; *Mormons and the Bible: The Place of the Latter-day Saints in American Religion*, updated ed., (New York: Oxford University Press, 2013).

5. On the origins of "atonement" see the Introduction. Cf. David Rolph Seely, "William Tyndale and the Language of At-one-ment," in *The King James Bible and the Restoration*, edited by Kent P. Jackson (Provo, UT: BYU Religious Studies Center, 2011): 25–42.

6. The traditional Hebrew name derives from Lev. 23:27, "the tenth day of this seventh month is the day of atonement" (NRSV).

7. Jacob Milgrom, *Leviticus 1–16* (New Haven: Yale University Press, 1998), 1082. Milgrom has also written about this generally in an LDS context, "The Temple in Biblical Israel: Kinships of Meaning," in *Reflections on Mormonism: Judaeo-Christian Parallels*, edited by Truman G. Madsen (Provo, UT: BYU Religious Studies Center, 1978), 57–66. Cf. Martha T. Roth, editor in charge, *The Assyrian Dictionary of the Oriental Institute of the University of Chicago (The Chicago Assyrian Dictionary)*, 21 vols. (Chicago: University of Chicago Press, 1921–2011), volume 8, for "kapāru" meaning "to wipe off," "to smear on," and in a related form, *kuppuru*, "to wipe off, to clean objects, to rub, to purify magically."

8. Milgrom, *Leviticus*, 1083.

9. Baruch Levine, *The JPS Torah Commentary: Leviticus* (Philadelphia: Jewish Publication Society, 1989), 99.

10. Ezekiel 10 describes a vision of Yahweh abandoning the Israelite temple. Verse 18 records the "glory (presence) of Yahweh" physically leaving. In Ezekiel 11:22, Yahweh leaves the city as well.

11. See the *New International Dictionary of Old Testament Theology and Exegesis* (*NIDOTTE*) "[kāpar]" 2:689–709. Hugh Nibley, a Latter-day Saint scholar of the ancient Near East, provides an expansive interpretation of *kippēr* in "The Meaning of the Atonement" in *Approaching Zion*, edited by Don E. Norton (Salt Lake City: Deseret Book, 1989), 554–614.

12. Compare Bruce R. McConkie's usage and definition under "Salvation" and "Exaltation" in *Mormon Doctrine*, 2nd ed. (Salt Lake City: Deseret Book, 1966). McConkie writes under the latter topic that "Although salvation may be defined in many ways to mean many things, in its most pure and perfect definition it is a synonym for exaltation" (257). In the former, he distinguishes between "unconditional or general salvation" and "conditional or individual salvation" (669).

13. See for, example, Robert Millet's expression of this counterreaction. Robert L. Millet, "Joseph Smith's Christology: After Two Hundred Years," in *The Worlds of Joseph Smith*, edited by John Welch (Provo, UT: BYU Press, 2006), 233.

14. With three exceptions found in poetry (Job 5:4, 11, and Ps. 12:5) forms of *yāšaʿ* are always translated as *save, salvation,* or *saviour* in the KJV. Similarly, all forms of "save" are translated from forms of *yāšaʿ* except Genesis 19:19, Ecclesiastes 5:11, and Amos 9:8. In the latter two, KJV "saving" means "except, but for."

15. The phrase which becomes anglicized as "hosanna" does not actually appear in the Hebrew Bible, although a longer form is present in Psalms 118:25.

16. "Salvation and Deliverance Imagery" in *Dictionary of the Old Testament: Wisdom, Poetry, and Writings,* edited by Tremper Longman III and Peter Enns (Downers Grove, IL: InterVarsity Academic, 2008)

17. *The Oxford Bible Commentary*, edited by John Barton and John Muddiman (Oxford: Oxford University Press, 2001), on Psalm 21.

18. For an LDS exploration of this term, see John W. Welch, "What Was a 'Mosiah'?" in *Reexploring the Book of Mormon*, edited by John W. Welch (Provo, UT: FARMS, 1992), 105–07.

19. P. E. Satterthwaite, "Judges," in *Dictionary of the Old Testament: Historical Books*, edited by Bill T. Arnold and H. G. M. Williamson (Downers Grove, IL: InterVarsity, 2005)

20. New American Bible, Revised Edition (2010).

21. New Revised Standard Version.

22. The *Oxford English Dictionary* (OED), under "Redeem," section 7a, lists examples as far back as 1425 AD.

23. English "redeem" apparently comes from Latin through French *redimer*, which current French replaced with *racheter.*

24. The *OED* connects the specific usage of "redeem" with coupons to the U.S. in 1897, though the general idea goes back much farther.

25. *The Jewish Study Bible*, edited by Adele Berlin and Marc Zvi Brettler, 1st ed. (Oxford: Oxford University Press, 2004), note to Lev 25:24.

26. While a complicated subject, the Hebrew Bible rarely distinguishes between *ʾel/ʾelōhîm* (KJV "God") and *yahweh* (KJV "Lord" or 4x, "Jehovah"), and I do not distinguish here between their respective theophoric elements *ʾel* and *yah*, translating both simply as "God." The LDS adoption of Elohim and Jehovah to designate (respectively) the Father and the Son represents a conventional adaptation of these Hebrew terms and does not reflect either Old Testament usage or early LDS usage. Doctrine & Covenants 109 likely uses "Jehovah" as a reference to the Father, and as late as 1961 President McKay could (accidentally?) speak of "Jehovah and his son, Jesus Christ." For

this and other examples, see Barry R. Bickmore, "Of Simplicity, Oversimplification, and Monotheism," *The FARMS Review* 15:1 (2003): 215–58; Ryan Conrad Davis and Paul Y. Hoskisson, "Usage of the Title Elohim," *Religious Educator* 14:1 (2013), 109–27. Cf. Mark S. Smith, *The Early History of God: Yahweh and Other Deities in Ancient Israel*, 2nd ed. (Grand Rapids, MI: William B. Eerdmans, 2002).

27. In LDS theology, Jesus and all humans existed prior to birth as "spirit children" of God, Jesus being the "firstborn."

28. See Corbin Volluz, "Jesus Christ as Elder Brother," *BYU Studies* 45:2 (2006): 141–58. Volluz traces the earliest identification of Jesus as "our Brother" to Orson Pratt in 1844.

29. The typical translation of *'am* as "people" represents the endpoint of a three-stage process of semantic broadening. It first meant "paternal uncle" (and still does in modern Arabic) before semantic broadening to "kin/kinsman" and then "people."

30. Outside of Israel, these and other terms such as "father-in-law," and "mother" were used to similar ends. Had I encountered something like *ḥamiel*, "God is my father-in-law," I might have figured out sooner that my narrow paradigm was not properly calibrated.

31. Note that this is not *revenge*. The concept of *eye for an eye* served to set an upper limit on justice and prevent escalation. If you accidentally killed my cow, I could not escalate and kill your child in response. Furthermore, Numbers 35 distinguishes between accidental killing (or involuntary manslaughter) and murder. In the first case, the culprit could appeal to the community, which rendered judgment on culpability, and temporarily retreat to a city of refuge for safety; in the second case, the murderer was put to death by the kinsman upon the evidence of witnesses.

32. This is not explicit in extant Israelite law, but is implied in the book of Ruth, which is heavily focused on themes of redemption. Indeed, "The subject of redemption is more prominent in Ruth than in any other biblical book. . . . Boaz announces his marriage to Ruth. Such an extension of the notion of redemption to include marriage exceeds expectations and provides utmost security for an otherwise marginalized person, by integrating her fully into the household in the most respectable fashion. Although marriage is not elsewhere demanded in the Bible in conjunction with redemption, marriage as a metaphor for God's redemptive actions on Israel's behalf is integral to some prophetic writings, expressed, for example, in Isaiah 54:5, where God is husband and redeemer" (Tamara Cohen Eskenazi and Tikva Frymer-Kremsky, *The JPS Bible Commentary: Ruth* [Philadelphia: Jewish Publication Society, 2011], liiii and lv). Compare the language of Ruth 4:10 with Deut 25:6.

33. Scott Hahn, *Kinship by Covenant: A Canonical Approach to a Fulfillment of God's Saving Promises* (New Haven: Yale University Press, 2009), 3.

34. Victor H. Matthews and Don C. Benjamin, *The Social World of Ancient Israel, 1250–587 BCE* (Grand Rapids, MI: Baker Academic, 1993), 8.

35. Frank Moore Cross, "Kinship and Covenant in Ancient Israel," in *From Epic to Canon: History and Literature in Ancient Israel* (Baltimore: Johns Hopkins University Press, 1998): 11, emphasis added. Hershel Shanks provides an accessible summary and discussion of Cross in "God as Divine Kinsman: What Covenant Meant in Ancient

Israel," *Biblical Archaeology Review* 25.4 (July/Aug. 1999): 32–33, 60. Cf. Hahn, *Kinship by Covenant*.

36. Cross, "Kinship and Covenant," 12–13.

37. The simile curse aspects of the covenant-ratification ritual in Exodus 24 have long been noted. That is, one typical aspect of covenant rituals was a physical reenactment of the curse to be carried out for violation thereof. In this case, the throats of animals were cut, the blood collected (called "the blood of the covenant"), half splashed on the altar, and half on the people who had just agreed to the covenant. Scott Hahn connects this with kinship. "The sprinkling of blood is a ritualized oath-curse—in technical terminology, a *Drohitus*. The sprinkled blood of the slain animals represents the curse of death that both parties invoke upon themselves should they prove unfaithful to their covenantal obligations. The mutual sprinkling of blood may also convey the idea that both parties now share one blood—that is, they have become kin." Hahn, *Kinship by Covenant*, 47.

38. Marriage was covenant-based and established kinship.

39. Cross, "Kinship and Covenant," 7.

40. *The Jewish Study Bible*, note to Lev 25:24.

41. See *NIDOTTE*, "[gā'al]" 1:789–94.

42. A verb with similar breadth of meaning which results in a large variety of translational glosses is *pāqad*. See Stuart Creason, "PQD Revisited," in *Studies in Semitic and Afroasiatic Linguistics Presented to Gene B. Gragg*, edited by Cynthia L. Miller, volume 60 of *Studies in Ancient Oriental Civilization* (Chicago: Oriental Institute of the University of Chicago, 2007), 27–42.

43. Note, however, that not every unnamed redeemer in the text is divine. The unnamed kinsman whom Boaz consults in Ruth 4:1–2 is one obvious example. More controversial would be the well-known passage enshrined in Handel's *Messiah*, Job 19:25–26, "I know that my Redeemer liveth." Michael Austin examines it as part of a larger analysis, concluding that the redeemer in question is a human defender of Job. See chapter 8 of his *Re-reading Job: Understanding the Ancient World's Greatest Poem* (Salt Lake City: Greg Kofford Books, 2014), 103–18.

44. Extra-scriptural metaphors are not inherently contrary to scripture or faulty, but they do tend to impose ideas or frameworks that scripture itself does not warrant, as well as preempt the actual metaphors used in the scriptures themselves.

45. George Handley, *Home Waters: A Year of Recompense on the Provo River* (Salt Lake City: University of Utah Press, 2010), xiii. My thanks to Kristine Haglund for this reference. See further E. Calvin Beisner et al., "A Biblical Perspective on Environmental Stewardship," Acton Institute, accessed March 21, 2023, http://www.acton.org/public-policy/environmental-stewardship/theology-e/biblical-perspective-environmental-stewardship.

46. One of my Jewish professors noted that "cleanness" and "uncleanness" carried misleading English implications. One could be spotlessly fresh from a shower but ritually impure or "unclean." By contrast, the dirtiest, stinkiest Boy Scout recently back from a showerless week in the mountains might be "clean" or ritually pure.

47. "In the context of a society which is concerned with purity and in which contact with the impure carries with it significant consequences, Jesus' touching of 'sinful' people, lepers, corpses, and others who in various ways were understood to be cultically compromised is indeed remarkable and warrants investigation." Craig A. Evans, "Who Touched Me? Jesus and the Ritually Impure," in *Jesus in Context: Temple, Purity, and Restoration,* edited by Bruce David Chilton and Craig A. Evans (Leiden: Brill, 1997), 360.

48. See, for example, Eric A. Seibert, *The Violence of Scripture: Overcoming the Old Testament's Troubling Legacy* (Minneapolis: Fortress, 2012). A popular treatment is provided by Peter Enns, *The Bible Tells Me So: Why Defending Scripture Has Made Us Unable to Read It* (San Francisco: HarperOne, 2015), especially chapter 6. On violence and other problems of scripture, see Kenton Sparks, *Sacred Word, Broken Word: Biblical Authority and the Dark Side of Scripture* (Grand Rapids, MI: William B. Eerdmans, 2012).

49. The Latter-day Saint version of the King James Version does not include cross-references to these two passages quoted in Matthew 37:28–29.

CHAPTER 2

Latter-day Saints and the Atonement in the New Testament

ERIC D. HUNTSMAN

While Latter-day Saints derive much, if not most, of their atonement theology from the Book of Mormon and seek the guidance of the spirit in applying it in their own lives, the New Testament writings nonetheless provide them with the basic "facts" of Jesus's atoning suffering, death, and resurrection.[1] In fact, despite the doctrinal preeminence of the Book of Mormon, because Joseph Smith and other early Latter-day Saints began with basic Christian, especially Protestant, understandings of the salvific work of Jesus Christ, New Testament propositions and images undergird Latter-day Saint atonement theology. In addition, atonement models developed by traditional Christianity have persisted in Mormon thinking.[2]

New Testament texts use a variety of soteriological terms in attempting to explain Jesus's salvific acts. Readers of the King James Bible, the version used by Joseph Smith and the earliest Mormons and still the official Bible of English-speaking Latter-day Saints today, often observe that although the word "atonement" occurs frequently throughout the Old Testament of that version, it only appears once in the New Testament, at Romans 5:11, where it is actually a rendering of the Greek term for reconciliation (*katallagē*). Similarly, the expression "atoning sacrifice" is the closest the New Revised Standard Version (NRSV) of the New Testament comes to using that explicitly talks about "atonement" (1 John 2:2; 4:10). Instead, with the idea that atonement refers to "the saving significance of Jesus's death" understood broadly,[3] New Testament authors employed a number of different verbs, nouns, and an adjective to express ideas to describe the saving actions of God or Jesus Christ and their effects upon people (see Table 1). These word groups included the ideas of rescuing and salvation (*sō̧zō/sōtēria*), ransoming and redemption (*lytroō//lytron/lytrōsis*;

exagorazō), justifying and acquittal (*dikaioō/dikaiōsis/dikaiōma/dikaiosynē*), expiation (*hilaskomai/hilastērion/hilasmos*), reconciling and reconciliation (*katallassō/katallagē*), and healing (*iaomai/iasis*). Further, New Testament passages frequently expand Jesus's saving actions beyond his death to include his resurrection and even ascension and glorification, an approach consonant with the Latter-day Saint approach of seeing atonement more broadly as everything that Jesus did to make us more like God.

Since Aulén (1879–1977), these models have often been grouped into three overarching categories: Christus Victor, which proposes that Jesus's atoning sacrifice and resurrection defeated sin, death, the power of Satan, and other cosmic forces;[4] an objective model, first proposed by Anselm (c. 1033–1099) as a satisfaction theory and then further developed by Protestant reformers after Luther as the idea of penal substitution model;[5] and a subjective model, first championed by Abelard (c. 1079–1142), which focuses on how Jesus's atoning work transforms believers through its moral influence.[6] In recent decades, in view of criticism by feminist and womanist thinkers of these models, especially the satisfaction model, some New Testament scholars have proposed other paradigms such as nonviolent and bloodless atonement.[7] These new paradigms nevertheless can help us discern additional aspects of the atonement beyond the persistent ideas of vicarious sacrifice and punishment, and these aspects may yet provide fruitful additional approaches useful for Latter-day Saints soteriology.

Despite the usefulness of both Aulén's three templates and much of the new thinking about salvation, the most productive course for understanding New Testament teaching on atonement is to examine and consider the more diverse models used by the New Testament authors themselves (see Table 2). Their models were drawn from the spectrum of common human experiences and relationships in the ancient world that often line up closely with the soteriological terms that they were trying to illustrate. These include the ideas of rescue, the redemption of enslaved individuals or groups, sacrifice in public worship, trials in courts of law, the reconciliation of estranged parties, participation or cooption into groups, and incidents of miraculous healing.[8] Nevertheless, while these models are illustrative and help us conceptualize what is not otherwise fully comprehensible, as metaphors they are necessarily limited. As Baker and Green put it, "Metaphors are two-edged: they reveal and conceal, highlight and hide,"[9] and their very number and diversity cautions us against assuming that any one was a perfect or comprehensive expression of how the atonement worked or what it did.

Considering the use of these soteriological terms and models in their assumed chronological order reveals a development or evolution in how New Testament authors struggled to understanding the saving work of Jesus Christ.

Much of this material comes from the Pauline corpus, which has also had perhaps the most significant influence on later Christian theology. Of course, the Synoptic Gospels, though written after the Pauline epistles, contain the only narrative accounts of what Jesus did. Although they contain fewer terms and models, they also appear to have preserved some of the historical Jesus's own statements on his mission. All these ideas are developed in the Johannine Writings, as well as some of the remaining New Testament books, especially 1 Peter and Hebrews. Examining the relevant passages—together with their interpretation not only with Aulén's three overarching categories but also in the light of the contributions of newer bloodless and nonviolent models—may provide fertile ground for a new consideration of the topic of atonement in restoration scripture and Latter-day Saint discourse.

The Pauline Epistles

The Pauline letters, both those generally agreed to have been written by him and the later letters attributed to the apostle, arguably provide the largest amount of material for our discussion of atonement in the New Testament. They begin with the basic Christian proclamation that Jesus died for humankind and then triumphed over death so that we too could live again. They then develop different models to illustrate the significance and function of these salvific acts. Because most of the letters are occasional in nature, to some extent these models developed in response to the different situations facing the individual communities to which they were addressed.[10] On the other hand, the evolution of these models over time suggests a certain trajectory in Pauline thought as it becomes more sophisticated. For this discussion, a working chronology of these letters begins with 1 and perhaps 2 Thessalonians followed by Galatians, Philippians, and Philemon,[11] 1 and 2 Corinthians, and then Romans. The authorship of the later letters attributed to Paul—perhaps 2 Thessalonians as well as Colossians, Ephesians, Titus, and 1 and 2 Timothy—is still disputed by many scholars: some maintain that they were actually written by Paul; some propose that they were DeuteroPauline in the sense that they represented Paul's ideas even if they were written by close associates towards the end of his ministry or shortly after his death; and an increasing number of scholars assert that they are pseudonymous, being written considerably after his death.[12] Regardless, even in the latter two cases, as examples of *Wirkungsgeschichte*, or "effective reception history," these later letters may well reflect Paul's developed thinking on atonement or the lasting impact of his positions.[13]

While the secure letters of Paul are some of the earliest New Testament texts, the redemptive role of Jesus's suffering and death was already part of the earlier *kērygma*, or apostolic preaching tradition, leading Paul to write, "For I handed on to you as of first importance what I in turn had received: that *Christ died for our sins in accordance with the scriptures,* and that he was buried, and that *he was raised on the third day in accordance with the scriptures*" (1 Cor 15:3–4, emphasis added).¹⁴ The expression "the scriptures" here referred not only to the Old Testament as interpreted and applied by the earliest Christians but also to the earliest Christian oral tradition.¹⁵ Paul taught this basic Christian message about salvation and resurrection in his earliest preserved letter when he wrote, "For God has destined us not for wrath but for obtaining salvation through our Lord Jesus Christ, *who died for us,* so that whether we are awake or *asleep we may live with him*" (1 Thess 5:9–10, emphasis added). Similarly, in another early letter he wrote that Jesus "gave himself *for our sins to set us free* from the present evil age" (Gal 1:4, emphasis added), and elsewhere he taught that Jesus died "for us" or "for our sins" (1 Cor 8:11; Rom 5:6–8). While Paul developed the idea that Jesus died as some kind of sacrifice in 1 Corinthians and especially in Romans, in its earliest expressions he follows the basic kerygmatic tradition of proclaiming what Jesus did without explicating how it functioned.

Perhaps his earliest attempt to explain how the atonement changed the condition or standing of believers was the juridical model that Paul first advanced in Galatians. One of his earliest letters, written in the mid-50's CE or perhaps as early as 47 or 48, Galatians was composed much like a courtroom speech, as Paul defended himself and the gospel he had preached against opponents who seem to have been teaching that the largely Gentile congregation should still be observing aspects of the Mosaic law.¹⁶ This juridical model thus appropriately centers on a word group surrounding the Greek verb *dikaioō*. In Classical Greek this was a legal term usually used in a negative sense, meaning "to condemn." However, in the Septuagint, or Greek translation of the Hebrew Bible, it was used to translate words deriving from the root *ṣdq* and described acting in accordance with the requirements of law and custom towards one's fellow beings and in accordance with the demands of God.¹⁷ When used in a legal sense in the Septuagint, *dikaioō* was almost always used positively, indicating that its subject rendered a favorable verdict or vindicated its object.¹⁸ This seems to have governed Paul's usage, which, however, is almost always in the passive.¹⁹ As an example of what is sometimes called "the divine passive" where God is presumed to be the agent, believers were thus vindicated by God. Paul thus famously declared to the errant Galatians, "Yet we know that a person is justified not [Greek, *ou dikaioutai*] by the works of the law but through faith in Jesus Christ. And we have come to believe in Christ Jesus, so that we might be justified by faith in Christ [*hina dikaiōthōmen ek pisteōs Christou*]" (Gal 2:16–17; cf. Gal 3:8, 24). Such language of justification, so important to Martin Luther and other Protestant reformers, was taken as a given by early

Latter-day Saints, as seen in its use in a revelation delivered by Joseph Smith at the organization of the Church on April 6, 1830 (see D&C 20:30),

Paul thus explains that God vindicates or declares believers "not guilty" not because of the works of the law, which in this context seems to be referring to the outward, ceremonial requirements of the law of Moses, but because of either their faith *in* Christ or because of the faithfulness *of* Christ (which is another intriguing rendering of *ek pisteōs Christou*).[20] Implicit in all three occurrences of *dikaioō* in Galatians is that believers are brought back into harmony with God and in some sense declared "righteous," but nowhere in this letter nor in the single occurrence of the term in 1 Corinthians (6:11) does Paul make it clear how this vindication or forgiveness comes about. Rather it is later in Romans, Paul's longest and most theologically developed letter written in 57 or 58,[21] that he makes his clearest statement that Jesus's death brings about justification: "Much more surely then, now that we have been justified *by his blood*, will we be saved through him from the wrath of God" (Rom 5:9). Forms of *dikaioō* appear frequently in this letter (3:24–25, 28, 30; 4:5, 22–25; 5:1; 6:7; 8:30, 33) as do the adjective and noun forms derived from it (see Table 1). Thus, in Romans, Paul uses *dikaioō* to refer to God's vindication of the believer, declaring him or her both "not guilty," or forgiven in an individual sense, and part of a new, inclusive covenant family that includes both Gentiles and believing Jews thanks to the death and saving blood of Christ.[22]

Despite the importance of justification in later, particularly Reformed, theology, outside of Galatians and Romans justification recedes as the primary model and is largely replaced by the verb *sōzō*, meaning to rescue or save,[23] and the noun *sōtēria*, describing deliverance, preservation, and salvation.[24] This focus on rescue is anticipated in the opening of Galatians, where Paul describes Jesus Christ "who gave himself for our sins *to set us free* from the present evil age" (Gal 1:4, emphasis added), although here he uses a form of the verb *exaireō* that the Septuagint had used referring to Moses' call to deliver Israel from its bondage in Egypt (Exod 3:8; cf. Acts 7:34). The evil age or world (Greek, *aiōn*) from which believers were to be delivered was one dominated by elemental powers (Greek, *stoicheia*), spiritual forces also characterized in the later Paulines as rulers, authorities, powers, and dominions (Col 2:10, 15, 20; Eph 1:20–22; 2:2). A ruler, whether a Hellenistic king or a Roman emperor, had the responsibility of rescuing his people from an enemy or delivering them from a natural catastrophe, a role frequently recognized by the political title "Savior" (Greek, *Sōtēr*).[25] For Paul, Christians would survive the destruction of the wicked at the end of the world because they were "expecting *a Savior*, the Lord Jesus Christ. He will transform the body of our humiliation that it may be conformed to the body of his glory, by the power that also enables him to make all things subject to himself" (Phil 3:20–21, emphasis added). Indeed, nothing was more powerful than Jesus, who triumphed over all powers that might try to come between us and the love of God: "I am convinced that neither death, nor life, nor angels, nor rulers, nor things present, nor things to come, nor powers, nor height, nor depth, nor anything else in all creation, will be able to separate us from the love of God in Christ Jesus our Lord" (Rom 8:38–39).

Again drawing upon the imagery of the deliverance from Egypt, Paul used the freeing of Israel from slavery and its being "passed over" by the angel of death as images for our being delivered from the bondage of sin and death, both of which are themselves depicted not only as states of being but as powers themselves. For Paul, beginning in Galatians and then especially in Romans, when "sin" appears in the singular, it refers not so much to individual wrong acts as it does to an actual cosmic force or power that holds humanity in bondage (Gal 2:17; 3:22; Rom 3:9; 5:21; 6:12–14; 7:14; 8:3).[26] He also seems to have conceived of death as a power (1 Cor 15:54–56; Rom 5:12), one which Christ began to defeat with his own resurrection and over which Christ's victory will be complete in the end when "The last enemy to be destroyed is death" (1 Cor 15:26). Not only is this image of a triumphant Christ the basis of the Christus Victor model, it is also one that has resonance with the Book of Mormon, where Jacob exclaimed, "O how great the goodness of our God, who prepareth a way for our escape from the grasp of this awful monster; yea, that monster, death and hell, which I call the death of the body, and also the death of the spirit" (2 Ne 9:10).

The shift from justification to salvation in Paul's writings also seems to indicate a broadening of his discussion of the atonement. Whereas his use of the forensic metaphor of justification in Galatians makes particular sense because of that letter's occasional situation, *dikaioō* is rare in 1 Corinthians and in Romans generally appears in counter position to *sōzō*. In the latter letter, justification refers to past forgiveness or declarations of righteousness, while being saved is more transformative and refers to either a continuing process or a future, eschatological state, a pattern that generally holds elsewhere in the Pauline correspondence.[27] Because of their reliance upon the KJV, this pattern is not always apparent to Latter-day Saints. For instance, what the KJV translates as, "For the preaching of the cross is to them that perish foolishness; but *unto us which are saved* it is the power of God," the NRSV correctly renders with a present participle as "to us who *are being saved*" (1 Cor. 1:18, emphasis added; see also 1 Cor 15:2; 2 Cor 2:15). Further, salvation seems to be broader, referring to present and future forgiveness of sins, future freedom from physical death, and eternal glory.

Another atonement model used by Paul is based upon the idea of redemption. In a classical context, this word-group refers primarily to purchasing someone's freedom after capture or in the slave market,[28] but for Paul and other Jewish Christians it was also heavily influenced by the Exodus narrative, which saw YHWH, or "Jehovah," redeeming his people from slavery and death in Egypt.[29] While the secure letters of Paul do not use specific words for freeing someone through a ransom based upon the verb *lytroō/lytoomai* as do later New Testament authors,[30] he does write that Christ has "bought back" (Greek, *exagorazō*) believers from the curse or power of the law (Gal 3:13; 4:4–5), and he tells the Corinthians, "For you were bought with a price [*ēgorasthēte gar timēs*]; therefore glorify God in your body" (1 Cor 6:20; cf. 7:23). Paul does use the more formal diction representing redemption (Greek, *apolytrōsis* in 1 Cor 1:30; Rom 3:24; 8:23) as do the later Paulines (Col 1:14; Eph 1:7, 14; 4:30; also, *lytroomai* at Tit 2:14). All these passages conjure up images of an enslaved humanity that needs to be "bought back," though the figure to whom the price is paid, unlike the later satisfaction or penal substitution models, is never explicit.

The fractious situation in the Corinthian Christian community availed Paul of another important image to understand and teach atonement. The church there was riven by cliques and was estranged from Paul himself on more than one occasion.[31] After he and the Corinthian saints had been reconciled, he used their experience to teach how Christ had bridged the divide between God and humanity:

> All this is from God, who reconciled us to himself through Christ, and has given us the ministry of *reconciliation*; that is, in Christ God *was reconciling* the world to himself, not counting their trespasses against them, and entrusting the message of *reconciliation* to us. So we are ambassadors for Christ, since God is making his appeal through us; we entreat you on behalf of Christ, *be reconciled* to God (2 Cor. 5:18—20, emphasis added).

The idea of reconciliation—expressed here by the noun *katallagē* and forms of the verb *katallassō*—describes the restoration of individuals to renewed intimacy and friendship after an earlier relationship was ruptured.[32] For instance, Paul uses "reconcile" in terms of bringing together two estranged spouses at 1 Corinthians 7:11: "But if she does separate, let her remain unmarried or else be reconciled to her husband." As Dunn expresses it, when applied to atonement theory, the reconciliation model presents God not "as an angry opponent having to be cajoled or entreated, but of God, the injured partner, actively seeking reconciliation."[33] Further, rather than paying a debt or volunteering for vicarious punishment, it presents Christ as a mediator stepping in to bring two estranged partners together. This relational approach to atonement is important in Latter-day Saint discourse, with reconciliation language prominent in the Book of Mormon (e.g., 2 Ne 10:24; 25:23; 33:9; Jacob 4:11) and Jesus's mediating role often stressed in the speaking of Latter-day Saints leaders, as seen particularly in Boyd K. Packer's talk "The Mediator," though he proceeded to explicate it largely through the prevailing language of penal substitution.[34]

The idea of repairing a relationship between a loving God and his wayward children *and* within the relationships of those children themselves is attractive,[35] and if it occurred only in the context of 2 Corinthians, it would be particularly useful to proponents of a nonviolent atonement. Still, it is clear from Paul's use of the reconciliation model in Romans that it still requires the death of the intermediary, although it does not explain *why* that death is necessary.[36] In a moving passage, Paul linked the death of Christ, past justification, reconciliation, and a future, transformative salvation that will bring life:

> For while we were still weak, at the right time Christ died for the ungodly . . . Much more surely then, now that *we have been justified* by his blood, *will we be saved* through him from the wrath of God. For if while we were enemies, *we were reconciled to God through the death of his Son*, much more surely, having been reconciled, *will we be saved by his life*" (Rom 5:6–10, emphasis added).

This image of reconciliation expands in the later Paulines, where the blood of Christ resolves the hostility between Gentiles and Israel, bringing both to God (Eph 2:11–16) and reconciling not only humanity but all creation to God through the blood of his cross (Col 1:19–20).[37]

What is striking is that explicit sacrificial imagery for atonement appears only in letters to the early Christians in Corinth and Rome, two communities that had large Jewish contingents. To the former, Paul describes Christ as "our paschal lamb" who "has been sacrificed" (1 Cor 5:7). While the Passover sacrifice was not strictly offered for sins, because it commemorated the deliverance of Israel from bondage in Egypt, by the time of Ezekiel 45:18–22, it was seen as somehow representing deliverance of the worshiper from sin.[38] Paul's description of the institution of the Lord's Supper (1 Cor 11:20–26), the oldest New Testament account, was written long before any of the Gospel accounts (see Mark 14:22–26; par Matt 26:26–29; Luke 22:19–20). In all these accounts not only did the Passover setting associate Jesus with the paschal lamb, but the phrase, "This cup is the new covenant in my blood" (1 Cor 11:25; cf. Mark 14:24; Matt 26:28; Luke 22:20), also echoes the sacrifice by which Moses established the covenant with Israel at Sinai (see Exod 24:8). Paul might also have used language connecting Christ to the Mosaic sin offering when he wrote to the Romans, "For God has done what the law, weakened by the flesh, could not do: by sending his own Son in the likeness of sinful flesh, and *to deal with sin*, he condemned sin in the flesh" (Rom 8:3, emphasis added). The phrase "to deal with sin" in the NRSV, which the KJV simply translates as "for sin," renders in English the Greek phrase *peri hamartias*, which the Septuagint regularly uses as a translation for "a sin offering" (Hebrew, *ḥaṭṭā't*).[39]

Paul's strongest sacrificial image is also the only one where he actually uses explicit language connected with "atonement" in the Old Testament. To the Romans he wrote of Christ "whom God put forward as *a sacrifice of atonement* [Greek, *hilastērion*] by his blood" (Rom 3:25). Earlier English translations such as the KJV and the NASB (New American Standard Bible) rendered *hilastērion* as "a propitiation," but this has largely been abandoned as theologically fraught, conjuring as it does the image of needing to placate an angry God. Originally an adjective meaning "propitious" or "well-disposed" in Classical Greek, *hilastērion* was used in the Septuagint for the Hebrew *kappōret*, which described the golden lid of the Ark of the Covenant. Also known as the "mercy seat" in English, this was the place where the high priest sprinkled the blood of the Day of Atonement sacrifice (see Lev 16). This in turn derived from *kpr*, which originally included the sense of "covering" sins and by the time of the Septuagint and New Testament meant "expiation" rather than "propitiation." In other words, with sin rather than God being its object, the sacrifice covered or removed sin rather than appeasing God.[40] Paul's single use of this term, which only appears in Hebrews 9:5 elsewhere in the New Testament, is significant because as the *hilastērion*, Christ is the new mercy seat, the *place* where atonement takes place. As Hultgren has described it, "Christ is both atoning sin offering and the place of atonement . . . the theological 'moment' of greatest significance in this metaphor is not sacrifice as such but that in Christ's death the justice and mercy of God meet. The atoning sacrifice at the *hilastērion* is the demonstration of divine justice and mercy, united in one event, one person."[41]

Perhaps Paul's most intriguing atonement model is that of participation.[42] The germ of the idea occurs early, in Galatians, when Paul wrote, "I have been crucified *with Christ*; and it is no longer I who live, but *it is Christ who lives in me*" (Gal 2:19b, emphasis added). Then, just as we die with Christ, God made Christ one with us, "For our sake he made him to be sin who knew no sin, so that in him we might become the righteousness of God" (2 Cor 5:21). The roots of this identification might have stemmed from an important aspect of Mosaic sacrifice. Bell observes, "The Israelite through the laying on of hands is identified with the sacrificial animal to such an extent that the death of the animal is the death of the Israelite and by passing through this judgement of death, the Israelite is able, via the blood rite, to have fellowship with God."[43] But the participation model then finds its fruition in Romans that goes beyond mere identification: through such identification, just as humanity participated with Adam in sin and death, so believers will participate with Jesus's triumph over these powers (Rom 5:14–15).[44]

Paul's crowning expression of this model, which occurs in his discussion of the significance of baptism, is worth quoting in full:

> Do you not know that all of us who have been baptized into Christ Jesus *were baptized into his death*? Therefore we have been buried with him by baptism into death, so that, *just as Christ was raised from the dead* by the glory of the Father, so *we too might walk in newness of life*. For if we have been united with him in a death like his, we will certainly be united with him in a resurrection like his. We know that our old self was crucified with him so that the body of sin might be destroyed, and we might no longer be enslaved to sin. *For whoever has died is freed from sin*. But if we have died with Christ, we believe that we will also live with him. We know that Christ, being raised from the dead, will never die again; death no longer has dominion over him. The death he died, he died to sin, once for all; but the life he lives, he lives to God. *So you also must consider yourselves dead to sin and alive to God in Christ Jesus* (Rom 6:3–11, emphasis added).

The power of this model is that Christ's death represents not so much a payment or punishment as it does an end to something, and I have argued elsewhere that as such, when we die with Christ our old man or woman—and everything associated with it—dies too. Christ carries not only our sins but also our suffering, pain, and sorrows to the cross, where they have an end.[45] Then, as Bell observes, "We see here that the atonement for Paul is achieved by the death and resurrection of Christ . . . by participating through faith in Christ's death, the believer is made a new creation."[46] But the believer is not only a new creation in mortality; the new Christian life is a symbol and foretaste of the eternal life that follows resurrection.

Although some of these models are less familiar to us today, they all had meaning in the lived experience of Paul's original audiences. In the classic summation by Martin Hengel, Pauline atonement drew upon central features of that world: *justification* from the forensic realm, *redemption* from the realm of human rights and freedom, *expiation* from the cultic realm, and *reconciliation* from the political-social realm.[47] While the occasional situation may have favored one model over another in a specific letter, reconciliation and especially participation appear later in the Pauline corpus and seem to reflect more developed thinking. Interestingly, both these models provide material for advocates of a more nonviolent atonement,[48] and they are arguably more amenable to the Latter-day Saint images of God as the literal, loving Parent and Christ as a Savior whose purpose is to make us more like himself. Still, earlier models do not disappear, and the indispensable role of Jesus's sacrificial death pervades the Pauline corpus.[49]

The Synoptic Gospels

The Gospel according to Mark, assumed by most scholars to be the first of the three Synoptic Gospels, likely served as the narrative foundation for the Matthean and Lucan accounts, although the order of these other two gospels and their exact relationship to the Marcan prototype and to each other is still debated.[50] Mark may have first taken form sometime in the late 60's, not long after Peter and Paul's martyrdoms in Rome sometime between 64 and 68. According to tradition, it was written by John Mark, the translator of Peter, and in many ways it reflects the pattern Peter's kerygmatic preaching, at least as portrayed by his sermons in Acts, which laid out how God sent his Son Jesus, who went about doing good, was crucified, and was then raised from the dead (cf. Acts 10:36–43).[51] In this sense, although Mark was written after the secure letters of Paul, it reflects the same early, relatively unadorned apostolic proclamation seen in the most simple Pauline statements about Jesus's death already discussed (e.g., 1 Thess 5:9–10; Gal 1:4; 1 Cor 8:11; 15:3–4; Rom 5:6–8). Unlike the developing ideas on atonement in the Pauline corpus, however, Mark puts forward little direct doctrinal exposition on the meaning of the death of Jesus, leaving it to the Gospel's narrative structures to reveal the significance of its atonement theology.[52] Martin Kähler's famous observation that "one could call the Gospels passion narratives with extended introductions"[53] is particularly the case with Mark, some twenty percent of which focuses on Jesus's final days and hours. The "extended introduction" that precedes this sets Jesus's death into the context of Jesus's ministry of serving and liberating especially the lowest of society, despite the risks this created in the face of both the Jewish and Roman governing authorities. Only two sayings of Jesus, however, attribute specific meaning to his death, and these are not explicitly connected to the forgiveness of sins.[54]

The first of these sayings follows three passion predictions in which Jesus explains to his disciples that when they arrive in Jerusalem he will be betrayed, killed, and then rise again (Mark 8:31; 9:30–31; 10:32–34). After the third prediction, which is the most detailed, Jesus then proclaims, "For the Son of Man came *not to be served but to serve*, and *to give his life a ransom* for many" (Mark 10:45). The reference to serving connects the passion narrative that follows with the ministry of service and liberation that preceded in Jesus's Galilean ministry,[55] but it is the word "ransom" (Greek, *lytron*) that gives his prophesied death significance. While the term Jesus used in his native Aramaic is unknown, Mark used this technical, but non-Pauline, Greek term.[56] His presumably Gentile audience would have connected *lytron* with the Roman slave trade, where it referred specifically to buying a slave's freedom.[57] Still, in Jesus's mind and in the ears of his first Jewish followers, the idea of ransom might have primarily brought to mind the Exodus story, in which case "ransom" would have meant more release from bondage than a payment made to a previous owner.[58] Both of these ideas—ransom from slavery and liberation from bondage—fit the larger narrative picture of Mark, in which Jesus has come to deliver people from captivity, whether it be from economic and social oppression or from the bondage of Satan and unclean spirits.[59] While Jesus's forgiving sins (Mark 2:1–12) was part of that mission, Mark does not explicitly connect being released from this kind of spiritual bondage to the ransom Jesus is going to pay, indicate to whom it is owed, or whether it is simply the price of standing up to the political, religious, and supernatural powers that Jesus faces in his service of the powerless. Read without the soteriological reflections of other texts, in Mark "his life as a ransom" could well suggest that Jesus's death came at the hands of the authorities of his day because of his activism on behalf of the oppressed.

The other saying of Jesus that seeks to give meaning to his death is found in his words at the Lord's Supper, when he declares, "This is my blood of the covenant, *which is poured out* for many" (Mark 14:24). As with Paul's account of the Lord's Supper, the Passover setting of the Last Supper connects this saying closely with the paschal sacrifice and, more broadly, with the Exodus story.[60] While this story implied that Jesus's blood would deliver from bondage and death, the Marcan version adds "which is poured out" to the earlier Pauline formulation, which connects it even more closely with the institution of the Mosaic covenant at Exod 24:6–8, which uses the same verb for pour (Greek, *ekcheō*) in the Septuagint.[61] Still, the implication of this saying is unclear. While the blood of sacrificial victims was certainly poured out (Exod 29:12; Lev 4:7, 18, 25, 30, 34; 8:15; 9:9), so was the blood of animals slaughtered for food in non-sacral settings (See Lev 7:13; Deut 12:16, 24; 15:23). Further, the New Testament refers to the blood of righteous martyrs (Matt 23:35; Luke 11:50; Acts 22:20), who are in many ways prototypes of Jesus who dies, though innocent. Still, as Smith has observed, the narrative of Mark vividly illustrates the effects of that death: at the moment Jesus expires, the rending of the temple veil (Mark 15:39; parallels Matt 27:51; Luke 23: 45) connects his death to the entrance of the high priest to the Holy of Holies (and, by extension, to God's presence) on the Day of Atonement, and the centurion's declaration, "Truly this man was God's Son!" (Mark 15:39), reveals how Jesus's death transforms the soldier.[62]

The Gospel of Matthew appears to have drawn upon the basic Marcan narrative, interweaving it with additional sayings of Jesus and some additional unique material.[63] Matthew takes over the two sayings of Jesus about the meaning of his death found in Mark, but it places them in a greater soteriological context. First, Matthew directly establishes Jesus's saving mission at the beginning of his gospel when an angel declares to Joseph that Mary "will bear a son, and you are to name him Jesus, for *he will save his people from their sins*" (Matt 1:21, emphasis added). Matthew adopts the Marcan ransom saying without significant change in Matthew 20:28,[64] though his earlier direct quotation of Isaiah 53:4, in which the Suffering Servant figure "has borne our infirmities and carried our diseases," make stronger the possible allusion to Isaiah 53:10–12 in the ransom being for "for many."[65] Matthew does make a significant change in the Last Supper saying: "For this is my blood of the covenant, which is poured out for many *for the forgiveness of sins*" (Matt 26:28, emphasis added). While Matthew's rendering of the saying retains the connection with the institution of the Mosaic covenant, the addition of "for the forgiveness of sins" indicates that Matthew clearly understands that Jesus's death is an act of expiation, perhaps analogous to the Mosaic sin offering.[66] It also strongly echoes Isaiah 53:10–12, where the Servant makes his life an offering for sin and bears the iniquities of and makes intercession for transgressors.[67] This emphasis on dealing with sin has led Heider, using Aulén's rubric, to propose that Matthew presents a primarily objective model of atonement.[68] Nevertheless, despite Matthew's more explicit soteriology and its clearer connection of Jesus's death to forgiveness, this gospel presents Jesus's entire ministry of service, rather than solely his sacrificial death, as salvific.[69]

Scholars remain divided as to whether Luke and Matthew acted independently in drawing upon the Marcan narrative and some collection of Jesus's sayings, or whether Luke drew upon the latter largely from Matthew.[70] Nevertheless, Luke has more unique material than the other two gospels, claims to have consulted multiple sources, and is part of a two-volume work that includes Acts.[71] Surprisingly, both Luke and Acts have few references to the salvific significance of Jesus's death but focus more on his resurrection and ascension,[72] an emphasis that finds a parallel with the Book of Mormon's emphasis on resurrection its discussion of atonement.[73] Luke omits the ransom saying found in both Mark and Matthew, and instead of adding "for the forgiveness of sins" to the Lord's Supper saying, he writes, "This cup that is poured out for you is the *new* covenant in my blood" (Luke 22:20, emphasis added), which connects the event more clearly with the prophecy of Jeremiah 31:31–33. Later, when the disciples on the road to Emmaus express despair at Jesus's death, the Risen Lord makes clear that he was the one meant to redeem Israel in spite of this seemingly unexpected, ignominious death: "Was it not necessary that the Messiah should suffer these things and then enter into his glory?" (Luke 24:26). The kerygmatic speeches of Peter in Acts emphasize that Jesus's enemies killed him rather than portraying that death as a vicarious sacrifice, and they give equal, or more weight, to the resurrection, portraying it as God's vindication of Jesus.[74] As with Matthew, Jesus's salvific role includes the totality of his life and then extends it beyond the resurrection.[75] Although this should not minimize the role of Jesus's death in salvation,[76] Baker and Green have observed, "For Luke, the totality of Jesus's ministry—his coming, his public mission, his death, his exaltation, and his present activity via the Spirit—play" the role of bringing about the redemption on humanity.[77] The change that this works in people as the subjects of atonement has led Heider to see Lucan atonement as representing a more subjective model.[78]

This broader view of Jesus's saving work, though apparent in Matthew and most clear in Luke, appears in all three Synoptics through Jesus's healing ministry. The Lord as healer is a prominent motif in the Hebrew Bible, especially in the explicit prophecy about Isaiah's Servant figure, who was to bear infirmities, carry diseases, and heal bruises, which is particularly apparent in Jesus's reading from Isaiah in the synagogue in Nazareth (Luke 4:18–19).[79] Healings indeed comprise the largest proportion of Jesus's miracles, providing immediate physical relief to their recipients as well as serving as types of the emotional and spiritual fruits of the atonement.[80] Healing is particularly prominent in Luke, with the verb *iaomai* "to heal" appearing in that text almost as much as in the rest of the New Testament combined (see Table 1). For Latter-day Saints, the atonement as healing is an important soteriological contribution of the Book of Mormon (see esp. Alma 7:11–12), where the younger Alma expands upon the Servant's role in Isaiah 53,[81] and healing is an important subjective model in the work of Terryl and Fiona Givens.[82] Jesus's work of healing, reclaiming the lost, championing the poor, defending the oppressed, and modeling compassion are important aspects of atonement for proponents of nonviolent atonement, providing for Weaver a model that he calls "Narrative Christus Victor" offers a transformative example for believers.[83]

The Johannine Writings

Early tradition ascribed the Gospel according to John, 1–3 John, and Revelation to the apostle John. While the authorship of each of these books and their connections to each other continue to be debated,[84] of these Johannine Writings, the gospel, the first letter, and the apocalypse share a high Christology; persistent dualism in their portrayals of light and darkness, good and evil, and spiritual life and death; and certain other shared images, such as Jesus as the Word and the Lamb of God. They also demonstrate similar soteriology, presenting the atonement as both a sacrifice and a triumph over the powers of darkness.

Of the four New Testament Gospels, John portrays a Jesus who is more consistently divine and unified with the Father. The *Logos* Hymn (John 1:1–18) that opens the gospel establishes its high Christology with its portrayal of the Divine Word who becomes flesh in order that he could make those who believe in him the children of God (v. 12). Through the rest of the gospel, Jesus, as the Incarnate Word, thinly veiled in flesh, remains powerful, seemingly all-knowing, and perfectly obedient to and one with his Father.[85] This divine, eternal figure paradoxically becomes a sacrificial lamb, dying that those who accept him might live. This lamb imagery is explicit at the beginning of the gospel, when the prophet John, known in the Synoptics as the Baptist, declares, "Here *is the Lamb of God* who takes away *the sin* of the world!" (John 1:29) and then on the next day repeats this identification to two of his followers (1:36). Interestingly, the lamb has come to remove sin (in the singular) in a way that is reminiscent of Christ's triumph over the power of cosmic sin in Paul's letters to the Galatians and Romans (Gal 2:17; 3:22; Rom 3:9; 5:21; 6:12–14; 7:14; 8:3). Lamb of God imagery is then implicit at the end of the Gospel, where the timing of Passover, Jesus's blood on the wood of the cross, and the detail of none of his bones being broken in the Johannine passion narrative portray Jesus's death as that of the ultimate paschal lamb.[86] Accordingly, on one level John's Lamb of God imagery portrays Jesus's death as something other than a vicarious sacrifice for sin. The blood of lambs on the first Passover was meant to preserve life, causing the angel of death to "pass over" the children of Israel (Exod 12:3–14, 21–29).

John's Jesus came to give life, eternal and abundant (John 3:15–16, 36; 4:14; 5:21; 6:33–58; 10:10, 28; 11:25–26; 14:6; 17:1–3), achieving union of the believers with the divine (John 17:3, 9–11, 21). The Johannine passion narrative is also arguably less violent than the Synoptic narratives. Although John 18:1–19:37 does not pass over the abuse that he suffers at the hands of the Jewish and Roman authorities, it omits Jesus's anguish in Gethsemane, and he carries his own cross and hangs on the cross for only three hours rather than six as in the Synoptics. Jesus is both the sacrifice and the sacrificer: earlier he announced that he had power to lay his life down and take it up again (John 10:17–18), and in John 19:30, he announces, "It is finished," giving up his spirit rather than having his life taken from him (John 19:30). The blood and water pouring from Jesus's side then represent the eternal life flowing from him (19:34–35).[87]

The first letter of John twice explicitly calls Jesus "the atoning sacrifice for our *sins* [Greek, *hilasmos peri tōn hamartiōn hēmōn*]" (1 John 2:2; 4:10, emphasis added), with sins in the plural. While the KJV familiar to most English-speaking Latter-day Saints renders this as "the propitiation for our sins," *hilasmos* is closely related to Paul's *hilastērion* of Romans 3:25. Again, instead of propitiating a wrathful God, Jesus's atoning sacrifice covers or expiates sin. The plural "sins" must refer to individual wrong acts rather than to the power of cosmic sin that fit so well the dualism of the gospel, but if 1 John can be read partly as a commentary on the Gospel of John, then the Lamb of God imagery in the latter is more than just a paschal symbol. While we have seen that in Ezekiel 45:15 the Passover had begun to be seen as an offering for sin, it is also likely that in the Johannine writings all the lambs of the Old Testament—the Passover, the daily *tāmîd* offering, the Suffering Servant in Isaiah, and even the ram that took the place of Isaac—combine in the figure of the Lamb of God.[88]

The Lamb of God is also, of course, a very prominent image in Revelation. The only one of the Johannine writings that actually identifies its author by the name John (Rev 1:1, 4, 9; 22:8), its Greek, style, and genre are very different from the gospel of that name.[89] Revelation also uses one Greek word for lamb, *arnion*, while the gospel uses another, *amnos*. Nevertheless, the image of "a Lamb standing as if it had been slaughtered" (Rev 5:6) who conquers, redeems, provides, and is worshipped together with the Father (Rev 7:17; 15:3; 19:9; 21:23; 22:1; 22:3),[90] fits very well the composite Lamb of God in the Gospel of John. The triumph of the apocalyptic Lamb over Satan and his hosts throughout Revelation also finds subtle parallels in references in John and 1 John to Jesus's promised victory over Satan, who is described as the thief, the ruler of this world, and explicitly as the devil (John 8:44; 10:10; 12:31; 14:30; 16:11; 1 John 3:8). This powerful image of a dying lamb conquering the power of death accords with Aulén's later Christus Victor image, as Heider observed.[91] Revelation also serves as an important lynchpin in Weaver's theory of Narrative Christus Victor as an important nonviolent atonement model.[92]

The General Epistles and Hebrews

The letters of Jude and James contribute little, christologically or soteriologically, to the discussion of atonement. In fact, Martin Luther famously referred to James as "an epistle of straw,"[93] apparently because it made only two references to the name of Jesus Christ, once to help identify the book's author (1:1) and then to warn that their belief in Jesus Christ should be without favoritism (2:1; KJV, "with respect of persons"). Still, some Latter-day Saints are fond of quoting the declaration "faith, if it hath not works, is dead" (Jas 2:17) as a control on Pauline passages that base justification on faith and salvation on grace (Gal 2:16; Eph 2:9–10), but in the context of James 2, the works described are the works of charity without which the poor cannot be saved from nakedness and hunger rather than means to the salvation of the giver.[94] References to justification and saving in both letters are not directly connected to Jesus's suffering, death, or resurrection (see Table 1); in the closing of Jude it is God, not Jesus, who is referred to as Savior (1:25). On the other hand, 1 Peter and Hebrews both make significant statements about Jesus's atoning work.

Attributed to the chief apostle, the first Petrine letter combines a ransom model and paschal imagery, declaring, "You know that *you were ransomed* [Greek, *elytrōthēte*] from the futile ways inherited from your ancestors, not with perishable things like silver or gold, but with the precious blood of Christ, like that of *a lamb without defect or blemish*" (1 Pet 1:18–19). Using a form of the technical verb *lytroomai* for ransom, in this passage believers have been delivered not from bondage in Egypt but from the wickedness of their previous lives through the blood of Christ, who appears, as in the Johannine Writings, as a perfect lamb. Then, in a striking passage, the author combines vicarious death for sins with a quotation about the healing Servant of Isaiah who rescues lost sheep: "He himself *bore our sins in his body on the cross*, so that, free from sins, we might live for righteousness; *by his wounds you have been healed*. For you were going astray like sheep, but now you have returned to the shepherd and guardian of your souls (1 Pet 2:24–25, emphasis added; Isa 53:3–6).[95] Finally, while Jesus's blood ransoms, his cross pays for sins, and his wounds heal, the letter also includes the resurrection in its view of atonement. In an interesting connection of resurrection with baptism reminiscent of Paul's arguments in Romans 6:4–5, the author proposes that the resurrection of Jesus, which precedes his triumphant ascent into heaven, saves (1 Pet 3:21–22).

Because of its powerful use of priestly and sacrificial symbolism, in some ways Hebrews is the crowning jewel of New Testament atonement imagery.[96] The book is an enigma: difficult to date, more of a theological treatise than a letter, and its author unnamed.[97] It was not attributed to Paul before Jerome (c. 347–420) and is significantly different from any of the Pauline letters in topic and the style of its Greek. Still there is at least one connection in its use in Hebrews 9:5 of *hilastērion* for the mercy seat, using the same term that Paul had used in Romans 3:25. Priestly and temple imagery pervades the text, with expiation at times combined with elements of recapitulation and Christus Victor:

> Since, therefore, the children share flesh and blood, *he himself likewise shared the same things*, so that through death *he might destroy the one who has the power of death, that is, the devil* . . . Therefore he had to become like his brothers and sisters in every respect, so that he might be a merciful and faithful high priest in the service of God, *to make a sacrifice of atonement* [Greek, *hilakesthai*; KJV, "make reconciliation"] for the sins of the people. Because he himself was tested *by what he suffered*, he is able to help those who are being tested (Heb 2:14–18, emphasis added).

The idea of suffering (Greek, *paschō*) being part of Jesus's saving work is particularly prominent in Luke,[98] which is also the one gospel that, in the final form of its text at least, significantly expands the Gethsemane incident in a way familiar to Latter-day Saints from restoration scripture (Luke 22:39–44; see Mos 3:7; D&C 19:16–19).[99] If the suffering in Hebrews 2 refers Jesus's experience in the garden, the next passage in Hebrews 5 takes on new import:

> In the days of his flesh, Jesus offered up prayers and supplications, with loud cries and tears, to the one who was able to save him from death, and he was heard because of his reverent submission. Although he was a Son, he learned obedience *through what he suffered*; and having been made perfect, he became the source of eternal salvation for all who obey him (Heb 5:7–9, emphasis added).

Yet perhaps the strongest image from Hebrews is that of Jesus performing the Day of Atonement sacrifice once and for all, which contrasts with the annual obligation of mortal high priests who passed through the veil separating the Holy Place from the Holy of Holies with the blood of the Yom Kippur sacrifices, stood to minister before the mercy seat, but then withdrew again. Jesus, on the other hand, entered the Holy of Holies with his own blood, symbolically opening the presence of God to all in a way that vividly draws together an Old Testament expiation and New Testament redemption, reconciliation, and participation models (Heb 9:1–14). This temple imagery is particularly potent in view of the Latter-day Saint temple ceremony. While many Protestants view the rending of the temple veil at the death of Jesus (Mark 15:39; parallels Matt 27:51; Luke 23:45) as a sign that the temple's function was superseded and Christians now had free access to God's presence, Latter-day Saints see the rending more as a parting of the veil rather than its destruction, symbolizing that God's presence can now be accessed through Jesus Christ and his salvific blood. Thus, by making and keeping sacred covenants in order to more fully follow Jesus, participants in the modern temple ceremony believe that they are more fully benefitting from the saving and exalting power of Christ's atonement as they symbolically pass from an ordinance room where the ceremony is held into the temple's celestial room, which, like the Holy of Holies in the earlier Jerusalem Temple, symbolizes God's presence.[100]

Prospects for Latter-day Saint Approaches to Atonement

These New Testament terms, images, and models constituted the standard repertoire from which the early Latter-day Saints, like other Christians, drew their understanding of the atonement. Nevertheless, their breadth and differences are unfamiliar to many members today. In addition, certain models—particularly vicarious substitution, drawn from our largely Protestant cultural heritage as well as from Book of Mormon discussions of satisfying the mercy and justice of God (e.g., 2 Ne 2:10–12; Mos 15:9; Alma 42:13–25)—sometimes overshadow other possibilities that restoration scripture and latter-day revelation afford. While some popular contemporary Latter-day Saint models continue to focus on objective models such as paying a debt or compensating for shortfalls, there has been increasing interest in subjective models focusing on grace, compassion, and healing,[101] including those put forward in the second half of this collection. In addition, Latter-day Saint apocalypticism, which both sees an ongoing battle between good and evil yet also takes literally the eschatology of Revelation, continues to find resonance with the image of Christus Victor. Indeed, the different examples in the New Testament reminds us of the need for multiple models, which as metaphors can only partially describe the indescribable.

In addition, some early Christian developments, such as the evolution of Paul's thinking, can provide a template for understanding the expansion of doctrinal understanding in the Restoration tradition, such as the shift in Joseph Smith's revelations that Ostler has observed from his early use of Pauline categories, especially justification and sanctification, to more Johannine concepts, including transformation and becoming one with, and perhaps even like, God and Christ (see John 17: 17:3, 9–11, 21; 1 John 3:2).[102] Indeed, transformation and the deification of the individual—rich fruits of Restoration theology—extend further New Testament models such as Pauline participation and Johannine unity with the divine. As Laughton and Haws discuss in their essays below (chapters 3 and 6), for Latter-day Saints, participation in and sharing of the divine nature goes beyond the kind of *theosis* contemplated by later Christian thinkers like Irenaeus or that found in Eastern Orthodox thought.[103] Nevertheless, returning to New Testament teachings about becoming "joint heirs with Christ" (Rom 8:16–17; cf. Eph 4:13; 2 Tim 2:10–12; 1 John 3:2) anchors such a lofty view of exaltation in the atonement worked by Jesus Christ. In the end, not only salvation but also exaltation are products of his grace. While the Latter-day Saint expectation of deification is audacious, it nonetheless is believed to arise from "him that loved us, and washed us from our sins in his own blood, And hath made us kings and priests unto God and his Father; to him be glory and dominion for ever and ever" (Rev 1:5b–6 KJV). §

Table 2.1. Key New Testament Soteriological Terms

Lexical Entry	English Meanings	1 Thess	2 Thess	Galatians	Philippians	Philemon
agorazō	bought, purchased					
exagorazō	redeem, buy back			3:13; 4:5		
dikaioō	justify; treat as just, acquit			2:16 (3x), 17; 3:8, 11, 24; 5:4		
dikaiōma	justification					
dikaios	just, in harmony with law; righteous; right, proper			3:11	1:7; 4:8	
dikaiōsis	justification					
dikaiosynē	justification / righteousness			2:21; 3:6, 21; 5:5	1:11; 3:6, 9 (2x)	
exaireō	deliver, set free			1:4		
hilaskomai	propitiate, conciliate					
hilastērion	means of expiation, place of propitiation					
hilasmos	appeasement, expiation					
iaomai	heal					
iasis	healing					
katallassō	reconcile					
apokatallassō	reconcile					
katallagē	reconciliation					
lyō	loose, free (from sin or bondage)					
apolytrōsis	redemption					
lytroō/lytroomai	purchase freedom with a ransom					
lytron	ransom, redemption					
lytrōsis	redemption					
ryomai	rescue, deliver	1:10	3:2			
Sōtēr	Savior, deliverer				3:20	
sōtēria	deliverance, salvation	5:8, 9	2:13		1:19, 28; 2:12	
sōtērion	deliverance, salvation					
sō̧zō	save, rescue	2:16	2:10			
		1 Thess	2 Thess	Galatians	Philippians	Philemon

a All three James references are to being "justified by works"
b Instances where sō̧zō seems to mean "heal" from context
c Instances where sō̧zō seems to mean both "heal" and "saved"

Table 2.1. (continued)

Lexical Entry	English Meanings	1 Cor	2 Cor	Romans	James	Colossians
agorazō	bought, purchased	6:20; 7:23				
exagorazō	redeem, buy back					4:5
dikaioō	justify; treat as just, acquit	4:4; 6:11		2:13; 3:4, 20, 24, 26, 28, 30; 4:2, 5; 5:1, 9; 6:7; 8:30 (2x), 33	2:21, 24, 25[a]	
dikaiōma	justification			1:32; 5:16		
dikaios	just, in harmony with law; righteous; right, proper			1:17; 2:13; 3:10, 26; 5:7, 19; 7:12	5:6, 16	4:1
dikaiōsis	justification			4:25; 5:18		
dikaiosynē	justification / righteousness	1:30	3:9; 5:21; 6:7, 14; 9:9, 10; 11:15	1:17; 3:5, 21, 22, 25, 26; 4:3, 5, 6, 9, 11 (2x), 13, 22; 5:17, 21; 6:13, 16, 18, 19, 20; 8:10; 9:30 (3x), 31; 10:3 (3x), 4, 5, 6, 10; 14:17	1:20; 2:23; 3:18	
exaireō	deliver, set free					
hilaskomai	propitiate, conciliate					
hilastērion	means of expiation, place of propitiation			3:25		
hilasmos	appeasement, expiation					
iaomai	heal				5:16	
iasis	healing					
katallassō	reconcile	7:11 (of husband and wife)	5:18, 19, 20	5:10 (2x)		
apokatallassō	reconcile					1:20, 21/22
katallagē	reconciliation		5:18, 19	5:11; 11:15		
lyō	loose, free (from sin or bondage)					
apolytrōsis	redemption	1:30		3:24; 8:23		1:14
lytroō/lytroomai	purchase freedom with a ransom					
lytron	ransom, redemption					
lytrōsis	redemption					
ryomai	rescue, deliver		1:10 (1x, 2x)	7:24; 11:26; 15:31		
Sōtēr	Savior, deliverer					
sōtēria	deliverance, salvation		1:6 (2x); 6:2 (2x); 7:10	1:16; 10:10; 11:11; 13:11		
sōtērion	deliverance, salvation					
sō$_1$zō	save, rescue	1:18, 21; 3:15; 5:5; 7:16 (2x); 9:22; 10:33; 15:2	2:15	5:9, 10; 8:24; 9:27; 10:9, 13; 11:14, 26	1:21; 2:14 (read in context!); 4:12; 5:15, 20	1:13
		1 Cor	2 Cor	Romans	James	Colossians

[a] All three James references are to being "justified by works"
[b,b] Instances where sō$_1$zō seems to mean "heal" from context
[c] Instances where sō$_1$zō seems to mean both "heal" and "saved"

Table 2.1. (continued)

Lexical Entry	English Meanings	Ephesians	Titus	1 Tim	2 Tim	Jude
agorazō	bought, purchased					
exagorazō	redeem, buy back	5:16				
dikaioō	justify; treat as just, acquit		3:7		3:16	
dikaiōma	justification					
dikaios	just, in harmony with law; righteous; right, proper	6:1	1:8	1:9	4:8	
dikaiōsis	justification					
dikaiosynē	justification / righteousness	4:24; 5:9; 6:14	3:5	6:11	2:22; 3:16; 4:8	
exaireō	deliver, set free					
hilaskomai	propitiate, conciliate					
hilastērion	means of expiation, place of propitiation					
hilasmos	appeasement, expiation					
iaomai	heal					
iasis	healing					
katallassō	reconcile					
apokatallassō	reconcile	2:16				
katallagē	reconciliation					
lyō	loose, free (from sin or bondage)					
apolytrōsis	redemption	1:7, 14; 4:30				
lytroō/lytroomai	purchase freedom with a ransom		2:14			
lytron	ransom, redemption					
lytrōsis	redemption					
ryomai	rescue, deliver				3:11; 4:17, 18	
Sōtēr	Savior, deliverer	5:23	1:3, 4; 2:10, 13; 3:4, 6	1:1; 2:3; 4:10	1:10	1:25
sōtēria	deliverance, salvation	1:13			2:10; 3:15	1:3
sōtērion	deliverance, salvation	6:17	2:11			
sōzō	save, rescue	2:5, 8 (past but perfect-with lasting result)	3:5	1:15; 2:4, 15; 4:16	1:9; 4:18	1:5, 23
		Ephesians	Titus	1 Tim	2 Tim	Jude

ᵃ All three James references are to being "justified by works"
ᵇ Instances where sōzō seems to mean "heal" from context
ᶜ Instances where sōzō seems to mean both "heal" and "saved"

Table 2.1. (continued)

Lexical Entry	English Meanings	1 Pet	2 Pet	Mark	Rev	Matt
agorazō	bought, purchased	2:1			5:9; 14:3, 4	
exagorazō	redeem, buy back					
dikaioō	justify; treat as just, acquit					11:19; 12:37;
dikaiōma	justification					
dikaios	just, in harmony with law; righteous; right, proper	3:12, 18; 4:18	1:13; 2:7, 8 (2x)	2:17; 6:20	15:3; 16:5, 7; 19:2; 22:11	1:19; 5:45; 9:13; 10:41 (3x); 13:7, 43, 49; 20:4; 23:28, 29, 35 (2x); 25:37, 46; 27:19 (NRSV "innocent")
dikaiōsis	justification					
dikaiosynē	justification / righteousness	2:24	1:1; 2:5, 21; 3:13		19:11; 22:11	3:15; 5:6, 10, 20; 6:1, 33; 21:32
exaireō	deliver, set free					
hilaskomai	propitiate, conciliate					
hilastērion	means of expiation, place of propitiation					
hilasmos	appeasement, expiation					
iaomai	heal	2:24		5:29		8:8, 13; 13:15; 15:28
iasis	healing					
katallassō	reconcile					
apokatallassō	reconcile					
katallagē	reconciliation					
lyō	loose, free (from sin or bondage)				1:5 (wash/free from sins)	16:19 (2x); 18:18 (2x)
apolytrōsis	redemption					
lytroō/lytroomai	purchase freedom with a ransom	1:18				
lytron	ransom, redemption			10:45		20:28
lytrōsis	redemption					
ryomai	rescue, deliver		2:7, 9			6:13; 27:43
Sōtēr	Savior, deliverer		1:1, 11, 20; 3:2, 18			
sōtēria	deliverance, salvation	1:5, 9, 10; 2:2	3:15		7:10; 12:10; 19:1	
sōtērion	deliverance, salvation					
sō̧zō	save, rescue	3:21; 4:18		3:4; 5:23[b], 28[b], 34[c]; 6:56[b]; 8:35 (2x); 10:26, 52[c]; 13:13, 20; 15:30, 31 (2x); 16:16		1:21; 8:25; 9:21[b], 22[c] (2x); 10:22; 14:30; 16:25; 19:25; 24:13, 22; 27:40, 42 (2x), 49
		1 Pet	2 Pet	Mark	Rev	Matt

[a] All three James references are to being "justified by works"
[b] Instances where sō̧zō seems to mean "heal" from context
[c] Instances where sō̧zō seems to mean both "heal" and "saved"

Table 2.1. (continued)

Lexical Entry	English Meanings	Luke	Acts	Hebrews	John	1 John
agorazō	bought, purchased					
exagorazō	redeem, buy back					
dikaioō	justify; treat as just, acquit	7:29, 35; 10:29; 16:15; 18:14	13:39			
dikaiōma	justification	1:6				
dikaios	just, in harmony with law; righteous; right, proper	1:6, 17; 2:25; 5:32; 12:57; 14:14; 15:7; 18:9; 20:20; 23:47 (NRSV "innocent"), 50	3:14; 4:19; 7:52; 10:22; 22:14; 24:15	10:38; 11:4; 12:23	5:30; 7:24; 17:25	1:9; 2:1, 29; 3:7 (2x); 3:12
dikaiōsis	justification					
dikaiosynē	justification / righteousness	1:75	10:35; 13:10; 17:31; 24:25	1:9; 5:13; 7:2; 11:7, 33; 12:11	16:8, 10	2:29; 3:7, 10
exaireō	deliver, set free		7:34			
hilaskomai	propitiate, conciliate	18:13		2:17		
hilastērion	means of expiation, place of propitiation			9:5		
hilasmos	appeasement, expiation					2:2; 4:10
iaomai	heal	5:17; 6:18, 19; 7:7; 8:47; 9:2, 11, 42; 14:4; 17:15; 22:51	9:34; 10:38; 28:8, 27	12:13	4:47; 5:13; 12:40	
iasis	healing	13:32	4:22, 30			
katallassō	reconcile					
apokatallassō	reconcile					
katallagē	reconciliation					
lyō	loose, free (from sin or bondage)	13:16 (bent woman healed)	2:24 (loosing bands of death)		11:14 (loosing Lazarus from grave clothes)	
apolytrōsis	redemption	21:28		9:12, 15		
lytroō/lytroomai	purchase freedom with a ransom	24:21				
lytron	ransom, redemption					
lytrōsis	redemption	2:38				
ryomai	rescue, deliver	11:4				
Sōtēr	Savior, deliverer	1:47, 69; 2:11	5:31; 13:23		4:42	4:14
sōtēria	deliverance, salvation	1:69, 71, 77; 19:9	4:12; 7:25; 13:26, 47; 16:17; 27:34	1:14; 2:3, 10; 5:9; 6:9; 9:28; 11:7	4:22	
sōtērion	deliverance, salvation	2:30; 3:6	28:28			
sō̧zō	save, rescue	6:9; 7:50[c]; 8:12, 36, 48[c], 50[c]; 9:24 (2x); 13:23; 17:19[c]; 18:26, 42[c]; 19:10; 23:35 (2x), 37, 39	2:21, 40, 47; 4:9[b], 12; 11:14; 14:9[b]; 15:1, 11; 16:30, 31; 27:20, 31	5:7; 7:25	3:17; 5:34; 10:9; 11:12; 12:27, 47	
		Luke	Acts	Hebrews	John	1 John

[a] All three James references are to being "justified by works"
[b] Instances where *sō̧zō* seems to mean "heal" from context
[c] Instances where *sō̧zō* seems to mean both "heal" and "saved"

Table 2.1. (continued)

Lexical Entry	English Meanings	2 John	3 John
agorazō	bought, purchased		
exagorazō	redeem, buy back		
dikaioō	justify; treat as just, acquit		
dikaiōma	justification		
dikaios	just, in harmony with law; righteous; right, proper		
dikaiōsis	justification		
dikaiosynē	justification / righteousness		
exaireō	deliver, set free		
hilaskomai	propitiate, conciliate		
hilastērion	means of expiation, place of propitiation		
hilasmos	appeasement, expiation		
iaomai	heal		
iasis	healing		
katallassō	reconcile		
apokatallassō	reconcile		
katallogē	reconciliation		
lyō	loose, free (from sin or bondage)		
apolytrōsis	redemption		
lytroō/lytroomai	purchase freedom with a ransom		
lytron	ransom, redemption		
lytrōsis	redemption		
ryomai	rescue, deliver		
Sōtēr	Savior, deliverer		
sōtēria	deliverance, salvation		
sōtērion	deliverance, salvation		
sō̧zō	save, rescue		
		2 John	3 John

^a All three James references are to being "justified by works"
^b Instances where sō̧zō seems to mean "heal" from context
^c Instances where sō̧zō seems to mean both "heal" and "saved"

Table 2.2. New Testament Atonement Models

Models	Christus Victor / Rescue Model			
	Over Satan/Ruler of This World	Over Sin (also Law and Flesh)	Over Death, Fear of Death	Over Other Powers and Cosmic Forces
Proponents	Gustaf Aulén (1931)	Irenaeus (2nd half of 2C)		
OT precedents	Gen 3:15			Ps 110:1
Author/Text Group (Authors and text groups appear in probable historical order)				
James				
Pauline		Rom 3:9; 6:6 (7–12); 7:14–25; 8:3	Rom 8:19–22	Gal 1:4; 4:3, 9; 1 Cor 15:23; 2 Cor 10:3–4
Pauline Passover (both sin and death)		1 Cor 5:7–8		
Pastorals				
DeuteroPauline	Eph 4:8; Col 2:15	Eph 2:3–5; 4:8		Col 2:10, 15, 20; Eph 1:20–22; 2:2, 5; 6:12
Petrine				
Mark				
Johannine Apocalypse				
Matthew		1:21		
Luke	4:18; 11:21–22	19:10		
Acts			20:28	
Hebrews	2:14–15		2:14–15	
John	12:31; 16:11		10:10	
Johannine Lamb of God		John 1:28; 19:14		
Johannine Letters	1 John 3:8			

Table 2.2. (continued)

Models			Objective/Anselm	
	Ransom/ Redemption (Paid to Satan or God?)	Salvation through Resurrection and Exaltation	Satisfaction / Propitiation (Including Saving from God's Wrath)	Penal Substitution
Proponents	Origen, Patristic	Nonviolent Atonement!	Anselm (1097)	Calvin
OT precedents	Ps 103:4			Is 53:3–5; see laying on of hands in Lev 1–7
Author/Text Group (Authors and text groups appear in probable historical order)				
James				Jas 2:10
Pauline	Gal 3:13; 4:4–5; 1 Cor 11:23–25		1 Cor 11:25a; Rom 3:23–25 KJV (NRSV has "sacrifice of atonement" for ἱλαστήριον)	Gal 3:10–14; 1 Cor 15:3; Rom 3:22–26; 5:26
Pauline Passover (both sin and death)				
Pastorals				
DeuteroPauline	Col 1:14; Tit 2:14		Col 1:20a	
Petrine				
Mark	10:45; 14:22–24 (est. of covenant relationship)			
Johannine Apocalypse				
Matthew	20:28; 26:26–29			
Luke	22:19–20	24:26		22:37
Acts		2:32–36; 5:30–31; 10:38–43		
Hebrews	9:15b		7:22; 8:6; 9:15a	9:1–10:18
John			3:36	1:29
Johannine Lamb of God				
Johannine Letters				

Table 2.2. *(continued)*

Models		Subjective/Abelard		
	Expiation/Make Atonement/Cover Sins	Justification? (Declared/ Changed to Be Innocent)	Reconciliation	Participation (Connected with *Christus Victor*?)
Proponents		Luther		Again, Irenaeus; Greek Orthodox *Theosis*
OT precedents				
Author/Text Group (Authors and text groups appear in probable historical order)				
James				
Pauline		Gal 2:16–17; 3:8, 24; 1 Cor 6:11; Rom 3:24; 4:22–25; 5:9; 6:7	2 Cor 5:18–20; Rom 5:6–10 ; 11:15	Gal 2:19–21; 2 Cor 5:14–15, 17, 21; Rom 6:3–11; 8:3, 14–17 **maybe 1 Cor 15:3, Rom 5:14–15 a la Ridderbos, 84–88
Pauline Passover (both sin and death)				
Pastorals		Tit 3:7		2 Tim 2:12
DeuteroPauline			Col 1:20a; Eph 2:16	
Petrine				1 Pet 4:13–16
Mark				
Johannine Apocalypse				Rev 5:10
Matthew				
Luke				
Acts				
Hebrews				2:14–15
John				
Johannine Lamb of God				
Johannine Letters				

Table 2.2. (continued)

Models	Subjective/Abelard		
	Healing	Revelation / Moral Influence	Moral Example
Proponents		Abelard (1079–1142)	Socinus (1539–1604)
OT precedents	Exod 15:26; Hos 6:1–2; Is 53:5b; Ps 103:2–3		
Author/Text Group (Authors and text groups appear in probable historical order)			
James			
Pauline			
Pauline Passover (both sin and death)			
Pastorals			
DeuteroPauline			
Petrine	1 Pet 2:24–25	1 Pet 2:19–21; 3:16–17; 4:1–2, 13–16; 1 Pet 2:20; 4:13–14; 5:10	
Mark	2:9–11		
Johannine Apocalypse			
Matthew	8:17; 9:5–6, 35		
Luke	4:18–19, 32; 7:50; 8:48	Luke's narrative, e.g. 24:25–27, emphasizes illumination	
Acts			
Hebrews			
John		1:9	
Johannine Lamb of God			
Johannine Letters			

Notes

1. Eric D. Huntsman, *Becoming the Beloved Disciple: Coming unto Christ through the Gospel of John* (Springville, UT: Cedar Fort, 2018), 1.

2. For the historical development of these models, see chapter 3 of this book, "'He Shall Find Satisfaction Through His Knowledge': Atonement in Early Christianity and the Middle Ages," by Ariel Bybee Laughton.

3. Mark D. Baker and Joel B. Green, *Recovering the Scandal of the Cross: Atonement in New Testament and Contemporary Contexts*, 2nd ed. (Downers Grove, IL: InterVarsity Press Academic, 2011), 53.

4. Gustaf Aulén, *Christus Victor: An Historical Study of the Three Main Types of the Idea of Atonement*, translated by A. G. Herbert (New York: Macmillan, 1931; reprinted, Eugene, Oregon: WIPF & Stock, 2003), 4–7, 143–59. Aulén first published his book in his native Swedish as *Den kristna försoningstanken* (Svenska Kyrkans Diakonistyrelses Bokförlag, 1930). See also the discussion of James Beilby and Paul R. Eddy, eds., *The Nature of the Atonement: Four Views*, (Downers Grove, IL: InterVarsity Press Academic, 2006), 12–14, and Gregory A. Boyd, "Christus Victor View," in Beilby and Eddy, *The Nature of the Atonement*, 23–53, as well as Baker and Green, *Recovering the Scandal of the Cross*, 143–51.

5. See Beilby and Eddy, *Nature of the Atonement*, 14–18; Thomas R. Schreiner, "Penal Substitution View," in Beilby and Eddy, *Nature of the Atonement*, 67–98; Baker and Green, *Recovering the Scandal of the Cross*, 151–61.

6. See Beilby and Eddy, *The Nature of the Atonement*, 18–20; Baker and Green, *Recovering the Scandal of the Cross*, 161–64.

7. See, for instance, the essays collected in Brad Jersak and Michael Hardin, eds., *Stricken by God? Nonviolent Identification and the Victory of Christ* (Grand Rapids: Eerdmans, 2007), and J. Denny Weaver, *The Nonviolent Atonement*, 2nd ed. (Grand Rapids: Eerdmans, 2011).

8. Baker and Green, *Recovering the Scandal of the Cross*, 123, describe these areas including "the court of law (e.g., justification), commercial dealings (e.g., redemption), personal relationships (whether among individuals or groups—e.g., reconciliation), worship (e.g., sacrifice), and the battleground (e.g., triumph over evil)." Each of these, and some additional spheres, will be discussed below. See also Joseph A. Fitzmeyer, "Reconciliation in Pauline Theology," in *No Famine in the Land: Essays in Honor of John L. McKenzie*, edited by J. W. Flanagan and A. W. Robinson (Missoula, MT: Scholars Press, 1975), whose proposed categories are salvation (sōtēria), expiation (hilastērion), ransom/redemption (apolytrōsis), sanctification (hagiasoms), freedom (eleutheria), justification (dikaiōsis), transformation (metamorphōsis), new creation (kainē ktisis), and reconciliation (katallagē).

9. Baker and Green, *Recovering the Scandal of the Cross*, 118.

10. Eric D. Huntsman, "The Occasional Nature, Composition, and Structure of Paul's Letters," in *How the New Testament Came to Be*, edited by Kent P. Jackson et al., (Salt Lake City: Deseret Book, 2006), 191–95.

11. As "imprisonment letters," Philippians and Philemon are usually assumed to have

been written late in Paul's ministry when he was imprisoned in Rome, presumably shortly before his martyrdom. Paul was imprisoned repeatedly, however, and geographic placement of their recipients as well as the letters' style and the themes of Philippians might actually place them closer to Galatians towards the beginning of his middle ministry. See Raymond E. Brown, *Introduction to the New Testament* (New York: Doubleday, 1997), 493–96, 507–509, and Peter T. O'Brien, *The Epistle to the Philippians*, New International Greek New Testament Commentary (Grand Rapids, MI: Eerdmans, 1991), 19–26. See Brown, *Introduction to the New Testament*, 507–9, for similar arguments that have been made about the dating of Philemon.

12. Brown, *Introduction to the New Testament*, 585–89; Garwood P. Anderson, *Paul's New Perspective: Charting a Soteriological Journey* (Downers Grove, IL: InterVarsity Press Academic, 2016), 182–87; Stanley E. Porter, *The Apostle Paul: His Life, Thought, and Letters* (Grand Rapids, MI: Eerdmans, 2016), 156–78.

13. Anderson, *Paul's New Perspective*, 187–225.

14. Unless otherwise noted, all biblical references are to the New Revised Standard Version (NRSV).

15. Herman Ridderbos, "The Earliest Confession of the Atonement in Paul," in *Reconciliation and Hope*, edited by Robert Banks (Milton Keynes, England: Paternoster, 1974) 81–84.

16. Brown, *Introduction to the New Testament*, 468–73; Huntsman, "The Occasional Nature, Composition, and Structure of Paul's Letters," 192–93; Porter, *The Apostle Paul*, 185–200.

17. Liddell and Scott, "dikaioō," in Walter Bauer, *A Greek-English Lexicon of the New Testament and Other Early Christian Literature*, edited by Frederick William Danker, translated by William F. Arndt, F. Wilbur Gingrich, and F. W. Danker, 3rd edition (Chicago: University of Chicago Press, 2000), 429; Karl Kerteleg, "dikaioō," in Horst Balz, *Exegetical Dictionary of the New Testament*, 3 vols. (Grand Rapids, MI: Eerdmans, 1990–93), 1:330–34; Bauer, "dikaioō," *Greek-English Lexicon*, 249.

18. See the discussion of James B. Prothro, "The Strange Case of Δικαιόω in the Septuagint and Paul: The Oddity and Origins of Paul's Talk of 'Justification,'" *Zeitschrift für die neutestamentliche Wissenschaft und die Kunde der älteren Kirche* 107.1 (2016): 50–58.

19. F. Blass and A. Debrunner, *A Greek Grammar of the New Testament and Other Early Christian Literature*, translated and revised by Robert W. Funk (Chicago: University of Chicago Press, 1961), 72 §130 (1) and 164–65 §313, assert that this usage arose out of the practice in Aramaic and might have reflected a desire to avoid frequent use of the divine name. For both this proposal and some controls upon it, see Daniel B. Wallace, *Greek Grammar beyond the Basics: An Exegetical Syntax of the New Testament* (Grand Rapids, MI: Zondervan, 1996), 437–38.

20. Wallace, *Greek Grammar*, 115–16.

21. Brown, *Introduction to the New Testament*, 559–64; Huntsman, "The Occasional Nature, Composition, and Structure of Paul's Letters," 194–95; Porter, *The Apostle Paul*, 291–311.

22. N. T. Wright, "New Perspectives on Paul," in *Pauline Perspectives: Essays on Paul 1878–2013*, edited by Bruce L. McCormack (Minneapolis: Fortress Press, 2013), 285–89.

23. Liddell and Scott, "sōzō," *Greek-English Lexicon*, 1748; Bauer, "sōzō," *Greek-English Lexicon*, 982–83; Walter Radl, "sōzō," *Exegetical Dictionary*, 3.319–321.

24. Liddell and Scott, "sōtēria," in Bauer, *Greek-English Lexicon*, 1751; Bauer, "sōtēria," *Greek-English Lexicon*, 985–86; Karl Hermann Schelkle "sōtēria," in Balz, *Exegetical Dictionary*, 3.327–29.

25. Liddell and Scott, "sōtēr," in Bauer, *Greek-English Lexicon*, 1751; Bauer, "sōtēr," *Greek-English Lexicon*, 985; Karl Hermann Schelkle "sōtēr," in Balz, *Exegetical Dictionary*, 3.326–27. For the occurrences and meanings of sōtēr in both the Old and New Testaments, see *Thou Art the Christ, the Son of the Living God: The Person and Work of Jesus in the New Testament*, edited by Eric D. Huntsman, Lincoln Blumell, and Tyler J. Griffin (Provo, UT: Religious Studies Center; Salt Lake City: Deseret Book, October 2018), 404–5.

26. James D. G. Dunn, *Theology of Paul the Apostle* (Grand Rapids, MI: Eerdmans, 1998), 111–14; Baker and Green, *Recovering the Scandal of the Cross*, 122.

27. See the detailed discussion of Anderson, *Paul's New Perspective*, 298–308. By Anderson's analysis, *sōtēria/sōzō* are past-referring in 2 Corinthians 6:2; Titus 3:5; and 2 Timothy 1:9 and present-referring in 1 Corinthians 1:18 and 15:2; 2 Corinthians 2:15 and 6:2. All of the remaining 39 occurrences are future-referring or are nonspecific, global, or atemporal.

28. Liddell and Scott, "lytron" and "lytroō," in Bauer, *Greek-English Lexicon*, 605–6; Karl Kertelege, "lytron," in Balz, *Exegetical Dictionary*, 2:365–66.

29. Dunn, *Theology of Paul the Apostle*, 227–28; N. T. Wright, "Redemption from the New Perspective? Towards a Multilayered Pauline Theology of the Cross," in *Pauline Perspectives: Essays on Paul 1878–2013* (Minneapolis: Fortress, 2013), 300–301.

30. Although "Redeemer" (Hebrew, go'al) is a common title for YHWH in the Old Testament, interestingly the Greek word, *lytroumenos*, never occurs in the New Testament. See Huntsman, Blumell, and Griffin, *Thou Art the Christ*, 403–4.

31. Brown, *Introduction to the New Testament*, 511–15, 541–48; Huntsman, "The Occasional Nature, Composition, and Structure of Paul's Letters," 193; Porter, *The Apostle Paul*, 253–59, 278–82; Anderson, *Paul's New Perspective*, 244–48, 272–75.

32. Liddell and Scott, "katallassō," in Bauer, *Greek-English Lexicon*, 899; Bauer, "katallagē" and "katallassō," *Greek-English Lexicon*, 521; Helmut Merkel, "katallassō," in Balz, *Exegetical Dictionary*, 2:261–63. See also Fitzmeyer, "Reconciliation in Pauline Theology," 157.

33. Dunn, *Theology of Paul the Apostle*, 229.

34. Packer, "The Mediator," *Ensign* (May 1977): 54–56.

35. Fitzmeyer, "Reconciliation in Pauline Theology," 167, has written, "For Christians in particular the motivation for this is found in Paul's idea of reconciliation, in the breaking down of the barriers between men (and by implication, between nations) . . . on another level of dealings between groups and individuals within a given national or ethnic society there is still further need for reflection on the Pauline message of reconciliation."

36. Fitzmeyer, "Reconciliation in Pauline Theology," 160–62.

37. Ralph P. Martin, "Reconciliation and Forgiveness in the Letter to the Colossians," in Banks, *Reconciliation and Hope*, 109–15

38. Dunn, *Theology of Paul the Apostle*, 216–17.

39. Dunn, *Theology of Paul the Apostle*, 216.

40. Dunn, *Theology of Paul the Apostle*, 214–15; Stephen Hultgren, "*Hilastērion* (Rom. 3:25) and the Union of Divine Justice and Mercy, Part II: Atonement in the Old Testament and in Romans 1–5," *Journal of Theological Studies* 70.2 (Oct. 2019): 557–63.

41. Hultgren, "*Hilastērion* (Rom. 3:25) and the Union of Divine Justice and Mercy," 597–98.

42. Dunn, *Theology of Paul the Apostle*, 390–412. Participation is closely connected with another atonement model, that of recapitulation, wherein Christ, as the New or Second Adam, successfully reenacts the human experience, succeeding where Adam failed.

43. Richard H. Bell, "Sacrifice and Christology in Paul," *Journal of Theological Studies* 53.1 (2002), 4; see also Dunn, *Theology of Paul the Apostle*, 219–21.

44. Christopher D. Marshall, *Beyond Retribution: A New Testament Vision for Justice, Crime, and Punishment* (Grand Rapids, MI: Eerdmans, 2001), 61, puts it this way: "It is true . . . that Paul sees a substitutionary dimension to Christ's death. But it is substitutionary not in the sense of one person replacing another, like substitutes on a football team, but in the sense of one person representing all others, who are thereby made present in the person and experience of their representative. Christ died not so much instead of sinners as on behalf of sinners, as their corporate representative."

45. Eric D. Huntsman, "Preaching Jesus and Him Crucified," in *His Majesty and Mission*, edited by Nicholas J. Frederick and Keith J. Wilson (Provo, UT: Religious Studies Center; Salt Lake City: Deseret Book, 2017), 64–67.

46. Bell, "Sacrifice and Christology in Paul," 8–9; Brad Jersak, "Nonviolent Identification and the Victory of Christ," in Jersak and Hardin, *Stricken by God*, 43–49.

47. Martin Hengel, "Der Kreuzestod Jesu Christi als Gottes souveräne Erlösungstat Exegese über 2 Kor 5,11–21," in *Theologie und Kirche. Reichenau-Gespräch der Evangelischen Landessynode Württemberg* (Stuttgart: Caler Verlag, 1967), 83–84; cf. Helmut Merkel, "katallassō," in Balz, *Exegetical Dictionary*, 2:263.

48. For obvious reasons, participation is appealing for those uncomfortable with bloody sacrificial and penal satisfaction models, and advocates of nonviolent models of atonement often nuance other images to reflect more of a participation model. For instance, Jersak, "Nonviolent Identification and the Victory of Christ," 39–42, writes "that paschal lambs, which served as the central course of a festal meal, and many other Levitical offerings such as the sin and peace offerings, that provided elements for sacrificial meals that worshipers ate in God's presence, serve as ways of providing communion with deity, much as the sacrament of the Lord's Supper does for Christians."

49. See, for instance, the very different conclusions of Stephen H. Travis, *Christ and the Judgement of God* (Peabody, MA: Hendrickson, 2008), 199, who writes, "Rather than saying that in his death Christ experienced retributive punishment on behalf of humanity, Paul more often says that he entered into and bore on our behalf the destruc-

tive consequences of sin. Standing where we stand, he bore the consequences of our alienation from God. In doing so he absorbed and exhausted them, so that they should not fall on us. It is both true and important to say that he 'was judged in our place'—that he experienced divine judgement on sin in the sense that he endured the God-ordained consequences of human sinfulness. But this is not the same as to say that he bore our punishment," and Jarvis Williams, "Violent Atonement in Romans: The Foundation of Paul's Soteriology," *Journal of the Evangelical Theological Society* 53.3 (Sept. 2010)," 598, who continues to maintain "that Jesus' death was a necessary, violent, penal sacrifice of atonement for sin that absorbed God's wrath to achieve salvation for those for whom he died has historical precedent in the Greek, Greco-Roman, and Jewish world that preceded Paul and in the Greco-Roman and Jewish world in which Paul lived and wrote Romans."

50. Brown, *Introduction to the New Testament*, 111–22; Stanley E. Porter and Bryan R. Dyer, eds., *The Synoptic Problem: Four Views* (Grand Rapids, MI: Baker Academic, 2016), 1–26. While Marcan priority is accepted by most scholars, there is still considerable debate over the existence of a hypothetical Q document as the source for the sayings of Jesus common to Matthew and Luke, and which of these Gospels was written first. For the Two Source Hypothesis, which assumes that Mark and Q were sources for both Matthew and Luke, see Craig A. Evans, "The Two Source Hypothesis," in Porter and Dyer, *The Synoptic Problem*, 27–46. For a development of the Farrer Hypothesis, which does not posit the existence of Q and proposes that Luke drew upon both Mark and Matthew, see Mark Goodacre, "The Farrer Hypothesis," in Porter and Dyer, *The Synoptic Problem*, 47–66.

51. Brown, *Introduction to the New Testament*, 127, 158–67; Eric D. Huntsman, "The Petrine Kērygma and the Gospel according to Mark," in *The Ministry of Peter, the Chief Apostle*, edited by Frank F. Judd Jr., Eric D. Huntsman, and Shon D. Hopkin (Provo, UT: BYU Religious Studies Center; Salt Lake City: Deseret Book, 2014), 170–75, 177–82.

52. Julie M. Smith, "Narrative Atonement Theology in the Gospel of Mark," *BYU Studies Quarterly* 54.1 (2015), 29–30.

53. Martin Kähler, *The So-Called Historical Jesus and the Historic Biblical Christ*, translated by Carl E. Braaten (German original, 1896; Philadelphia: Fortress, 1964), 80 n. 11.

54. Sharyn Dowd and Elizabeth Struthers Malbon, "The Significance of Jesus' Death in Mark: Narrative Context and Authorial Audience," *Journal of Biblical Literature* 125.2 (2006), 271.

55. Dowd and Malbon, "The Significance of Jesus' Death in Mark," 277–82.

56. Adela Yarbro Collins, "Mark's Interpretation of the Death of Jesus," *Journal of Biblical Literature* 128.3 (2009): 547–48, points out the connections of *lytron* with the Septuagint, where the singular occurs in Leviticus 27:31; Proverbs 6:35 and 13:8; and in the plural in Exodus 21:30 (twice); Exodus 30:12; Leviticus 19:20; 25:24, 26, 51, 52; Numbers 3:12, 46, 48, 49, 51; 18:15; 35:31, 32; and Isaiah 45:13. Exodus 30:12–16 is particularly significant because it equates ransom money with "atonement money" used to "to make atonement for your lives" and serve as "a ransom for your lives."

57. Baker and Green, *Recovering the Scandal of the Cross*, 58. Adela Yarbro Collins,

"The Signification of Mark 10:45 among Gentile Christians," *Harvard Theological Review* 90.4 (1997), 373–82, documents epigraphic evidence that also reveals that lytron was widely used in religious contexts, where ritual acts "ransomed" people who were burdened with the weight of divine pleasure.

58. Baker and Green, *Recovering the Scandal of the Cross*, 118.

59. Dowd and Malbon, "The Significance of Jesus' Death in Mark," 271, 284–85.

60. Baker and Green, *Recovering the Scandal of the Cross*, 58–63.

61. Christopher J. Edwards, *The Ransom Logion in Mark and Matthew* (Tübingen: Mohr Siebeck, 2012), 118.

62. Smith, "Narrative Atonement Theology in the Gospel of Mark," 30–36.

63. Brown, *Introduction to the New Testament*, 170–73; Porter and Dyer, *The Synoptic Problem*, 19–21, 28–44, 47–53.

64. Dowd and Malbon, "The Significance of Jesus' Death in Mark," 293. The only difference in the Greek text is the more frequent substitution of the more elegant *hösper* for the Marcan *kai gar*.

65. Michael J. Wilkins, "Isaiah 53 and the Message of Salvation in the Four Gospels," in *The Gospel According to Isaiah 53: Encountering the Suffering Servant in Jewish and Christian Theology*, edited by Darrell L. Bock and Mitch Glaser (Grand Rapids, MI: Kregel Academic & Professional, 2012), 122–26.

66. Collins, "Mark's Interpretation of the Death of Jesus," 550.

67. Wilkins, "Isaiah 53 and the Message of Salvation in the Four Gospels," 128.

68. George C. Heider, "Atonement and the Gospels," *Journal of Theological Interpretation* 2.2 (2008), 263–66.

69. Birger Gerhardsson, "Sacrificial Service and Atonement in the Gospel of Matthew," in Banks, *Reconciliation and Hope*, 25–26, 33–35.

70. Porter and Dyer, *The Synoptic Problem*, 19–21, 28–44, 51–66.

71. Brown, *Introduction to the New Testament*, 225–26.

72. See various views as summarized by David Peterson, "Atonement Theology in Luke-Acts: Some Methodological Reflections," in *The New Testament in Its First Century Setting: Essays on Context and Background*, edited by P. J. Williams, Andrew D. Clarke, Peter M. Head, and David Instone-Brewer (Grand Rapids, MI: Eerdmans, 2004), 57–59.

73. See Nicholas J. Frederick, "Atonement' in the Book of Mormon," chapter 4 herein.

74. See Acts 2:14–36, 38–39; 3:12–26; 4:8–12; 5:29–32; 10:34–43

75. Passages that emphasize salvation in all of Jesus's life include Luke 1:77 (the prophecy of Zacharias), Luke 4:18–19 (Jesus's quotation of Isa 61:1–2), and Luke 19:9–10 (Jesus's declaration that salvation has come to the house of Zacchaeus).

76. Peterson, "Atonement Theology in Luke-Acts," 59–71.

77. Baker and Green, *Recovering the Scandal of the Cross*, 127.

78. Heider, "Atonement and the Gospels," 266–68.

79. Isa 53:4–5; also Exod 15:26; Ps 103:2–3; Isa 53:5b; Hos 6:1–2. Wilkins, "Isaiah 53 and the Message of Salvation in the Four Gospels," 122–25.

80. See Bruce R. Reichenbach, "Healing View," in Beilby and Eddy, *Nature of the Atonement*, 117–42, and Eric D. Huntsman, *The Miracles of Jesus* (Salt Lake City: Deseret Book, 2014), 41–63, 87–103, 129–33.

81. Thomas A. Wayment, "The Hebrew Text of Alma 7:11," *Journal of Book of Mormon Studies* 14.1 (2005): 101–3.

82. While their suggestion that *sōzō* can be translated as "heal" is potent (Terryl and Fiona Givens, *The Christ Who Heals: How God Restored the Truth that Saves Us* [Salt Lake City: Deseret Book, 2017], 63–72; see also Fiona Givens, "Atonement and Retributive Justice," chapter 9 herein), in some cases it needs modification. Often, the term can only mean "save" or "rescue" (Matt 8:25; 14:30), and in other instances where it can be understood to mean heal, as the Givenses intriguingly suggest, it also means more broadly "saved." See Huntsman, *The Miracles of Jesus*, 58, 63, 110, 112, and Radl, "sōzō," in Balz, *Exegetical Dictionary*, 320, who notes "This shows that Jesus's *sōzein* effect not only physical healing, but well-being in a broader sense."

83. J. Denny Weaver, "The Nonviolent Atonement: Human Violence, Discipleship and God," in Jersak and Hardin, *Stricken by God?*, 321–44. Interestingly, Weaver also reads Revelation as a Narrative Christus Victor text and suggests that it and the Gospels provide "bookends" for the New Testament, encouraging us to read this model into many, if not most, of its writings.

84. R. Aland Culpepper, "An Introduction to the Johannine Writings," in *Johannine Literature*, edited by John M. Court, Ruth Edwards, and Barnabas Lindars (London: Bloomsbury T&T Clark, 2000), 9–29; Paul A. Rainbow, *Johannine Theology: The Gospel, the Epistles, and the Apocalypse* (Downers Grove, IL: InterVarsity Press Academic, 2014), 27–71.

85. Eric D. Huntsman, "The Lamb of God: Unique Aspects of the Passion Narrative in John," in *Behold the Lamb of God*, edited by Richard Neitzel Holzapfel, Frank F. Judd Jr., and Thomas A. Wayment (Provo, UT: Religious Studies Center, 2008), 51–52.

86. Huntsman, "Lamb of God," 52–55, 62–64.

87. Huntsman, "Lamb of God," 59–65.

88. George L. Carey, "The Lamb of God and Atonement Theories," *Tyndale Bulletin* 32 (1981): 101–11.

89. Because of references in restoration scripture that identify John the seer with the apostle John (e.g., 1 Ne 14:18–27; Ether 4:16; D&C 7; D&C 77:1–15; D&C 88:141), Latter-day Saints have a particular investment in connecting the Fourth Gospel and the Apocalypse. One possibility is that an early Neronian date in the 60s (CE) and the rough, heavily Semitic Greek of Revelation might make it an actual composition by the apostle, whereas the Gospel, with John as the ultimate source but not necessarily the author, might have been written by another as late as the 90s.

90. See Charles E. Hill, "Atonement in the Apocalypse of John: A Lamb Standing as if Slain," in *The Glory of the Atonement, Biblical, Historical and Practical Perspectives*, edited by Charles E. Hill and Frank A. James III (Downers Grove, IL: InterVarsity Press, 2004), 190–208; Nicholas J. Frederick, "The Paradoxical Lamb and the Christology of John's Apocalypse," in Huntsman, Blumell, and Griffin, *Thou Art the Christ*, 260–74.

91. Heider, "Atonement and the Gospels," (2008), 261–63.

92. Weaver, *The Nonviolent Atonement*, 20–35.

93. Brown, *Introduction to the New Testament*, 725.

94. Brown, *Introduction to the New Testament*, 732–34; Peter H. Davids, *The Epistle of James*, The New International Greek Testament Commentary (Grand Rapids, MI: Eerdmans, 1982), 119–34.

95. Craig A. Evans, "Isaiah 53 in the Letters of Peter, Paul, Hebrews, and John," in Bock and Glaser, *The Gospel According to Isaiah 53*, 157–59.

96. For detailed discussions, see Simon J. Kistemaker, "Atonement in Hebrews: 'A Merciful and Faithful High Priest'" in Hill and James, *The Glory of the Atonement*, 163–75, and Steve Motyer, "The Atonement in Hebrews," in *The Atonement Debate: Papers from the London Symposium on the Theology of Atonement*, edited by Derek Tidball, David Hilborn, and Justin Thacker (Grand Rapids, MI: Zondervan, 2008), 136–53.

97. Brown, *Introduction to the New Testament*, 683, 689–701; Paul Ellingworth, *The Epistle to the Hebrews*, The New International Greek Testament Commentary (Grand Rapids, MI: Eerdmans, 1993), 3–33.

98. Luke 9:22; 17:25; 22:15; 24:26, 46; see Table 1 for the appearance of *paschō*, "to suffer," elsewhere in the New Testament.

99. For the textual problems associated with Luke 22:43–44, see Bruce M. Metzger, *A Textual Commentary on the Greek New Testament*, 2nd ed. (Stuttgart: United Bible Societies, 1994), 151. For a defense of the passage by a Latter-day Saint scholar, see Lincoln H. Blumell, "Luke 22:43–44: An Anti-Docetic Interpolation or an Apologetic Omission?" *A Journal of Biblical Textual Criticism* 19 (2014): 1–35.

100. See Church of Jesus Christ of Latter-day Saints, "Inside Temples," accessed March 23, 2023, https://www.churchofjesuschrist.org/temples/inside-temples, and "About the Temple Endowment," accessed March 23, 2023, https://www.churchofjesuschrist.org/temples/what-is-temple-endowment; see also Devery S. Anderson, ed., *The Development of LDS Temple Worship: 1846–2000: A Documentary History* (Salt Lake City: Signature Books, 2011), xxv–vi.

101. Examples include Stephen E. Robinson, *Believing Christ: The Parable of the Bicycle and Other Good News* (Salt Lake City: Deseret Book, 1994); Tad R. Callister, *The Infinite Atonement* (Salt Lake City: Deseret Book, 2000); Blake T. Ostler, *Exploring Mormon Thought, Volume 2: The Problems of Theism and the Love of God* (Salt Lake City: Greg Kofford Books, 2006), 189–230, some of which is critiqued by Deidre Green, "Got Compassion? A Critique of Blake Ostler's Theory of Atonement," *Element* 4.1 (2008): 1–21; and again, Terryl and Fiona Givens, *The Christ Who Heals* (n. 82, above).

102. Blake T. Ostler, "The Development of the Mormon Concept of Grace," *Dialogue* 24.1 (Spring 1991): 57, 68–84.

103. Instead, later revelations in the Doctrine and Covenants radically redefine the definition of eternal life, speaking not only of salvation but also of exaltation, defined as actual, potential deification that includes inheriting all power and glory and receiving eternal increase (e.g., D&C 75:5; 76:52–70; 130:2; 132:19–20, 24, 29, 37; 138:51). For further discussion, see chapter 3, Ariel Bybee Laughton, "He Shall Find Satisfaction Through His Knowledge," and chapter 6, J.B. Haws, "'This Perfect Atonement': Agency, Law, Theosis, and Atonement Theology," below.

CHAPTER 3

"He Shall Find Satisfaction Through His Knowledge"

Atonement in Early Christianity and the Middle Ages

ARIEL BYBEE LAUGHTON

In 1930, Gustaf Aulén, professor of systematic theology at the University of Lund, delivered a series of eight lectures at the University of Uppsala that were published in English the following year under the title *Christus Victor*. In these lectures, Aulén laid out a history of the development of what he understood to be the three prevalent theories of Christ's atonement from Jesus's time to the nineteenth century in order to argue that a "Christus victor" theory, or the idea that emphasized Christ's atonement as God's triumph over Satan, was the most ancient and thus the most authoritative.[1] His work became one of the foundational theological texts for study of atonement throughout the twentieth century. Taking what he considered to be a "scientific" and impartial approach, Aulén collapsed the ideas of nearly two thousand years of Christian writers into three categories in order to formulate a comprehensive argument for his theological views.[2]

Many modern scholars have pointed out the numerous problems with Aulén's work, including his gross oversimplification of the rich and diverse ideas, images, and arguments about Christ's atonement that are made over several centuries of Christianity.[3] In response to projects such as Aulén's, historical theologian John McGuckin has described patristic soteriology (or the teachings of the Church Fathers on the salvific work of Christ) as being "bigger," "looser," and more "organically diffuse" than it has been portrayed, and argued that "to impose systematic order on this wildly vivid kerygmatic witness is often inappropriately scholastic."[4]

At the risk of being "inappropriately scholastic," this chapter will nevertheless attempt to tease out some of the ways in which ancient and medieval

Christians understood the salvific work of Jesus Christ. Because of the limited scope of this essay, it will not be possible to do true justice to the large and variegated body of soteriological thought during late antiquity and the Middle Ages. Instead, my objective is to highlight the ideas of several theologians whose writings were most influential and enduring in the Christian tradition and make some preliminary suggestions as to how these ideas may find resonance with Latter-day Saint scripture and theology. By resisting the grouping of thinkers into rigid categories as Aulén did, I hope to convey something of the "bigness" and "looseness" of the body of Christian thought on atonement, both in the ancient church as well as in The Church of Jesus Christ of Latter-day Saints.

The Apostolic Fathers: A Miscellany of Thought

Of the writings of the Apostolic Fathers, some of the earliest extracanonical Christian writings that date from the late first and second centuries, very few address the subject of Christ's salvific work at any length, but some expound Christ's atonement in unique and interesting ways. For example, the anonymous *Epistle to Diognetus* draws heavily upon Pauline language and ideas of the atonement but also presents a somewhat unique and more detailed salvation narrative than most other writings from this period.[5] God, having already laid out a divine plan with his Son in his mind, allows for a period that humans might fall into sin and be led astray by their own pleasures and desires. When it becomes clear to humans that all they could expect as recompense for their sins was punishment and death, God creates in the present an "age of righteousness" by sending his Son as a ransom to hide humanity's sins.[6] According to *Diognetus*, the Son is a pre-contemplated gift of God sent to save sinners from what they have justly earned by both ransoming them (from an unnamed creditor) and covering up their sins.[7]

The *Epistle of Barnabas* also provides some insight into early Christian thought on Jesus's atonement. The author of *Barnabas* allegorically reads numerous stories and symbols from the Hebrew Bible as signifiers of Christ's atonement in order to demonstrate that Judaism is a false religion and that the Christians are God's covenant people. These include his understanding of Abraham's sacrifice of Isaac as a type for the sacrifice of Jesus,[8] his explanation of Moses's outstretched arms as a symbol of Christ's cross,[9] and his complex reading of Christ into the scapegoat ritual on the Day of Atonement drawn from both the Hebrew Bible and the Talmud.[10] *Barnabas* asserts that "the Son of God suffered, that *by being beaten* he might give us life," emphasizing the physical pain of Jesus's suffering as he took upon himself the penalty justly owed to humankind.[11] He admonishes Christians to heed the signs given to ancient Israel which have been abandoned by the Jews so that they might be numbered among the chosen, as "this is why the Lord allowed his flesh to be given over to corruption, that we might be made holy through the forgiveness of sins, which comes *in the sprinkling of his blood*."[12] Christ allowed his flesh to die so that sinners may be cleansed of their sin by his blood.

The letters of Ignatius of Antioch also present some interesting perspectives on Jesus's atonement. Ignatius writes of Christ as having been "truly nailed for us in the flesh" and that "we ourselves come from the fruit of his divinely blessed suffering."[13] As other Christian writers of his time, he extols the real flesh of Jesus and his corporeal suffering when speaking of atonement. In addition, Ignatius emphasizes the participatory nature of Jesus's sacrifice. He commends the Smyrneans for having faith so unshakeable it is "as if you were nailed to the cross of the Lord Jesus Christ in both flesh and spirit."[14] True Christians must "choose to die voluntarily in his suffering" so that his life is in us.[15] In his letters, Ignatius refers to himself three times as a "ransom," suggesting that he sees his own suffering and anticipated martyrdom as sharing in and testifying of Jesus's suffering and atoning death.[16]

The *Epistle of Barnabas*'s understanding of Hebrew scripture as a series of types and symbols for Jesus's atonement resonates strongly in Latter-day Saint scripture. The Book of Mormon also reads Abraham's sacrifice of Isaac as a prefiguration of God's offering of his Only Begotten Son (Jacob 4:5). Christ is frequently portrayed as a sacrifice laid upon the altar to appease the broken law (2 Ne 2:7, cf. Alma 34:13). The Levitical rituals of sacrifice are read as types for the great and final sacrifice to be made by the Son of God (D&C 138:12–13, Alma 34:10–15). In the *Pearl of Great Price*, after expulsion from the Garden of Eden, Adam and Eve are commanded to sacrifice the first of their flocks to the Lord, and an angel teaches them that "this thing is a similitude of the sacrifice of the Only Begotten of the Father, which is full of grace and truth" (Moses 5:5–7). Hebrew figures, rituals, and language are reiterated in relationship to the atonement of Jesus Christ. In addition, the Apostolic Fathers' understandings of Christ's atonement as a "ransom" for sin and the idea that Jesus took upon himself the punishment justly incurred by humanity will become better developed by Christian writers in the coming centuries and also have profound influence upon Latter-day Saint atonement theologies later on.

Justin Martyr and Tertullian: Penal Substitution Theory

Outside of the traditional canon of Apostolic Fathers, other writers of the second century emphasized the penal nature of Jesus's atonement. In his *Dialogue with Trypho*, Justin Martyr, one of the earliest Christian apologists in Rome, is questioned by a Christian detractor named Trypho about whether Christ is not cursed for being hung upon a tree, as Deuteronomy 21:22–23 asserts. Justin responds that Jesus, being sinless, was the only one who has lived who did not bear the curse of God for disobedience to the law, and therefore was able to take upon him the divine curses that rightfully belonged to human beings and suffer for their sins. "If, then, the Father of all wished His Christ for the whole human family *to take upon Him the curses of all* . . . why do you argue about Him, who submitted to suffer these things according to the Father's will, as if He were accursed, and do not rather bewail yourselves?" Justin asks.[17] For him, Christ's salvific work was to comply with the Father's wish that he take upon himself the punishments of God that were humanity's due. Justin articulates the atonement of Jesus in a way that emphasizes Jesus's suffering in the place of sinners.[18]

Tertullian, a Roman Christian writer of the second century, is often overlooked for his contributions to atonement theology since the majority of his writings focus on the subjective dimension of Christ's work—what the Christian must do to receive salvation—rather than the meaning or mechanics of Christ's atonement.[19] But there are a few important exceptions. In his *Against Marcion,* Tertullian responds to Marcion and others who deny Christ's corporeality by emphasizing Jesus's suffering and death in the flesh so that he might bring to pass the forgiveness of sins and the resurrection of the physical body.[20] Elsewhere, he urges Christians not to pay monetary ransoms to avoid persecution. "How unworthy is it of God and his ways of acting, who spared not his own Son for you, that he might be made a curse for us . . . All this took place that He might redeem us from our sins." Tertullian invokes the language of Isaiah 53 in context of explicating Christ's patient endurance of physical pain and humiliation as he suffered scourging, smiting, spitting, and ultimate deliverance to death on the cross to pay for the sins of his people. Those who attempt to escape persecution through monetary bribes insult Christ and all of the good things that he obtained for humankind through the great "ransom" of Jesus's precious blood.[21]

Both Justin Martyr and Tertullian emphasized Christ's corporeality and his physical pain and suffering as he took upon himself the "curse" and suffered for the sins of humanity. Christ took upon himself the penalty or punishment that was due to human beings on account of their sins and suffered in their place to expiate them. Both writers largely understood Jesus's atonement as an act of penal substitution, or that the punishment due to humans on account of their sin was taken on by Christ and paid for through his sufferings.[22]

Several passages of Latter-day Saint scripture develop a similar view of Jesus's sacrifice. In the Book of Mormon, the prophet-king Benjamin prophesies that Christ will take upon himself bodily suffering greater than any man could suffer without dying as he bled from every pore of his body to atone for the sins and abominations of his people (Mos 3:7). Another Book of Mormon figure, Alma, explains that Adam's and Eve's first sins of disobedience in the Garden of Eden had brought upon all humankind the penalty of death, and that God himself would atone to appease the demands of justice that cut them off from his presence (Alma 42:7, 12–15, cf. Mos 3:11). A similar penal substitutionary view of atonement is developed at length in the Doctrine and Covenants, where Christ speaks to his own pain and suffering while making atonement for sin:

> For behold, I, God, have suffered these thing for all, that they might not suffer if they would repent; But if they would not repent they must suffer even as I; Which suffering caused myself, even God the greatest of all, to tremble because of pain, and to bleed at every pore, and to suffer both body and spirit—and would that I might not drink the bitter cup, and shrink—Nevertheless, glory be to the Father, and I partook and finished my preparations unto the children of men (D&C 19:16–19).

In his own voice, Jesus describes the agony of suffering the sins of all in order to prevent this penalty from falling upon them on the condition of repentance. This understanding of Jesus's atonement as the suffering of the penalty justly due to humankind is prominent in contemporary Latter-day Saint theology as well.[23]

Irenaeus of Lyons: Recapitulation and *Theosis*

Irenaeus of Lyons, a second century bishop of Greek origins who lived in modern-day France, was the first Christian writer to set forth a fully developed theory of atonement. For Irenaeus, Christ represented the "recapitulation" of Adam, or the means by which God undoes and redoes all that Adam did or failed to do as the head of humanity.[24] All aspects of history, including the preexistent Word, the Old Testament prophets, the Fall, Christ's incarnation at birth, his life's work, his suffering and death, his resurrection, and the ultimate glorification of humankind as fully living beings partaking in incorruptibility and the glory of God were all aspects of God's divine, grand economy and revealed the mystery of Christ's work through which he recapitulated all things and brought them into a single narrative.[25]

In Irenaeus's *Against Heresies,* God creates earth life to be a pedagogical tool for human beings in which all things ultimately work for good on account of Christ's predetermined work of mercy.[26] In fact, for Irenaeus, the Word is not only a preordained means of redemption for humankind but is the very purpose for the creation of humanity from the beginning: "For inasmuch as He had a preexistence as a saving being, *it was necessary that what might be saved should also be called into existence*, in order that the Being who saves should not exist in vain."[27] Since the Word pre-existed earth life as a saving being, something for him to save had to be created so that his existence was not without purpose. Therefore, he created humankind so that he would have something to save. For this reason, Irenaeus rejects the notion that the Fall of Adam was an unforeseen catastrophe and reads it as part of the long narrative of Christ's atonement in God's overarching plan. He argues that God intended from the beginning that Adam's transgression and expulsion from Paradise allow for Christ to come as the recapitulation of Adam to conquer death and set humanity free.[28] The divine Word takes a human body in order to join humanity to divinity so that man, "having been blended with the Word of God, and receiving the adoption, might become the son of God. For by no other way could we have received incorruptibility and immortality, *except by having been united to incorruptibility and immortality*."[29] Through the blending of man and God in Christ, the human race is "adopted" and thus redeemed from the corruption of death and sin that they had incurred through the fall of Adam in a participatory model of salvation.

For Irenaeus, Christ's unique position as incarnate Word-Son, related to both God the Father and humankind, allows him to impute not only sanctification but something of the divine nature itself to human beings. Irenaeus teaches that the Word of God had "become what we are, that he might bring us to be even what he is himself."[30] The divine infusion into humanity through Jesus Christ allows human beings who were united with Christ to see and comprehend God and thus participate in him, partaking of his divine nature and enjoying his goodness.[31]

Similar to Irenaeus's idea of divine economy, much of modern Latter-day Saint theology centers around a "plan of salvation" doctrine that outlines the process by which God has and continues to work to bring about the salvation of his children. Latter-day Saint scripture asserts the existence of the souls of human beings before the creation of the earth and explains God's intended purpose of earth life to be a testing ground to allow his children to prove their obedience to his will, with the promise that the greater glories of immortality and eternal life would be added to their first estate should they succeed (Abr 3:22–26, Moses 1:39). In this economy of salvation, Jesus Christ holds a pivotal salvific role from the beginning. Numerous Latter-day Saint leaders have taught that Jesus, the first of all the sons of God, volunteered and was designated to atone for the inevitable fall of humanity from God's presence in the Garden of Eden as well as for all sins that undoubtedly would be committed by God's human children as they were tested on earth.[32] Through Christ's atonement, human beings may be reconciled again to a oneness of heart and mind with God and receive his forgiveness, immortality, and an eternal life in his presence.[33]

Irenaeus taught that the Word had become human to enable humans to become what he is. In similar fashion, Latter-day Saint prophet Lorenzo Snow (1814–1901), fifth president of the Church, taught that, "as man is, God once was. As God is, man may become," claiming to have received this teaching from church founder Joseph Smith.[34] Whereas Irenaeus's understanding of *theosis* relied heavily upon his notion of Christ's salvific adoption of all humanity by the Word's joining of his divine nature to human nature, Latter-day Saint scripture teaches that the divine potential of human beings provided by Jesus Christ exists in a more literal (and more radical) sense: that Christ became human, atoned for sin, and was resurrected in the flesh to provide a means whereby human beings might receive "exaltation," or become gods like unto the Father and the Son in their own right (D&C 76:50–70; 132:19–20, 24).[35]

Athanasius of Alexandria and Gregory of Nyssa: Incarnation Soteriology

Like Irenaeus, Athanasius of Alexandria and Gregory of Nyssa, two influential Christian writers who lived in the fourth century, also understood Christ's salvific work for humanity not on the cross but rather at the incarnation of the Word in flesh at the birth of Jesus. Both Athanasius and Gregory premise their soteriologies on a perceived transformation of humanity that took place at the moment that the Word became flesh and then diverge, developing their theories of atonement in distinctive ways.

For Athanasius, bishop of Alexandria, humans were made mortal *ex nihilo* but graciously endowed by God with his image at their creation, or made rational by his Word, to stop their natural mortality from devolving into death. This rationality—a divine knowledge—would have allowed them to abide in blessedness forever in paradise, being incorrupt through his grace.[36] Yet at the Fall, this image of God is lost and therefore also the sustaining rationality that had prevented it from disintegrating into death and corruption.[37] As a result of Adam's sin, it became incumbent upon the Word, who at first imparted the image of God to human beings and is the sole image of the Father, to restore that image and make again incorrupt the natural corruption of humanity.[38]

> And thus taking from our bodies one of the same nature, because all were under penalty of the corruption of death, he gave that nature over to death in the place of all, and offered it to the Father. He did this, moreover, out of his loving-kindness, to the end that, first, all being considered to have died in him, the law involving the ruin of men might be undone (inasmuch as its power was fully spent upon the Lord's body, and had no longer holding-ground against men, his friends), and that, secondly, he might turn them again toward incorruption, and quicken them from death *by the appropriation of*

his body and by the grace of the resurrection, banishing death from them like straw from the fire.[39]

The incorrupt and incorporeal Word condescended to take a human body so that he is able to die and offer a sinless life as an offering to the Father in the place of all human beings. While his human body is able to die, it is united with the powerful, immortal nature of the Word, so death fully exhausts itself and is broken upon the body of Christ. Because he has become one with sinful humanity through his human body, the Word is conjoined to all people and thus his death is able to remove their natural corruption and impart to them the grace of resurrection. In addition to the destruction of death, the Word's incarnation restores the image of God—the lost rationality or knowledge of God—through teaching and revealing God and salvation by making God visible to humanity in Christ.[40] Once humans possess this knowledge again, the image of God is recreated within them and they are "adopted and deified through the Word." The Word makes humans into the image of God once again as they had been intended to be from the beginning. As the image of God, they are able to participate in the divine life of the Trinity.[41] In this sense, Athanasius understands Christ's atonement as a second salvation, a re-creation through the second conferral of saving grace after the bounty of God's salvific image was conferred at its first creation.

Paraphrasing Irenaeus, Athanasius wrote, "He [the Word] was made Man, that we might be made god."[42] While Irenaeus had been the first to suggest that Christ's atonement resulted in human theosis or divinization, Athanasius fully develops this idea in his later work, *Against the Arians,* which gives a more complex account of Christ's salvific work. In the Incarnation, the perfect Word of God clothes himself in an imperfect body in order that he might pay the debt humans owe and perfect within himself what is imperfect in the human nature he takes on.[43] Jesus perfects or "deifies" his human self through his sacrifice on the cross and his resurrection and so becomes the first to experience human redemption in himself before allowing those who believe in him to participate in his own perfection.[44] Sanctified and exalted, Christ shares the grace of his deified state with those who are united with him, so that they too may rightly be called "gods," not because they are equal to God but because they were "adopted and deified through the Word."[45] In this more complex soteriology, Athanasius maintains the importance of the incarnation for the salvation of humankind but gives greater emphasis to the work of the cross and the resurrection, which are for him the means by which the Word perfects his own humanity and divinizes human beings. Those who have received this deification through unity with Christ share in the divine life of Father, Son, and Holy Spirit as they were intended to from the very beginning.

Like Athanasius, Gregory of Nyssa, a fourth-century bishop in Asia Minor, understood Christ's atonement to find its primary expression in the incarnation of the Word.[46] In his *Great Catechetical Oration,* Gregory explains in great detail the "trick" of incarnation that Jesus played upon the devil to bring about the salvation of humankind while yet maintaining the justice of God. For Gregory, human beings were designed at their creation in the image of the divine nature and as a result had freedom of will and a natural attraction to beauty. But Satan used this attraction to deceive humanity into thinking that vice was beauty, and Adam was caught by this deception. He unwittingly sold himself into slavery to the Deceiver, becoming subject to the power of death and hell. To redeem humankind from this situation while yet preserving his own justice, Gregory argues, God must offer a ransom to the slaveholder.[47] But God knew that Satan, who suffers from "the special passion of pride," would only accept as a ransom something superior to what he already holds in thrall. For Nyssa, only Christ, who is the Word made flesh, could tempt Satan to make such a bargain. Christ's perfect life—his purity, his power, his miracles—make him an irresistible exchange for humans "shut up in the prison of death" through the Fall.[48] But Christ's body of flesh obscured Satan's ability to perceive that he was in fact God incarnate:

> Therefore, *in order to secure that the ransom in our behalf* might be easily accepted by him who required it, the Deity was hidden under the veil of our nature, that so, as with ravenous fish, the hook of the Deity might be gulped down along with the bait of flesh, and thus, life being introduced into the house of death, and light shining in darkness, that which is diametrically opposed to light and life might vanish.[49]

For Nyssa, the incarnation was essentially God disguising himself in human flesh in order to trick Satan into taking him into his realm of death so that he might destroy it by the power of his divine presence. Already anticipating objections to his assertion that God could use deception to defeat Satan, Nyssa returns again to his arguments about God's justice: "By the reasonable rule of justice, he who practiced deception receives in return that very treatment, the seeds of which he had himself sown of his own free will."[50] Since God is just, Nyssa argues, it is fitting that he deal deceitfully with Satan, who chose by his own free will to deceive man in the first place. Furthermore, Satan will not be likely to dispute God's actions in this matter since he must acknowledge that what God did was not only just but also salutary. Even Satan is healed through Christ's incarnation, Nyssa asserts, since God's "fish hook" has acted upon him as the refiner's fire.[51]

In his writings, Gregory of Nyssa mainly constructs his theory of atonement upon the concept of ransom. Ransom language is found in connection with

Christ's atonement in the earliest Christian writings, but Nyssa is among the first to present a fully developed soteriology in which Christ's atonement is understood as a ransom paid by God to the devil in exchange for the freedom of an enslaved mankind. Following the lead of Origen of Alexandria, Nyssa's ransom theory focused on Christ's atonement as the remedy for the problems of death and the loss of the image of God incurred at the Fall rather than as a payment for the everyday sins of humanity.[52]

Irenaeus, Athanasius, and Gregory all highlighted the incarnation of the Word—the joining of God to human flesh—as a critical aspect of salvation for humanity. While Latter-day Saint atonement theology largely focuses on Gethsemane and Golgotha, the Book of Mormon prophet Abinadi emphasized the importance of the divine incarnation to Christ's atonement. Abinadi prophesies that God himself would come down to redeem his people and would be called the Son of God because he would dwell in flesh (Alma 15:1–2). He would be both Father and Son, being "the Father" since he was conceived by God's power and "the Son" because he dwelt in the flesh, yet being "one God, yea the very Eternal Father of heaven and of earth" (15:3–4). While Athanasius and Gregory envisioned this joining of God to humanity to recreate the image of God in human souls, Abinadi explains the aim of the incarnation of God to be submission rather than restoration. When God comes to dwell in a human body, he subjects the flesh to the will of God and "flesh becom[es] subject to the Spirit, or the Son to the Father, being one God" (15:2, 5). This divine incarnation, this utter submission of human body to God, yields flesh that cannot only perfectly withstand temptation and tribulation (15:5) but also can willingly submit to crucifixion and death, a manifestation that the will of the Son has been fully consumed by the will of the Father (15:7). It is in this state of the Son's complete submission, body and soul, to the Father, that the Son is filled with mercy and compassion for humankind, has power to satisfy justice on behalf of all people, and claims victory over death (15:8–9). Abinadi understands the end purpose of God's incarnation to provide a shelter of divine love and mercy rather than a payment of ransom to the devil or a pathway to theosis. While Athanasius and Nyssa saw the joining of God and human flesh to enable the transformation of all that is corrupt and fallen in human nature, Abinadi understands the incarnation of the Son as the divine remodeling of human flesh in a manner that makes capable the full submission of the Son that is required for him to become merciful intercessor between humankind and justice.

For Athanasius and Nyssa, the Son's atonement effected a restoration of the divine image of God, lost at the fall of Adam and Eve, to the souls of human beings. The Book of Mormon prophet Alma explains Christ's transformative power upon the human soul in similar terms. The preaching of Christ's gospel to the people engenders within them a "mighty change" of heart, or transformative spiritual rebirth, which results in the image of God being written upon their countenances (Alma 5:13–14). This appearance of the image, however, is not the return to a primal participation in divinity lost at the Fall but is understood as the mark that one has turned toward God, has repented of all sin, and is exercising faith and righteous works with the intention of retaining that image in order to be found clean and pure at the day of final judgment (5:15–19). For Alma, the image of God is not remade in all humanity through the joining of the Word with flesh. It is the gift given immediately and individually to each person who receives Jesus Christ, and it can be lost and regained time and again through the exercise of personal agency.

Augustine of Hippo: Double Redemption and Legal Justification

In the West, outside the influence of the Alexandrian legacy and incarnational soteriology, Christian writers would deal with the problems of justice and God's punishment in Christ's atonement in very different ways. Augustine of Hippo, a fifth-century North African bishop and arguably the most influential theologian of Late Antiquity, never composed a work solely dedicated to the subject of Christ's atonement, but he constructed numerous and diverse theories of atonement throughout his writings on other subjects during his very long and prolific career. Two of these theories, both developed in his *On the Trinity*, are worthy of note here for their uniqueness and their resonance with Latter-day Saint atonement theologies.

Among the earliest of these is his idea of Christ's work as a response to humanity's "double death." Similar to Gregory of Nyssa and Athanasius, Augustine asserts that humans were intended from their creation for participation in the Word and the contemplation of God.[53] But the devil deceived man by appearing to be powerful and important, and he appealed to man's pride to convince him to choose power over righteousness.[54] For Augustine, this choice brought about a "double death": death in both soul and body. "For as the soul dies when God leaves it, so the body dies when the soul leaves it; whereby the former becomes foolish, the latter lifeless."[55] The devil applied his single death—"the death of his spirit through ungodliness," as he did not have flesh to die a second death—to bring about this double death in humanity and to gain dominion over us.[56] When Christ offers himself as a ransom for humanity, Satan, who possesses by right a double authority over the souls and bodies of sinners, essentially trades his "inner" authority over human beings for the "outer" authority to kill Christ's body. Yet Christ dies a single death that answers both aspects of the double death of humanity, providing the cleansing of repentance to the human soul and a resurrection of the human body.[57] Augustine understands atonement as God becoming human in a limited sense in order to reconcile humanity to himself and make humans partakers in his divinity once more. Christ's divinity combines with his sinless human flesh to make possible ultimately a single death capable of answering to God for both human deaths.[58]

For Augustine, humanity's participation in the crucifixion of Christ on the cross by repentance allows their inner ungodliness to be crucified. The death of the soul is therefore destroyed by the death of Christ's physical body. While the death of the mortal physical body cannot be escaped, Augustine reassures us that Christ "meets us at the end to which we have come" in death and provides for the resurrection of the outward man in his own resurrection.[59] This double redemption of both soul and body allows humans to be recreated in the image of God and participate in the contemplation of divine truth.[60]

One of Augustine's later and more well-developed atonement theories in his *On the Trinity* invokes legal concepts and the language of justice to explain Christ's redemption of human beings. As a result of the sin of Adam, death comes upon all humanity as a just and deserved punishment. Augustine portrays God as the judge who passes the sentence of death upon man, not to appease his own justice but because of the desert of the crime. But Christ enters into this legal scenario and shifts the balance of power in a dramatic way:

> He, having been put to death himself although innocent, by the unjust one who was acting against us by just right, *might by a most just right overcome him*, and so might lead captive the captivity caused by sin, and free us from a captivity that was just on account of sin, by blotting out the handwriting, and redeeming us who were to be justified although sinners, through his own righteous blood unrighteously poured out.[61]

As a man, Christ allowed himself to be tempted by Satan to show us how to resist temptations, but when Satan failed to lead Christ into sin he became determined to effect death upon Christ. But in killing Christ, the devil overreaches and violates divine justice. Since Christ has no sin, he owes nothing to justice and is not subject to death so Satan's power over death is broken and his dominion over human beings is forfeit.[62] While Nyssa's sense of divine trickery is echoed in this scenario, Augustine does not explain Christ's atonement as a ransom paid (either to Satan or God) on humanity's behalf but rather a kind of legal transaction in which Christ outmaneuvers Satan by manipulating justice to free human beings.[63] Christ's atoning death "blot[s] out the handwriting" as though canceling a legal contract between Satan and humanity.

In contrast to Athanasius and Gregory of Nyssa, Augustine shifts the focal point of Christ's atonement away from incarnation and toward the death of Christ on the cross and its functions. Among Augustine's many ideas and interpretations of atonement are his understanding of Christ's single death to save the human soul and body and his legal reestablishment of justice in humanity's favor. Unlike Nyssa, who portrayed Satan as slaveholder over humanity on account of the Fall, Augustine's legal soteriology casts Satan as plaintiff against man in the court of God's justice, where the devil only holds human beings bound on account of their guilt before the law and exercises no authority or equality with God. God is the only one to whom any penalty or ransom must be paid. "Wherefore God, made a righteous man, *interceded with God for man the sinner*," Augustine later explained.[64] In his legal theory of atonement, Christ removes human sin by taking upon himself the punishment demanded by God's justice.[65] For Augustine, Christ's death on the cross is a gross violation of justice that is given as a voluntary sacrifice out of obedience on behalf of the human race.[66]

As with Augustine's writings, Latter-day Saint scripture asserts a primeval "double death" of humanity in both body and spirit at the fall of Adam and Eve which left all in the thrall of "that monster, death and hell" and the devil (2 Ne 9:8–10; cf. Alma 42:7–9, 11). Christ's atonement, completed at his resurrection from the grave, forces death and hell to deliver up their dead and restore the spirits of humankind to their bodies once again. Human beings must choose to participate in Jesus's death on the cross through repentance and patiently enduring the "crosses of the world" (2 Ne 9:18, 23; cf. Jacob 1:8, Alma 39:9; 3 Ne 12:30) if they would escape the "second death," a state of permanent subjection to the devil where Christ's redemption has no claim upon the sinner (Jacob 3:11; Alma 12:16, 32; Hel 14:16–18; cf. Alma 13:30; D&C 63:17–18).

In his later writings, Augustine explained Christ's resurrection and resulting victory over all human death as the inevitable outcome of God's justice. Latter-day Saint theology often invokes the language of God's justice and legalistic concepts and imagery similar to those found in *On the Trinity* to explain the mechanics of divine atonement. In the Book of Mormon, Alma imagines individuals brought before a "tribunal of God" to be judged of their works and to display whether the image of God can be found upon their countenances (Alma 5:15–19). Elsewhere, Alma explains that the fall of all humankind in the Garden of Eden, brought about by disobedience to the law he had given Adam and Eve, resulted in humans being permanently cut off from God on account of God's justice (Alma 42:7, 12, 14). In order to appease the demands of justice, "God himself atoneth for the sins of the world, to bring about the plan of mercy, to appease the demands of justice, that God might be a perfect, just God, and a merciful God also" (Alma 42:15). Christ's atonement extends mercy to fallen humanity without robbing justice of what it is rightly owed, bringing to pass the resurrection of the dead and returning all humankind to

God's presence to have their works judged by the law and by his justice (Alma 42:23). While Augustine sees Christ's crucifixion as a violation of God's justice that is righted with the resurrection of all humanity, Alma explains Jesus's atonement as the means by which mercy might be extended by a benevolent God to a fallen humankind without creating an injustice that would cause God to "cease to be God" (Alma 42:25). Drawing on these Book of Mormon teachings, Boyd K. Packer (1924–2014), a member of the Council of the Twelve from 1970 until his death, has expounded Jesus Christ's role as "the Mediator," an intercessor uniquely prepared to make a payment that satisfies the demands of divine justice even while extending salvific mercy to humankind.[67]

Anselm of Canterbury and Peter Abelard: Protecting God's Sovereignty

For most writers of the Middle Ages, the idea that the Son of God would have to descend to pay ransom to the devil demeaned the honor and omnipotence of God. Anselm of Canterbury (1033/34–1109), an eleventh-century bishop, disliked the suggestion that Satan was an independent legal party whose rights could possibly be set over God's, a notion inherent to many earlier soteriologies.[68] In response to these issues, Anselm formulated a "satisfaction" theory of atonement protective of God's absolute omnipotence and omniscience, locating the reasons and motives for Christ's work in God's honor rather than a debt owed to Satan, as earlier ransom theories had done.[69] In his *Cur Deus Homo?* (*Why God Became Man?*), Anselm represents God as a feudal lord to whom humans, as his vassals, owe submission and obedience. Sin arises when humans fail to give to God these duties that are owed him.[70]

Like earlier writers, Anselm understood sin's consequences to be both a loss of the eternal blessedness that humankind is intended for and also physical death. But in *Cur Deus Homo?*, Anselm adds to the list of these resulting problems of sin an even larger one: God is dishonored by sin and so injustice and disorder are created in the universe.[71] The return of man's submission to God is simply not enough to restore the honor due to God. Justice and order can only be restored to the universe through providing satisfaction. Under the law, a thief must restore not only what was stolen but also make amends in proportion to the crime.[72] Human beings, fallen in nature and finite, are incapable of providing this recompense.[73] Only Christ, who is God and man, can make the necessary satisfaction by providing amends for the dishonor of God and mitigating the death and loss of blessedness that have come upon mankind.[74] Christ chooses to let himself be killed and in doing so gives the whole of himself—both his divine and human natures—as an infinite sacrifice capable of counterbalancing the sins of all human beings, producing a gift that is offered to God on behalf of humanity.[75] The Father in turn gives the Son a reward for his great voluntary benevolence, but since Christ is in need of nothing, he mercifully bestows a remission of sin upon human beings.[76] Thus, Christ's sacrifice both saves humankind and satisfies God's honor.

Like Anselm, Peter Abelard (c. 1079–1142), a twelfth-century theologian, strongly objected to the notion that Satan had or ever could hold some power or right of debt over God and, by extension, human beings.[77] As God is the only one with authority over us, Abelard reasoned, it would only be right that a ransom be paid only to God, as Anselm's satisfaction theory and others had proposed. But Abelard also found it nonsensical that God could be considered a creditor that would demand a debt from himself, since in such a scenario, no payment or actual ransom would be taking place at all. Furthermore, it would be unjust and cruel of God to demand the blood of an innocent person as ransom for other people's wrongdoing. It would be even more absurd, Abelard argued, to think that God would accept the death of his Son as a means of reconciliation with the world when man had forced the Son of God to endure so much suffering and a violent and shameful death on the cross, an incident that would have justifiably caused God to be "all the more angry with man because men forsook him so much more in crucifying his Son."[78]

In response to the many aspects of other theories he found illogical and demeaning of God's absolute power and goodness, Abelard formulated a "moral exemplar" theory of atonement that emphasized the importance of Christ's work as a pedagogical tool. In his interpretation of Romans 3, he reads Paul's statements on righteousness and justice as a doctrine of divine love and its salvific power.

> Nevertheless it seems to us that in this we are justified in the blood of Christ and reconciled to God, that it was through this matchless grace shown to us that his Son received our nature, and in that nature, *teaching us both by word and by example*, persevered to the death and bound us to himself even more through love, so that when we have been kindled by so great a benefit of divine grace, true charity might fear to endure nothing for his sake . . . Each one is also made more righteous after the Passion of Christ than before; that is, he loves God more, because the completed benefit kindles him in love more than a hoped-for benefit. Therefore, our redemption is that supreme love in us through the Passion of Christ, which not only frees us from slavery to sin, but gains for us the true liberty of the sons of God, *so that we may complete all things by his love rather than by fear.*[79]

Through the grace of God, Christ received human nature and taught humanity with the example of his life. The divine love Christ exhibited through his Passion and death incites human beings to love God and to desire to emulate

Christ. The love that is kindled by viewing Christ's suffering and death binds man to God and makes him righteous.[80] Abelard passes over the idea that Christ's cross was about making ransom or satisfaction to God or Satan. After all, he asserts, if God wills to forgive sin, he can simply forgive it, and Abelard implies that Christ has chosen to do so.[81] Instead, he emphasizes the salvific power of viewing the example of Christ's life and the love it manifested. Seeing the supreme act of love in Christ's atonement, now not only hoped for but come to pass in the flesh, inspires in man that greater love which transforms him to be more righteous than before Christ came.[82] For Abelard, the function of Christ's atonement is to gift human beings with the love that inspires them to turn more fully to God and receive a forgiveness of sins.[83]

Most Latter-day Saint models of atonement understand Christ's sacrifice to be critical to ongoing balance and order in the universe. Like Abelard, however, some modern Latter-day Saint writers have emphasized the exemplary power of his atoning work. Most notable among these was Eugene England, for whom "the effects of the Atonement were not metaphysical but moral and spiritual."[84] England perceived the problem of sin to be not in the moral failing itself but in the resulting alienation that one personally feels from God and from oneself after its commission. God, intimately aware and concerned with human suffering for sin, sent his Son to demonstrate empathetic suffering with humanity in order to give human beings power to forgive themselves and be reconciled to God and their own true natures. "We do not repent in order that God will forgive us and atone for our sins," he wrote, "but rather God atones for our sins . . . in order that we might repent and thus bring to its conclusion the process of forgiveness."[85] As Terryl Givens has noted, England's teachings were a basic revision of Abelard's moral influence theory that emphasized individual transformation in response to the "shock of eternal love" demonstrated by Christ's sacrifice.[86]

Thomas Aquinas: Satisfaction Theory and Beyond

In the writings of Thomas Aquinas (1225–1274), the most prolific Christian scholar of the medieval period, a number of earlier theories of atonement coalesce and find greater development. Like Abelard, Aquinas understood Christ's atonement as a manifestation of God's love which inspires those who see it to love him in return, and which also provides them with an example of obedience and other virtues.[87] Yet this is only one aspect of his complex understanding of Christ's work. Aquinas's writings also display Anselm's understanding of atonement as an act of satisfaction. For Aquinas, the sin of human beings causes a disorder in their relationship with God that needs to be reestablished by their offering compensation that can make up for the debt of sin even after the sin has been forgiven.[88] To make such an offering capable of providing satisfaction to God's justice, Christ offered more to God than was demanded in recompense for all the sins of humanity, since he suffered voluntarily, his life was of such great dignity, and his suffering and pain were infinite in scope.[89] Since sin is offense of the infinite divine majesty, proper satisfaction can only be made by someone divinely infinite.[90] Because Christ was both divine and sinless human, he was able to make satisfaction for the whole human race.[91]

While many of these principles were founded upon Anselm's thought, Aquinas's teaching on the satisfaction of Christ diverges from Anselm's thought in many significant ways. Aquinas was not satisfied that Anselm had adequately protected God's sovereignty in finding Christ's atonement fundamentally necessary. He stressed that neither God nor Christ had been or could be compelled in any way and that God certainly could have freed all people from sin merely by willing it as he is omnipotent. Furthermore, he argued, for God to do so would not have been unjust, just as it is not unjust but rather merciful for someone to forgive another who has given offense.[92] Aquinas asserted that satisfaction was necessary simply because God ordained that it should be so. This manner of bringing people to God was superior, he reasoned, as it was in accordance with God's justice and his mercy rather than just his mercy, as a divine willing of the forgiveness of sin would have been.[93]

In a further departure from Anselm, Aquinas formulated a hybrid theory of atonement that incorporated aspects of earlier ransom and satisfaction theories.[94] According to Aquinas, humans were held in the bondage of sin both by personal transgression and by sin incurred at the Fall, when Satan overcame man and induced him to sin, subjecting him to the devil's bondage.[95] But they also were constrained by a debt of punishment—not only payment to discharge the debt but also the compensation for harm done—owed to God's justice. Christ's atonement creates "a sufficient and a superabundant" payment for the debt of humanity, so it not only provides the ransom that releases humanity from the devil's bondage but it also satisfies the punishment that is owed to God's justice.[96] The copious amount of mercy produced by Christ's passion exceeds that which would have been available to humanity had God simply willed the forgiveness of all sin.[97] Since Christ actually offered more to God than what was demanded as recompense for humanity, his sacrifice provided not only the basic payment owed but also the excess compensation required to make full satisfaction to God's justice, not requiring God to just forgive out of mercy.[98] In addition, the great bounty of mercy produced by Christ "overflowed from him to others, so that the Son of God, made human, might make people gods and sons and daughters of God."[99] Aquinas envisioned Christ as the Head of the Church and human beings are the bodily members of a "single mystic person." In this way, Christ's merit extends into all who are united with him through the spiritual regeneration of baptism.[100] For Aquinas, this extension of merit from Christ to his body is an infusion of grace that saves people from both past sin and also serves as a "remedy for the avoidance of sin" in the future.[101]

Aquinas's multifaceted theory of atonement also incorporated earlier ideas of penal substitution and incarnation soteriology. "From the beginning of His conception, Christ merited our eternal salvation, but on our side there were some obstacles, whereby we were hindered from securing the effect of His preceding merits. Consequently, in order to remove such hindrances, *it was necessary for Christ to suffer*," he concludes.[102] For Aquinas, Christ had extended grace to humanity at the moment the Word became incarnate, as Athanasius had maintained. But the merit of the incarnation was not enough to remove some obstacles to human salvation, and Christ had to suffer to clear the pathway for humankind. While Aquinas was careful to delineate between the suffering of Christ's human nature and his impassive divine one,[103] he placed great emphasis on the physical suffering of the atonement.

In attempting to demonstrate that the pain of Christ's passion was the very greatest of all pain, he calls for consideration of the various sources of Christ's extreme suffering: how Christ's pain was both external and internal, how his death on the cross is the most bitter of all deaths since the nails are driven into his most sensitive parts, how the duration of crucifixion prolonged his suffering, how his human nature must have been horrified at the prospect of death, how his suffering was magnified by his acutely honed senses of physical touch and spiritual empathy, how he did not use his higher faculty of reason to mitigate his sufferings, and finally, how the magnitude of Christ's pain was proportionate to the magnitude of his achievement in delivering the whole human race from sin. In this way, Christ redeemed humanity not only by his power to forgive but also according to justice.[104] He accepted voluntarily this great quantity of pain and sorrow to bring about men's deliverance from sin. Elsewhere, Aquinas reads the animal sacrifice rituals of the Hebrew Bible to explain that Christ is both priest and victim in that he offers himself as a "victim for sin" to blot out transgressions and extend the grace of salvation to humankind.[105] As the substitutionary victim, Christ gives to human beings both an infusion of grace that turns their hearts toward God and also full justification inasmuch as he has "borne our infirmities and carried our sorrows (Isa 53:4)."[106]

Aquinas's emphasis on Christ's pain and suffering reflects his attempt to reconcile earlier precepts of incarnational soteriology with the idea that Christ's passion was the significant and critical moment in salvation history. While Aquinas concedes that the incarnation brings salvation in some form, the passion of Christ is clearly for him the locus for forgiveness of sin, the satisfaction of God's justice, and humankind's release from the bondage of Satan rather than Christ's incarnation. Christ's extreme pain is a manifestation of its salvific significance. In emphasizing the sufferings of Christ as a means whereby humankind receives salvation, Aquinas seems to propose a type of penal substitution theory of atonement that echoes the writings of Justin Martyr and Tertullian. For Aquinas, Christ's incarnation is not enough to remove all (or even most of) the obstacles to human salvation. Rather, he teaches that God's justice demands satisfaction through payment of a penalty of suffering, and that Christ satisfies God by offering himself as the sacrificial victim to pay through his passion. While Aquinas explicitly rejects the notion that Christ's suffering is penal because it was voluntary and not personal (meaning that God did not demand it of humans themselves nor of Christ, but rather allowed that Christ suffer to generally remit sin),[107] his writings nevertheless lay important groundwork for Reformation thinkers like Martin Luther and John Calvin in whom penal substitution theory will realize its full development.

Conclusion: The Christian Heritage of The Church of Jesus Christ of Latter-day Saints

Thomas Aquinas's writings stand as a monument to over one thousand years of Christian thought on the significance of Jesus Christ's atonement. In the *Summa Theologiae*, his great "summary of theology," Aquinas reiterated aspects of penal substitution, theosis, incarnation, ransom, justification, satisfaction, moral exemplarism, and many others and wove them together into a complex and multifaceted soteriology reflecting both the richness of the Christian tradition as well as the eternal mystery of God's work among humankind. While Aquinas attempted to systematize and standardize doctrine, his *Summa* clearly reflects the "bigness" and "looseness" of Christian atonement theory when considered in context of many of the thinkers and authors that preceded him.

Like Aquinas, some Latter-day Saint theologians have attempted to harmonize or standardize church doctrine concerning the atonement of Jesus Christ.[108] But Latter-day Saint scripture, with its diversity of ideas and understandings, resists systematization, and the Church's strong emphasis of God's continued prophetic revelation to the ecclesiastical leadership and the great value placed upon personal revelation means that past and contemporary understandings are constantly subject to revision by both the leaders and laymen. Even a very preliminary consideration of Latter-day Saint teachings on atonement in context of earlier Christian soteriologies reveals the rich diversity of Latter-day Saint atonement theology and suggests possible connections to earlier Christian understandings. Despite its claims to the knowledge and authority of primitive Christianity, Latter-day Saint theology represents an amalgamation of many different thoughts and ideas about the Son's salvific mission that reflect the Church's shared intellectual heritage with other Christian denominations. This chapter has attempted to summarize some of the most important soteriologies of Christianity's first millennium and suggest some likely relationships between early Christian teachings on atonement and Latter-day Saint teachings. Other authors in this volume will consider in greater detail the cultural and intellectual contexts of Latter-day Saint atonement theories to further illuminate some of the ways in which Christians of all stripes have labored to understand the work of Christ and their own relationships to God.

Notes

1. Gustaf Aulén, *Christus Victor: An Historical Study of Three Main Types of the Idea of the Atonement*, translated by A. G. Herbert (New York: Macmillan, 1957), 4–6.

2. Aulén viewed his endeavor as a purely historical one and his method to be objective and scientific in nature. In his estimation, the tidy historical narrative presented in *Christus Victor* was merely the result of facts being uncovered and brought to light once again. Aulén's historiographic aspirations clearly reflect the entrance of ideas and methods of the German empirical school of history into the discipline of theology. Empiricist historians such as Leopold von Ranke advocated an objective, methodical approach to the past and thought that by looking at documents and primary sources, a historian would be able to gather facts and reveal a definitive narrative picture of what actually happened in the past. Such an approach is now considered deeply problematic by modern historians. See Elizabeth A. Clark, *History, Theory, Text: Historians and the Linguistic Turn* (Cambridge, MA: Harvard University Press, 2004), 9–13.

3. For example, see Roland Spjuth, "Gustaf Aulén," in *T&T Clark Companion to Atonement*, edited by Adam J. Johnson (London: Bloomsbury, 2017), 389–92; John Aliosi, "'His Flesh for Our Flesh': The Doctrine of the Atonement in the Second Century," *Detroit Baptist Seminary Journal* 14 (2009): 23–27; Joseph J. Anderlonis, *The Soteriology of Gustaf Aulén: The Origins, Development, and Relevancy of the Christus Victor Atonement View* (Rome: Pontificia Università Gregoriana, 1988).

4. John A. McGuckin, "St. Gregory of Nyssa on the Dynamics of Salvation," in Johnson, *T&T Clark Companion to Atonement*, 158.

5. On the influence of Paul's (and pseudo-Paul's) writings on the author of Diognetus, see Michael F. Bird, "The Reception of Paul in the Epistle to Diognetus," in *Paul in the Second Century*, edited by M. F. Bird and J. R. Dodson (London: T&T Clark, 2011), 70–90, and Andreas Lindemann, "Paulinische Theologie im Brief an Diognet," in *Kerygma und Logos: Beiträge zu den geistesgeschichtlichen Beziehungen zwischen Antika und Christentum*, edited by A. M. Ritter (Göttingen: Vandenhoeck & Ruprecht, 1979), 337–50.

6. *Epistle to Diognetus* 9.1–3 (Ehrman II, 148–50), emphasis added.

7. John Aliosi discusses how Diognetus's soteriology does not support Aulén's asser-

tion that the Christus Victor model was the only atonement theory taught and accepted by early Christian writers. See Aliosi, "'His Flesh for Our Flesh,'" 39.

8. *Epistle of Barnabas*, 7.3 (Ehrman II, 36).

9. *Barnabas*, 11.2–5 (Ehrman II, 52).

10. *Barnabas*, 7.1–8.7 (Ehrman II, 36–42). Maier, "The Apostolic Fathers," in Johnson, *T&T Clark Companion to Atonement*, 373–74, cites details of the scapegoat ritual recounted in *Barnabas* that don't pertain to the Hebrew Bible and parallel an account in the Babylonian Talmud (Yoma 4a-8b).

11. *Epistle of Barnabas*, 7.2 (Ehrman II, 36), emphasis added.

12. *Barnabas*, 4.14–5.1 (Ehrman II, 24–25), emphasis added.

13. Ignatius, *Letter to the Smyrneans*. 1.2 (Ehrman I, 296).

14. Ignatius, *Smyrneans*. 1.1 (Ehrman I, 296).

15. Ignatius, *Letter to the Magnesians*. 5.2 (Ehrman I, 245).

16. Maier, "Ignatius of Antioch," in Johnson, *T&T Clark Companion to Atonement*, 548–49.

17. Justin Dialogues 94.5, 95.1–3 in *Justin Martyr: Dialogue avec Tryphon, édition critique*, Vol. I, translated by Philippe Bobichon (Fribourg: Academic Press Fribourg, 2003), 444.

18. Many modern scholars mark Justin Martyr as the first advocate of a "penal substitution" understanding of Jesus's atonement. See Garry J. Williams, "Penal Substitutionary Atonement in the Church Fathers," *Evangelical Quarterly* 83.3 (2011), 196–99; Aliosi, "His Flesh for Our Flesh," 37.

19. See Gerald Lewis Bray, *Holiness and the Will of God: Perspectives on the Theology of Tertullian* (Atlanta: John Knox, 1979), 88–89. The distinction between objective and subjective dimensions of atonement is made by Geoffrey D. Dunn in his "A Survey of Tertullian's Soteriology," *Sacris Erudiri* 42 (2003): 61–86.

20. Tertullian, *Against Marcion*, Corpus Christianorum Series Latina (CCL), volume 1, 3.8.1 (CCL 1, 518).

21. Tertullian, *On Running Away from Persecution*, Corpus Scriptorum Ecclesiasticorum Latinorum (CSEL), volume 25, 12.3–5 (CSEL 25, 36–38).

22. As Stephen R. Holmes has explained, "Penal substitutionary atonement assumes the logic of the law court. Sin is understood as law-breaking, and so necessarily attracts a penalty, which is inevitably death. In dying on the cross, Jesus pays the penalty of death for all those who are saved, and so they are freed from their deserved punishment." See Holmes, "Penal Substitution," in Johnson, *T&T Clark Companion to Atonement*, 295.

Penal substitution theory of atonement is a matter of great controversy among modern writers for various reasons. Many theologians are anxious to distance ancient Christianity from this soteriology and attribute the invention of penal substitutionary theory to John Calvin (1509–1564), a Reformation writer. For this view, see Holmes, above, and also Derek Flood, "Substitutionary Atonement and the Church Fathers: A Reply to the Authors of *Pierced for Our Transgressions*," *Evangelical Quarterly* 82.2 (2010): 142–59. Others argue that it was taught in the earliest Christian churches and by the Catholic church fathers of late antiquity. See Steve Jefferey, Michael Ovey, and Andrew Sach, *Pierced for Our Transgressions: Rediscovering the Glory of Penal Substitution* (Nottingham,

UK: Inter-Varsity Press, 2007); Williams, "Penal Substitutionary Atonement in the Church Fathers"; Peter Ensor, "Justin Martyr and Penal Substitutionary Atonement," *Evangelical Quarterly* 83.3 (2011): 217–32, and Ensor, "Tertullian and Penal Substitutionary Atonement," *Evangelical Quarterly* 86.2 (2014): 130–42.

23. Former Latter-day Saint writer and apostle Bruce R. McConkie (1915–1985) taught that in taking upon himself "the pains and agonies of an infinite burden," Christ "ransomed penitent souls from the pains and penalties of sin" (McConkie, "The Purifying Power of Gethsemane," *Ensign* [May 1985]: 9–11). See also Boyd K. Packer, "The Mediator," *Ensign* (May 1977): 54–56, and also Gordon B. Hinckley, "The Wondrous and True Story of Christmas," *Ensign* (Dec. 2000): 2–6.

24. The origins of the concept of recapitulation appear to be from Paul's writings in Romans 5:12–21 and 1 Corinthians 15:45–50, while the Latin word "recapitulatio" was a translation of the Greek "anakephalaitosis" in Ephesians 1:10, which speaks of Christ summing up all things in himself. See Ben Pugh, *Atonement Theories: A Way through the Maze* (Eugene, OR: Cascade Books, 2014), 27–28.

25. John Behr, "Irenaeus of Lyons," in Johnson, *T&T Clark Companion to Atonement*, 569–70.

26. Irenaeus, *Against Heresies*, Patrilogia Graeca (PG), volumes 7a and 7b, translated by John Keble (London: James Parker & Co. and Rivingtons, 1872), 3.20.1 (PG 7a, 942).

27. Irenaeus, 3.22.3 (PG 7a, 958), emphasis added.

28. Irenaeus, 3.23.2–7 (PG 7a, 961–64); 3.18.6–7 (PG 7a, 936–38).

29. Irenaeus, 3.19.1 (PG 7a, 958), emphasis added.

30. Irenaeus, 5 pref. (PG 7b, 1119–120). Cf. 4.38.4 (PG 7a, 1109).

31. Irenaeus, 4.20.5 (PG 7a, 1034–1036). Anthony Briggman fleshes out this aspect of Irenaeus's soteriology to a greater extent in his *God and Christ in Irenaeus* (Oxford: Oxford University Press, 2019), 181–204.

32. See Jeffrey R. Holland, "Behold the Lamb of God," *Ensign* (May 2019): 44–46; L. Tom Perry, "The Plan of Salvation," *Ensign* (Nov. 2006): 69–71; Henry B. Eyring, "Tested, Proved, and Polished," *Ensign* (Nov. 2020): 96–99; Dallin H. Oaks, "The Great Plan," *Ensign* (May 2020): 93–96, et al.

33. Russell M. Nelson, "The Atonement," *Ensign* (Nov. 1996): 33–35 and James E. Faust, "The Supernal Gift of the Atonement," *Ensign* (Nov. 1988): 12–14.

34. Eliza R. Snow, *Biography and Family Record of Lorenzo Snow* (1884), 46. See also *The Teachings of Lorenzo Snow*, edited by Clyde J. Williams (1996), 1–9, and the discussion at The Church of Jesus Christ of Latter-day Saints, "Becoming Like God," https://www.churchofjesuschrist.org/study/manual/gospel-topics-essays/becoming-like-god.

35. See also Russell M. Nelson, "Salvation and Exaltation," *Ensign* (May 2008): 7–10; Theodore M. Burton, "Salvation and Exaltation," *Ensign* (July 1972): 78–79.

36. Athanasius, *On the Incarnation of the Word*, Patrilogia Graecus (PG), volume 25g, 3.3 (PG 25b, 100–102).

37. Athanasius, *Inc.* 4.4–5 (PG 25b, 1–3).

38. Athanasius, 7.4–5 (PG 25b, 108).

39. Athanasius, 8.4 (PG 25b, 109), emphasis added.

40. Athanasius more closely follows the second- and third-century Alexandrian intel-

lectuals Clement and Origen in his conflation of the image of God with rationality. See Walter J. Burghardt, "The Image of God in Man: Alexandrian Orientations," *Proceedings of the Catholic Theological Society of America* 16 (1961): 149–54.

41. Athanasius, *Against the Arians*, Patrilogia Graeca (PG), volume 25c, 3.19 (PG 25c, 561–64). Cf. *On the Incarnation of the Word* 14.2–7, 16.1–5 (PG 25b, 120–21; 124–25). Weinandy explains Athanasius's understanding of deification is "the making of humankind, through the indwelling of the Holy Spirit, into what it was meant to be from the very beginning, that is, the perfect image of the Word who is the perfect image of the Father, affected by being taken into the very divine life of the Trinity." See Thomas G. Weinandy, "Athanasius's Incarnational Soteriology," in Johnson, *T&T Clark Companion to Atonement*, 150.

42. Athanasius, *Inc.* 54.3 (PG 25b, 192). His teaching is likely a paraphrase of Irenaeus's teaching quoted above.

43. Athanasius, *Arians*, 2.66 (PG 25c, 285–88), 1.41 (PG25c, 96–97).

44. Athanasius, *Arians*, 2.61 (PG 25c, 276–77).

45. Athanasius, *Arians*, 3.19 (PG 25c, 361–64).

46. McGuckin notes that a "macro-context" of incarnational Christology in Gregory of Nyssa's thought that was heavily influenced by Athanasius and Origen. See John A. McGuckin, "St. Gregory of Nyssa on the Dynamics of Salvation," 156. As is customary among scholars of early Christianity, "Gregory of Nyssa" will be abbreviated hereafter to Nyssa rather than Gregory to keep him distinct from his good friend and contemporary, Gregory Nazianzen.

47. Gregory of Nyssa, *Great Catechetical Oration*, Patrilogia Graeca (PG), volume 45, 21 (PG 45, 57–60).

48. Gregory of Nyssa, 23 (PG 45, 61–64).

49. Gregory of Nyssa, 24 (PG 45, 64–65), emphasis added.

50. Gregory of Nyssa, 26 (PG 45, 68–69).

51. Gregory of Nyssa, 26 (PG 45, 68–69).

52. On Origen's soteriology, see Corine B. Milad, "Incarnation and Transfiguration: Origen's Theology of Descent," *Journal of Theological Interpretation* 12 (2018): 200–216. Nyssa not only emphasized the incarnation as the critical locus of salvation but also asserted that the crucifixion itself was most important for its allegorical meaning. He reads it as an allegory for the whole of creation and Christ's suspension upon the cross represents his lordship over all things. This allegorical interpretation blunts the violence and other physical dimensions of Christ's atonement. See Gregory of Nyssa, *Or. Cat.*, 32 (PG 45, 77–80).

53. Augustine of Hippo, *On the Trinity*, Corpus Christianorum Series Latina (CCL), volume 50, 4.4 (CCL 50, 169–72).

54. Augustine, *Trin.* 4.13 (CCL 50, 178).

55. Augustine, 4.5 (CCL 50, 165–69).

56. Augustine, 4.15 (CCL 50, 180–81).

57. Augustine, 4.4 (CCL 50, 163–64).

58. For Augustine, Christ was sinless both on account of his life without sin and also because of the manner of his incarnation. He explains elsewhere that Christ was born

free from the original sin of Adam transmitted through carnal concupiscence as he was conceived of a virgin. See Augustine, *Trin.* 13.23 (CCL 50a, 413–14).

59. Augustine, *Trin.* 4.15, 4.6 (CCL 50, 180–81; 166–69). In contrast to many other Christian writers of his era, Augustine claimed that the same bodies human beings possess in this life will rise with them in the resurrection. See Paula Fredriksen, "Vile Bodies: Paul and Augustine on the Resurrection of the Flesh," in *Biblical Hermeneutics in Historical Perspective*, edited by Mark S. Burrows and Paul Rorem (Grand Rapids, MI: William B. Eerdmans, 1991), 75–87.

60. Augustine, *Trin.* 4.24–25 (CCL 50, 191–94).

61. Augustine, 4.17 (CCL 50, 182–84), emphasis added.

62. Augustine, 13.14 (CCL 50a, 400–401). cf. 4.17 (CCL 50, 182–84).

63. Junius Johnson, *Patristic and Medieval Atonement Theory* (Lanham, MD: Rowman & Littlefield, 2016), 97.

64. Augustine, *Trin.* 4.4 (CCL 50, 163–65).

65. Junius Johnson has posited that Augustine's ideas construct a type of penal substitutionary model of atonement (Johnson, *Patristic and Medieval Atonement Theory*, 98). On the other hand, Adonis Vidu has persuasively argued that Augustine's understanding of atonement may more accurately be termed "representative sacrifice." While he concedes that Augustine's soteriology included ideas of divine retribution and propitiation, Vidu points out multiple reasons why Augustine's theology departs from classic penal substitution models. These include Augustine's understanding of the punishment of death as self-inflicted rather than meted out by God (*Trin.* 4.12), his insistence that Christ volunteers to atone instead of being compelled to suffer on our behalf (4.13), and his suggestion that God could have chosen to remove original sin without the atonement of Christ (13.10). See Adonis Vidu, *Atonement, Law, and Justice: The Cross in Historical and Cultural Contexts* (Grand Rapids, MI: Baker Academic, 2014), 35–41.

66. Vidu writes that "God is pleased that the Son, having assumed the human condition with everything it entails, including fearsome death, is utterly obedient to him even in the face of the destruction of the body. God takes delight not so much in seeing Christ punished as he does in beholding the attitude of the Son in the midst of our cursed condition." See Vidu, *Atonement, Law, and Justice*, 41.

67. Packer, "The Mediator," 54–56.

68. Anselm of Canterbury, *Why God Became Man* (*Cur Deus Homo* [*CDH*]), Patrilogia Graeca (PG), volume 158, 1.6–7 (PL 158, 76–77).

69. For a broader survey of the way atonement is understood in Anselm's work, see Marilyn McCord Adams, "Satisfying Mercy: St. Anselm's *Cur Deus Homo*, Reconsidered," *The Modern Schoolman* 62 (1995): 91–108, and Katherine Sonderegger, "Anselmian Atonement," in Johnson, *T&T Clark Companion to Atonement*, 175–94. In an older but very useful study, J. Patout Burns examines Anselm's theory of satisfaction in context of nine other Christian writers of the twelfth and thirteenth centuries in "The Concept of Satisfaction in Medieval Redemption Theory," *Theological Studies* 36.2 (1975): 285–304.

70. Anselm, *CDH* 1.14 (PL 158, 80).

71. Anselm, *CDH* 1.11–12 (PL 158, 79–81).

72. Anselm, 1.12, 14 (PL 158, 79–80; 80–81).

73. Anselm, 1.20 (PL 158, 84); 1.23 (PL 158, 85).

74. Anselm, *CDH* 2.6 (PL 158, 87–88); 2.8, 10 (PL 158, 88–90).

75. Anselm, 2.18 (PL 158, 93–94); 2.11 (PL 158, 90).

76. Anselm, 2.19 (PL 158, 95).

77. Peter Abelard reasoned that since humans are God's servants, if they should run away from him at the persuasion of another servant, they nevertheless continue to be his property rather than the property of the servant who persuaded them to run away. Any right Satan may have over man comes by permission of the Lord and with the same authority a jailer or torturer might have (Peter Abelard, *Commentary on the Epistle to the Romans*, Corpus Christianorum Continuatio Mediavalis (CCCM), volume 11, 2.3.26 [CCCM 11, 113–18]). All English translations of Abelard's commentary are taken from Stephen R. Cartwright's translation in volume 12 of *Fathers of the Church Medieval Continuations* (Washington, DC: The Catholic University of America Press, 2011).

78. Abelard, *Comm. Rom.* 2.3.26 (CCCM 11, 113–18).

79. Abelard, *Comm. Rom.* 3.26 (CCCM 11, 113–18), emphasis added.

80. Abelard, 4.25 (CCCM 11, 244).

81. Abelard, 4.26 (CCCM 11, 113–18).

82. Abelard, *Comm. Rom.* 3.25 (CCCM 11, 210): "Through this righteousness, that is, charity, we may obtain the forgiveness of sins, just as also the Truth said through itself concerning the blessed sinner, 'Her many sins are forgiven, because she loved much.'"

83. Many modern scholars have pointed out that Abelard's "moral influence" theory does not account for all or even the majority of his atonement theology. See Adam J. Johnson, "Peter Abelard," in Johnson, *T&T Companion to Atonement*, 357–60; Alister McGrath, "The Moral Theory of the Atonement: A Historical and Theological Critique," *Scottish Journal of Theology* 38 (1985): 205–20; Burns, "The Concept of Satisfaction," 289–91; Philip L. Quinn, "Abelard on Atonement: 'Nothing Unintelligible, Arbitrary, Illogical, or Immoral about It,'" in *Reasoned Faith: Essays in Philosophical Theology in Honor of Norman Kretzmann*, edited by Eleonore Stump (Ithaca, NY: Cornell University Press, 1993), 281–300. While this theory is only one aspect of Abelard's ideas on Christ's atonement, it is the most unique and innovative aspect of his soteriological writings and becomes the foundation for many theological discussions of atonement in the centuries to come.

84. Eugene England, as quoted in Terryl L. Givens, *Stretching the Heavens: The Life of Eugene England and the Crisis of Modern Mormonism* (Chapel Hill: The University of North Carolina Press, 2021), 127.

85. England, as quoted in Givens, *Stretching the Heavens*, 128.

86. Givens, 126–28. Givens also notes the similar, if less well known, ideas of B. H. Roberts, an earlier LDS church theologian and historian (Givens, 125–26, 128).

87. Brian Davies, *The Thought of Thomas Aquinas* (Oxford: Oxford University Press, 1992), 334.

88. Thomas Aquinas, *Summa Theologiae*, Ia2ae.87.1 ad 3 (Blackfriars v.27, 14); IIIa.48.2 (Blackfriars v.54, 78). All references to the *Summa Theologiae* in this section refer to the Blackfriars critical edition, 61 vols., (New York: McGraw-Hill, 1964–1981).

89. Aquinas, *Sum.* IIIa.48.2 (Blackfriars v.54, 76–78).

90. Aquinas, IIIa.1.2 (Blackfriars v.48, 8–14).

91. Davies, *The Thought of Thomas Aquinas*, 330.

92. Aquinas, *Sum.* IIIa.46.1, 2 (Blackfriars v.54, 2–10).

93. Aquinas, IIIa.46.3 (Blackfriars v.54, 10–14).

94. For a more detailed study of the various ways in which Aquinas incorporates Christus Victor or ransom theory motifs into his work, see Jonathan Morgan, "*Christus Victor* Motifs in the Soteriology of Thomas Aquinas," *Pro Ecclesia* 21.4 (2012): 409–21. Adam Johnson also discusses how Aquinas appropriated and rearticulated various current theories of atonement in "A Fuller Account: The Role of 'Fittingness' in Thomas Aquinas' Development of the Doctrine of Atonement," *International Journal of Systematic Theology* 12.3 (2010): 302–18.

95. Aquinas, *Sum.* IIIa.46.3 ad 3 (Blackfriars v.54, 10–14); IIIa.48.4 (Blackfriars v.54, 82–86).

96. Aquinas, IIIa.48.4 (Blackfriars v.54, 82–86).

97. Aquinas, IIIa.46.1 ad 3 (Blackfriars v.54, 6).

98. Aquinas, IIIa.46.1 ad 3 (Blackfriars v.54, 6).

99. Aquinas, *Sum.* IIIa.19.4 (Blackfriars v.50, 102–6).

100. Aquinas, IIIa.19.4 (Blackfriars v.50, 102–6), cf. IIIa.48.1 (Blackfriars v.54, 74–76).

101. Aquinas, Suppl.13.2. See also Charles Raith II, "Thomas Aquinas's Pauline Theology of the Atonement," in Johnson, *T&T Clark Companion to Atonement*, 195–212.

102. Aquinas, *Sum.* IIIa.48.1 ad 2 (Blackfriars v.54, 76), emphasis added.

103. Aquinas, IIIa.46.12 (Blackfriars v.54, 50–52).

104. Aquinas, IIIa.46.6 (Blackfriars v.54, 22–30).

105. Aquinas, IIIa.22.2 (Blackfriars v.50, 140–42).

106. Aquinas, *Sum.* IIIa.22.3 (Blackfriars v. 50, 142–46). Cf. IIIa.46.6 (Blackfriars v.54, 22–30).

107. Aquinas, Ia2ae.87.8 (Blackfriars v.27, 38–40). This is a point that was made earlier by Augustine, *Trin.* 4.13 (CCL 50, 178).

108. Two of the most notable of these are James E. Talmage, *Jesus the Christ: A Study of the Messiah and His Mission According to the Holy Scriptures Both Ancient and Modern* (Salt Lake City: Deseret Book Company, 1922) and Bruce R. McConkie, *Mormon Doctrine: A Compendium of the Gospel* (Salt Lake City: Bookcraft Publishing Company, 1952).

CHAPTER 4

"Atonement" in the Book of Mormon

NICHOLAS J. FREDERICK

The first Latter-day Saints were probably unaware of the great diversity concerning the atonement of Christ that existed in early Christian and Medieval thought. What they were familiar with were the basic atonement models articulated in the New Testament, but what increasingly became normative for them was use of the term "atonement" in the Book of Mormon, the movement's foundational text. This sensitivity toward the Book of Mormon's usage of "atonement" has become even more pronounced in the years since the 1980s, when Mormon leader Ezra Taft Benson made the serious engagement with the Book of Mormon a primary part of his message. While Latter-day Saints still rely upon the Bible for much of their theology, the Book of Mormon, with its not-so-subtle critique of nineteenth-century Christian organizations and traditions, paved the way for adherents to reach beyond the fortressed walls of canonicity to find theological truths. The text's presentation of atonement is no exception. The noun "atonement," the verb "atone/-eth," and the adjective "atoning" appear in the Book of Mormon a total of thirty-nine times. Of these thirty-nine usages, by far the most prominent is the noun "atonement," appearing a total of twenty-eight times. The verb "atone/-eth" appears eight times, and the adjective "atoning" only three times. Contrasting this number of occurrences with the single appearance of "atonement" in the New Testament of the King James Bible at Romans 5:11 immediately signals that atonement theology is going to be an explicit part of Book of Mormon teaching.

The Book of Mormon presents itself as the thousand-year record of a small group of Jewish refugees who fled Jerusalem around 600 BCE, shortly before the Babylonian captivity. Led by a prophet named Lehi, the party arrived somewhere in the Americas where it quickly split into two groups—the Nephites, led by Lehi's son Nephi, and the Lamanites, led by Laman, another of Lehi's sons. The next centuries would find the Nephites and Lamanites warring back and forth over political, social, and religious concerns. One of the Book of Mormon's key ideas is that the Nephites taught and lived a form of pre-Christian Christianity, even at points converting Lamanites to their cause. Nephite prophets such as Lehi, Jacob, Benjamin, and Abinadi, all men whose lives predate the founding of the Christian church, spoke with a very clear conception of who Jesus Christ would be and what his mission would entail, including multiple discussions of "atonement."

The concept of "atonement" in the Book of Mormon is built upon three key theological points, with each point introduced and developed by important Book of Mormon figures. First, Lehi and Jacob's concept of the atonement provided an important focus on the *physical death and physical resurrection* of Jesus Christ. Second, Abinadi's teaching put a powerful emphasis on the atonement being performed by a divine figure, "God himself," a point taken up by several subsequent authors. Third, while several Book of Mormon characters speak of atonement as the familiar act of the shedding of blood in sacrifice, one, King Benjamin, understood it not just as a sacrificial death but as "blood com[ing] from every pore," an apparent reference to Jesus's experience in Gethsemane that has become almost axiomatic in much current Latter-day Saint thinking.[1] By examining how each of the authors who use the term emphasize one or more of these points, we will see important contributions that the Book of Mormon makes to the many implications of Jesus's salvific work.

Approaching Atonement in the Book of Mormon

When considering the saving, healing, and transformative work of Jesus Christ in this foundational text, we should begin by presenting various Book of Mormon *theologies* of "atonement," rather than trying to construct a single Book of Mormon *theology* of atonement. To borrow from the language of Christian theology, this paper will not be arguing that the Book of Mormon, for example, promotes a Christus Victor theory of atonement or a substitution theory of atonement, or even a more contemporary governmental theory of atonement. This is not to say that such a study would not be a fascinating and worthwhile undertaking.[2] One could fruitfully analyze Jacob's extensive discussion of a Christus Victor view of atonement in 2 Nephi 9:7–12, or the possibility of a governmental position laid out by the Nephite patriarch Lehi in 2 Nephi 2:6–10. The Nephite prophet Alma's discussion of justice and mercy aimed at his son Corianton in Alma 42:14–26 is rife with the language and imagery of penal substitution, although the application is something far different.[3] Alma's missionary companion, the newly converted Amulek, provides one of the most fascinating discussions of atonement in the Book of Mormon, as he uses the vocabulary of satisfaction theory and the imagery of penal substitution in a remarkable sermon that somehow climaxes with one of the most poignant descriptions of a moral influence theory in all of Mormon scripture (Alma 34:15–41). All of this is to say that discussing how theories of atonement overlap within the Book of Mormon, while useful, in this case risks imposing too much upon the text and would involve looking not only at the terms "atone" and "atonement" but also specifically at other theologically loaded terms such as "reconcile," "redeem," and "grace." Although these are vital concepts in a broader discussion of atonement, instead I look only at places in the Book of Mormon where the terms "atonement," "atone/eth," and "atoning" are specifically found, using exegesis of those passages as a lens through which to understand different theologies of atonement in the Book of Mormon. Examining simply the word "atonement" and its derivatives yields additional understanding to a remarkably complex text, thereby laying the groundwork for future discussions of the Book of Mormon's overall treatment of Jesus's salvific work, even if it means omitting critical passages such as Alma 7:11–12 and its discussion of an empathetic atonement that has become, I would argue, the starting point for many Latter-day Saints when they conceptualize the implications of Jesus Christ's actions in the garden of Gethsemane.

In attempting any exegetical maneuvers in respect to the Book of Mormon, two key points must be made clear at the forefront: First, from a *linguistic* perspective, the Book of Mormon presents itself as an English translation of a text that claims to have been written in an otherwise unknown Egyptian script by a people who likely spoke some form of Hebrew (Morm 9:32–33). Presumably early conceptions of *kpr*[4] from the Hebrew Bible lay behind early Book of Mormon understanding of atonement, ideas that would have been reinforced by continued Nephite observance of the Law of Moses through much of their history. Similarly, the Greek New Testament concept of *katallagē*,[5] or reconciliation, provided one important foundation of the Christian understanding of atonement inherited by Joseph Smith, perhaps influencing the way that he either understood or rendered the Book of Mormon text.[6] But perhaps most important was Joseph Smith's own, nineteenth-century understanding of the term "atonement" itself, one that evidently appealed to him so much that the Book of Mormon uses it more frequently than any other book of Latter-day Saint canonized scripture except the Old Testament.[7] This understanding seems to have broadly referred to everything Jesus Christ did to make us one with God (at-one-ment),[8] a wide semantic range of meanings that he then applied to whatever terms the original authors had employed or concepts that they had explicated.[9]

Second, from a *theological* perspective, it is clear that from as early as 1 Nephi 10 (c. 600 BCE) the Nephites have access to a remarkable amount of information regarding Jesus Christ. Lehi teaches his sons not only that the Messiah will be baptized, but that he will be baptized by a man named John in a location "in Bethabara, beyond Jordan" (1 Ne 10:9). This theological trend, which could be viewed as something akin to a "realized messialogy," suggests that readers should not reconstruct Book of Mormon theology by simply separating the text into "pre-Christian" (1 Ne 1–3 Ne 11) and "post-Christian" (3 Ne 12-Moro 10).[10] Thus, a paper dealing with "atonement" in the Book of Mormon cannot simply assume that prior to 3 Nephi 11, where Jesus Christ himself first appears, any mention of the atonement should be understood as referring to an Israelite or early Jewish conception, while any usage of "atonement" after 3 Nephi 11 should be understood as referring to a Christian concept of atonement.

Lehi and Jacob: Emphasizing the Resurrection

The first mention of "atone" in the Book of Mormon comes in Lehi's discussion with his son Jacob in 2 Nephi 2. The purpose of Lehi's complicated discourse seems to be answering for Jacob *why* there needs to be a Messiah. As Lehi explains, humanity receives a sufficient amount of instruction on what is right and what is evil, but unfortunately as people exercise their agency they will occasionally choose evil, and thus find themselves in violation of the law and in an un-justified state. Fortunately, God has provided a means of redemption through "the righteousness of [the] Redeemer" (v. 3). Perhaps surprisingly, the first actual usage of "atonement" appears in 2 Nephi 2:10:

> And because of the intercession for all, all men come unto God; wherefore, they stand in the presence of him, to be judged of him according to the truth and holiness which is in him. Wherefore, the ends of the law which the Holy One hath given, unto the inflicting of the punishment which is affixed, which punishment that is affixed is in opposition to that of the happiness which is affixed, to answer the ends of the *atonement*.

Two things are of note here. First, Lehi teaches that humanity becomes justified through the sacrifice of the Messiah—"Behold, he offereth himself a sacrifice for sin, to answer the ends of the law . . . " (v. 7), and presumably this sacrifice that "answers the ends of the law" is the atonement, if readers understand "ends" teleologically as "purposes" or "aims." However, the second important point is that the sacrifice offered by the Messiah receives a specific focus in 2 Nephi 2:8:

> Wherefore, how great the importance to make these things known unto the inhabitants of the earth, that they may know that there is no flesh that can dwell in the presence of God, save it be through the merits, and mercy, and grace of the Holy Messiah, *who layeth down his life according to the flesh,* and *taketh it again by the power of the Spirit, that he may bring to pass the resurrection of the dead, being the first that should rise* (emphasis added).

Here Lehi carefully identifies the "sacrifice for sin" that will "answer the ends of the atonement" as the death *and* the resurrection of the Messiah. There is no notion in Lehi's words of a Gethsemane experience where the atoning blood of the Messiah is to be shed for sin prior to his sacrificial death; rather the redemptive acts that will bring salvation are the actual death and then, significantly, the resurrection of the Messiah. Lehi elaborates further: "Wherefore, he is the firstfruits unto God, inasmuch as he shall make intercession for all the children of men; and they that believe in him shall be saved" (v. 9). Again, Lehi states that intercession for humanity is fully realized only through the resurrection of the Messiah, his role as the "firstfruits unto God." This emphasis upon the resurrection of Jesus as the intercessory, salvific act may seem a bit strange to contemporary Latter-day Saints, who have, at least since the writings of Joseph Fielding Smith (1876–1972), been accustomed to associating intercession and salvation with Gethsemane.[11] Nevertheless, Lehi's teachings here, with their particular focus upon the death and subsequent resurrection of the Messiah as *the* salvific act, play a prominent part in Book of Mormon theology.[12]

The next Book of Mormon figure who uses the term "atone" is Jacob himself during his discourse in 2 Nephi 9–10. Specifically, Jacob uses the noun "atonement" five times over the course of his sermon. The first two usages come in 2 Nephi 9:7:

> Wherefore, it must needs be an infinite *atonement*—save it should be an infinite *atonement this corruption could not put on incorruption*. Wherefore, the first judgment which came upon man must needs have remained to an endless duration. And if so, this flesh must have laid down to rot and to crumble to its mother earth, to rise no more.

In this verse and the verse before, Jacob carefully walks his audience through the reality of death. Because of the fall of Adam, everyone dies. There is no exception. However, this "infinite" death is unacceptable to God, who, in his love, has instituted a "merciful plan." This merciful plan must serve to counteract the effects of death, so, as Jacob tells us, "there must needs be a power of resurrection." This leads him to verse 7, where he reiterates, in almost the exact same language, that "it must needs be an infinite atonement." The key to interpretation relies upon how readers understand the use of "it" in "it must needs be." It is fully possible that "it must needs be" is simply a rhetorical flourish, a way for Jacob to essentially say "it is important that."[13] However, based upon the similarity of language in verse 6, "it must needs be" seems to echo "there must needs be." If this is the case, then Jacob is essentially saying "the resurrection must needs be an infinite atonement," a point supported by the next clause, "this corruption could not put on incorruption," which appears to clearly indicate a resurrection experience. Notably, the remainder of 2 Nephi

9:7 explicitly explains the implications of an "infinite atonement" through the language of *physical death* and *physical rebirth*. Jacob argues that the lack of an infinite atonement would have caused "corruption" to be unable to "put on incorruption," and bodies "must have laid down to rot and to crumble, *to rise no more.*" This understanding of atonement as a messianic resurrection brings Jacob in line with what Lehi had taught in 2 Nephi 2.

Two additional usages of the noun "atonement" by Jacob are found in 2 Nephi 9:25–26:

> Wherefore, he has given a law; and where there is no law given there is no punishment; and where there is no punishment there is no condemnation; and where there is no condemnation the mercies of the Holy One of Israel have claim upon them, because of the *atonement*; for they are delivered by the power of him. For the *atonement* satisfieth the demands of his justice upon all those who have not the law given to them, that they are delivered from that awful monster, death and hell, and the devil, and the lake of fire and brimstone, which is endless torment; and they are restored to that God who gave them breath, which is the Holy One of Israel.

These loaded verses require a fair bit of unpacking. There are at least three key ideas in verse 25. First, Jacob explains that for individuals who live without being given a law, there is no condemnation. This exemption is due to their having received the "mercies of the Holy One of Israel." Second, the reason there is no condemnation is due to "the atonement." Finally, Jacob appears to equate both the "mercies of the Holy One of Israel" and "the atonement" with "the power of him." Put more simply, God, the "Holy One of Israel," has obtained a salvific power through completion of something termed "the atonement."

With the next verse, 9:26, Jacob implies that this sacrifice was requisite insofar as it "satisfieth the demands of justice." Both Amulek (Alma 34:9–16) and Alma the Younger (Alma 42:22–24) later explore the relationship between justice and mercy and how an atonement can appease justice. Here, Jacob presents something like this: God has a strict sense of justice, one that must be maintained. In order to do so, he establishes a law. Violation of this law leads to punishment. However, God recognizes that some people will not have access to a full understanding of the law, and desires to leave them exempt from his justice. The reason God can show mercy to those who violate his law is because of his "power" which he has obtained through the act of "atonement." Based upon what Jacob has said earlier in 2 Nephi 9, this act of "atonement" would be the divine resurrection of the Holy One of Israel.

The final usage of the noun "atonement" by Jacob in his sermon comes in 2 Nephi 10:25, a passage where the meaning of atonement might be better understood when it is shown enjambed, like a poem:

> Wherefore, may God raise you from death by *the power of the resurrection*,
> and also from everlasting death by the power of the *atonement*,
> that ye may be received into the eternal kingdom of God,
> that ye may praise him through grace divine. Amen (emphasis added).

With this statement, Jacob seems to make a distinction between "atonement" and "resurrection." On one hand, the "resurrection" is the power to "raise you from death." On the other, the "atonement" is the power to be raised "from everlasting death." The natural assumption would be to interpret the first "death" as a physical, temporal death—a death that would be overcome through Jesus regaining his physical body. The second death, the "everlasting death," would need to be a death with greater consequences than the "death" in the first clause. The best possible candidate would be spiritual death, which in the Book of Mormon is the idea that the unrepentant sinner is permanently separated from the presence of God following the resurrection. If this is the case, Jacob is teaching that the atonement is both different than resurrection and capable of overcoming spiritual death. This assertion would be contrary to how "atonement" has been understood both by Lehi and by Jacob earlier in his discourse.

There seem to be at least two possible ways of understanding this dissonance. First, Jacob states that during the night (between the sermon found in 2 Nephi 9 and the sermon found in chapter 10) he received additional information on the crucifixion and ministry of Jesus Christ. It is possible that a reorientation of the meaning of atonement came from this new experience. Second, Jacob could be employing a form of *synonymous parallelism* into his speech. Synonymous parallelism is a feature of Hebrew poetry where the poet makes a statement and then restates that statement in different language in the next line. One famous example from Isaiah is his millennial prediction that

> And he shall judge among the nations,
> and shall rebuke many people:
> and they shall beat their swords into plowshares,
> and their spears into pruninghooks:
> nation shall not lift up sword against nation,
> neither shall they learn war any more. (Isa 2:4)[14]

In three separate places in Isaiah 2:4, Isaiah makes a statement and then restates it for poetic purposes. Jacob obviously shares Nephi's love of Isaiah. Jacob spent the two chapters prior to 2 Nephi 9 quoting from Isaiah. It is clear he is familiar with Hebrew poetry. Perhaps he is ending his sermon where it began, with poetry. If this is the case, Jacob is simply asserting what he has been teaching the whole time, that the resurrection *is* the atonement, and that it saves humanity from ultimate, interminable death.

Jacob uses the noun "atonement" three additional times once he begins his own record. The first two usages appear in Jacob 4:11–12. As with 2 Nephi 9:7, Jacob appears to use "atonement" to mean "resurrection." He writes:

> Wherefore, beloved brethren, be reconciled unto him through the *atonement* of Christ, his Only Begotten Son, and *ye may obtain a resurrection*, according to the power of the resurrection which is in Christ, and be presented *as the first-fruits of Christ* unto God, having faith, and obtained a good hope of glory in him before he manifesteth himself in the flesh. And now, beloved, marvel not that I tell you these things; for why not speak of the *atonement* of Christ, and attain to a perfect knowledge of him, as to attain to the knowledge *of a resurrection* and the world to come? (Emphasis added.)

The first usage, in Jacob 4:11, echoes Nephi's statement in 2 Nephi 25:16 that the atonement is the means of reconciliation. This reconciliation will apparently lead to two results. First, the reconciled party may "obtain *a* resurrection, according to *the* power of the resurrection" (emphasis added). While the resurrection of Christ provides new life to all, the reconciled party will receive a particular resurrection, the first resurrection that presents him or her "as the first-fruits in Christ unto God" (cf. Mos 15:21–26). Two key factors in this reconciliatory process are "faith" and "a good hope of glory in him." However, unlike 2 Nephi 9, it is not Jesus's resurrection that is intended by Jacob. Rather, it is the glorious resurrection of the believer that comes through the atonement.

The second usage, in 4:12, again couples "atonement" with "resurrection." Jacob rhetorically asks his readers why he should not speak of the atonement of Christ. In doing so, he and his readers can "attain to a perfect knowledge of him," an experience synonymous with attaining "to the knowledge of a resurrection and the world to come." One of Jacob's primary purposes in this chapter is to convince his Jewish audience of why they stumble. According to Jacob, they "look beyond the mark" and refuse to understand the greater meaning behind the law. Essentially, they have rejected the fully revealed word of God through his prophets in favor of their exegesis of the prophets' written words alone. Jacob's discussion of the atonement and the resurrection are points along that trajectory. If we have a knowledge and understanding of the atonement revealed to us, Jacob argues, it is only for our betterment, our improved standing before God, because our "faith" and our "hope" can now be centered around the correct principles. As with the previous verse, Jacob links the atonement of Jesus Christ with the resurrection of those who believe. Perhaps a cleansing from overcoming *spiritual* death is meant to be implicit in his teachings, that Jesus's suffering and death for sin is part of the "perfect knowledge of him," but Jacob's (and Lehi's) words only (with the exception of 2

Ne 10:25) ever explicitly point to *resurrection*, Jesus's and that of all humanity, as the key point in understanding the *atonement*.

Jacob returns to the term "atonement" one final time, in his discussion with Sherem in Jacob 7:12:

> And this is not all—it has been made manifest unto me, for I have heard and seen; and it also has been made manifest unto me by the power of the Holy Ghost; wherefore, I know if there should be no *atonement* made all mankind must be lost.

This chapter almost serves as a sequel to Jacob 4, as Jacob again returns to the themes of prophecy and revelation and the stubborn state of those who refuse to recognize their reality. Sherem claims that he believes the scriptures and gives no indication of being anything other than a follower of the Law of Moses without any messianic expectations, yet he refuses to believe in the coming of a messiah: "I know that there is no Christ, neither has been, nor ever will be" (7:9). Jacob claims a messianic knowledge not through scripture but through "the power of the Holy Ghost." This knowledge leads Jacob to make the unequivocal claim that "if there should be no atonement made, all mankind must be lost" (v. 12). Jacob does not clarify here how he understands atonement, as a resurrection overcoming physical death or as a sacrifice for sin, but based upon his earlier teachings, the former would seem the most likely option.

Abinadi and Amulek: A Divine, Eternal Atonement

Abinadi is a strikingly ambiguous figure in the Book of Mormon. He appears seemingly out of nowhere and then proceeds to deliver one of the most theologically and politically charged speeches in the Book, one resulting in his execution. He is also important in a discussion of how to understand the term "atonement" in the Book of Mormon. While sequentially Abinadi follows Benjamin in the narrative, chronologically their positions are reversed—Abinadi precedes Benjamin, and thus must be dealt with first.[15] Abinadi's speech before the priests of King Noah attempts to move them away from their position that the Law of Moses alone can bring salvation. In making this argument, Abinadi makes three key points: First, there will be an atonement made, and without that atonement the Law of Moses has no effect. Second, God himself, as both *Father* and *Son*, will descend and perform this atonement. Finally, because of the atonement all humanity will be resurrected.

Throughout the course of his speech, Abinadi makes his one mention of "atonement" in 13:28:

> And moreover, I say unto you, that salvation doth not come by the law alone; and were it not for the *atonement*, which God himself shall make for the sins and iniquities of his people, that they must unavoidably perish, notwithstanding the law of Moses.

Here, Abinadi provides the second theological point in the Book of Mormon's understanding of "atonement." By identifying that the act of "atonement" will be performed by "God himself," a claim that leads him into a lengthy quotation of Isaiah 53, Abinadi highlights the condescension of God (the Book of Mormon is, notably, quite comfortable referring to Jesus Christ as "God") and its role in the atonement.[16] Significantly, Abinadi does not link the "atonement" with any images of the shedding of blood. In fact, the only shedding of blood he mentions is his own (17:10). Once Abinadi concludes his discussion of how Jesus can be both "Father" and "Son," he mentions that Jesus will bear the sins of all humanity and thus redeem his people (15:18). He emphasizes that "were it not for the redemption which he hath made for his people, which was prepared from the foundation of the world, I say unto you, were it not for this, all mankind must have perished" (15:19). At this point, Abinadi joins the train of thought introduced by Lehi and Jacob and their emphatically creation-affirming view of atonement. Abinadi explicitly links this redemptive power with the overcoming of *physical* death and the *physical* resurrection: "But behold, the bands of death shall be broken, and the Son reigneth, and hath power over the dead; therefore, he bringeth to *pass the resurrection of the dead*" (Mos 15:20, emphasis added). A crucial summation is made in 15:24:

> And these are those who have part in the first resurrection; and these are they that have died before Christ came, in their ignorance, not having salvation declared unto them. And thus the Lord bringeth about the restoration of these; and they have a part in the first resurrection, or have eternal life, being redeemed by the Lord.

Here Abinadi links "redemption" with "eternal life," which is having "a part in the first resurrection." Abinadi appears to accept Lehi and Jacob's teachings that the "atonement" and the "resurrection" are synonymous, emphasizing the pivotal idea that the being who will make atonement is a divine being, God himself.[17]

With Amulek, readers encounter a Book of Mormon speaker who, in Alma 34, uses "atonement" six times, twice as a verb and four times as a noun:

> And now, behold, I will testify unto you of myself that these things are true. Behold, I say unto you, that I do know that Christ shall come among the children of men, to take upon him the transgressions of his people, and that he shall *atone* for the sins of the world; for the Lord God hath spoken it (Alma 34:8).

> For it is expedient that an *atonement* should be made; for according to the great plan of the Eternal God there must be an *atonement* made, or else all mankind must unavoidably perish; yea, all are hardened; yea, all are fallen and are lost, and must perish except it be through the *atonement* which it is expedient should be made (Alma 34:9).
>
> Now there is not any man that can sacrifice his own blood which will *atone* for the sins of another. Now, if a man murdereth, behold will our law, which is just, take the life of his brother? I say unto you, Nay (Alma 34:11).
>
> But the law requireth the life of him who hath murdered; therefore there can be nothing which is short of an *infinite atonement* which will suffice for the sins of the world (Alma 34:12, which resonates with the approach of Anselm).

In these verses, Amulek makes two important moves. First, he continues Abinadi's emphasis upon the *divine nature* of the one performing the atonement in Alma 34:8, with reference to "Christ shall come down among the children of men." In Alma 34:10–11 Amulek states that an infinite atonement "shall not be a human sacrifice; but it must be *an infinite and eternal* sacrifice," apparently because any mortal, finite being shedding his or her own blood as atonement would lack any substantial efficacy and not be able to "atone for the sins of another."

This emphasis upon divinity leads Amulek into his second important move, which is to emphasize that the atonement can successfully cover the sins of the world because it is a "sacrifice of his own blood," and several subsequent Book of Mormon characters will similarly emphasize a "bloody" or "sacrificial" element in atonement, which echoes the Eucharistic words of Jesus in Mark 14:24 (parallel Matt 26:28).[18] Here Amulek links these two points together: atonement *must* be performed by a divine, infinite being, and atonement *must* involve the shedding of blood, for only by the shedding of divine blood can the atonement "suffice for the sins of the world." Amulek appears to see this emphasis on the shedding of blood as arising out of Mosaic sacrifice, for he says in Alma 34:13:

> Therefore, it is expedient that there should be *a great and last sacrifice*, and then shall there be, or it is expedient there should be, a stop to the shedding of blood; *then shall the law of Moses be fulfilled*; yea, it shall be all fulfilled, every jot and tittle, and none shall have passed away (emphasis added).

Amulek reframes "infinite atonement" as a "great and last sacrifice," a sacrifice which will once and for all put an end to "the shedding of blood" and, in the process, fulfill the Law of Moses.

Benjamin: Bleeding from Every Pore

Mosiah 3 continues a speech delivered by the Nephite King Benjamin to the people of Zarahemla. Over this course of this chapter, Benjamin will use "atonement" twice, "atoneth" twice, and "atoning" once. In the process he adds for the first and only time an additional dimension to the Book of Mormon's idea of "atonement" by focusing on the atoning act of shedding blood "from every pore." This added dimension is first seen in Benjamin's use of the verb "atoneth" in Mosiah 3:11:

> For behold, and also his blood *atoneth* for the sins of those who have fallen by the transgression of Adam, who have died not knowing the will of God concerning them, or who have ignorantly sinned.

With this statement, Benjamin explicitly links "atonement" with "sins," the "transgression of Adam," and Jesus's blood. The difficulty in understanding what Benjamin means when he talks about "blood" atoning for sins comes from the preceding verses. Benjamin's statement that "blood atoneth" could simply be a reference to Jesus's crucifixion and death, and thus be in line with what we saw with Lehi and Jacob. This view is supported by the verses immediately preceding 3:11:

> And lo, he cometh unto his own, that salvation might come unto the children of men even through faith on his name; and even after all this they shall consider him a man, and say that he hath a devil, and shall scourge him, and shall crucify him. And he shall rise the third day from the dead; and behold, he standeth to judge the world; and behold, all these things are done that a righteous judgment might come upon the children of men (vv. 9–10).

Here Benjamin specifically speaks of Jesus's crucifixion and resurrection, events which bring to pass a "righteous judgment." However, the only place in chapter 3 where Benjamin directly mentions "blood" itself comes in Mosiah 3:7:

> And lo, he shall suffer temptations, and pain of body, hunger, thirst, and fatigue, even more than man can suffer, except it be unto death; for behold, *blood cometh from every pore*, so great shall be his anguish for the wickedness and the abominations of his people.

When contemporary Latter-day Saint readers take this verse together with Luke 22:44 and D&C 19:18,[19] the context is clearly the Gethsemane experience, where Jesus bled "from every pore." Like Lehi and Jacob, the messianic resurrection is still a pivotal event, but Benjamin has placed equal emphasis upon the particular event in Gethsemane, the importance of which sometimes leads modern Latter-day Saints to tend to refer to the experience in Gethsemane *as being the atonement itself*.

Whether Jesus's atoning "blood" is understood to refer specifically to the bloody sweat of Gethsemane or is expanded to include all of Christ's blood shed up through his suffering and death on the cross, Benjamin's emphasis on blood as part of the atonement is clear in a series of statements echoing Mosiah 3:7 and 3:11

> And many signs, and wonders, and types, and shadows showed he unto them, concerning his coming; and also holy prophets spake unto them concerning his coming; and yet they hardened their hearts, and understood not that the law of Moses availeth nothing except it were through *the atonement of his blood* (Mos 3:15).
>
> And even if it were possible that little children could sin they could not be saved; but I say unto you they are blessed; for behold, as in Adam, or by nature, they fall, even so *the blood of Christ atoneth for their sins* (3:16).
>
> For behold he judgeth, and his judgment is just; and the infant perisheth not that dieth in his infancy; but men drink damnation to their own souls except they humble themselves and become as little children, and believe that salvation was, and is, and is to come, in and through *the atoning blood of Christ*, the Lord Omnipotent (3:18).

A final use of "atone" in Mosiah 3, 3:19, is the only use of "atone" that isn't coupled with blood but does continue Benjamin's emphasis upon *spiritual* rebirth only being possible through an act of Jehovah, the Messiah:

> For the natural man is an enemy to God, and has been from the fall of Adam, and will be, forever and ever, unless he yields to the enticings of the Holy Spirit, and putteth off the natural man and becometh a saint through *the atonement of Christ the Lord*, and becometh as a child, submissive, meek, humble, patient, full of love, willing to submit to all things which the Lord seeth fit to inflict upon him, even as a child doth submit to his father.

Three more uses of "atone" follow in Mosiah 4. Two of them, 4:6 and 4:7, are spoken by Benjamin himself:

> I say unto you, if ye have come to a knowledge of the goodness of God, and his matchless power, and his wisdom, and his patience, and his long-suffering towards the children of men; and also, the *atonement* which has been prepared from the foundation of the world, that thereby salvation might come to him that should put his trust in the Lord, and should be diligent in keeping his commandments, and continue in the faith even unto the end of his life, I mean the life of the mortal body—I say, that this is the man who receiveth salvation, through the *atonement* which was prepared from the foundation

of the world for all mankind, which ever were since the fall of Adam, or who are, or who ever shall be, even unto the end of the world.

Both uses of "atone" in Mosiah 4:6–7 stress the eternal nature of the atonement, that it was not God's "Plan B" but was always the primary plan. Benjamin also declares that the atonement has application to *everyone* who has lived on Earth, not just those who have lived since the atonement. In a way, he is working out the implications of what Jacob may have intended by an "infinite atonement," an act with universal temporal application.

Notably, Mosiah 4 includes a direct statement made by the audience of Benjamin's speech. Having fallen to the earth, they declare with one voice, "O have mercy, and apply the *atoning blood* of Christ that we may receive forgiveness of our sins, and our hearts may be purified; for we believe in Jesus Christ, the Son of God, who created heaven and earth, and all things; who shall come down among the children of men" (Mos 4:2). Their statement recapitulates two important themes emphasized by Benjamin in the preceding chapter. First, the mechanism for "atonement" is the "blood of Christ." It must be shed or there can be no forgiveness of sins. Second, the being who will perform this atonement is the divine creator, who will condescend to mortality.

As we survey where the Book of Mormon understanding of "atone" stands by the conclusion of Benjamin's reign, we can see the following progression: First, Jacob and probably Lehi understood "atone" as synonymous with an act of *physical death* followed by a *physical resurrection*. Abinadi maintained the emphasis upon *physical death* followed by a *physical resurrection* but added, along with Amulek, the important emphasis that God himself is the one who dies and rises from death, as well as providing elaboration on a "first" and a "second" resurrection. Finally, Benjamin sustained the previous teachings about the identity of the atoner and the remedy from death through resurrection, but he places, for the first time, an emphasis upon an act of shedding blood as the means of atonement. It is fully possible that other previous prophets were aware of this concept of "atonement" as an act of shedding blood, but Benjamin is the first one to explicitly develop it. These three concepts will provide the baseline for all future discussions of "atonement" in the Book of Mormon.

The Importance of the Shedding of Blood in Later Authors

While many additional Book of Mormon writers still allude to Lehi and Jacob's discussion of the resurrection and Abinadi and Amulek's emphasis of its being accomplished by a divine being, their main emphasis seems to be on the role of the blood shed by Jesus in his atoning work. Without any explicit mention of bleeding "from every pore" such as King Benjamin describes, the most natural view of the shedding of blood would be to see it as a sacrificial death, thereby referring to the suffering and death of Jesus on the cross.[20]

Alma the Younger uses the terminology of "atonement" seven times: four times as a noun and three times as a verb. The first usage comes in his Ammonihah address:

> Or in fine, in the first place they were on the same standing with their brethren; thus this holy calling being prepared from the foundation of the world for such as would not harden their hearts, being in and through the *atonement* of the Only Begotten Son (Alma 13:5).

Here we see emphasized Abinadi's second theological point, that only a divine being, in this case the "Only Begotten Son," could provide adequate atonement. His next usage, Alma 33:22, is more complex:

> If so, wo shall come upon you; but if not so, then cast about your eyes and begin to believe in the Son of God, that he will come to redeem his people, and that *he shall suffer and die to atone* for their sins; and that he shall rise again from the dead, *which shall bring to pass the resurrection*, that all men shall stand before him, to be judged at the last and judgment day, according to their works.

In this statement—the first time readers encounter the infinitive form "to atone" —Alma certainly emphasizes resurrection and divinity. There is an understanding of "atonement" as involving a physical death and physical resurrection, as well as the clear understanding that it will be a divine figure, the "Son of God," who will provide the atonement. The question is how Alma understands "suffer and die." Does this suffering refer to the beginning of the work of redemption in Gethsemane when Jesus took upon himself the crushing weight of humanity's collective sins, infirmities, disappointment, and pains, to the shedding of his blood in the crucifixion, or to both? In his Zarahemla discourse, Alma stated that believers "garments must be purified until they are cleansed from all stain, through the blood of him of whom it has been spoken by our fathers, who should come to redeem his people from their sins" (Alma 5:21, cf. Alma 5:27), but is Alma equating "blood" with "redeem," or is the act of redemption the physical death and physical resurrection of Jesus? The text remains ambiguous.

Because the fourth usage of "atone," Alma 36:17, mentions "atonement" only in passing, we must turn to Alma 42, which is the conclusion of Alma the Younger's lengthy doctrinal discussion with his inquisitive youngest son, Corianton. Corianton appears to be struggling over the reality of punishment for sin, and so Alma lays out for him, in a discourse that, at least on the surface, has resonances with penal substitution or even satisfaction models of atonement, the relationship between justice and mercy. Over the course of this discussion, Alma uses "atonement" four times:

> And now, the plan of mercy could not be brought about except an *atonement* should be made; therefore God himself *atoneth* for the sins of the world, to bring about the plan of mercy, to appease the demands of justice, that God might be a perfect, just God, and a merciful God also (Alma 42:15).
>
> But God ceaseth not to be God, and mercy claimeth the penitent, and mercy cometh because of the *atonement*; and the *atonement* bringeth to pass the *resurrection* of the dead; and the resurrection of the dead bringeth back men into the presence of God; and thus they are restored into his presence, to be judged according to their works, according to the law and justice (42:23).

Alma informs Corianton that the "atonement" is requisite for God's mercy to be in effect, and that the "atonement" covers the sins of the world. In the final two examples, Alma lays out an understanding of "atonement" that correlates well with the positions of both Lehi and Jacob and that of Abinadi, namely that the atonement brings to pass a resurrection of the dead. However, unless we use Alma 5:21 and connect "blood" to "redeem" and then "redeem" to "atone" in Alma 33, it is difficult to see King Benjamin's blood "from every pore" in Alma's teaching.

Mormon also includes two verses summarizing the teachings of Aaron, a brother of Ammon, in which "atonement" is used.

> Now Aaron began to open the scriptures unto them concerning the coming of Christ, and also concerning the resurrection of the dead, and that there could be no redemption for mankind save it were *through the death and sufferings of Christ*, and *the atonement of his blood* (Alma 21:9, emphasis added).
>
> And since man had fallen he could not merit anything of himself; but *the sufferings and death* of Christ *atone* for their sins, through faith and repentance, and so forth; and that he breaketh the bands of death, that the grave shall have no victory, and that the sting of death should be swallowed up in the hopes of glory; and Aaron did expound all these things unto the king (22:14, emphasis added).

The first verse, Alma 21:9, sees Aaron speaking of the role of "Christ," the "resurrection of the dead," and an atonement specifically "of his blood." What is curious about the statement is whether or not Aaron/Mormon is explicitly separating "death and sufferings" and "the atonement of his blood," a question similar to the one raised by Alma the Younger in Alma 33:22. Does he see them as two different events? Or is "the atonement of his blood" simply meant to specify the "sufferings and death of Christ?"

Unfortunately, the second verse, Alma 22:14, provides little clarity. Present again is an emphasis upon resurrection and divinity, with a mention of

"Christ" and references to the resurrection. But this verse notably lacks explicit mention of any atonement "of blood," and instead seems to echo Jacob rather than Benjamin. Aaron teaches that the "sufferings and death" atone because they allow Jesus to break "the bands of death," with the result that "the grave shall have no victory, and the sting of death should be swallowed up in the hopes of glory." One could argue that "sufferings and death" is simply a way of saying "Gethsemane and Calvary," but while that may work for Alma 22:14 it does not for Alma 21:9, where the text explicitly separates "sufferings and death" from "the atonement of his blood." Because Jesus's experience on the cross certainly included "sufferings" as well as "death," the easiest reading of these verses is that they are speaking specifically about the cross.

King Anti-Nephi-Lehi, in a speech given to his Lamanite people, says the following:

> Behold, I say unto you, Nay, let us retain our swords that they be not stained with the blood of our brethren; for perhaps, if we should stain our swords again they can no more be washed bright *through the blood of the Son of our great God*, which shall be shed for the *atonement* of our sins (Alma 24:13, emphasis added).

The king states that "atonement" will be made through the shedding of blood by "the Son of our great God." He makes no mention of the death or physical resurrection of that Son. This omission does not necessarily indicate that he doesn't possess a knowledge of the resurrection. Rather, King Anti-Nephi-Lehi thoughtfully chooses to contrast his people's covenant to no longer shed blood with the divinely shed blood that allows them to repent and have the stain of their former sins removed. Inasmuch as the king's people had "shed blood" through the murder of their brethren, the natural reading would be that the shed blood of the Son of God likewise refers to his own death.

In his final words to his sons Nephi and Lehi, Helaman instructed them about the absolute necessity for atonement:

> O remember, remember, my sons, the words which king Benjamin spake unto his people; yea, remember that there is no other way nor means whereby man can be saved, only through the *atoning blood of Jesus Christ*, who shall come; yea, remember that he cometh to redeem the world (Hel 5:9).

In this brief mention of atonement, Helaman mentions by name "Jesus Christ, who shall come" and references the "atoning blood" of Jesus Christ. Because Helaman instructs his sons to "remember . . . the words which King Benjamin spoke," clearly he has Benjamin's teachings on "atonement" in mind. What is not clear is whether Helaman's reference to "the atoning blood of Jesus Christ" refers specifically to Benjamin's single image of "bleeding from every pore" or to

Benjamin's other references to the sacrificial death of the Messiah. It may well be that contemporary Latter-day Saints are preconditioned to read into the text the former because of their outside understanding of the Gethsemane experience. Instead, the general equation of shedding blood to death, undergirded by the use of the shed blood of slain victims in Mosaic sacrifices, probably underlays later Book of Mormon authors' use of the expression "atoning blood."

Mormon: The Resurrection and the Redemption

The final Book of Mormon figure to use the term "atone" is Mormon himself. In two separate epistles to his son, preserved in Moroni 7 and 8, Mormon uses the noun "atonement":

> And what is it that ye shall hope for? Behold I say unto you that ye shall have hope through the *atonement of Christ* and *the power of his resurrection*, to be raised unto life eternal, and this because of your faith in him according to the promise (Moro 7:41, emphasis added).
>
> "And he that saith that little children need baptism denieth the mercies of Christ, and setteth at naught the *atonement of him* and *the power of his redemption* (8:20, emphasis added).

In the first usage, Moroni 7:41, Mormon links "atonement" with the resurrection as had Lehi and Jacob, holding these out as areas where true believers should place their hope. Yet while atonement and resurrection are clearly connected, they could be read as two discrete salvific acts: atonement, narrowly defined as overcoming sin and spiritual death, and resurrection, as the means of overcoming physical death. However, in the second passage Mormon couples atonement with redemption. Is redemption here only redemption from sin or is it also redemption from the grave? While Mormon may perhaps have used these different salvific terms broadly in overlapping fashion, perhaps atonement is used expansively in both instances and then defined in each context, emphasizing in the resurrecting power of the atonement in the first passage and demonstrating how the resurrection raises us to eternal life. In the second, with its references to mercy and the imputed innocence of little children, the redeeming power of the atonement is emphasized.

Contributions of the Book of Mormon to Our Understanding of the Atonement

Book of Mormon authors thus provide three important emphases to our understanding of Jesus's saving work. First, Jacob, developing Lehi's teachings, emphasized the connection between "atonement" and "resurrection," an association that is absent in many atonement theories. As an act of overcoming *physical death* through a *physical* resurrection, atonement opens the door to eternal life, particularly when repentance and grace lead to a glorious resurrection, making us what Jacob terms "the firstfruits of Christ unto God." Second, Abinadi stressed the importance of a *divine* atonement, something that others, notably Amulek, later stress. The "atonement" will be an act performed by "God himself." Third, while many Book of Mormon authors refer to the blood of Christ shed at his death, Benjamin introduces the particular idea that the "atonement" includes bleeding "from every pore." Following Benjamin's address, subsequent Book of Mormon authors talked about "atonement" in language involving one or more of these theological points. The point most consistently emphasized was the idea that a divine being, Jesus Christ, the Son of God, must perform the atonement and that his atoning blood, shed most clearly in his death, was salvific. While the connection between the "atonement" and the resurrection is less prominent among later authors, resurrection regains its importance in Mormon's two epistles.

Significantly, Benjamin's single statement about blood "from every pore" in Mosiah 3:7 has made the most distinguishing impact on Latter-day Saint thinking about the atonement. Because for many contemporary modern Latter-day Saints speaking of "the atonement" is to speak of the Gethsemane experience, Douglas J. Davies has noted, "Amidst Christian traditions Mormonism stands out both iconographically and theologically, in the way it gives priority to Christ in Gethsemane rather than to Christ on the cross."[21] Nevertheless, unless one's *a priori* assumption is that Jesus experienced infinite suffering prior to the crucifixion, subsequent Book of Mormon references to "the shedding of blood" refer broadly to death and to sacrifice in particular, and no other Book of Mormon author *in a discussion of the term "atonement"* explicitly separates Gethsemane from Calvary. It remained for subsequent revelation (D&C 19:16–19) and the writings of twentieth century religious leaders to expand upon what Benjamin taught. To read the Book of Mormon on its own terms is to discover a very different concept of "atonement," one rooted in Jesus's divinity, death on the cross, and subsequent resurrection.

Notes

1. See S. Kent Brown, "Gethsemane," *Encyclopedia of Mormonism*, vol. 2, edited by Daniel H. Ludlow (New York: MacMillan) 2.542–43. While the preeminence of Gethsemane in Latter-day Saint atonement thinking, at least as the starting point of Jesus's atoning work, is taken for granted by many contemporary Latter-day Saints, some scholars have argued that this focus upon Gethsemane at the expense of the Cross is largely a twentieth century development rooted in the speaking and writing of Joseph

Fielding Smith and Bruce R. McConkie. See, for example, John Hilton III and Joshua P. Barringer, "The Use of 'Gethsemane' by Church Leaders: 1859–2018," *BYU Studies Quarterly* 58.4 (2019): 49–76.

2. For example, see Lorin K. Hansen, "The 'Moral' Atonement as a Mormon Interpretation," *Dialogue* 27.1 (1994): 195–227.

3. See discussion in Mark Ellison, "Beyond Justice: Reading Alma 42 in the Context of Atonement Theories," in *Give Ear to My Word,* edited by Kerry M. Hull et al., (Provo, UT: BYU Religious Studies Center, 2019), 21–49; Jacob Morgan, "The Divine Infusion Theory: Rethinking the Atonement," *Dialogue* 39.1 (Spring 2006): 57–81.

4. For more on the theological background of *kipper,* see B. Lang, "s.v. kipper," in Johannes G. Botterweck, Helmer Ringgren, and Heinz-Josef Fabry, eds., *Theological Dictionary of the Old Testament* (Grand Rapids, MI: William B. Eerdmans, 2020), 7:288–303.

5. For more on the theological background of *katallagē,* see Friedrich Buchsel, "s.v. katallassō," in Botterweck, Ringgren, and Fabry, *Theological Dictionary of the New Testament,* 1:254–59.

6. See Eric D. Huntsman, "After All We Can Do? Grace and the Book of Mormon," in *Mormons and Grace,* edited by Sheila Taylor (Salt Lake City: Greg Kofford Books, forthcoming).

7. While "atonement" occurs approximately eighty times in the King James version of the Old Testament, this is almost always in the cultic sense of *kpr* (See T. Benjamin Spackman, "The Israelite Roots of Atonement Terminology," *BYU Studies Quarterly* 55.1 [2016]: 47–48). In contrast, "atonement" appears only once in the KJV of the New Testament (Rom 5:11), though *katallagē* and its derivatives appear approximately ten times. Nevertheless, "atonement" appears twenty-eight times in the Book of Mormon, three times in the Doctrine Covenants, and once in the Pearl of Great Price.

8. For the neologistic nature of "atonement," see Spackman, "The Israelite Roots of Atonement Terminology," 46–47.

9. For example, Charles Buck's *Theological Dictionary* (Philadelphia: Joseph J. Woodward, 1829) defines "atonement" as "the satisfying of Divine Justice by Jesus Christ giving himself a ransom for us, undergoing the penalty due to our sins, and thereby releasing us from that punishment which God might justly inflict upon us" (37). Adam Clarke understood "atonement" to refer to "the sacrificial death of Christ." See *The New Testament of our Lord and Saviour Jesus Christ: A Commentary and Critical Notes* (Nashville: Abingdon, 1824), 2:69.

10. I borrow "realized messialogy" from New Testament theological discussions of eschatology, where "realized eschatology" refers to the kingdom of God as existing within a sort of "already/not yet" tension. Throughout the Book of Mormon Jesus and his atonement exist in a sort of proleptic fashion, as the Nephites who live hundreds of years prior to Jesus's birth discuss the atonement as if it has already occurred (Jarom 1:11; Mos 16:6). See discussion in John Christopher Thomas, *A Pentecostal Reads the Book of Mormon: A Literary and Theological Introduction* (Cleveland, TN: Center for Pentecostal Theology, 2016), 199–204.

11. See, for example, Joseph Fielding Smith, *Doctrines of Salvation*, 3 vols. (Salt Lake City: Bookcraft, 1954), 1:130.

12. This clear synthesis of atonement and resurrection mirrors that of modern twentieth-century theologians such as Thomas Torrance. See Paul D. Molnar, "Resurrection and Atonement in the Theology of Thomas F. Torrance," in Adam J. Johnson, ed., *T&T Clark Companion to Atonement,* (New York: T&T Clark, 2017), 35–56.

13. The phrase "it must needs be" appears twenty-six times in the Book of Mormon.

14. Perhaps coincidentally, Isaiah 2 will be quoted in full by Nephi in 2 Nephi 12.

15. According to the dates in the footnotes of the Book of Mormon, Abinadi delivered his speech "about 148 BC," while Benjamin delivered his "about 124 BC."

16. The idea that the atonement would be performed by a divine being does not begin with Abinadi. Nephi's apocalyptic vision, in particular 1 Nephi 11, taught him about the "condescension of God." Jacob has already discussed the idea of atonement and its relationship to Jesus Christ. The reason for the focus upon Abinadi is that he seems to be the first one to explicitly insist that "atonement" will only work if "God himself" performs it. For Nephi and Jacob this realization was a part of their larger theology; for Abinadi it seems to be the foundation of it, a claim that can be seen through his use of Isaiah and his discussion of Jesus's roles as Father and Son.

17. It is fair to ask if this theological move by Abinadi is an attempt by the Book of Mormon to avoid the thorny and (to some) offensive theological issue of penal substitution, with its implied violence of the Father toward the Son.

18. See the discussion in chapter 2, Eric D. Huntsman, "Latter-day Saints and the Atonement in the New Testament."

19. Lincoln H. Blumell, "Luke 22:43–44: An Anti-Docetic Interpolation or an Apologetic Omission?" *A Journal of Biblical Textual Criticism* 19 (2014): 1–35.

20. Although not discussed in this paper, one additional character who does use "atonement" is Korihor in Alma 30:17–18.

21. Douglas J. Davies, *The Mormon Culture of Salvation: Force, Grace and Glory* (Burlington, VT: Ashgate Publishing Company, 2000), 46.

CHAPTER 5

Saving the House of Israel

Collective Atonement in the Book of Mormon

SHARON J. HARRIS

Since 1982 The Church of Jesus Christ of Latter-day Saints has printed the Book of Mormon with a subtitle, "Another Testament of Jesus Christ." Numerous studies have considered Christ in the Book of Mormon with several emphasizing Christ's atonement, especially how Christ and the atonement may save individuals. But such a focus risks overlooking a broader salvation story told in the Book of Mormon, one of communal covenant. The title page of the Book of Mormon announces that it is "written to the . . . remnant of the house of Israel" and for "the convincing of the Jew and Gentile that Jesus is the Christ, the Eternal God, manifesting himself unto all nations." The message of the Book of Mormon as portrayed in the title page is that it is scripture centered on Christ as a communal or collective Savior, one who saves nations through covenants. Furthermore, nations will be saved through scriptural records that come forth to testify of Christ and unite those who enter into covenant with him.

Before continuing, a couple of notes about terminology and an introduction to Book of Mormon peoples are in order: Salvation and atonement are, of course, related, but not the same. This essay asks what collective salvation looks like and considers salvation—collective and individual—as an outcome of atonement. Thus, I refer to collective salvation and collective atonement to explore how the atonement saves groups, turning to the Book of Mormon as an exemplary case study. Here, "collective atonement" is used literally, that Christ expiated for personal sins and suffering *and* for the sins and suffering caused by groups. The idea of collective atonement assumes that groups have emergent properties, attributes that are more than the sum of the attributes of the individuals who make up the group. Speaking of groups, one of the primary peoples in the Book of Mormon are the Lehites, descended from Lehi and Sariah through Joseph in Egypt (1 Ne 5:14; 6:2; 2 Ne 3:4), who traveled from Jerusalem to a promised land in the Americas around 600 BCE. Not long after their arrival, the Lehites divided into the Lamanites and Nephites. In general, Nephites adopt Christian beliefs, and Lamanites reject them. The narrative of the Book of Mormon is told almost entirely from the perspective of Nephites.

When Jesus appears to the Lehites shortly after his death, he talks little about his passion and crucifixion, the traditional events of the atonement, and instead emphasizes communal salvation. Specifically, he reminds them of the interdependence of the Lehitic Book of Mormon covenant. As Jesus puts it, "the work of the Father [shall] commence among *all* the dispersed of my people . . . which the Father hath led away out of Jerusalem" (3 Ne 21:26, emphasis added). In spite of the Book of Mormon's Nephite-centric narrative, the account Jesus gives is not exclusively a story of the righteous and tragically besieged Nephites who act as saviors to wayward Lamanites. Salvific needs operate in both directions. Without the Lamanites' redemption as a remnant in the latter days, the Nephites (and Lehites as a whole) will be lost altogether. This interdependence sets up a model of salvation that is tied to Jesus and to right relations among God's children. It does so through the covenant outlined in the Book of Mormon about the Book of Mormon's role in the salvation of a latter-day Lehite remnant. This is familiar territory in Book of Mormon studies, but what has not been fully appreciated is how this familial interdependence maps onto Lehite belief in Christ in a way that reveals the political and theological stakes of this relationship. In this chapter I first sketch out what is meant by the Book of Mormon covenant and how this covenant is understood in the Book of Mormon, including through a reading of Jacob 5. Then I consider how Christ and Christian belief shape Lehite relations across the span of the Book of Mormon and how belief in Christ is politicized to divide the Lehites at express cross-purposes with the Book of Mormon covenant. The chapter ends by reflecting on how the Book of Mormon's self-referential prophecies require undoing the politicization of Christ that it has narrated, and that this happens through collective atonement.

The Book of Mormon Covenant

The Book of Mormon covenant is laid out in the title page and in the book of Enos. The title page explains that the Book of Mormon is scripture "written to the Lamanites" and contextualizes the Lamanites as "a remnant of the house of Israel." Specifically, the Book of Mormon is to show unto this remnant "how great things the Lord hath done for their fathers, and that they may know the covenants of the Lord." It self-referentially traces its status as a record of the Lehites and also as part of God's covenant to the Lehites. They must be righteous as a people or be swept off the land. If or when they are destroyed, however, a remnant will be preserved to return to God and the covenant in the latter-days. Nephi prophesies about the record coming from his people: "the words of the Lamb shall be made known in the records of my seed" (1 Ne 13:41; see also vv. 34–35, 39–41). Enos resecures a covenant from God that ensures the future remnant will be brought back into the covenant:

> If it should so be that my people the Nephites should ... by any means be destroyed and the Lamanites should not be destroyed that the Lord God would preserve a record of my people the Nephites ... that it might be brought forth at some future day unto the Lamanites, that perhaps they might be brought unto salvation (Enos 1:13; see also vv. 14–17).

Enos and other Book of Mormon prophets are concerned with preserving and reintegrating the Lamanites into the covenant.[1] But this prayer for the Lamanites is in the context of the Nephites' destruction. The Lamanites' salvation is not just for them; it is the means of saving and recuperating the entire Lehite family. The focus of the Book of Mormon covenant, or the communal salvation of the Lehites, comes through the atonement. Although the Book of Mormon focuses on the Lehites, it shows that the atonement offers communal salvation to anyone in covenant. Nephi makes this clear as his first use of the word *atonement* explains that it is infinite "for all mankind" and that it will serve to gather the Jews (2 Ne 25:16).[2] The atonement includes individual salvation, but it also exceeds it. Jesus can save everyone in every way.

The Book of Mormon follows the Lehite covenant and weaves together this thread with the story of the Lehites' relationship with Christ. Ultimately, the record suggests that the peoples who thrive are those who embrace Christ and his salvation as communities; those who do not will be destroyed. This is the Book of Mormon covenant and the Book of Mormon's account of collective salvation. It includes sermons and accounts of individuals who are saved and born again in Christ, to be sure, but the Book of Mormon is also rife with discussions of the salvation of families, of ancestors and descendants, of remnants, and of groups' righteousness or wickedness. In short, while the Book of Mormon provides beloved accounts of individuals' relationships with Christ, it is also thoroughly invested in collective salvation.

From this focus on the Book of Mormon covenant and the Book of Mormon's portrayal of Jesus's atonement as communal, this chapter proceeds with an illustration of how these themes coincide and reinforce one another in the allegory of the olive trees, found in Jacob 5. From there, we can see how the larger project of the Book of Mormon concerns itself with communal salvation through its quotations of Isaiah and its own self-referential prophecies. But in order to understand the origins of these groups' differences and need for one another, first we must also explore how belief in Christ became politicized and a means of dividing the Lehite family. As this becomes clear, the project of gathering, loving, and saving through covenant with Christ emerges as the telos and hope of the Book of Mormon.[3]

The Allegory of the Olive Trees

Jacob's tale of the olive trees, drawn from the extrabiblical prophet Zenos, is cooperative and boasts a cast of characters. Instead of one person—a sinner, lost sheep, silver coin, or prodigal son—the tree that opens the story represents the entire house of Israel: "thus saith the Lord, I will liken thee, O house of Israel, like unto a tame olive tree which a man took and nourished in his vineyard" (Jacob 5:3). As the tree ages and begins to decay, the Lord hopes to encourage new, young growth. Soon a servant joins the master of the vineyard in caring for the tree, and their first strategy to save it involves mixing the branches with other trees in the vineyard. Throughout this allegory, salvation is a group project, and, apparently, not the kind in which one laborer can do all the work alone.

As the story progresses, what began as care for one tree grows to include more and more of the vineyard. The Lord expands his focus from the tree representing the house of Israel to its branches. This perspective increases to become care for all the trees and the vineyard as a whole. Initially the Lord takes interest exclusively in the tame olive tree saying multiple times, "It grieveth me that I should lose this tree" (vv. 7, 11–13; see also v. 18). But once it has been cross-grafted—its branches spread throughout the wild trees and wild branches grafted into the tame tree's roots—the master evaluates the results, carefully checking each transplant site. He travels to the nethermost parts of the vineyard: "Behold these! . . . Take of the fruit thereof . . . that I may preserve it unto mine own self," and "Look hither and behold another branch also which I have planted" (vv. 20, 24; see also vv. 14, 21–26). Scattering the tame tree's branches multiplies his care for the entire vineyard, such that when all the trees fail to produce good fruit, the Lord of the vineyard weeps. Instead of referring to just the one tree, he repeatedly asks, "What could I have done more for my vineyard?" (vv. 41, 47). The enterprise of saving the tame olive tree widens to that of saving the entire vineyard. The allegory suggests that the trees' success is interdependent, that what affects one ultimately has an impact on the rest of the vineyard too. In short, concern for one tree must spread to concern for all if any of the trees are to survive.

The tame roots are necessary for the wild branches to produce good fruit. In like manner, the grafted wild branches revitalize the decaying tame tree. As Deidre Green writes of the allegory,

God's covenant with Israel will not be fulfilled if those within the covenant isolate themselves from others. The tame olive trees that represent Israel cannot flourish or even survive without the new life introduced by the wild branches. Far from being disposable, the wild olive trees alone are capable of saving the tame olive trees from being deemed "good for nothing" and cast out.[4]

If any part of the vineyard is to be spared, the various trees, branches, and roots need each other. The master designs them into productive relations, and the servant encourages the master to give the endeavor enough time to grow.

Not only are the trees interdependent with one another but also the lord and servant's relationship is collaborative. When the Lord despairs that all his trees produce bad fruit, the servant urges and persuades him to wait, make new attempts, and still try to save the vineyard. When the Lord says to "pluck off the branches that have not brought forth good fruit and cast them into the fire," the servant replies, "Let us prune it and dig about it and nourish it a little longer, that perhaps it may bring forth good fruit unto thee" (v. 27). When the lord sees the trees as good for nothing and is ready to hew them all down, the servant coaxes, "Spare it a little longer" (v. 50). The Lord agrees and, with renewed resolve, plans to regraft some branches and clear away others (vv. 52, 54, 65). He engages additional servants "that we may labor with our mights in the vineyard" (v. 61). This is a different picture than a singular, omnipotent God who dispenses individual permission slips into heaven. This is a picture of "all hands on deck" for sweat and problem-solving; for backbreaking, dirty work and undetermined experiments; and for head-scratching frustration combined with arboricultural acumen. Jacob (through Zenos) presents salvation as an ambitious family home-improvement project that must be figured out together. *This* is the story Jacob tells of how the lord and his followers work out salvation.

If we pluck the allegory out as a self-contained story, we may not readily categorize it as an account of Christ as Savior. But Jacob connects the allegory of the olive trees to Christ directly. In context, the transnational and transtemporal allegory of the olive trees is not presented as a sweeping story of a global Abrahamic covenant, although it can be read as such. Rather, Jacob tells the allegory of the olive tree to show how the house of Israel returns to Christ. In the previous chapter, he writes, "for why not speak of the atonement of Christ and attain to a perfect knowledge of him?" (Jacob 4:12). And from this query, he explains how one branch of the house of Israel would not accept Christ. The premise for the allegory of the olive trees arises as Jacob circles back to ask, "how is it possible that these, after having rejected the sure foundation, can ever build upon it that it may become the head of their corner?" (Jacob 4:17). He proceeds to answer that question through the example of communal salvation in the allegory. As Jacob frames it, the story of the olive trees *is* about the

Savior of each individual sinner, the one lost sheep, the single silver coin, and the one prodigal son, but the allegory is also an illustration of how an entire lost people may be redeemed through other peoples.

Connecting Christ to Communal Covenants

The allegory of the olive trees exemplifies the Book of Mormon's emphasis on how Christ's atonement saves in and through networks. But Jacob is not the first Book of Mormon author to teach about the atonement this way; Nephi precedes him. This may surprise us because we know Nephi for his boldness, visions, and love of Isaiah but not necessarily for bringing families together. The antipathy between Nephi and Laman is the original fraternal conflict of the Book of Mormon.

Nephi details the Lord's covenants to Lehi and Sariah's family and reads these covenants into Isaiah's prophecies and vice versa.[5] Although certain parts of Isaiah have traditionally been linked to Christ (even where the historical-textual justification for doing so is tenuous), Nephi generally does not quote from these passages.[6] Put another way, discussions of Nephi's focus on Isaiah typically tie this theological priority to his interest in large covenants rather than to Christology. Even so, when Nephi first tells Book of Mormon readers of his focus on Isaiah, he writes, "I did read many things unto them which were in the Books of Moses. But that I might *more fully persuade them to believe in the Lord their Redeemer*, wherefore I did read unto them that which was written by the prophet Isaiah" (1 Ne 19:23, emphasis added). Nephi understands Isaiah's words as the way of persuading his people to believe in their Redeemer, and he frames his multi-chapter quotation of Isaiah in these terms. Thus, in the opening books of the Book of Mormon, the first authors position a Christological interpretation of Judahite prophecy and embed Christological readings into a covenantal context for the house of Israel. This is how the Book of Mormon maps the outset of the Lehite Christological project, and this frame shapes Book of Mormon atonement theology.

This is not to say that personal forgiveness and individually changed hearts are unimportant in Book of Mormon accounts of salvation. It's just that they are beginnings, not endings. Enos receives forgiveness of his sins, and *then* he continues to pray in "many long strugglings" for the Nephites and then the Lamanites (Enos 1:11). Alma$_1$ believes the words of the prophet Abinadi and then begins recruiting others to the faith. Alma$_2$ repents after seeing the angel and engages in lifelong reparations for his former efforts to undermine the church. Likewise, the sons of Mosiah undertake to share their conversion to Christ with the Lamanites. The Anti-Nephi-Lehies change their name, move to Jershon, volunteer their sons, and raise resources to support the Nephites.

Time after time, the Book of Mormon depicts belief in Christ as the catalyst to further salvific work. If students of the Book of Mormon focus too narrowly on the initial experience of forgiveness as the end-stopped experience with the atonement, they risk remaining in the proverbial anteroom of the household of God, never advancing far beyond the entrance.

These differences between collective and individual focus ebb and flow across the Book of Mormon. Joseph Spencer identifies related changes in how prophets interpret Isaiah in the Book of Mormon. Nephi gives greater attention to the covenantal aspects of Isaiah, as already noted, whereas Abinadi reads Christ as a personal redeemer in Isaiah's words (see Mos 14). As we have seen, Jesus also quotes Isaiah during his visit to the Lehites, and in doing so, he returns to an emphasis on the covenant.[7]

When Jesus descends and teaches the survivors of the Book of Mormon apocalypse, he draws together the priorities of communal and individual covenants. He instructs his listeners that "great are the words of Isaiah" because "surely he spake as touching all things concerning my people which are of the house of Israel" (3 Ne 23:1–2). Jesus emphasizes Isaiah's discussion of the house of Israel, but with this he also combines teachings on individual salvation, namely, individual repentance and baptism. This is clearer if we consider a larger block of Jesus's preaching that includes the above passages regarding Isaiah's prophecies. Jesus says,

> Yea, a commandment I give unto you that ye had ought to search these things diligently, for great are the words of Isaiah. For surely he spake as touching all things concerning my people which are of the house of Israel. . . . And all things that [Isaiah] spake have been and shall be . . . Therefore give heed to my words. . . . And whosoever will hearken unto my words and repenteth and is baptized, the same shall be saved. Search the prophets, for many there be that testify of these things (3 Ne 23:1–5).

Notice that the Lord links the injunction to study Isaiah with heeding his own words, and that a person must study Isaiah in order to heed Christ's words. Christ points to these commandments in addition to repenting and being baptized in order to be saved. Popular and devotional Latter-day Saint discourse cite repentance and baptism as necessary to individual salvation so frequently that they can seem to be formulaic steps. Heeding and hearkening to Christ's teachings, as obvious as this may seem, however, is found less often on Latter-day Saints' how-to-be-saved lists, to say nothing of studying Isaiah. Jesus includes them here, though, suggesting that care for broader covenants, like that found in Isaiah, must accompany the individual covenant of baptism. Unexpected as this addition may be, it is not the end of the Lord's message about turning attention to groups, peoples, and covenants.

Jesus prioritizes still more scripture in a way that illustrates the Book of Mormon's unique position to highlight communal atonement and salvation. After enjoining his hearers to "Search the prophets," as found in the above passage, Jesus "expounded all the scriptures unto them which they had received" and then turned his attention to scriptures that they had received but had not written. Asking for and perusing their records, Jesus observed, "I commanded my servant Samuel the Lamanite that he should testify unto this people. . . . How be it that ye have not written this thing?" (3 Ne 23:9, 11). Jesus's interest in Samuel's prophecies reflects the dynamic of the Lehite covenant already mentioned. Just as the wild olive trees revitalized the decaying tame tree, the Lamanites are essential to the Nephites in order for the Lehite line to survive and remain in the covenant. Here, Jesus suggests that the Nephites also need the prophecies of a Lamanite and corrects them for omitting this from their records.

Without the Lamanites, the Nephites (and Lehites as a whole) will be lost altogether. Jesus implores his listeners to study the words of Isaiah and come to an understanding "concerning my people which are of the house of Israel" (3 Ne 23:2). Then he underscores his message that all members of the house of Israel are needed by commanding the Nephites to record Lamanite prophecy (3 Ne 23:13).[8] The hostility between the Nephites and Lamanites is well-known, beginning in just the first few chapters of the Book of Mormon. But, as the next section details, the fault lines that separate these fraternal groups run along theological lines that are intimately bound up in questions of individual versus communal redemption. What does the Lehites' relationship to the covenant look like across the Book of Mormon? The entire arc of the Book of Mormon showcases how God ministers to individuals but relies on the faithfulness of communities and peoples to help other communities and peoples. But within this arc, belief in Christ becomes a dividing line that demarcates Lehite communities, ecclesiology, race relations, and much more.

The Innovation of Christ in Lehite Scripture

To begin with the conclusion, Lehite belief or lack of belief in Christ becomes politicized. It follows original disagreements between Lehi and Sariah's sons and remains a way of identifying opposing sides of theological debates, which spill over into political and military conflicts. For the next few pages, I trace the genealogy of this friction, specifically the Christological interpretation of Jewish scripture, in order to give a better context for what the Book of Mormon illustrates about the stakes of communal atonement.

The Book of Mormon opens with Lehi having a series of experiences in which he sees "One descending out of the midst of heaven" (1 Ne 1:9) and learns of Jerusalem's impending destruction. He then preaches to "the Jews" about "their wickedness and their abominations" and declares that his visions "manifested plainly of the coming of a Messiah" (1 Ne 1:19). When the Jews hear Lehi's message, though, they become angry with him, and Lehi is instructed to flee with his family to the wilderness. Once out of Jerusalem, Laman and Lemuel criticize Lehi and defend Jerusalem and its inhabitants (1 Ne 2:11–13, 17:20–22). Nephi, however, comes to "believe all the words which had been spoken by [his] father" (1 Ne 2:16). And thus the Nephite and Lamanite antagonism begins to take shape.

We should note two things about the conflict: First, although we can infer something of the family dynamic, the text of 1 Nephi focuses on spiritual and religious disagreements rather than family friction *per se*. Second, as Grant Hardy points out, "Whatever else they may have been, Laman and Lemuel appear to have been orthodox [and] observant" religionists.[9] Hardy reminds us that Nephi never accused them of failure to observe Mosaic commandments and practices and that the majority of Jews of the time believed that the people of Jerusalem were living as God would have them.[10] As Laman and Lemuel put it, the people at Jerusalem "were a righteous people; for they kept the statutes and judgments of the Lord, and all his commandments, according to the law of Moses; . . . and our father hath judged them . . . " (1 Ne. 17:22). We can read Laman and Lemuel as religiously orthodox men increasingly at odds with their plausibly heretical father and younger brother. They were "like unto the Jews who were at Jerusalem" (1 Ne 2:13) who were "angry" when Lehi preached about the Messiah (1 Ne 1:19–20).

Once we begin looking for signs of this difference of opinion, we find them throughout the Book of Mormon. I share a few examples of this doctrinal distinction and then offer some theological readings of what it suggests.

Nephi's signature teachings of Isaiah and his commentary on Isaiah's prophecies suggest that his teaching about the Messiah was a conscious departure from the beliefs of the Jews in Jerusalem. He also notes that belief in the Messiah differentiated the Nephites from the Lamanites. Spencer's work on Nephi's record shows that Nephi prioritizes his quotations of Isaiah as the "more sacred things" of his record (1 Ne 19:5). However, Nephi reports that although "the Jews do understand the things of the prophets," Isaiah's prophecies "were hard for many of my people to understand" because "they know not concerning the manner of prophesying among the Jews" (2 Ne 25:1). The reason they do not understand is because Nephi has "not taught them many things concerning the manner of the Jews" (2 Ne 25:1–2, 5). Thus, even though the Jews understand the things of the prophets, and even though Nephi dedicates so much of his "more sacred things" to such prophecies, he is wary enough of Judahite customs and culture that he opts not to teach his people about them. Instead, he describes their works as "works of darkness" and their doings as "doings of abomination" (2 Ne 25:2).

Nephi contrasts "the manner of prophesying among the Jews" with "plainness." Nephi's "plainness" begins in 2 Nephi 25 and is an exegesis of Isaiah. He begins by identifying what the Jews will know, or what will be made plain to them, namely, the Messiah whom they will reject (see 2 Ne 25:18). The rest of the chapter continues this focus on Jesus Christ, identifying his name as the only one "whereby man can be saved" (2 Ne 25:20). Nephi explains,

> For we labor diligently to write, to persuade our children, and also our brethren, to believe in Christ, and to be reconciled to God.... And, notwithstanding we believe in Christ, we keep the law of Moses, and look forward with steadfastness unto Christ, until the law shall be fulfilled. For, for this end was the law given; wherefore the law hath become dead unto us, and we are made alive in Christ because of our faith; yet we keep the law because of the commandments. And we talk of Christ, we rejoice in Christ, we preach of Christ, we prophesy of Christ, and we write according to our prophecies, that our children may know to what source they may look for a remission of their sins. Wherefore, we speak concerning the law that our children may know the deadness of the law; and they, by knowing the deadness of the law, may look forward unto that life which is in Christ, and know for what end the law was given. And after the law is fulfilled in Christ, that they need not harden their hearts against him when the law ought to be done away (2 Ne 25:23–27).

Note that Nephi focuses extensively on Christ in an attempt to persuade two groups to believe in Christ: "our children, and also our brethren." The clear implication is that the brethren, the Lamanites, *do not* believe in Christ. Furthermore, note Nephi's care to contextualize their Mosaic practices *within* their belief in Christ. Nephi's insistence that they follow the law of Moses seems a little defensive: "And notwithstanding we believe in Christ, we keep the law of Moses" (2 Ne 25:24). Nephi suggests that belief in Christ has been added to his people's practice of keeping Mosaic law. But the word "notwithstanding," indicates that others who keep the law may view Nephi and his followers' Christian beliefs as a different belief system altogether. Where Nephi and Lehi seem to think that they have incorporated an additional (albeit transformative) belief to their Judahite practices or that they have interpreted prophecy and scriptures through a Christological lens, Laman and Lemuel may have viewed this change as a fuller departure from the faith, an apostate rejection of their native people and land that resulted in the family's irreversible exile.

Christ Politicized

Book of Mormon accounts portray belief in Christ as a Nephite innovation and characteristic. When the sons of Mosiah approach their father about proselytizing to the Lamanites, they hoped to "bring [the Lamanites] to the knowledge of the Lord their God," suggesting that the Lamanites did not know much about, much less believe in Christ (Mos 28:2). Indeed, the Lamanite king Lamoni's paradigm focuses on the earth rather than the heavens and acknowledges only a "Great Spirit" (see Alma 18:24–29). Transition to belief in Christ is a benchmark and pivot point of Lamanite conversion in several details in this story. Abish, a servant of Lamoni who is instrumental in bringing the news of Lamoni's conversion to her fellow Lamanites, was different because she had already "been converted to the Lord for many years" (Alma 19:16). When Lamoni and the queen rise after having fallen unconscious in the spirit, Lamoni declares, "behold, I have seen my Redeemer" and goes on to certify Jesus's birth and mission (Alma 19:12–13). When the queen awakes, she first exclaims, "O blessed Jesus, who has saved me from an awful hell!" (Alma 19:29). Aaron's preaching of Christ seems to be what triggered his expulsion (see Alma 21:9–11). When Aaron eventually teaches the king over all the Lamanites, it seems that the king has not held any firm belief in a god (see Alma 22:7 and 18) but is especially interested in the need for a redeemer (see Alma 22:6). In each of these cases belief in and conversion to Jesus is the distinction between the Lamanites' former way of life and their acceptance of the Nephite faith system.

Notably, after the Lamanites' conversion, we find an editorial explanation from Mormon that these new converts kept "the law of Moses as yet, for it was not all fulfilled" (Alma 25:15). He is quick, however, to assure the reader that "notwithstanding the law of Moses, they did look forward to the coming of Christ," and regarded the law of Moses as "a type of his coming" (Alma 25:15). Mormon slips into pedantry by continuing to explain: "Now they did not suppose that salvation came by the law of Moses; but the law of Moses did serve to strengthen their faith in Christ" (Alma 25:16). Modern readers may take this relationship between Mosaic practice and Christian belief for granted, but Mormon's anxiety about explaining suggests that holding both was unusual and required additional clarification, even during Mormon's lifetime, hundreds of years after Nephi.

If we understand that belief in Christ served as the founding difference between the Lamanites and Nephites, it is easy to see examples of how this difference split other Book of Mormon peoples. Belief in Christ not only separated the Nephites from the Lamanites but also Nephites from other dissenters.

In the next generation after Nephi, Sherem, an opponent of this Christian movement among the Nephites, approaches Jacob and accuses him of

> preaching that which ye call the gospel or the doctrine of Christ. And ye have led away much of this people, that they pervert the right way of God and keep not the law of Moses, which is the right way, and convert the law of Moses into the worship of a being which ye say shall come many hundred years hence. And now behold, I, Sherem, declare until you that this is blasphemy (Jacob 7:6–7).

Sherem spells out the rebuttal to Nephi and Jacob's position on Christ. We do not know where Sherem comes from, whether he is from the Nephites or another people, but we can speculate that his arguments are similar to what Laman and Lemuel proffered: The doctrine of Christ converts the law of Moses into something blasphemous, the worship of a being that has yet to come. Predictably, Jacob and Sherem dispute whether or not the scriptures testify of Christ, and their dispute is, at least partly, exegetical. Once again, the conflict can be understood in terms of different interpretations of scripture.

Centuries later, Zeniff, a Nephite adventurer, and his followers return to the land of the Lamanites, where, having established a colony there, they may have adopted related approaches to the scriptures. The priests of King Noah, Zeniff's son and successor, cross-examine Abinadi with the passage, "the Lord hath comforted his people; he hath redeemed Jerusalem" (see Mos 12:20–24). They may be testing whether Abinadi believes in Christ and whether he regards Jerusalem as a place of wickedness or righteousness. The debate follows now-familiar fault lines; Abinadi asks what the priests teach the people and they respond that they teach the law of Moses (Mos 12:27–28). Abinadi then sidesteps much of the well-trod exegetical standoff by asking not how they understand the law but why they do not keep it. This leads naturally to Abinadi citing the Ten Commandments, keeping his preaching firmly rooted in Hebrew scripture but eventually connecting it to how the law of Moses was a preparatory law for belief in Christ (see Mos 13:27–35).

One generation later Noah's son Limhi shows the tension between Hebraic tradition and acceptance of Christ. He grounds his people's belief in the faith of Israel when he praises the "God of Abraham, and Isaac, and Jacob; and also that God who brought the children of Israel out of the land of Egypt" (Mos 7:19). Limhi lists several miracles, and notes that the same God "brought our fathers out of the land of Jerusalem" (Mos 7:20). However, Limhi also explains details of Abinadi's prophecies of Christ—that Christ would "take upon him the image of a man" and that thus "God should come down among the children of men" (Mos 7:27). Limhi ties Abinadi's prophecies of Christ directly to the people's violent rejection of Abinadi and his message: "and now because he said this, they did put him to death" (Mos 7:28). Over 450 years had passed since Lehi and Sariah's family had left Jerusalem, but preaching of Christ constituted a dire offense to this group of Nephites who had returned to land occupied by Lamanites.

Other dissenters revert to Jewish nostalgia, pointedly oppose Nephite Christianity, or both.[11] When the Amlicites secede from the Nephites, they build a city and name it Jerusalem. It is not clear if followers of Nehor turn to Jewish customs, but they persecute people who "had taken upon them the name of Christ" (Alma 1:19). The Zoramites keep neither the law of Moses nor the "performances of the church" (Alma 31:10) but they emphatically "do not believe in the tradition of our brethren which was handed down to them by the childishness of their fathers" and declare in their prayers, "thou hast made it known unto us that there shall be no Christ" (Alma 31:16). Captain Moroni notes that his people are despised by the Nephite dissenter Amalickiah and his followers "because we take upon us the name of Christ" (Alma 46:18). This military leader likewise adopts a Christian reading of Genesis as the people covenant their commitment to Christ by rending their garments in a type of Joseph of Egypt's torn coat (see Alma 46:21–24).

The Nephites' allusion to Joseph of Egypt as a vow of their Christianity is suggestive of a well-known historical Christian interpretive tradition that renders Joseph as a Christ figure, drawing parallels between Joseph and Jesus and showing how both acted as a savior.[12] This scene of covenant in the Book of Mormon points not only to Joseph as an individual but also to the descendants of Joseph as a remnant. Seeking to unite his troops, Moroni exhorts them,

> Yea, let us preserve our liberty as a remnant of Joseph. Yea, let us remember the words of Jacob before his death. For behold, he saw that a part of the remnant of the coat of Joseph was preserved and had not decayed. And he saith: Even as this remnant of garment of my son's hath been preserved, so shall a remnant of the seed of my son be preserved by the hand of God and be taken unto himself, while the remainder of the seed of Joseph shall perish, even as the remnant of his garment. . . . And now, who knoweth but what the remnant of the seed of Joseph which shall perish as his garment are those which have dissented from us; yea, and even it shall be us if we do not stand fast in the faith of Christ (Alma 46:24, 27).

Rather than an individual messianic figure, Moroni recalls an ancient patriarch's prophecy that an entire people would serve as a saving remnant in the typology of Joseph. Moroni rallies his people with the hope that they, who call themselves Christians, might be that surviving remnant (see Alma 46:13–15). Of course, Mormon's literary craft as an editor shines through with painful poignancy here. Just one chapter earlier, Alma$_2$ had prophesied to his son Helaman that the Nephites would, indeed, "dwindle in unbelief" and "become extinct"

(Alma 45:10, 11). The Nephites will not be the eventual surviving remnant. That distinction belongs, instead, to their ever-reliable foes, the Lamanites.

Atonement Is Communal

The Book of Mormon announces self-referential prophecies of its destiny to gather in a Lehite remnant and thereby reunite the Lehite branch of Israel. Readers encounter this message on its title page, in its final chapter of Moroni 10, and throughout the volume. But the narrative arc of the volume details the tragedy of how this branch of Israel destroyed itself. It tells how the Lehites could not be relied on to help save one another. Thus, the Book of Mormon asserts the necessity of collective salvation while demonstrating the Lehites' failure to achieve it. What is more, for years they failed precisely because they permitted belief in Christ to separate them from one another rather than uniting them. Ultimately, in their separation and the subsequent Nephite extinction, Christ disappeared altogether. The Book of Mormon suggests that whatever individual salvation the atonement makes possible, Christ requires collective care from his covenant disciples for other communities. Without it, and for all the atonement's efficacy, over time groups (and the individuals who comprise them) collectively fail to embrace Christ and the covenant. Eventually the Nephites rejected Christ just as the Lamanites had. While Christ's atonement is infinite, those lost to the wash of history in this way must be brought back to it by some other means.

Perhaps the centuries between the destruction of the Nephites and the latter-day reception of the Book of Mormon are the means for the book to finally fulfill its own prophesied covenant. Perhaps it takes that long for the divisive identities of Nephites and Lamanites to be reduced by time and for this family to reemerge as a branch of Israel that must be redeemed by Christ. The Book of Mormon's portrayal of atonement and salvation could double as a cautionary tale against hoarding Christ and lording Christian belief over and against others in such a way that it aligns with or even constitutes definitive political and social differences. The number of times that Christ became a divisor between the Nephites and others suggests that this was a regular danger within the Nephite Christian project.

Or perhaps the account of the Book of Mormon makes a greater demand of latter-day Christians than mere communal equanimity. Perhaps they must learn to be saved in Christ and yet not expand the victory of their own individual salvation to a sense of superiority. Consider this plot twist, for example: Sixty-six years after Captain Moroni's Christians vow, in fervent devotion, to triumphantly carry the banner of their forebear Joseph, a prophet, also from Joseph, comes forward foretelling the birth of Christ. But that chosen messenger is not one of them. He is a Lamanite. Given that "the more part of [the Nephites] did not believe in the words of Samuel" (Hel 16:6), some of same descendants of Moroni's band who agreed that they would perish "if we do not stand fast in the faith of Christ" probably rejected Samuel the Lamanite's Christian annunciation. The Book of Mormon shows that self-satisfaction in individual salvation through Christ risks misrecognizing the path of collective Christian salvation. Theologically, those who are secure in their Christian belief may need to hold more lightly to their saved status and see how others, especially those they do not expect, have more salvation to offer them.

This reversal, requiring humility, forgiveness, and repentance, typifies how the atonement works in the Book of Mormon. More than offering a doctrinal description or platitude, the Book of Mormon sets up a kind of collective atonement lab. Although it includes masterful sermons on the atonement, when it comes to saving peoples, the Book of Mormon authors are especially invested in laying out the practical particulars among these groups that must be negotiated. All must come to Christ—Nephites, dissenters, and Lamanites alike—and they need each other to get there. Salvation through the atonement in the Book of Mormon looks like a family of God, often imperfect but interdependent. This restoration scripture seems to say that individual discipleship to Christ is necessary but insufficient. Atonement—and salvation—are communal.

Notes

1. Jacob invites the Lamanites as a group, "Wherefore, beloved brethren, be reconciled unto him through the atonement of Christ" (Jacob 4:11). Jacob's address to the Lamanites in this written sermon is not commonly recognized. Jacob 4 opens as the transition from Jacob's sermon at the temple to his writings and identifies three groups at the outset: 1. His own people, the Nephites, to whom he was preaching in the previous chapters (v. 1); 2. Their children (v. 2); 3. Their "beloved brethren" (v. 2). These "beloved brethren" must be the Lamanites. They are the obvious remaining audience after Jacob has referred to the Nephites and their posterity. Jacob also knows from Nephi's prophecies that this record is destined to go to a remnant of the Lamanites. And Jacob anticipates that these plates will give them "a small degree of knowledge concerning us or concerning their fathers" (v. 2). See Jarom 1:2 for another example. Alma$_2$ cites the record as a contributing factor to the conversion of many Lamanites in his day and could help do the same for dissenting Nephites. See Alma 37:9–10.

2. Although the word *atonement* appears earlier in the Book of Mormon than here, those uses are in quotations of Lehi and Jacob. Nephi's depiction of atonement here shares parallels with Paul's account of saving Israel in Romans 8–11.

3. A topic of this theological significance and scriptural scope necessarily spills over the bounds of one chapter. It can, and I hope will, fill several books and studies. What I sketch here is only the most preliminary of outlines.

4. Deidre Nicole Green, *Jacob: A Brief Theological Introduction* (Provo, UT: Neal A. Maxwell Institute for Religious Scholarship, 2020), 102.

5. Joseph Spencer has shown how Nephi reinterprets the brass plates, including Isaiah's prophecies, through the lens of his visions and understands his prophecies through his reading of Hebrew scripture. See Joseph M. Spencer, *The Vision of All: Twenty-Five Lectures on Isaiah in Nephi's Record* (Salt Lake City, UT: Greg Kofford Books, 2016), and Joseph M. Spencer, *1st Nephi: A Brief Theological Introduction* (Provo, UT: Neal A. Maxwell Institute for Religious Scholarship, 2020), especially chapter 1.

6. Isaiah 53, with its discussion of the suffering servant, is perhaps the most prominent example. But Nephi does not quote Isaiah 53. He devotes the majority of his Isaiah quotations to First Isaiah, focused on God's work with Israel through Assyria and Hezekiah's Davidic inheritance. First Isaiah is much more concerned with the historical development of Israel and God's hand in shaping his covenant people, especially in producing a remnant, than it is in explicitly Christological ideas. As with the olive tree allegory, the interest here is in the needs of an entire people rather than individual devotion. See Spencer, *The Vision of All*, 25–28 for a discussion of Isaianic theology in the Restoration tradition, and John Goldingay, *The Theology of the Book Called Isaiah* (Downers Grove, IL: InterVarsity, 2014) for a discussion of theological themes in Isaiah more broadly.

7. See Joseph M. Spencer, *An Other Testament*, 2nd ed. (Provo, UT: Neal A. Maxwell Institute for Religious Scholarship, 2016).

8. A small but provocative detail: we may still reap the consequences of dismissing Samuel's contribution. The original chapter break ends after 3 Nephi 23:13 with the Lord's commandment to include Samuel's prophecies. Orson Pratt, however, included the subsequent sentence in that same chapter and placed the chapter break one verse later. The original chapter break punctuated the emphasis on Samuel's prophecies by ending the chapter on that topic, but Pratt's chapter break embeds it within the chapter, making it less prominent.

9. Grant Hardy, *Understanding the Book of Mormon: A Reader's Guide* (Oxford: Oxford University Press, 2010), 39.

10. Julie M. Smith discusses how Huldah's reforms only a couple of decades earlier probably contributed to the peoples' confidence that they were living righteously. See "Huldah's Long Shadow" in *A Dream, a Rock, and a Pillar of Fire: Reading 1 Nephi 1*, edited by Adam S. Miller (Provo, UT: Neal A. Maxwell Institute for Religious Scholarship, 2017), 1–16.

11. For more discussion of Nephite dissenters' rejection of Christ, see Matthew Bowman, "The Profession of Nehor and the Holy Order of God: Theology and Society in Ammonihah," in *A Preparatory Redemption: Reading Alma 12–13*, edited by Matthew Bowman and Rosemary Demos (Provo, UT: Neal A. Maxwell Institute for Religious Scholarship, 2018), 1–12, and Kylie Nielson Turley, *Alma 1–29: A Brief Theological Introduction* (Provo, UT: Neal A. Maxwell Institute for Religious Scholarship, 2020), especially chapter 2 of Turley, "Numbered among the Unbelievers," 20–35.

12. For one example, see Kristian S. Heal, "Joseph as a Type of Christ in Syriac Literature," *BYU Studies* 41.1 (2002): 29–49.

CHAPTER 6

"This Perfect Atonement"

Agency, Law, Theosis, and Atonement Theology in the Doctrine and Covenants

J.B. HAWS

Arguably no book of scripture in the canon of The Church of Jesus Christ of Latter-day Saints better represents the expansiveness of Latter-day Saint atonement theology than does the Doctrine and Covenants. The Doctrine and Covenants envisions the atonement's temporal reach as extending backward, into a pre-earth life, as well as forward, into a postmortal spirit world.[1] The Doctrine and Covenants extends Jesus's atonement outward, too, to the inhabitants of worlds, plural.[2] And the Doctrine and Covenants' framing of the atonement's salvific impact opens up for readers a hopeful quasi-universalism that upends traditional soteriological categories. Significantly, in the Doctrine and Covenants, atonement theology culminates in an invitation to participate fully in the divine life, to experience theosis. All this in a book that also contains detailed dimensions for the building of a church printing office; instructions for the timing of the sale of a church member's farm; and a statement in support of fair, representative public government.[3]

This is to say that the Doctrine and Covenants is wonderfully eclectic—and given its composition, it could hardly have been otherwise. Readers unfamiliar with the Doctrine and Covenants will quickly discover that it is a collection of around one hundred and thirty revelations recorded or dictated by Joseph Smith, plus a handful of revelations to his successors in the Church's prophetic office. The revelations address a host of issues, from church polity to behavioral guidelines to visions of the afterlife. The revelations often came in answer to questions that Joseph Smith and his associates faced in the course of organizing and leading a new church, one that believers saw as the reconstitution of *the* church of Christ.

It is something of a truism to acknowledge that while the Book of Mormon gave the Latter-day Saint movement its most recognizable nickname, the Doctrine and Covenants gave the movement its most recognizable theological distinctives. Whereas the Book of Mormon—despite all its implications about an open canon—is regularly characterized, even by outside observers, as traditional and orthodox in its Christian worldview and outlook, the Doctrine and Covenants is noteworthy for revelations that take Latter-day Saints in distinctly nontraditional directions.[4] Perhaps as telling as anything as to the way that the Doctrine and Covenants functions in the religious lives of believers is this description of the book from a late twentieth-century Latter-day Saint apostle, Neal A. Maxwell (1926–2004): "In the Doctrine and Covenants we receive the voice as well as the word of the Lord. We can almost 'hear' him talking.... Thus, in many ways the Doctrine and Covenants is the modern equivalent of the thundering directness of Sinai."[5] What Maxwell thus memorably captured about the book's format is that the majority of the revelations are voiced in the first person—and Jesus is most often the speaker identified.

That means that even a revelation whose principal concern is something as seemingly mundane as the best way for a group of church missionaries to travel from Missouri to Ohio can still open with a lofty introduction like this one: "Behold, and hearken unto the voice of him who has all power, who is from everlasting to everlasting, even Alpha and Omega, the beginning and the end. . . . I the Lord forgive sins, and am merciful unto those who confess their sins with humble hearts" (D&C 61:1–2). For Latter-day Saints, there is a seamless mixing of the transcendent and the tasks of the day; this speaks to a classic passage in Doctrine and Covenants 29:34: "all things unto me are spiritual, and not at any time have I given unto you a law which was temporal."[6] For Latter-day Saint readers, too, this makes atonement theology in the Doctrine and Covenants a mixture of the infinite and the intimate, since they would hold that many of the relevant passages are in the voice of the Atoner himself.

But the book's makeup also means that the sheer abundance of atonement-related passages can understandably be obscured across pages that address such wide-ranging concerns and interests. Hence this essay aims to draw out some of the key atonement-related passages and themes in the book, especially to represent some of the ways that those Doctrine and Covenants passages and themes shape Latter-day Saint atonement theology—namely offering to readers a substitutionary model of the atonement that is different than the *penal* substitution model. That is a central point toward which the essay will build. The approach here aims, too, to portray something of a Latter-day Saint mindset when approaching the Doctrine and Covenants. Most of all, it aims to suggest to readers that a concentrated, focused read-through of the Doctrine and Covenants in search for atonement-related commentary will not go unrewarded.

Redeemer, Redemption

First, a few facts about the text: perhaps surprisingly, considering the claims just made, the word "atonement" appears in just three Doctrine and Covenants verses—but they are three significant appearances. Doctrine and Covenants 74:7 emphasizes a crucial Latter-day Saint tenet about accountability and children. Latter-day Saints reject inherited guilt, and this passage underscores that: "But little children are holy, being sanctified through the atonement of Jesus Christ." Doctrine and Covenants 76:69 captures the ultimate hope that believers have in Jesus, and offers a superlative modifier for the atonement that is unique in all scripture (and the source of this essay's title): "These are they who are just men made perfect through Jesus the mediator of the new covenant, who wrought out this *perfect* atonement through the shedding of his own blood." Doctrine and Covenants 138:4 makes the connection between human obedience and the efficacy of Christ's atonement, in a passage very reminiscent of the Church's third Article of Faith: "That through his atonement, and by obedience to the principles of the gospel, mankind might be saved." (This attention to obedience will certainly make another appearance later in this essay.)

Other forms of the word "atone" appear in two Doctrine and Covenants verses (D&C 29:1; D&C 138:2), but the infrequency of the word itself belies just how present in the text attention to Jesus's saving work really is. Other verbs and other name-titles stand out instead.

For example, the word "redeem" appears twenty-seven times in the Doctrine and Covenants; "redemption" thirty-eight times; "Redeemer" twenty-three times. The title "Redeemer" first appears in a very early revelation from April 1829, a year before the Church was organized (the revelation is now D&C 8:1). The prevalence of this "redemption"/"Redeemer" terminology prompts some additional thoughts and some additional comparisons.

The word "Redeemer" appears eighteen times in the King James Version of the Old Testament but does *not* appear in the King James Version of the New Testament. Significantly, thirteen of those eighteen Old Testament usages come from the pages of the book of Isaiah. That seems worthy of note. Observers have considered the Old Testament echoes in Joseph Smith's revelations and in the overall project of restoring Christ's church—and the connections to Isaiah are strong throughout.[7] Those Old Testament echoes are worth keeping in mind—and will reverberate later.

In the Doctrine and Covenants, "Redeemer" even slightly outstrips "Savior" in usage (twenty-three to twenty instances). Without making too much of this, it does seem worth emphasizing something important about the Doctrine and Covenants: "redemption" is the mood of the revelations as much as "rescue." It is telling that in the Doctrine and Covenants, "redeem" is the principal verb, "Redeemer" the principal descriptor, and "redemption" the principal outcome. (See Ben Spackman's discussion of Old Testament meanings of "redeem" in chapter 1 herein.) "Redeem" has the connotation of bringing back something that was precious and had been temporarily lost or pawned; the connotation of utilizing something to bring forth full value; the connotation of being set on a path with a newness of life and innocence and potential. All of this, as will be seen, fits well in a Doctrine and Covenants cosmology.

It is also instructive to look at the sections of the Doctrine and Covenants with the greatest concentration of "redemption" verbiage. These sections are the revelations dealing with a devastating episode in the history of The Church of Jesus Christ of Latter-day Saints. In the summer and fall of 1833, armed groups of concerned citizens in Jackson County, Missouri used violence and harassment to force several hundred Latter-day Saint settlers—relative newcomers to the area—to abandon their homes and farms in the county; the county was the spot Joseph Smith had designated by revelation as the eventual gathering place of Zion. "Redemption" is used in the revelations that addressed this loss (the word appears in ten different verses in D&C 103 and 105) as both *rescue* of beleaguered Saints in Missouri and as *restoration* of Saints to their rightful inheritance. The promised, future redemption of Zion is both a regaining of that which is lost and a renewed hope in that which had not yet been realized. This, again, feels very reminiscent of Isaiah, where redemption of Israel as a *people* matters—and that idea of collective salvation, of covenant community, is a Doctrine and Covenants theme, too.[8]

If, then, the revelations in the Doctrine and Covenants emphasize redemption and rescue, the obvious next question is, just from what situation does humanity need to be redeemed? From what peril does humanity need to be rescued? In other words, *why* is the atonement of Jesus Christ necessary for our salvation?

Alternatives to Substitution

These questions are *the* questions when it comes to atonement theology. They are the questions that drive every model of the atonement that thinkers, for the past two millennia, have proposed to get at the metaphysical mechanics, so to speak, of Jesus Christ's saving act—the *how* and *why* of that act.[9] A number of essays in this volume do well at introducing and explaining a variety of those models—vicarious satisfaction, moral influence, divine empathy—and readers can find passages in the Doctrine and Covenants that reinforce or line up well with these theories of atonement. The Doctrine and Covenants, like the New

Testament, offers a variety of models and metaphors for thinking through Christ's salvific work.

For example, Doctrine and Covenants 45:3–5 sounds very much like a "vicarious satisfaction" passage: "Listen to him who is the advocate with the Father, who is pleading your cause before him—Saying: Father, behold the suffering and death of him who did no sin, in whom thou wast well pleased; behold the blood of thy Son which was shed, the blood of him whom thou gavest that thyself might be glorified; Wherefore, Father, spare these my brethren that believe on my name, that they may come unto me and have everlasting life." Doctrine and Covenants 6:36–37 seem to partake of the "moral influence" atonement theory: "Look unto me in every thought; doubt not, fear not. Behold the wounds which pierced my side, and also the prints of the nails in my hands and feet; be faithful, keep my commandments, and ye shall inherit the kingdom of heaven." And then Doctrine and Covenants 62:1 seems to resonate with the "divine empathy" model of the atonement: "Behold, and hearken, O ye elders of my church, saith the Lord your God, even Jesus Christ, your advocate, who knoweth the weakness of Man and how to succor them who are tempted."[10]

For Latter-day Saints, these passages work together to signal that the atonement of Jesus Christ is bigger than any one model or metaphor. Latter-day Saints would find much to agree with in Christian theologian Peter Schmiechen's observation—in a treatise on the "theories of atonement" that Schmiechen classified as "sacrifice," "justification by grace," and "penal substitution"—that "the language of the three [theories] is often intertwined in scripture, liturgy, hymnody, and preaching. Indeed, many Christians would assume that all three are part of one common theme. All move to the same conclusion: on the cross Jesus died for us and for our salvation."[11] This description of an intertwining of language seems likewise apt for the Doctrine and Covenants—and seems, in the Latter-day Saint mind, a reminder that it can be practically, religiously productive to remember that Jesus does rescue humanity, he does ransom us, his example should motivate us to repent, he does feel deep and perfect empathy for us, and so on. But still, the atonement is more than each of these models, more than all of them combined.

Some would say, then why parse it out? Why quibble about these various models and theories? One answer is that professional theologians and professing believers alike can take—and have taken—these models too far, in detrimental ways. In that vein, one model that has come under consistent criticism is the penal substitution model—and recent theological work has offered an important escape from some of the dangerous implications that can grow out of such a model. Think, here, of the work of Gustaf Aulén, identified in this volume's introduction. Or, for example, this line in a 1995 survey of the field of atonement theology: "there is an almost universal consensus that explanations along the lines of compensation (or satisfaction), ultimately traceable to St. Anselm, are now untenable. This applies to his own straightforward legalistic theory of quasi-compensation to God for the affront done to his honour by sin, and also to theories of penal substitution in which Christ is deemed to have taken on himself the punishment for the sins of the human race."[12]

Some Latter-day Saint thinkers have been just as dissatisfied with penal substitution, too. Dennis Potter, for example, wrote a well-known 1999 essay aimed at Book of Mormon believers that took the penal substitution model of the atonement to task. Potter acknowledged that this model finds frequent expression in both the discourse and thinking of many Christians, including many Latter-day Saints, primarily because so many scriptures seem to speak of substitution; Isaiah 53:5 is one such classic passage. But Potter pulls everyone up short with some fundamental questions. Essentially, in what world would it ever be considered just to punish an innocent person in place of a guilty person, and then to consider justice served? Additionally, Potter points out, "The real problem comes with explaining what it is that is owed."[13] Who or what is being satisfied here? What eternal penalty or "fine" is Jesus paying? And perhaps most disconcerting, why cannot a perfect, loving God waive that penalty or fine out of love, when very mortal and very imperfect parents or judges seem to be able to do that very thing? Why can humans who are moved by compassion forgive debts and *not* demand payments?

Potter goes on to argue for an empathy model of the atonement—in essence, Jesus suffered all that he did in order to understand the full depth of the human experience so that he can be a compassionate and empathetic judge. There is much to commend this approach. But Potter admits to an incompleteness, one that is also present in the penal substitution theory: "I admit that in the last step [of laying out the empathy theory] this reading [of a key passage in Alma 42 in the Book of Mormon] goes a little beyond the actual text. Really, this text alone does not make it clear *why* the atonement paves the way for mercy." In the end, Potter calls for more work in the direction of a coherent model that could replace the penal substitution model.[14]

Potter's call seems well placed for Latter-day Saint readers. That is because while not every atonement-related passage in the Doctrine and Covenants comes with substitutionary language, there are enough passages that *do* come with such language that substitution cannot be ignored. Here is one striking example—and it comes in the first-person directness so typical of the Doctrine and Covenants. This very early revelation (1829) was directed to Martin Harris—one of the original supporters of Joseph Smith's Book of Mormon translation project—when Harris faced a difficult decision. Harris was weighing whether or not he should mortgage his farm to finance the publication of the Book of Mormon. In response to that concern, the revelation that followed proclaimed, among other things, "I, God, have suffered these things for all, that they might not suffer if they would repent. But if they would not repent, they must suffer, even as I, which suffering caused myself, the greatest of all, to tremble because of pain, and to bleed at every pore, to suffer both body and spirit, and would that I might not drink the bitter cup and shrink—nevertheless, glory be to the Father, and I partook, and finished my preparations unto the children of men" (D&C 19:16–19).

The substitutionary aspects of this passage seem inescapable. The Savior suffered for humanity so that our suffering would be reduced; he took upon himself suffering that was due us, and that *will occur* if we do not repent. In other words, the implications of this passage seem clear: a requisite amount of suffering must be borne by someone. But why? Only for the Savior to be able to understand us, as important as that is?

In 2006, another Latter-day Saint writer, Jacob Morgan, published in *Dialogue: A Journal of Mormon Thought* a very insightful articulation of just what the Doctrine and Covenants can add to traditional theories of atonement. So much of what he wrote is relevant here. In setting out what was, in effect, a subjective, transformational model of atonement, Morgan's focus was on divine light, and on the way that the atonement of Jesus Christ can make possible in each human an infusion of that divine light; as will be seen, his approach resonates deeply with the themes at hand. Morgan, too, was dissatisfied with the penal substitution theory—but he was also dissatisfied with stopping at the empathy theory. "The principal problem with the empathy theory," he wrote, "is that it gives the atonement no direct influence on humankind. The only person directly affected by the atonement was Christ. How then, does the atonement save us? The empathy theory seems to answer by saying that Christ saves us by judging us fairly. This strikes me as inadequate."[15] Yet Morgan also "readily concede[d], however, that the [divine infusion] theory does not explain *why* suffering was required to accomplish this infusion. I simply accept that it does on the authority of scripture."[16]

It is to these very questions left hanging in the air—*Why* does the atonement pave the way for mercy? Why was suffering *required*?—that the Doctrine and Covenants can, it seems, offer a significant response.

Again, there is much to commend the empathy theory, but it still feels incomplete in addressing the language of important Doctrine and Covenants passages (let alone passages in other books of scripture). The "*must* suffer" imperative in the Doctrine and Covenants 19 passage quoted above makes the suffering feel inexorable, inescapable, absolutely necessary. Why would that be? (And again, punishing an innocent person to make amends for the culpability of another feels somehow worse.)

An Alternative Substitution Model of the Atonement

That brings us to what could be the Doctrine and Covenants' chief contribution to a Latter-day Saint atonement theology: the offering to readers of a substitutionary model of the atonement that is different than the *penal* substitution model. Here's the difference: what if this model is not about a punishment imposed by any personal figure, any judge—or a debt claimed by any personal creditor? What if this model is based around consequences that flow naturally, simply because every choice *must* have a consequence? Guided by Terryl Givens's important work, this alternative model might be called "the guarantor of agency" model, or the "agency-consequence-substitution" model. What makes the Doctrine and Covenants so critical in the coherence of this model is the book's presentation of a wholly distinct cosmology, a wholly distinct view of the universe in which the atonement of Jesus Christ bears sway.

Before moving to that discussion about cosmology, then, there needs to be first a note about Terryl Givens's approach to this question of atonement. In his book, *By the Hand of Mormon*, Givens dedicated two chapters to the theological contributions that the Book of Mormon can offer to the Christian world.[17] His case was persuasive. He argued that the Book of Mormon takes a new tack when it comes to the absolute necessity of the atonement of Jesus Christ by returning to the sticking point for any kind of penal substitution theory of the atonement: why cannot a perfect God forgive in the same way that an imperfect human can forgive? Why does a punishment have to be exacted?

Givens asserts that the Book of Mormon's answer is *human agency*. In order for agency to have any meaning or validity, humans must be able to get what they choose. If they make choices, but they cannot obtain what they choose, those choices are not really choices at all. Human agency would then be an illusion, a sham. Realized consequences, therefore, manifest the reality of agency, and the reality of agency demands connected consequences.

In Givens's skilled hands, "the justice of God" really means agency guaranteed, a consequence for every choice. God is the guarantor of agency, ensuring that genuine agency really does obtain in the universe. Punishment is not mandated because of God's vindictiveness, nor his injured sense of right and wrong. The "punishment affixed" to sin represents instead the consequence of a freely chosen act—and without a consequence attached to a choice, agency would be nullified.[18] This, Terryl Givens argues, is the Book of Mormon's contribution to the question of atonement—Latter-day Saint theology's contribution, really.[19]

It is not unlikely that readers who have made it this far might be asking themselves if Terryl Givens's passages in *By the Hand of Mormon* are really offering anything that is substantively different from the penal substitution model. The contention of this essay is that there is a substantive difference, but that response only makes sense—only has coherence—in the cosmology that the Doctrine and Covenants sets forth. And that is the point. The Doctrine and Covenants is adamant about the indispensability of agency—and that theological starting seed grows into a robust way of thinking about the atonement of Jesus Christ. This Doctrine and Covenants cosmology is one of eternally coexistent intelligences, a cosmology that rejects creation *ex nihilo*.

That cosmology largely came together during a remarkably prolific fifteen months in Joseph Smith's prophetic career. Historian Richard Bushman, in his biography of Joseph Smith, *Rough Stone Rolling*, titled the chapter that dealt with these fifteen months, simply, "Exaltation."[20] The beginning of that period can be marked by Joseph Smith's February 1832 vision of a three-tiered heaven (now D&C 76); and the closing of that period can be marked by a May 1833 revelation about the nature of human existence (now D&C 93). That last revelation carried this message: "man was also in the beginning with God. Intelligence, or the light of truth, was not created or made, neither indeed can be. All truth is independent in that sphere in which God has placed it, to act for itself, as all intelligence also; otherwise there is no existence" (D&C 93:29–30).[21] These lines have stunning implications for Latter-day Saint theology. God does not—apparently *cannot*—create or make intelligence or the light of truth. What He *can* do is place truth and intelligence into spheres of existence to "act for itself." Without that very independence to act, Doctrine and Covenants 93 is saying, there is no existence. For Latter-day Saints that rings true, on a deep level. If real, meaningful existence means a degree of self-awareness, then real, meaningful existence seems inextricably tied to choices, to agency, to self-determination, to independence to act.

This matters especially in the discussion at hand because in the Doctrine and Covenants, salvation and exaltation are clearly portrayed as states of being at which a person arrives because a person has *become* such. In other words, those who inherit the celestial kingdom—the highest degree of heaven described in the February 1832 vision—naturally belong there because this is who they have become. They are not there because divine election has so designated it; they are there because they have chosen it—freely chosen it. They have grown "from grace to grace" until that is who they *are* (D&C 93:20). "Unto every kingdom," another of the revelations that came in this same year declared, "is given a law; and unto every law there are certain bounds also and conditions.

All beings who abide not those conditions are not justified" (D&C 88:38–39). The verse that follows starts with a very telling, very instructive connector: "For," the next verse starts, "intelligence cleaveth unto intelligence; wisdom receiveth wisdom; truth embraceth truth; virtue loveth virtue; light cleaveth unto light; mercy hath compassion on mercy and claimeth her own; justice continueth its course and claimeth its own; judgment goeth before the face of him who sitteth upon the throne and governeth and executeth all things" (D&C 88:40). The sequence links the "law" with "likeness"—in other words, abiding by the conditions of the law that pertains to a certain kingdom means being in the likeness of the inhabitants of that kingdom.

This passage is but one more reminder that the mood of the Doctrine and Covenants is one of law and obedience—that mood, and even that terminology, is everywhere in the book.

Given this mood, this emphasis on law, readers familiar with the "governmental theory of atonement" will likely hear some echoes here. Terryl Givens has even suggested that "the historic atonement theory closest to Mormonism's may be the Governmental Theory"; the essence of this model, in E. Brooks Holifield's helpful summary, is that "Christ died not to redeem a debt but to preserve the dignity of the divine government. Having promulgated a moral law, God could not permit its subversion without allowing the destruction of the moral order itself. When Christ died to vindicate the honor of the law, he made it possible for God to forgive sinful rebels without upsetting the moral order."[22] This approach to atonement is often associated with the work of Hugo Grotius in the seventeenth century. Grotius reasoned that "it is part of the Justice of a Governour to keep Laws," which is an absolute necessity for "the Preservation of Good Order." Order is based on law, on trustworthiness, on the immutability of promises, and because God, "as a Governor, . . . cannot do this"—break promises, that is—he "is therefore called faithful, because he keeps his Promises."[23]

Some of Jonathan Edwards's theological successors favored this view for its emphasis on God's sense of justice and goodness and order rather than his wrath over sin and the connected need for appeasement.[24] Many nineteenth-century Methodists favored this view for its implications about the *universal* impact of the atonement in maintaining the divine order of government, in contradistinction to any model of a limited atonement that would be efficacious only for the elect.[25] Influential Latter-day Saint thinker B. H. Roberts used Doctrine and Covenants passages to put a uniquely Latter-day Saint cosmological overlay on the governmental theory. Roberts entitled a chapter on atonement in his *The Truth, the Way, the Life*, "In Harmony with a Reign of Law," and he wrote in that chapter that "inexorableness is of the essence of law. There can be no force in law, only as it is inexorable. What effect is to cause in the physical world, so penalty or consequence must be to violation of law in the moral and spiritual kingdom. That inexorableness of law is at once both its majesty and glory; without it neither majesty nor glory could exist in connection with law; neither respect, nor sense of security, nor safety, nor rational faith."[26]

Yet it is precisely because of that cosmological overlay that it feels like what Terryl Givens is arguing for in his "guarantor of agency" approach—and what the Doctrine and Covenants is ultimately presenting—is still slightly more than this. It is B. H. Roberts's mention of the cause-and-effect aspect of natural processes that resonates here more than the need for God to preserve his standing as a respecter of law.[27] A focus on agency moves the discussion beyond the governmental theory, beyond the potential chaos that would hypothetically result if some kind of disregard for law on God's part would threaten His reign or His order.[28] In focusing on agency, the discussion moves, in the Latter-day Saint worldview, to a fundamental characteristic of existence itself. If agency is real and if agency is essential to the plan of God, consequences simply *happen*. And that is the dilemma which the atonement of Jesus Christ answers.

That is why the passage from Doctrine and Covenants 88:38–40, quoted above, is also a reminder that the idea of "law" takes on a different cast in the Doctrine and Covenants. Law, in the Doctrine and Covenants, seems to have a descriptive function as much as a prescriptive one. Laws are axiomatic statements because they describe the nature of things *as they really are*. The Doctrine and Covenants links metaphorical and metaphysical synonyms in a way that signals overlap and continuity more than differentiation and precise categorization; "law" and "spirit" and "light" and "truth" and "intelligence" are all used interchangeably. "The glory of God is intelligence, or, in other words, light and truth" (D&C 93:36). "For you shall live by every word that proceedeth forth from the mouth of God. For the word of the Lord is truth, and whatsoever is truth is light, and whatsoever is light is Spirit, even the Spirit of Jesus Christ" (D&C 84:44–45). "And the light which shineth, which giveth you light . . . which light proceedeth forth from the presence of God to fill the immensity of space—the light which is in all things, which giveth life to all things, which is the law by which all things are governed" (D&C 88:12–13). "Truth is knowledge of things as they are, and as they were, and as they are to come" (D&C 93:24). And finally, the book reasserts itself by circling back again to where this started: "Intelligence, or the light of truth, was not created or made, neither indeed can be" (D&C 93:29). In the Doctrine and Covenants' conception of this, there is something real and concrete about truth—it describes things as they really are. Hence, it exists independently; it corresponds to reality.

This is "law" in the King Follett Discourse sense. In that well-known 1844 funeral sermon—occasioned by the death of a Latter-day Saint named King

Follett—Joseph Smith characterized the plan of salvation as God's marking of the path for "weaker intelligences"—but *coeternal* intelligences—to progress as far as they would wish.²⁹ Hence, grace for grace progression is simply the nature of obtaining a fullness—and anyone who wants to obtain a fullness must follow that law; the law simply describes the process. If salvation is about *becoming*, about pursuing a path that is freely chosen, then it becomes clear why controverting agency would destroy the very plan God has laid out. Independent actors cannot *become* something except through processes built on choice after choice after choice. Agency must be preserved or there could be no *becoming* and hence no salvation—there could be no existence. The pointlessness of a world without agency becomes clear. That is why, for Latter-day Saints, the entire plan of God hinges on human agency.

But agency is both gift and curse, because—to reinforce again Terryl Givens's approach to this—every choice must have a consequence to make it a real choice and not some illusion of a choice. It follows, therefore, that the same revelation that affirms the eternality of human existence (D&C 93) also puts readers face to face with the question of the utter necessity of the atonement of Jesus Christ: "Behold, here is the agency of man, and here is the condemnation of man; because that which was from the beginning is plainly manifest unto them, and they receive not the light" (D&C 93:31). Agency thus is also the condemnation of humanity, because "every man whose spirit receiveth not the light is under condemnation" (D&C 93:32). Why condemnation? Because in the Latter-day Saint cosmology, losing light and truth is the natural consequence of rejecting light and truth—and the choice of not receiving light naturally leads away from light, truth, the glory of God, the presence of God; humans thus condemn themselves by *choosing* to be where God is not. What Jesus did in his atoning sacrifice, then, in some miraculous and still-incomprehensible way, was to assume—suffer—the damning *consequences* for humans' evil, misguided, wrong choices, thus leaving humans free, mercifully, to make new choices; in a word, to *repent*—in the original sense of the word, meaning to change one's mind or course, reorienting oneself towards God.

Christians have long noted that one key problem with ransom theory or penal substitution theory is that there is always a *personal* figure demanding payment—and that personal figure inevitably takes on the vague outlines of either a too-vindictive God or a too-powerful Satan; some*one*, in those models, must be satisfied, must be paid. Imagine instead a scenario where law simply describes the nature of things. Imagine, for example, a person who is Jeeping in an abandoned mine shaft. Breaking all rules and warnings, he drives deeper into the mine. He sees a support beam extending from floor to ceiling. He disregards a placard posted on the support beam and knocks it out of the way so that his Jeep can pass. Naturally—and that is the key word here—the ceiling begins to cave in, and the person in our story barely has time to get his shoulders under the cross beam. He can but momentarily slow the cave-in; his demise is imminent. But a rescuer finds him—an infinitely capable and willing rescuer, strong beyond our comprehension. (It is worth noting here that both the Book of Mormon and the Doctrine and Covenants use another Isaiah phrase that is unique to that biblical book: "mighty to save.")[30] It will tax the rescuer desperately, but still this rescuer can hold up the cross beam and restore the support, if the unlucky soon-to-be victim will but move out of the way. The crushing weight is not coming down because a divine God wants to teach the Jeeper a lesson, or because God demands that the Jeeper pay for disobeying orders and warnings and thus restore God's injured honor; rather, the consequence follows naturally and inexorably from a choice—it is like the law of gravity that is simply in operation. But mighty shoulders can assume these burdens and can restore what was broken and lost.

Another metaphorical pass at this: imagine a second unwise adventurer who is in a country where a brutal civil war has just ended. As part of the cleanup, UN peacekeepers have cordoned off miles and miles of land-mine strewn battlefields. The fences around these areas are high and strong, but our adventurer feels lucky. She snips a hole through the fence, and knowing (but perhaps not fully appreciating) the risks, enters the desolate erstwhile battlefield. Twenty steps in, she hears a distinctive, sickening click as she sets a foot down; she has triggered a pressure mine. If she lifts her foot, she will be ended. Thus, she is stuck in place, desperately, thoroughly doomed. But then imagine a rescuer comes, an infinitely capable and willing rescuer, strong beyond comprehension—"mighty to save." He can skillfully step on the mine in place of this once-doomed adventurer. The rescuer assures her that, after she is a safe distance away, the rescuer can detonate the land mine and absorb the blow. The rescuer's unique constitution is such that it will wound him terribly, but it will not kill him. He will recover; this way, both can live and continue forward with life.[31]

It cannot be stressed enough that no metaphor or model can do justice to what is at stake here. Latter-day Saints of all stripes repeatedly affirm that the *how* of the atonement of Jesus Christ is incomprehensible in humanity's current sphere of existence—it seems to operate on a level that is currently out of grasp.[32] This transcendence, too, is highlighted in the Doctrine and Covenants (see, for example, D&C 50:40–42). But what this essay is arguing is that the Doctrine and Covenants works in the religious lives of Latter-day Saints to give them new resources to apprehend more closely the *why* of the atonement of Jesus Christ. What is aimed at in these hypothetical situations are scenarios where severe, debilitating, destructive, paralyzing consequences put people in places where they are no longer free to make new choices. These consequences are not imposed by the edict of a vindictive God, or even an *impartial* God. They simply happen in natural course, because choices really do have consequences; cause and effect are real.

But, coming full circle, some might still ask, Why even in this cosmology could not God just do away with the consequences of the choices? Why not intervene and "block" the consequences, for example? Is not this essentially the same as saying that he must impose punishments for wrongdoing when an earthly father, or a court judge, can mercifully vacate a penitent perpetrator's sentence? Here is the coherence of this "guarantor of agency" model, to use Terryl Givens's important language again—and this is deeper than just semantics. In this Doctrine and Covenants worldview, God cannot "block" or simply dispense with consequences, or else he would violate agency; a choice is only a choice if the chooser can get what he or she chooses, if a consequence really follows from every choice. And, to close this circle, the Doctrine and Covenants makes plain that disallowing in that way the reality of choice—the reality of one's being "independent . . . to act for itself"—would compromise existence itself ("otherwise there is no existence"). God is not—nor can be—a God of compulsion. The theological dilemma in this model is, of course, what happens when humans realize they do not *want* the consequences of their sinful choices? If consequences must obtain for every choice, and those consequences could prove damning to individuals who have chosen those paths but come to wish that they hadn't, what can God do in the "guarantor of agency" model? What God can do—did do—instead of dispensing with consequences, is provide his Son, "in whose name alone salvation can be administered to the children of men" (D&C 109:4). Jesus—uniquely, miraculously—is able to assume these consequences; more will be said on that later. He alone is the means by which all consequences—which are simply *there* because of choice—really do obtain, such that agency can be held inviolate, and thus he alone is also the means by which repentance can still be possible for those who *choose* it.

In other words, as an 1805 hymn put it, "God will force no man to heaven."[33] Doctrine and Covenants 88 proves emphatic on this same point. "Bodies who are of the celestial kingdom"—note that "celestial kingdom" here becomes something of a descriptor of belonging, of an identity—"may possess it [a sanctified earth, from the preceding verses] forever and ever; for, for this intent was it [the earth] made and created, and for this intent are they sanctified." Hence, it follows that "they who are not sanctified through the law which I have given unto you, even the law of Christ, must inherit another kingdom, even that of the terrestrial kingdom, or that of a telestial kingdom" (D&C 88:21). Those souls inherit another kingdom *not* because God cannot be merciful to sinners, but rather because He will not compel anyone to abide in a kingdom that he or she does not choose, that he or she is "not willing to enjoy"; instead, his plan is that each of us will inherit what we "are willing to receive" (D&C 88:32).[34]

For Latter-day Saints, this defines the point of humanity's whole probationary experience on earth—a chance for humans to work out, and then pursue, that which we are willing to enjoy, that which we are willing to receive. But it is not all so straightforward. Humans are enticed on both sides so that we can make choices that reflect what we really want—and the Doctrine and Covenants makes clear that if it were not for real enticements and real choices, we "could not be agents unto [our]selves, for if they never should have bitter they could not know the sweet." (D&C 29:39–40). We humans are here, now, to determine what we love, to decide what we love, to act for what we love, to become what we love, to choose our love.[35]

Why is it that those who "love darkness rather than light" "cannot be redeemed"? Because of choice—"because they repent not" (D&C 29:44–45). Doctrine and Covenants 76:102 puts a finer point to this: "Last of all, these all are they who *will not* be gathered with the saints." The will is eternally respected, eternally inviolate. "That which breaketh a law . . . and willeth to abide in sin, and altogether abideth in sin, cannot be sanctified by law, neither by mercy, justice, nor judgment. Therefore, they must remain filthy still" (D&C 88:35).[36]

But what of those who wake up, in a sense, and "willeth [*not*] to abide in sin"? What then? Misused agency is still "the condemnation of man" (D&C 93:31). In this Doctrine and Covenants framing of things, when we come to ourselves, like the Prodigal Son, and realize how each of us, all of us, have been enticed to pursue—at least at times—those other paths, we come to understand how desperately we need Jesus's intercession because of the consequences that still must follow and that we cannot escape otherwise—but that *he* can assume. And these moments of realization and regret and "re-choosing" are repentance.[37]

This view of things explains why repentance is such a dominant theme in the Doctrine and Covenants—so much so that the injunction in an early revelation is to "say nothing *but* repentance" (D&C 6:9; emphasis added). Repentance represents choice, represents turning in a new direction. As with Zion, the Doctrine and Covenants implies, humanity's promised redemption is both a regaining of that which is lost and a renewed hope in that which has not yet been realized. Utterly indispensable in all of this is the atonement of Jesus Christ. The Doctrine and Covenants makes it clear that Jesus's atonement opens the way for repentance and mercy: "For behold, the Lord your Redeemer suffered death in the flesh; wherefore he suffered the pain of all men, *that* all men might repent and come unto him" (D&C 18:11; emphasis added). The Redeemer has "suffered these things for all"—the crushing consequences of our evil, misguided choices—"that they might not suffer if they would repent." This prompts an alternate, expanded reading of Doctrine and

Covenants 19:16–17: "I, God, have suffered these things for all [that is, I have assumed all of the eternally consequential and potentially damning results of your choices; I have descended below all things], that they might not suffer [that is, receive the eternally consequential and potentially damning results of their choices] if they would repent [that is, re-choose]. But if they would not repent, they must suffer [that is, deal with those consequences] even as I" (D&C 19:16–19).

A Savior Who Is Uniquely Mighty to Save—and to Heal

In this Doctrine and Covenants model, then, Jesus was wounded with humanity's stripes *not* because stripes are necessary to appease an indignant God. Jesus was wounded with our stripes because every choice we make has real consequences, and some of those consequences are "stripes" that we could not bear and yet live, or at least live in God's presence when sin disqualifies us from God's presence (see D&C 1:31). In other words, all humans make choices that, absent the atonement of Jesus Christ, would result in condemnation. Jesus assumed the consequences of these damning choices. Humans' choices still have consequences, but they are consequences that Jesus chose to bear in our place.

How did Jesus do this? For Latter-day Saints as for other Christians, that surely is the mystery and the miracle. But in this choice-consequence model, there are some hints, in thinking about a few observable consequences of bad choices we've all made—shame, injustice, injury, alienation. A passage that was at the heart of Jacob Morgan's aforementioned essay stands out here: "He that ascended up on high . . . also descended below all things, in that he comprehended all things, that he might be in and through all things" (D&C 88:6). This corresponds with the biblical witness: Jesus descended below all things; he bore the shame of sin, though he was without sin, thus he felt injustice more deeply than anyone else could feel; he felt injuries more deeply than anyone could feel; he felt irony and alienation more than anyone else could feel; he felt the loss of divine light to a degree no one else could feel.[38] Thus he "comprehendeth all things," in every sense of that phrase. The resultant connection is profound and total: he is "in and through all things."

Doctrine and Covenants 19 seems to offer an important clue as to how Latter-day Saint theology can approach this question. Again, the revelation is in Jesus's first-person voice in relating his own suffering to Martin Harris's loss of the Spirit—and in describing that loss of the Spirit for Harris as the smallest taste of what Jesus's ultimate suffering had entailed (D&C 19:20). In other words, if the consequence of sin is loss of light—divine light, being cut off from the presence of God (a parallel phrase in D&C 121:37 is "the heavens withdraw themselves")—Jesus assumed that consequence in infinite proportions. He cried out, "My God, my God, why hast thou forsaken me?"[39]

At this point, though, and to do justice to Latter-day Saint atonement theology, all of this still calls for caveats. Even as this model of the atonement is emphatic that no judge (and no God) is imposing these consequences on humans *or* on Jesus, Latter-day Saint proponents of this model still feel the difficulty of explaining this. Even as this model insists that these consequences are not waivable offenses—these are consequences that just happen—this still leaves believers at a loss to explain just how Jesus could step in and absorb them.

And Latter-day Saints have submitted that this is how it should be. "The Savior's Atonement cannot become commonplace in our teaching, in our conversation, or in our hearts," Elder Dieter Uchtdorf said in a 2015 General Conference address. "I have tried to understand the Savior's Atonement with my finite mind, and the only explanation I can come up with is this: God loves us deeply, perfectly, and everlastingly. I cannot even begin to estimate 'the breadth, and length, and depth, and height . . . [of] the love of Christ.'"[40] Or as Eugene England put it movingly: "Although we certainly can't begin to understand all that happened in Gethsemane, especially how it happened, we can begin to feel the impact in our hearts of the divine love expressed there."[41] Even after spending significant time in outlining this "agency-consequence-substitution" model, it would be unfaithful to the whole premise of this essay to say that this is *it*, that this comprehends the atonement of Jesus Christ in Latter-day Saint theology. There still is more. The very fact of this volume is exhibit A that there is still more.

Another essential caveat in the Latter-day Saint worldview that Terryl Givens has put into apt words is this one: "we never make choices with a perfect fulness of understanding or with agency that is perfectly untainted by circumstance, ignorance, genetic impairments, bodily limitations, and so on. . . . Because our agency is seldom perfect and undiluted, Christ can intercede on our behalf without violating our agency; he can take upon himself the consequences of our poor choices" so that "our *ultimate* choices are validated and honored."[42] This is yet another reason why so many aspects of the empathy theory of the atonement resonate deeply with Latter-day Saint thought; in Potter's words, "Why should the atonement open up the possibility of mercy? Perhaps because the atonement makes our judge aware of our reasons for sinning (i.e., the mitigating circumstances), of our intense remorse for the harm that we have done, and of our willingness to change our hearts."[43] That is surely why Jesus's declaration in Doctrine and Covenants 110—"I am he who was slain; I am your advocate with the Father"—can bring such relief to believers.

The Doctrine and Covenants also speaks of Jesus's work as healing.[44] A passage from Doctrine and Covenants 112, in the context of all that has been discussed here, stands out: "And after their temptations and much tribulation, behold, I, the Lord, will feel after them, and if they harden not their hearts, and stiffen not their necks against me, they shall be converted, *and I will heal them*" (D&C 112:13; emphasis added). Notice how this divine offer of healing connects, crucially, with choice, with response, with receptivity.

Healing also fits well with passages about redemption in the Doctrine and Covenants, specifically with the redemption of the body that comes through that key aspect of Jesus's atoning work that is the resurrection. In Doctrine and Covenants 88, the resurrection cannot be separated from salvation in the various kingdoms of heaven, and that is instructive: "And the spirit and body are the soul of man. And the resurrection from the dead is the redemption of the soul. And the redemption of the soul is through him which quickeneth all things, in whose bosom it is decreed that the poor and the meek of the earth shall inherit it" (D&C 88:17). In the Doctrine and Covenants framework, Jesus's conquering work heals both body and spirit—heals all of creation. If sin creates wounds in the divine image,[45] Christ's atonement enables him to heal those wounds that otherwise cannot be healed—and thus wounded, humans could never become like God.

One final, imperfect analogy that again might give insight into a Latter-day Saint mindset on this: imagine a man who loves to cook on a propane grill, but also loves his recliner, so against all warning labels—and prompted by his love of creature comforts—he moves his grill into his family room, so that he can cook without getting out of his chair or moving away from his television. As surely as the warning labels predicted, his family room fills with deadly carbon monoxide. The man succumbs. He is discovered unconscious—but still barely breathing—by a rescuer, one who is uniquely mighty to save. The rescuer brings the unwise cook back to consciousness, but the cook is nauseous and barely hanging on. The rescuer rushes the man to a nearby hospital. This rescuer is utterly unique. His body produces red blood cells at an unprecedented rate, and so he offers his blood in a life-saving transfusion. The victim, awe-struck, tearfully, humbly agrees. The rescuer's blood takes the place of the tainted, inevitably life-threatening blood—the victim is saved from doom, able to continue forward. The transfusion taxes the rescuer almost to death, but he will recover—his unique nature allows him to take on the consequences that would have obtained if he had not intervened. This is a substitutionary assumption of the consequences that naturally followed a bad choice, consequences that simply derived from the nature of being. This, too, is healing and redemption.

One key piece in all of these analogies is that the rescuer has to be uniquely qualified to do things that no one else can do. What does the Doctrine and Covenants offer in response to that question, the question of why *is* Jesus "mighty to save"? It bears repeating that for Latter-day Saints, something miraculous and beyond our limited understanding is at work here. The full answer feels just beyond our reach, in that the answer presently can only be given in parts. His utter uniqueness seems to be a factor of his identity, his inheritance, his intent, his innocence—and yet it seems apparent that in this case the whole of the truth is still greater than the sum of its parts.

For one, Jesus alone "did no sin" (D&C 45:3), such that he, for his own part, was not under the burden of self-inflicted consequences; he was free from any self-inflicted alienation from God. He himself had "[done] no sin" (D&C 45:4). If, as the Doctrine and Covenants posits, refusing God's light is the "condemnation of man," Jesus was under no such condemnation (D&C 93:31). Not only that, but in the first-person language of the Doctrine and Covenants, Jesus affirms that he is "God, the greatest of all" (D&C 19:18). One more turn to Hugo Grotius's seventeenth-century writings on atonement seems relevant here. Grotius proposed that Jesus could assume our punishments because of the incarnation—his being made flesh gave him a connection to us, a "consanguinity" with us. Grotius then argued for "another much greater Conjunction between Christ and us [that] was decreed by God; for he was appointed of God, that he should be the Head of the Body of which we are Members"—and thus it follows that the head could naturally suffer the pain that afflicted any member of the body.[46] Latter-day Saints would take that consanguinity one step further, into pre-earth existence; thus the Doctrine and Covenants passage that has Christ pleading for "my *brethren*" (D&C 45:5; emphasis added) carries a literalness in Latter-day Saint thinking about humanity's natural kinship with Christ, even as Jesus stands apart from all other premortal intelligences: "I was in the beginning with the Father, and am the *Firstborn*" (D&C 93:21; emphasis added). He "received a fulness of the glory of the Father": "The Father . . . gave me of his fulness, and. . . . I was in the world and made flesh my tabernacle" (D&C 93:4, 16). This singular inheritance and identity meant that Jesus, the "Only Begotten of the Father, full of grace and truth" (D&C 93:21), could take on "eternal punishment" and emerge triumphant to "[finish]" his work, to "subdue all things unto myself," to "[retain] all power, even to the destroying of Satan and his works" (D&C 19:2, 3, 11).[47] His divinity made him equal to the "suffering and death" he faced (D&C 45:3).[48] Another allusive phrase drawn from the book of Isaiah—one that makes its appearance three separate times in the Doctrine and Covenants—has resonance here: "I have *overcome* and trodden the wine-press *alone*" (D&C 76:107, emphasis added; see also D&C 88:106; D&C 133:50; compare Isa 63:3). The Doctrine and Covenants' witness is that Jesus—empowered by, and inheritor of, the Father's fullness—did this alone, and he alone could do this.

Telos: Light and Theosis

What the analogies in this essay have also aimed at is the Doctrine and Covenants' sense of how desperately humans need Christ, because of just how, well, *consequential* human choices are. That desperate need, it seems, must be highlighted at least in part because an emphasis on agency and law and obedience could be taken as too strong a celebration of the individual will—or lead to the conclusion that, in the Doctrine and Covenants cosmology, humans *earn* salvation, or we *deserve* our salvation for our own righteousness. Latter-day Saints have often been accused of holding just those views, especially when others hear Latter-day Saints speak of becoming gods. But that sense of "deserving salvation" is not the mood of the Doctrine and Covenants.

It is true that *theosis*—human deification—is a theological thread that weaves its way through the Doctrine and Covenants. And in this way the Doctrine and Covenants puts Latter-day Saints in company and in dialogue with Christians—especially Christians in the tradition of Eastern Orthodoxy—who repeat what Athanasius (c. 296–373) famously said: "God became man so that men might become gods."[49] The atonement of Jesus Christ in the cosmology of the Doctrine and Covenants makes little sense without that admittedly breathtaking end in mind. Certainly there are significant differences between the way that Latter-day Saints and Orthodox Christians conceive of God's nature and essence—that should not be downplayed here. Orthodox Christians (like Roman Catholics and Protestants) hold to God's utter and transcendent and insuperable "Otherness"; as already noted here, Latter-day Saints do not ascribe to God that kind of ontological difference. But despite this different ontological starting point (an undeniably important difference), Latter-day Saints and Orthodox Christians both affirm that the endpoint of human salvation is theosis. "We are each destined to become a god," twentieth-century Greek Orthodox theologian Cristoforos Stavropolous wrote, "to be like God himself . . . to become just like God, a true God."[50] This is striking language—and it resonates with Latter-day Saints. Often, though, similar Latter-day Saint affirmations about theosis cause more serious consternation among other Christians, in part because of the very fact Latter-day Saints do *not* hold to God's ontological Otherness. But there seems to be another part to this consternation. Admittedly, too, sometimes Latter-day Saints, in their exuberance for proclaiming what seems to be this best news of the good news of the gospel, have not always carefully represented the humility that the Doctrine and Covenants also calls for, in its teachings about exaltation. This is a point, therefore, that must not be missed: Latter-day Saints believe that humans become gods only by grace.[51]

That matters on several levels. Latter-day Saints do not commonly speak of "prevenient grace," this sense that God made possible human free will by a preliminary extension of grace.[52] Yet there are echoes of this concept, not necessarily with theological precision, all throughout the Doctrine and Covenants.[53] This sense of prevenient grace is especially strong around the Doctrine and Covenants' "light" motif. "The Spirit giveth light to every man that cometh into the world" is how Doctrine and Covenants 84 frames this initial and universal extension of divine grace (D&C 84:46). Here again, though, human powerlessness is not the mood of the Doctrine and Covenants, either; agency, responsiveness, choice is. Thus, "he that receiveth light, and continueth in God, receiveth more light—and that light groweth brighter and brighter until the perfect day" (D&C 50:24). This is the "growing from grace to grace unto a fulness" model of Doctrine and Covenants 93; this is Jacob Morgan's "divine infusion of light" model. The concept of *light* is a central element when the Doctrine and Covenants points to the aim, the telos, of the atonement of Jesus Christ: "And if your eye be single to my glory, your whole bodies shall be filled with light, and there shall be no darkness in you; and that body which is filled with light comprehendeth all things" (D&C 88:67). That phrase—"comprehendeth all things"—also appears just two dozen verses earlier, in describing "him who sitteth upon the throne and governeth and executeth all things. *He* comprehendeth all things . . . and all things are by him, and of him, even God, forever and ever" (D&C 88:41; emphasis added). The parallel phrasings are no accident. What they indicate—what the whole of the Doctrine and Covenants indicates—is that the "why" of the atonement of Jesus Christ is, ultimately, theosis, becoming like God.

That same revelation, Doctrine and Covenants 88, puts the matter in these superlative terms, in a context of eschatological and soteriological culmination: "And again, another angel shall sound his trump, which is the seventh angel, saying: It is finished; it is finished! The Lamb of God hath overcome and trodden the winepress alone, even the winepress of the fierceness of the wrath of Almighty God. And then shall the angels be crowned with the glory of his might, and the saints shall be filled with his glory, and receive their inheritance and *be made equal with him*" (D&C 88:107; emphasis added). Being "made equal" with the Lamb of God is the point.

Yet, crucially, God is always doing the deify*ing*, the "[making] equal." Doctrine and Covenants 132, a section that proclaims as clearly as any other that saved humans "shall be gods, because they have no end; . . . shall be gods, because they have all power" (v. 20), still reminds hearers of their utter reliance on the saving power of God, when only four verses later, the revelation speaks of the uniqueness of God and Jesus Christ: "this is eternal lives—to know *the only* wise and true God, and Jesus Christ, whom he hath sent. I am he. Receive ye, therefore, my law" (v. 24; emphasis added). Despite all the expansiveness about human potential, there is, in this language of the Doctrine and Covenants, an implied qualitative distinction—perpetually so—between God and deified humanity.[54] Doctrine and Covenants 76, one of Joseph Smith's earliest revelations on deification, declared that saved and exalted humans "are gods, even the sons of God—wherefore, all things are theirs . . . and they are Christ's, and Christ is God's" (D&C 76:58–59). That order signals something important in the cosmology of the Doctrine and Covenants about relationship, about reliance, about eternal indebtedness.

Concluding Notes: Quasi-universalism, Sacramentalism, and Hope

With that last passage in mind, it seems like Doctrine and Covenants 76 is the right place to conclude for a number of reasons, as it captures so many of the thematic threads of atonement theology in the Doctrine and Covenants. This vision of a multitiered heaven simply stands out in the Doctrine and Covenants, especially when a reader arrives there in a sequential read of the book. It feels like a class of its own, a rupture from what had preceded it. Of course, the revelation to Joseph Smith that is now Moses 1 (in the Church's canonical book, the *Pearl of Great Price*) had predated Doctrine and Covenants 76 by more than a year and a half, so a number of these cosmological themes were already part of the revelations of Joseph Smith. But in terms of reading through the Doctrine and Covenants, section 76 feels like a pivot point.

For one thing, the revelation emphasizes the sheer breadth of Jesus's saving reach. With the exception of those "sons of perdition" who willfully, knowingly refuse to be saved, "*all the rest* shall be brought forth by the resurrection of the dead, through the triumph and the glory of the Lamb who was slain, who was in the bosom of the Father before the worlds were made" (D&C 76:39; emphasis added). The proposition that "all the rest" will inherit a degree of heaven, depending upon their choices, their agency, represents a quasi-universalism that matches Doctrine and Covenants 88's notion of inheriting that which we are "willing to receive" (D&C 88:32). "To hell there is an exit," Doctrine and Covenants 76 reminds readers.[55] This concept gets a fuller expression in Doctrine and Covenants 138, a revelation to Joseph F. Smith (1838–1938), Joseph Smith's nephew and fifth in the line of Joseph Smith's successors. This 1918 revelation declared that in a postmortal spirit world "the gospel" is "preached to those who had died in their sins, without a knowledge of the truth, *or in transgression, having rejected the prophets*" (D&C 138:32; emphasis added). In this way, "it was made known among the dead, . . . *the unrighteous as well as the faithful*, that redemption had been wrought through the sacrifice of the Son of God upon the cross" (D&C 138:35). In the Latter-day Saint plan of salvation, this is joyous news—"the dead who repent will be redeemed" (D&C 138:58).

Doctrine and Covenants 76 also connects salvation to the receipt of ordinances, and thus envisions heaven as a saved community bound together through ritual participation. Those who inherit the celestial kingdom are those "who received the testimony of Jesus, and believed on his name and *were baptized* after the manner of his burial" (D&C 76:51; emphasis added). "They are they who are the church of the Firstborn" (D&C 76:54). In reading the Doctrine and Covenants, the connection between priesthood rites and the saving power of God is inescapable: "In the ordinances [of the priesthood], the power of godliness is made manifest. And without the ordinances thereof, the power of godliness is not manifest unto men in the flesh. For without this no man can see the face of God, even the Father, and live" (D&C 84:20–22). This priesthood authorization is a key that unlocks. "The power and authority of the higher, or Melchizedek Priesthood, is to hold the keys of all the spiritual blessing of the church . . . to commune with the general assembly and church of the Firstborn, and to enjoy the communion and presence of God the Father, and Jesus the mediator of the new covenant" (D&C 107:19). Even the "dead who repent will be redeemed *through obedience to the ordinances* of the house of God" (D&C 138:58). We circle back to what a number of commentators have noted in all of this: the Old Testament echoes of sacrifice and ritual and priesthood reverberate throughout the Doctrine and Covenants. Atonement theology in the Doctrine and Covenants is inextricably tied to sacramental theology. Sacraments—ordinances, rites—are for Latter-day Saints the acts that mark the making of covenants and the entering into new relationships with God. They are moments when humans can demonstrate their agency, their free choices, to reorient their lives. These are acts of re-choosing, repenting—and thus they open channels of grace through which Jesus's redeeming power, his promised vicarious assumption of the natural consequences of sin, can flow.[56]

And finally, Doctrine and Covenants 76 instills hope in readers with the proposition that saved individuals are "just men who are made perfect through Jesus the mediator of the new covenant" (D&C 76:69). This key Latter-day Saint tenet is that God is the one who is doing the "making"—his grace is the means, the only means, by which humans can be made perfect.

It seems fitting to close here on the same note that introduced this entire volume, which was Joseph Smith's statement that "the fundamental principles of our religion is the testimony of the apostles and prophets concerning Jesus Christ, 'that he died, was buried, and rose again the third day, and ascended up into heaven'; and all other things, are only appendages to these, which pertain to our religion."⁵⁷ Joseph Smith could have been describing the Doctrine and Covenants itself. If the Doctrine and Covenants is a book that certainly gives ample attention to those "appendages," a careful reading suggests that it is also a book that gives even more attention to the "fundamental principles" surrounding what the book calls, significantly, the "perfect atonement."

Notes

1. See, for example, D&C 29:46 or 93:38 on the pre-earth life; see D&C 138:57–59 on the postmortal world.

2. See D&C 76:22–24.

3. See D&C 95:11; D&C 64:21; and D&C 134.

4. It should be noted that there are important works by Latter-day Saints who challenge the notion that the Book of Mormon is wholly traditional and orthodox in its Christian worldview and suggest that the Book of Mormon has been underappreciated for its theological contributions. See, for example, Terryl Givens, *By the Hand of Mormon: The American Scripture that Launched a New World Religion* (New York and Oxford: Oxford University Press, 2002). See also the recent series published by the Neal A. Maxwell Institute at Brigham Young University, The Book of Mormon: Brief Theological Introductions (Provo, UT: 2020).

5. Neal A. Maxwell, "The Doctrine and Covenants: The Voice of the Lord," *Ensign* (Dec. 1978): 5–6.

6. See, for example, Richard Lyman Bushman, *Joseph Smith: Rough Stone Rolling* (New York: Alfred A. Knopf, 2005), 210.

7. See, for example, Terry B. Ball and Spencer S. Snyder, "Isaiah in the Doctrine and Covenants," in *You Shall Have My Word: Exploring the Text of the Doctrine and Covenants*, edited by Scott C. Esplin, Richard O. Cowan, and Rachel Cope (Provo, UT: BYU Religious Studies Center; Salt Lake City: Deseret Book, 2012), 108–110: "Our survey of the D&C found that nearly two-thirds of the sections, 86 out of 138, share some characteristic language, phrases, or terms with the words of Isaiah." On the theme of redemption in Joseph Smith's revelations, with attention to Old Testament parallels, see Jennifer C. Lane, "Redemption's Grand Design for Both the Living and the Dead," in *The Doctrine and Covenants: Revelations in Context*, edited by Andrew H. Hedges, J. Spencer Fluhman, and Alonzo L. Gaskill (Provo, UT: BYU Religious Studies Center; Salt Lake City: Deseret Book, 2008), 188–211. For observations about the Old Testament elements and tenor of Joseph Smith's work overall, see Jan Shipps, *Mormonism: The Story of a New Religious Tradition* (Urbana: University of Illinois Press, 1985), especially chapters 3 and 4. Much attention has been given to Isaiah in the Book of Mormon. For one recent standout treatment, see Joseph M. Spencer, *The Vision of All: Twenty-Five Lectures on Isaiah in Nephi's Record* (Draper, UT: Greg Kofford Books, 2016).

8. See, especially, Terryl L. Givens, "Latter-day Saint Covenant Theology," chapter 2 of *Feeding the Flock: The Foundations of Mormon Thought: Church and Praxis* (New York and Oxford: Oxford University Press, 2017), 14–44. See also Lane, "Redemption's Grand Design," 190–95.

9. In addition to a number of excellent essays in this volume, for a helpful summary of various atonement theories see Eric M. Vail, *Atonement and Salvation: The Extravagance of God's Love* (Kansas City, MO: Beacon Hill Press, 2016).

10. See Vail, *Atonement and Salvation*, 18, for brief descriptions of the models listed here.

11. Peter Schmiechen, *Saving Power: Theories of Atonement and Forms of the Church* (Grand Rapids, MI: William B. Eerdmans, 2005), 15.

12. Michael Winter, *The Atonement: Problems in Theology* (Collegeville, MN: Liturgical Press, 1995), vi.

13. R. Dennis Potter, "Did Christ Pay for Our Sins?" *Dialogue* 32.4 (Winter 1999): 79.

14. Potter, "Did Christ Pay for Our Sins?" 86; emphasis added.

15. Jacob Morgan, "The Divine Infusion Theory: Rethinking the Atonement," *Dialogue* 39.1 (Spring 2006), 62. Note, though, the significant way that Eugene England's essay, "That They Might Not Suffer," offers an important expansion to the divine empathy theory and speaks to that question of whether "the only person directly affected by the atonement was Christ . . . Because the love is unconditionally offered and comes freely from the same person who gives us our standard of right and will eventually judge us, it has the power to release man from the barrier of his own guilt and give him the strength to repent" (Eugene England, "That They Might Not Suffer: The Gift of Atonement," *Dialogue* 1.3 (Fall 1966): 147).

16. Morgan, "The Divine Infusion Theory," 70.

17. Givens, chapters 7 and 8 of *By the Hand of Mormon*. Givens's model of the atonement that is summarized here comes from pages 205–207 of *By the Hand of Mormon*. He has also recently reprised these important themes in a podcast interview with Spencer Fluhman, "Atonement and Grace," Faith Matters Foundation, YouTube video, April 7, 2019, https://youtu.be/-YVgZH46kgg; and in Terryl Givens, *2nd Nephi: A Brief Theological Introduction* (Provo, Utah: Neal A. Maxwell Institute for Religious Scholarship, 2020), 68–80.

18. These phrases come from Alma 42 in the Book of Mormon.

19. After this present chapter was written but before it was sent off to print, an important new book appeared. Adam Miller's *Original Grace* (Salt Lake and Provo: Deseret Book and BYU Maxwell Institute, 2022) is a significant contribution to Latter-day Saint theology on sin and suffering. The book worries that the concept of "original sin" can often determine—and almost unconsciously so—the way that Latter-day Saints think of justice and suffering and the atonement of Jesus Christ. Miller's argument hinges on an idea that justice might be conceived of as God's giving what is *needed* rather than what is *deserved*. *Original Grace* is focused on the nature of suffering and the logic of love—and thus has healing as a key aim of Jesus's salvific work, something this essay will discuss below—but there is much in *Original Grace's* discussion of the "material order" of the universe that resonates here. See, for example, this passage: "Sin is self-inflicted suffering. As a result, sinful actions always result in unnecessary suffering. In other words, our moral choices always have natural consequences in the material order of things. I'm arguing those natural consequences are dictated by the material order of things, not by the moral

order of things. . . . But again, this suffering is a natural self-inflicted consequence of sin, not a moral obligation required by justice. The moral order never demands punishment as an ethical obligation to return evil for evil" (40). *Original Grace's* strong push against a penal substitution model is another evidence of the theological alternatives offered by Latter-day Saint scripture and teachings. I also thank Steven Harper for an insightful conversation about this.

20. Bushman, *Joseph Smith: Rough Stone Rolling*, chapter 10, 195–214.

21. For a helpful overview, see Kenneth L. Godfrey, "The History of Intelligence in Latter-day Saint Thought," in *Pearl of Great Price: Revelations form God*, edited by H. Donl Peterson and Charles D. Tate Jr. (Provo, UT: BYU Religious Studies Center, 1989), 213–36. What seems to be central in Latter-day Saint thinking is that God does not create individual identity and agency, even if he initiates it or awakens it in some way. Here is apostle Joseph Fielding Smith's summation: "the intelligent part of man was not created, but always existed." For this line, and for a succinct statement of Latter-day Saints' official agnosticism on the nature of eternal intelligence/intelligences, see Joseph Fielding Smith, *Church History and Modern Revelation*, 4 vols. (Salt Lake City: Council of the Twelve Apostles of The Church of Jesus Christ of Latter-day Saints, 1946–1949), 1:401. See also Catholic philosopher Stephen H. Webb's treatment of these Latter-day Saint beliefs about pre-existent intelligence, "on the level of answering some of the perennial questions of human identity," in his *Mormon Christianity: What Other Christians Can Learn from the Latter-day Saints* (New York: Oxford University Press, 2013), especially 170–74.

22. Terryl L. Givens, *Wrestling the Angel: The Foundations of Mormon Thought: Cosmos, God, Humanity* (New York and Oxford: Oxford University Press, 2014), 228; E. Brooks Holifield, *Theology in America: Christian Thought from the Age of the Puritans to the Civil War* (New Haven: Yale University Press, 2003), 132–33.

23. Hugo Grotius, *A Defence of the Catholick Faith Concerning the Satisfaction of Christ. Written Originally by the Learned Hugo Grotius, and Now Translated by W. H.: A Work Very Necessary in These Times for the Preventing of the Growth of Socinianism* (London: Printed for Thomas Parkhurst and Jonathan Robinson, 1692), 84, 125.

24. See Mark Noll, "New England Theology," in Walter A. Elwell, ed., *Evangelical Dictionary of Theology* (Grand Rapids, MI: Baker Books, 1984), 76, for Noll's discussion of the elements of a governmental view of atonement in the work of Jonathan Edwards's students Joseph Bellamy and Samuel Hopkins. See also Holifield, *Theology in America*, 147–48, for a discussion of Bellamy's and Hopkins's positions and that especially of Jonathan Edwards Jr., who argued that the governmental theory of atonement opened the way for more appreciation of God's grace.

25. See Holifield, *Theology in America*, 267: "Governmental images pleased many Methodists because the idea of Christ's having died to preserve moral government suggested a universal effect for Christ's death. Their overriding aim was to argue that he died for all, not for the elect alone."

26. B. H. Roberts, *The Truth, the Way, the Life: An Elementary Treatise on Theology: The Masterwork of B. H. Roberts*, edited by Stan Larson (San Francisco: Smith Research Associates, 1994), 460. Roberts's contemporary, church apostle John A. Widtsoe, also

focused on the centrality of law in his approach to the divine plan of salvation. See, for example, Widtsoe, *Rational Theology as Taught by The Church of Jesus Christ of Latter-day Saints*, Signature Mormon Classics edition (Salt Lake City: Signature Books, 1997), 19–22, 39. *Rational Theology* was originally published by the Church as a course of study in 1915.

27. That felt difference from the governmental theory, as Givens himself notes, arises partly from a sense that "in the Mormon schema, the moral order may be independent of God"; in an important parenthetical aside, Givens points out that "not all Mormons have agreed on this point" (Givens, *Wrestling the Angel*, 228). For a helpful summary of "law" in Latter-day Saint thought, see Givens, "Laws Physical and Spiritual," chapter 7 of *Wrestling the Angel*, 62–65. In a passage in a later section entitled "Reconciliation," Givens articulates it this way: "Eternal life, the kind and quality of life that God lives, is a natural and inevitable consequence of compliance with eternal principles, just as God's own standing as God is the natural and inevitable consequence of perfect harmony with eternal law" (232).

28. Latter-day Saint writer and educator W. Cleon Skousen linked Widtsoe even more strongly with a radical version of the governmental theory of atonement in a widely-circulated recorded address that Skousen gave in 1980, "A Personal Search for the Meaning of the Atonement" (one version of the address has been distributed in CD format as *A Personal Search for the Meaning of Atonement* [Provo, Utah: Ensign Productions, Sounds of Zion, 2002].) However, a number of Latter-day Saint thinkers have found Skousen's theory to be problematic for the way that it makes God's position so tenuous and contingent and dependent. See, for example, Sunstone, "Roundtable: How Does the Atonement 'Work'?" January 4, 2012, https://sunstone.org/roundtable-how-does-the-atonement-work/; James, "Cleon Skousen's 'Intelligence Theory' of Atonement," Lehi's Library, accessed March 27, 2023, https://lehislibrary.wordpress.com/2011/02/03/cleon-skousens-intelligence-theory-of-atonement/.; Morgan, "Divine Infusion Theory," 80, note 5.

29. Here is a relevant passage from Joseph Smith's King Follett Sermon: "I might with boldness proclaim from the housetops that God never had the power to create the spirit of man at all. God himself could not create himself. Intelligence is eternal and exists upon a self-existent principle.... God himself, finding he was in the midst of spirits and glory, because he was more intelligent, saw proper to institute laws whereby the rest could have a privilege to advance like himself. The relationship we have with God places us in a situation to advance in knowledge. He has power to institute laws to instruct the weaker intelligences, that they may be exalted with Himself . . . " This excerpt from the King Follett Sermon comes from a version published in the April 1971 *Ensign*, republished at the website of The Church of Jesus Christ of Latter-day Saints, https://churchofjesuschrist.org/study/ensign/1971/04/the-king-follett-sermon. See also the Joseph Smith Papers, "Accounts of the 'King Follett Sermon,'" accessed March 27, 2023, https://josephsmithpapers.org/site/accounts-of-the-king-follett-sermon.

30. See D&C 133:47; 2 Ne 31:19; Alma 7:14; Alma 34:18; and Isa 63:1.

31. I thank Laura Haws for this analogy.

32. See one example of this in a statement by then–church president Gordon B.

Hinckley at the Church's General Conference in October 2005: "The magnitude of that Atonement is beyond our ability to completely understand" ("Forgiveness," *Ensign* [Nov. 2005]: 84).

33. "Know This, That Every Soul Is Free," *Hymns of The Church of Jesus Christ of Latter-day Saints* (Salt Lake City: The Church of Jesus Christ of Latter-day Saints, 1985), number 240.

34. See D&C 88:33: "For what doth it profit a man if a gift is bestowed upon him, and he receive not the gift? Behold, he rejoices not in that which is given unto him, neither rejoices in him who is the giver of the gift."

35. Note, too, that the Doctrine and Covenants envisions this probationary period extending into a postmortal spirit world; the chance for repentance does not end at death. This is outlined most clearly in D&C 138, discussed below.

36. After quoting this same Doctrine and Covenants verse, Terryl Givens added this helpful commentary: "It isn't law itself, but the sanctity of choice (this 'will' to abide by law or not) that constrains the consequences of Christ's grace.... The spiritual fruits of Christ's atonement, ... salvation itself, can only unfold within the larger framework of human agency's inviolability" (Givens, *Wrestling the Angel*, 233).

37. Terryl Givens uses this phrase—"re-choosing"—in Fluhman, "Atonement and Grace."

38. See also this important recapitulation of Isa 63 that appears in D&C 133: "In all their afflictions he was afflicted. And the angel of his presence saved them; and in his love and in his pity, he redeemed them, and bore them, and carried them all the days of old" (D&C 133:53). See also Morgan, "The Divine-Infusion Theory," 69–70.

39. For a rich reading of Doctrine and Covenants 19 that highlights the pathos in Christ's recounting of his own suffering, see Eugene England, "Means unto Repentance: Unique Book of Mormon Insights into Christ's At-one-ment," in John L. Sorenson and Melvin J. Thorne, eds., *Rediscovering the Book of Mormon* (Provo, UT: FARMS, 1991), 158–59.

40. Dieter F. Uchtdorf, "The Gift of Grace," *Ensign* (May 2015), 107.

41. England, "That They Might Not Suffer," 147.

42. Givens, *2nd Nephi: A Brief Theological Introduction*, 76–77; italics added.

43. Potter, "Did Christ Pay for Our Sins?" 86.

44. Fiona Givens's essay, chapter 9, "Atonement and Retributive Justice," treats this at length. On this line of thinking, as with so much of this essay, I am indebted to the work of Terryl Givens and Fiona Givens. See, for example, "The Healing Christ," chapter 9 of their book *The Christ Who Heals: How God Restored the Truth that Saves Us* (Salt Lake City: Deseret Book, 2017).

45. See Ernst Benz, *The Eastern Orthodox Church: Its Thought and Life*, translated by Richard and Clara Winston (Garden City, NJ: Doubleday, 1963), 51: "Whereas the Western mind defines sin as a violation of the divinely established legal relationship between God and man, the Eastern mind defines it as a diminution of essence, ... a wound or infection of the original image of God, which man is and ought to be."

46. Grotius, *A Defence of the Catholick Faith Concerning the Satisfaction of Christ*, 95.

47. At first read, the phrase "eternal punishment" in Doctrine and Covenants 19 is

not directly referring to Jesus's atonement. However, it does not seem to do injustice to the full text of that revelation to make this connection. The phrase "eternal punishment" is explicitly equated with "God's punishment" for unrepentant sinners—and for them, their future "sufferings [will] be sore." But in the subsequent verse, Jesus declares that "I, God, have suffered *these things* for all"—the antecedent for "these things" seems rightly to encompass the "sufferings" of "eternal punishment" mentioned in the previous sentences. And this seems confirmed in the next verse: "But if they would not repent they must suffer even as I" (D&C 19:11–17; emphasis added).

48. Crucially, it's worth noting that these Doctrine and Covenants titles and descriptors for Jesus take on their full significance for Latter-day Saints only when they are read through the lens of the complete Latter-day Saint scriptural corpus (see, for example, Mos 3:7; or Moses 4:3). A key line from the Church's official website under the topic heading "The Atonement of Jesus Christ" reads this way: "From His mortal mother, Mary, He inherited the ability to die. From His immortal Father, He inherited the power to overcome death. He declared, 'As the Father hath life in himself; so hath he given to the Son to have life in himself' (John 5:26)" (The Church of Jesus Christ of Latter-day Saints, "Atonement of Jesus Christ," accessed March 27, 2023, https://www.churchofjesuschrist.org/study/manual/gospel-topics/atonement-of-jesus-christ).

49. In Daniel B. Clendenin, *Eastern Orthodox Christianity: A Western Perspective*, 2nd edition (Grand Rapids, MI: Baker Academic, 2003), 117. See the discussion about theosis in Eric Huntsman's essay on New Testament atonement theology—chapter 2 herein—and in Ariel Bybee Laughton's discussion of atonement in the Middle Ages, especially of Irenaeus—chapter 3 herein.

50. Cristoforos Stavropoulos, "Partakers of Divine Nature," in *Eastern Orthodox Theology: A Contemporary Reader*, edited by Daniel B. Clendenin (Grand Rapids, MI: Baker Academic, 1995), 184.

51. For more on these points of contact between Eastern Orthodox and Latter-day Saint theology, see J.B. Haws, "Doctrine and Covenants Theology, Eastern Orthodox Terminology: Seeking Clarity about Theosis/Deification," in *How and What You Worship: Christology and Praxis in Joseph Smith's Revelations*, edited by Rachel Cope, Carter Charles, and Jordan Watkins (Provo, UT: BYU Religious Studies Center; Salt Lake City: Deseret Book, 2020), 75–97. This paragraph and the next three are taken from that essay. See also Jordan Vajda, *Partakers of the Divine Nature: A Comparative Analysis of Patristic and Mormon Doctrines of Divinization* (Provo, UT: FARMS, 2002).

52. See this helpful summary of the Wesleyan concept of prevenient grace on the website of the United Methodist Church: "Prevenient grace . . . prepares our hearts and minds to hear and receive the gospel of Jesus Christ, and to respond in faith" (Joe Iovino, "God at Work before We Know It," March 2, 2018, https://www.umc.org/en/content/god-at-work-before-we-know-it-prevenient-grace).

53. See, for example, D&C 93:38; D&C 29:46–47; D&C 1:17. I am grateful to Richard Bennett for that last example of what might be viewed as God's gracious proactivity.

54. Recent Latter-day Saint apostles have also stressed this key point. Gordon B. Hinckley told the Church's General Conference audience, "This lofty concept [of deification/exaltation] in no way diminishes God the Eternal Father. He is the Almighty.

He is the Creator and Governor of the universe. He is the greatest of all *and will always be so*. But just as any earthly father wishes for his sons and daughters every success in life, so I believe our Father in Heaven wishes for his children that they might *approach* him in stature and stand beside him resplendent in godly strength and wisdom" (Hinckley, "Don't Drop the Ball," *Ensign* [Nov. 1994] 48; emphasis added). Boyd K. Packer highlighted that same distinction: "The Father *is* the one true God. *This* thing is certain: no one will ever ascend above Him; no one will ever replace Him. *Nor will anything ever change the relationship that we,* His literal offspring, *have with Him*. He is Elohim, the Father. He is God. Of him there is only one. We revere our Father and our God; we *worship* Him" (Packer, "The Pattern of Our Parentage," *Ensign* [Nov. 1984]: 69).

55. James E. Talmage, Conference Report, April 1930, 37. See also J. Spencer Fluhman, "The Triumph and the Glory of the Lamb: Doctrine and Covenants 76 in Historical Context," *Ensign*, October 2017, 65–71.

56. For one treatment of this, see "Sacramental Theology," chapter 3 of Givens, *Feeding the Flock*, 45–71.

57. "Questions and Answers, 8 May 1838," *Elders' Journal* (July 1838): 42–44; Mark Ashurst-McGee, David W. Grua, Elizabeth A. Kuehn, Alexander L. Baugh, and Brenden W. Rensink, eds., *Documents, Volume 6: February 1838–August 1839*, vol. 6 of the Documents series of *The Joseph Smith Papers*, 3.

CHAPTER 7

"I have, to be sure, been called to drink deep of the bitter cup"

Nineteenth-Century Latter-day Saint Women and Atonement

JENNIFER REEDER

Mary Fielding Smith (1801–1852) was long familiar with separation and grief: she lost her mother at a young age.[1] She crossed the Atlantic alone to join her brother and sister who had immigrated to Canada two years earlier. She left Methodism to be baptized into the Church of Christ—an early name for what is now known as The Church of Jesus Christ of Latter-day Saints—then parted with siblings Joseph and Mercy who left on missions.[2] She finished teaching a school term without future plans.[3] She married Hyrum Smith (1800–1844), brother of the Church's founding prophet Joseph Smith and a new widower with five children in 1837. Then, with the Saints, she was forced from her home in Missouri with a newborn baby and the stepchildren while Hyrum was in Liberty Jail in 1839. Communication between them at that time was sporadic, causing profound misunderstanding while Mary was in ill health following the delivery of her child.[4] Mary felt acutely alone. She poured out her concerns in a letter to her brother Joseph, detailing affliction as well as deliverance in terms reminiscent of Gethsemane: "I have, to be sure, been called *to drink deep of the bitter cup*; but you know, my beloved brother, this makes the sweet sweeter" (3 Ne 11:11; D&C 19:18).[5] In her distress, Mary relied on divine companionship, grace, and deliverance in order to survive. She developed an intimate familiarity with the Savior, who had also drunk of the bitter cup (Luke 22:42; D&C 19:18). She believed that with her baptism, she had covenanted to take the name of Christ (Mos 5:8–10).

Bitter—sweet; alone—together; incomplete—filled: opposition led Mary Smith and other nineteenth-century Latter-day Saint women to a pragmatic perspective of the atonement of Jesus Christ. While they may not have engaged in theological parlor discussions of expiation, they daily lived their religion, incorporating God into their beliefs, practices, and relationships—a holistic, spiritual framework—explaining causes for their troubles, divine assistance in their extremities, and hopes for their future. They demonstrated the atonement—grace, relief, delivery, reunion—with participation in the restoration, sacred worship, and salvation as found in the female Relief Society and in the temple. In providing grace, relief, and deliverance, in community with others, they learned to imitate Christ, physically reenacting his works.[6]

Restoration

Many early nineteenth-century women were familiar with the Bible. Elizabeth Ann and Newel K. Whitney (1800–1882 and 1795–1850) yearned for the primitivist practice of spiritual gifts found in the New Testament and prayed for divine direction. A vision opened to them and a voice from a great cloud told them to prepare to receive the Lord. "We marveled greatly," Elizabeth Ann wrote. "We knew the word of the Lord was coming."[7] Hannah Last [Cornaby] saw spectacles of light in the sky and sensed the arrival of greater knowledge.[8] As a child, Eliza R. Snow (1801–1887) memorized New Testament chapters for her Reformed Baptist Sunday School. "When studying the[se] interesting narratives," she remembered, "my heart yearned for the gifts and manifestations of which those ancient Apostles testified."[9] Whitney, Cornaby, and Snow were among many women of the time seeking a restored Church of Christ.[10] They looked for prophetic authority with Christian fellowship—reconnection with God and with his people.

Restorationism—reconstituting the ancient church and restoring Israelites to their promised land—became popular with budding denominations in the early nineteenth century.[11] Joseph Smith established a restoration with covenant theology, connecting mortal women and men with heavenly parents. Priesthood authority delivered from heavenly messengers, including God the Father and Jesus Christ, opened the heavens and restored communication to the earth. *Christian fellowship* was, by definition, a form of at-one-ment, reconciling believers with an ancient church and priesthood government, a grand unification of Zion.[12]

Another restoration particularly pertinent to women was the Relief Society, a female order or quorum of the priesthood.[13] Joseph Smith told Sarah Kimball (1818–1898) that "the organization of the Church of Christ was never perfect until the women were organized."[14] Snow used a New Testament reference to connect the society to a full restoration of the ancient Church. "Although the name may be of modern date, the institution is of ancient origin. We were told by our martyred prophet, that the same organization existed in the church anciently, allusions to which are made in some epistles recorded in the New Testament, making use of the title, 'elect lady.'"[15] Women participated in a complete restoration; they expanded ecclesiastical activity to include *salvific service*, as discussed below.

Restoration at-one-ment theology required both God's authority and Christian fellowship. In the fall of 1830, Smith preached the principle of gathering, first to "the Ohio," and then to Independence, Missouri, or Zion (D&C 37:3; 57:3), then to Illinois. The excitement among believers was palpable. Fifteen-year-old Bathsheba W. Bigler [Smith] remembered "the spirit of gathering … came upon me, and I became very anxious indeed to go."[16] Ann Marsh Abbott described Saints coming to Nauvoo in a letter to her brother: "When I reflect a moment & see what a scatard sheep we are I to fe[e]l a great desire. that we might [all] be gathered even with the body of the latter day saints. They are flocking from all parts of the Earth to Zion."[17] This Zion, they learned, was a physical location where they could be "of one heart and one mind," with "no poor among them" (Moses 7:18). Later, Joseph Smith told the Nauvoo Relief Society, "by *union of feeling* we obtain pow'r with God," connoting a type of social at-one-ment.[18]

Gathering to this new restoration movement, the Saints experienced tremendous sacrifice. Caroline and John Crosby moved to Kirtland despite separation from family and friends: "we had set our faces as flint Zionward and were ready to forsake all to gain that port."[19] The price to become a Saint was like that required of Christ: piercingly deep (D&C 132:32). Like Christ, these women called upon God *for deliverance and relief,* then partook of the bitter cup. Eliza Partridge Lyman suffered from malnutrition and became extremely ill after delivering her first baby in Winter Quarters. "I am now like a skeleton so much so that those who have not been with me do not know me," she noted. She lost her hair and four months later, she lost her son. "I will try to be reconciled," she wrote.[20] At the same time, Jane Snyder Richards was in Winter Quarters while her husband was on a mission. Her baby Isaac died, and soon, her daughter Wealthy followed. Jane was devastated. "My own life seemed a burden," she recorded. "I only lived because I could not die."[21]

These and countless other records witness the depression, loss, and discouragement that rent the hearts of so many women, yet they continued. As Lyman laid her son in an unmarked grave, she testified, "I believe that there is a power that watches over us and does things right."[22] Richards became a Relief Society leader in Ogden, Utah, where she testified of relief and deliverance.[23] God did not necessarily provide a literal escape from trials; many saw trials as the price they must pay to join "the fellowship of his sufferings" (Philip. 3:10). They turned their extremities to Christ, who suffered all things with them and for them (D&C 19:16–19).

These women knew the Bible. They trusted that God would compensate them for their sacrifices as he had for fellow ancient Saints. Temperance Bond Mack described her situation in Far West, Missouri in December 1838: "I am no better than the martyrs—they had to suffer the loss of all things." She went on, "If the scriptures are fulfilled the saints must suffer persecution and although we have suffered much and it looks dark ahead of us yet none of these things move me neither in my life dear if so be I can obtain a crown of glory."[24] Abbott said: "Now I can say that through all our trials and afflictions our faith is not lesond but strengthened . . . we have past through all this for Christ sake. . . . we have got to be tried and proved in all things so that we may stand or fall."[25] Profound trials tested the marrow of these women, who relied on deliverance and inseparable partnership with Christ and demonstrated a belief in compensatory suffering. Despite the cost, they were anxious to participate in the restoration by gathering to Zion, connecting them to a living God and his people.

Worship

Worship displayed an understanding and reverence for the atonement and a sense of gathering—a collective fellowship—uniting voices, hearts, and souls in shared devotion. Hymns and the sacrament, or eucharist, reveal the worshipful expression of conviction, both for the faith community as a whole and for individuals.[26]

God told Emma Smith in 1830, "my Soul delighteth in the song of the heart." He continued, "the song of the heart righteous is a prayer unto me," insinuating the power of music to show honor, devotion, adoration, and love. She was instructed to "make a selection of sacred hymns" (D&C 25:11–12).[27] Smith also received instructions to expound scripture and exhort the Church (D&C 25:7). While she didn't formally preach over a pulpit until the formation of the Relief Society in 1842, Smith expounded doctrine and exhorted the Church through her hymnal, shaping Latter-day Saint atonement devotion and worship.[28] *A Collection of Sacred Hymns for the Church of the Latter Day Saints* included songs from Methodist, Episcopalian, Baptist, Presbyterian, Congregational, Shaker, and Unitarian hymnals, as well as new hymns written by Latter-day Saints.[29] The hymns she selected gave words—voice—to the heart of the Church. According to her preface to the hymnal, she selected hymns "with an eye single to his glory." These hymns instructed Saints about the atonement: "Redeemer of Israel, Our only delight," "Praise to God, immortal praise," and "Now let us rejoice in the day of salvation."[30] The hymnal was printed for the Kirtland Temple dedication in 1836.[31]

Amanda Barnes Smith (1809–1886) was one of many who experienced a sense of relief through Emma Smith's hymnal. Three years after its publication Amanda Smith found herself in a desperate moment. Her husband and son were killed by a Missouri mob at a massacre at Hawn's Mill, when another son was critically injured, and the family lost their possessions. She snuck into a cornfield to pray, then heard a voice speaking words from a hymn included in the 1835 hymnal, "How Firm a Foundation":

> That soul who on Jesus hath leaned for repose,
> I cannot, I will not desert to its foes;
> That soul, though all hell should endeavor to shake,
> I'll never, no never, no never forsake![32]

"From that moment on," she said, "I had no more fear. I felt that nothing could hurt me."[33] Her experience sharpened her need, and her informal worship provided the courage to move forward, confident that she had divine assistance.

Hymns, sung collectively and individually, taught significant atonement doctrine found in both Protestant and Latter-day Saint hymns collected by Smith, including five sacrament hymns. These songs spoke of the body and blood of Christ and of sacrifice, sanctification, purification, salvation, "living food," and "new covenant of blood."[34] Throughout succeeding editions of Latter-day Saint hymnals, Eliza R. Snow contributed twenty-one evocative and instructive sacrament hymns.[35] The Father's "wisdom and the love" sent Christ "to suffer, bleed and die," she wrote. "His precious blood he freely spilt," she taught, in order to save a dying world. And after that bitter cup, experienced personally in so many different ways, all, too, sang, "How great, how glorious and complete, / Redemption's grand design; / Where justice, love and mercy meet / In harmony divine."[36] Snow described Christ's atoning blood, purchased with a price, yet freely spilled to save the world.[37] Worship through hymns verbalized a sacred sense of adoration for Christ's role in the atonement, both for individuals and for congregations. Singing together created a community of believers. Songs of the heart delighted and pleased God and were answered with blessings on their heads (D&C 25:11–12).

The sacrament service was a significant worship experience. Emma Smith's 1835 hymnal included a song by Isaac Watts: "The blessed Savior hath prepar'd a soul-reviving feast, and bid your longing appetites the rich provision taste."[38] In addition to writing, selecting, and singing sacrament hymns, women contributed to the sacred experience in distinct ways. While men blessed the sacrament of the Lord's supper, women provided the bread, torn to represent Christ's broken physical body; they pressed their own wine and created and washed the linens representing Christ's shroud. In this act, they embodied Mary, the mother of Jesus who delivered the body of the Savior, and Mary Magdalene who cared for his body after death. Nancy Tracy remembered the sacrament in Kirtland: "We baked a lot of bread."[39] Women prepared the sacrament, a holy form of unification, embodying Christ.

Salvation

A cogent component of restoration and worship occurred through the structures of the Relief Society and the temple. Both required women's participation, and both contributed to the concept of salvation. The Relief Society and the temple rites allowed women to understand and perform salvific work, again embodying Christ.

Relief Society organization drew upon Emma Smith's 1830 revelation when the Lord named her "an elect lady" (D&C 25:3). Elect, according to an 1828 dictionary, suggests someone who is chosen or selected, even predestined or foreordained.[40] This "election" formally occurred on March 17, 1842, when Emma was elected president of the Nauvoo Female Relief Society. Joseph Smith patterned the women's organization after the order of heaven to complete the restoration of God's church.[41] John Taylor rejoiced "to see this Institution organiz'd according to the law of Heaven."[42] Eliza R. Snow connected the Society to the New Testament church, citing Peter's recognition of "holy women" (1 Pet 3:3–5).[43]

Though there was some debate about the organization's name at the first meeting, *Relief* proved an apt term for a society connected to Jesus Christ; the women actively relieved or cared for the poor, embodying his earthly mission. *Relief* also coordinated another of Emma Smith's 1830 charges from the Lord: her "office" was to "comfort" those in "afflictions, with consoling words" (D&C 25:5). Again, according to the 1828 dictionary, an "office" was a duty, charge, or trust of a sacred nature, conferred by God. "Comfort" was to strengthen, invigorate, cheer, or enliven, with the noun definition as relief from pain.[44] Comfort, through the Holy Ghost, was what Christ promised his disciples before his death. "I will not leave you comfortless," He promised. "I will come to you" (John 14:18). Then, as Jesus suffered in Gethsemane, an angel appeared from heaven, "strengthening him" (Luke 22:43).

Relief or comfort was an integral part of Relief Society and provided significant opportunities for women to embody Christ, providing grace in Christian service. Mary Fielding Smith said, "the Institution had her hearty concurrence—that nothing was more laudable than feeding the hungry, clothing the naked &c.—that she desired to aid in accomplishing objects so generous." Not only did Mary help needy women find work, but a few weeks later, she began a weekly donation of one bushel of much needed cornmeal for the poor.[45] In 1843, Elizabeth Ann Whitney assigned the first "visiting" teachers to visit people in their geographic districts to ascertain needs, leaving no stone unturned.[46]

Nauvoo Relief Society women achieved Christian fellowship by working together. Joseph Smith promised: "if you live up to your privilege, the angels cannot be restrain'd from being your associates—females, if they are pure and innocent can come into the presence of God."[47] His mother, Lucy Mack Smith (1775–1856), also vocalized this mission: "we must cherish one another, watch over one another, comfort one another and gain instruction, that we may all sit down in heaven together."[48] Their purpose of relief and comfort connected them to each other and to Christ, coming to be at-one.

A significant example of shared Christian service and fellowship occurred on April 19, 1842. Presendia Buell, sister of Relief Society member Zina Jacobs, heard about the Society and traveled thirty miles to join. Eliza R. Snow promised Buell that though she would be at a distance from the core membership, "the Spirit of the Lord which pervades this Society [shall] be with her—she shall feel it and rejoice—she shall be blest wherever she is." Snow called on the Lord to magnify Buell's efforts, that she may "warm up the hearts of those who are cold and dormant." The women's fellowship warmed them all, and as Snow noted, "the spirit of the Lord like a purifying stream, refreshed every heart."[49]

Providing relief extended beyond mere service. Joseph Smith proposed a twofold purpose for Relief Society: to relieve the poor and to save souls.[50] The salvific mission further aligned the mission of Relief Society with Christ. Joseph taught the women that "the Society should move according to the ancient Priesthood, . . . Said he was going to make of this Society a kingdom of priests as in Enoch's day—as in Paul's day."[51] A month later he taught: "This Society is to get instruction thro' the order which God has established—thro' the medium of those appointed to lead—and I now turn the key to you in the name of God and this Society shall rejoice and knowledge and intelligence shall flow down from this time—this is the beginning of better days to this Society." He spoke to them of enlarging, magnifying, and expanding—all phenomena connected with the grace of Jesus Christ.[52] The women had authority and keys (the right to use and exercise that authority); they had a prophetic charge; the door was opened for them to stand up with intelligence and glory and join a community of holiness, close to the presence of God.

In Utah, Snow took the lead of the Relief Society. She quoted Joseph Smith's sermons from the Nauvoo minute book as she called women to draw upon their sacred responsibilities to embody Jesus Christ and find their own salvation. "If the sisters honored their calling as daughters of the Most-High God, all would be fulfilled that had been promised." She wanted them to remember that they were "the daughters of God bought with the blood of *his* Son."[53] She reminded young mothers that while childcare was their first duty, "no one needs the spiritual sustenance and strength imparted by these meetings, more than young mothers."[54] She wanted all women to know that they had to work out their own salvation, not depending on father, brother, or husband, and she taught all women: "You have the same access to God."[55]

Through providing relief, these women found relief—and salvation. They partnered with Christ and were enlarged, magnified, and enabled to deal with the troubles of life. In addition to service, the Nauvoo Relief Society also prepared the women for salvific temple ordinances. God told Emma Smith in 1830 to "lay aside the things of this world, and seek for the things of a better." He continued, "Lift up thy heart and rejoice, and cleave unto the covenants which thou hast made." Emma was promised "a crown of righteousness" (D&C 25:10, 13, 15). That crown would come through the development of salvific and exalting temple ordinances allowing Saints to enter the presence of God—a pinnacle of the atonement of Jesus Christ.

The organization of the Nauvoo Relief Society set in place an initiation for women into the Anointed Quorum, which had been previously established for select men. Soon after Joseph restored the endowment to these men, one of the new initiates, Newel K. Whitney, addressed the women, explaining that God "bestow'd upon man certain blessings peculiar to a man of God, of which woman partook, so that without the female all things cannot be restor'd to the earth it takes all to restore the Priesthood." Whitney went on to speak about the newly restored temple ordinances in veiled terms, implying the temple was a location of at-one-ment. "I rejoice that God has given us means whereby we may get intelligence and instruction . . . it is as much our privilege as that of the ancient saints."[56] "All those who receive my gospel are sons and daughters in my kingdom," God told Emma in 1830 (D&C 25:1).

On September 28, 1843, Emma Smith became the first Latter-day Saint woman to be initiated into the higher order of priesthood now connected to the temple, and to receive her endowment—a bequeathed gift opening the door, or using the key Joseph Smith turned to the women, to a higher realm with God.[57] In turn, she administered the ordinance to other chosen women, first Elizabeth Ann Whitney, Mary Fielding Smith, and Lucy Mack Smith in the fall of 1843, and in December, several others.[58] Joseph taught Mercy Fielding Thompson that the endowment would bring her "out of darkness into marvelous light."[59] Bathsheba Smith remembered Joseph Smith's teachings as well: he "wanted to make of us, as the women were in Paul's day, 'A kingdom of priestesses.' We have that ceremony in our [temple] endowments as Joseph taught."[60] In the endowment ceremony, men and women reenacted the creation, the fall of Adam and Eve, and their return to the presence of God. They also made covenants with God. The covenantal rituals gave Latter-day Saint women a new understanding of their role in the plan of salvation and in the Church.[61] The temple enabled the women to become at-one with God and his glory.[62] Such ordinances unlocked the door to a new realm of possibilities and connections, even the "crown of righteousness" promised to Emma (D&C 25:15).

Along with the restoration of the endowment ceremony, Joseph Smith also began sealing husbands and wives together for eternity. The sealing covenant—bonding wife and husband—expanded traditional Judeo-Christian conjugal unity, becoming "one flesh" (Gen 2:24). On May 28, 1843, Emma was sealed to Joseph Smith for time and all eternity. Others soon followed.[63] Sealing at this time included plural marriage or the idea of adoption, extending a kin network through a priesthood web, in the great eternal chain.[64]

Emulating Emma Smith's role in Nauvoo, Snow in Utah assumed the title Elect Lady, not only in Relief Society, but also in the temple, acting as a "priestess" in the Endowment House in Salt Lake City before the temple there was completed, delivering initiatory ordinances to women, and often acted as Eve in the ritual ceremony.[65] She viewed "celestial marriage" as a means of removing the curse of Eve, a contemporary view of Eve's cause of the fall.[66] Eve, having been the first to sin, in Snow's view, relegated her daughters to a secondary position in the fallen world.[67] The temple rituals, she taught, enabled women to rise up to their proper place as "Queen of Queens, and Priestesses unto the Most High God."[68]

Covenant ordinances connected saints with God and with loved ones. Proxy work enabled deceased family members, male and female, to join the priesthood chain, repairing the gap caused by the physical, spiritual, and mortal separation of families (see Isa 58:12). As Emma Smith's "office" was a "comfort" to her husband, so these women could reach out to comfort or strengthen their ancestors, turning and connecting hearts (D&C 5; Mal 4:6). Those who performed this work became "Saviors on Mount Zion," prophesied by Obadiah (1:21) and encouraged by Snow.[69] Jane and William Neyman's oldest son, Cyrus, died before his parents joined the Church. According to contemporary Christian theology, having not been baptized, the boy was damned. Jane heard Joseph Smith recite Paul's teachings to the Corinthians regarding the resurrection at a funeral (1 Cor 15:19–26). Smith then taught a concept new to the minds of those in attendance, but again, a vital part of the restoration, concerning baptisms for the dead.[70] Less than a month later, Jane was baptized for Cyrus in the Mississippi River.[71]

Temple ordinances for the dead extended beyond baptism, and they allowed women to participate in salvific work for deceased family members, gathering them as one family. The parents of Eliza R. Snow separated from the Latter-day Saints, thus dividing their family. In 1880, she attended the St. George temple, the first location set apart for proxy work for the dead, where she performed ordinances for her ancestors.[72] An anonymous writer wrote in the *Woman's Exponent* about the manner in which women could become "saviors upon Mt. Zion." She explained, "Not only are men favored with these great and sacred blessings but women also are saviors of women. There is no inequality in ministering for the dead. Woman acts in her sphere as man in his." She concluded with the same idea Newel K. Whitney taught the Nauvoo Relief Society: "Man not without the woman, nor the woman without the man in the Lord. The work of performing the ceremonies requires as much labor and falls with as much dignity upon women as man. Therein is the goodness of our Father to His daughters made manifest. Holy women now minister in the Temple of God."[73] As they served, they received their own salvation, and in so doing, they partnered with Christ. In becoming at-one with Christ and their fellow Saints, they breached gaps with family through proxy temple work.

Continuing in the Spirit (D&C 25:14)

Life in nineteenth-century America was hard. Lack of efficient transportation and timely communication, illness and death, and religious differences separated Latter-day Saint women from their families, geographically, emotionally, and spiritually. They discovered pragmatic ways to understand and participate in the atonement of Jesus Christ based on immediate need. And they found relief and deliverance in remarkable ways as they embodied Christ in his service, compassion, and sacrifice.

Once women knew of the restoration, joined the fellowship of Saints and worshipped with them, served and saved one another in Relief Society, and covenanted to become at-one with God and with their ancestors in temples, they wanted their posterity to know the good news and to join them in the priesthood chain. In 1881, Sarah M. Kimball (1818–1898) collected reminiscences for a Jubilee Memorial Box to be distributed thirty years later to the oldest living female descendants. Women wrote to future generations of their belief in atonement. As a "maternal progenitor," Elmina S. Taylor (1830–1904) hoped that her posterity would "number *thousands* who are building upon the foundation which we have laid."[74] Her written words crossed generations of time, well beyond her death, to link her family. Lydia Ann Wells (1828–1909) connected atonement, posterity, and resurrection: "I leave my blessing with my children & their posterity and pray them to be faithful & true to their faith & covenants in the Gospel that we may meet where there shall be no more parting."[75] Taylor and Wells were three of many women who sensed a pressing responsibility as sisters and mothers in Zion to link their families to the covenants that would seal them in the power of priesthood together, at-one.

Just as Mary Fielding Smith personally embodied Christ's bitter cup, her son and future prophet Joseph F. Smith (1838–1918) recognized her noble yet meek efforts: "My own, own Mother. O! she was good! She was true! She was indeed a Saint! A royal daughter of God! To her I owe my very existence, as also my success in life, coupled with the favor and mercy of God."[76] Only hope in a Christ who delivered her could deliver her children and her children's children. The work of restoration, worship, and salvation gave women pragmatic understanding of the atonement of Jesus Christ and of their embodiment of his hope and love.

Notes

The chapter title is in reference to a quote from Mary Fielding Smith to Joseph Fielding, June 1839, in Edward W. Tullidge, *The Women of Mormondom* (New York: Tullidge and Crandall, 1877), 255–56.

1. Rachel Ibbotson Fielding (Nov. 30, 1767–Oct. 15, 1828), memorial no. 130141164, Find A Grave database, accessed March 27, 2023, https://www.findagrave.com/memorial/130141164/rachel-fielding.

2. Tullidge, *The Women of Mormondom*, 249–50.

3. Mary Fielding Smith to Mercy Fielding Thompson, [Aug.–Sept. 1837], CHL; see Janiece Lyn Johnson, "'Give It All Up and Follow Your Lord': Mormon Female Religiosity, 1831–1843" (master's thesis, Brigham Young University, 2001), 47–48.

4. Tullidge, *The Women of Mormondom*, 252–55. Hyrum Smith to Mary Fielding Smith, March 16, 1839; Hyrum Smith to Mary Fielding Smith, March 19, 1839; Mary Fielding Smith to Hyrum Smith, April 11, 1839 (all of the foregoing sources are available at the CHL); see Jay A. Parry, "'Called to Drink Deep of the Bitter Cup': Mary Fielding Smith," in *Women of Faith in the Latter Days: Volume One, 1775–1820*, edited by Richard E. Turley Jr. & Brittany A. Chapman. (Salt Lake City: Deseret Book, 2011), 381–86.

5. Smith to Fielding, June 1839, emphasis added.

6. For an in-depth analysis of Latter-day Saint embodiment theology, see Benjamin E. Park, "Salvation through a Tabernacle: Joseph Smith, Parley P. Pratt, and Early Mormon Theologies of Embodiment," *Dialogue* 43.2 (Summer 2010): 1–44.

7. Elizabeth Ann Whitney, in Tullidge, *The Women of Mormondom*, 41–42; Elizabeth Ann Whitney, "A Leaf from an Autobiography," *Woman's Exponent* 7.7 (Sept. 1, 1885): 51. See Richard T. Hughes, ed., *The American Quest for the Primitive Church* (Urbana: University of Illinois Press, 1988).

8. Hannah Cornaby, *Autobiography and Poems* (Salt Lake City: J. C. Graham, 1882), 9–11. See a copy at the Internet Archive, https://archive.org/details/autobiographyan00corngoog/page/n12.

9. Eliza R. Snow, "Sketch of My Life," in *The Personal Writings of Eliza Roxcy Snow*, edited by Maureen Ursenbach Beecher (Logan, UT: Utah State University Press, 2000), 8.

10. See Ann D. Braude, "Women's History *Is* American Religious History," in *Retelling U.S. Religious History*, edited by Thomas Tweed (Berkeley: University of California Press, 1996), 87–107; Catherine Brekus, *Strangers and Pilgrims: Female Preaching in America, 1740–1845* (Chapel Hill: University of North Carolina Press, 2007); Ann Taves, *Fits, Trances, and Visions: Experiencing Religion and Explaining Experience from Wesley to James* (Princeton: Princeton University Press, 1999).

11. See Hughes, *The American Quest for the Primitive Church*.

12. See Terryl L. Givens, *Wrestling the Angel: The Foundations of Mormon Thought* (New York: Oxford University Press, 2015), 301–9; Jonathan Stapley, *The Power of Godliness: Mormon Liturgy and Cosmology* (New York: Oxford University Press, 2018), 12.

13. Nearly forty years after its initial organization, Eliza R. Snow stated that "Joseph Smith believed the Relief Society to be a part of the Priesthood as much as the Elders Chorum [Quorum] only that it belonged exclusively to the Sisters." Wellsville Ward, Cache Stake, Relief Society Minutes and Records (1868–1973), vol. 1 (1868–1886), Sept. 9, 1873, 60 (CHL).

14. Sarah M. Kimball, "Early Relief Society Reminiscence, Mar. 17, 1882," Relief Society Record, 1880–1892, CHL; Jill Mulvay Derr, Carol Cornwall Madsen, Kate Holbrook, and Matthew J. Grow, eds., *The First Fifty Years of Relief Society: Key Documents in Latter-day Saint Women's History* (Salt Lake City: Church Historian's Press, 2016), 4.10.

15. Eliza R. Snow, "Female Relief Society," *Deseret Evening News*, (Apr. 18, 1868) 127; eds. Derr et al., *First Fifty Years of Relief Society*, 3.6.

16. Bathsheba W. Smith, *Autobiography*, ca. 1875–1906 (CHL), typescript, 2–5.

17. Ann Marsh Abbott to Nathan Marsh, June 20, 1843, private collection. See Johnson, "Give It All Up and Follow Your Lord."

18. Nauvoo Female Relief Society, 1842–1844, June 9, 1842, 60, in Derr et al., eds., *First Fifty Years of Relief Society*, 78, emphasis added.

19. Caroline Barnes Crosby, in *No Place to Call Home: The 1807–1857 Life Writings of Caroline Barnes Crosby, Chronicler of Outlying Mormon Communities*, edited by Edward Leo Lyman, Susan Ward Payne, and S. George Elsworth (Logan, UT: Utah State University Press, 2005), 35–37.

20. Eliza P. Lyman, Journal, 1846–1885, 33–35, CHL; Janiece Johnson and Jennifer Reeder, *Witness of Women: Firsthand Experiences and Testimonies of the Restoration* (Salt Lake City: Deseret Book, 2016), 191–92.

21. Jane Snyder Richards, *Reminiscences of Mrs. F. D. Richards*, holograph, 1880, 20–21, CHL; *Witness of Women*, 192–93.

22. Eliza P. Lyman, Journal, 1846–1885, 33–35; Johnson and Reeder, *Witness of Women*, 191–92.

23. See Emmeline B. Wells, "Weber Stake," *Woman's Exponent* 13.23 (May 1, 1885): 182; "Relief Society Conference," *Woman's Exponent* 19.20 (Apr. 15, 1891): 156; "Relief Society Conference," *Woman's Exponent* 20.20 (May 1, 1892): 156–57; "General Relief Society Conference," *Woman's Exponent* 21.1–2, (June 1 and 15, 1898): 290; "General Conference Relief Society," *Woman's Exponent* 32.12 (May 1904): 95.

24. Temperance Mack to Harriett Whittemore, Dec. 30, 1838, Whittemore Family Papers, Michigan Historical Collections, University of Michigan, Ann Arbor; Janiece L. Johnson, *"Give It All Up and Follow Your Lord": Mormon Female Religiosity, 1831–1843* (Provo, UT: BYU Studies, 2008), 51–53.

25. Abbott to Marsh, June 20, 1843.

26. Noah Webster, ed., *An American Dictionary of the English Language* (New York: S. Converse, 1828).

27. Revelation to Emma Smith, July 1830. Strikethrough text appears in original manuscript. Joseph Smith, Revelation Book 1 [ca. Mar. 1831–July 1835], 34–35, CHL.

28. Rachel Cope, "A Sacred Space for Women: Hymnody in Emma Hale Smith's Theology," *Journal of Religious History* (2017), 5–6.

29. Nancy J. Andersen, "Mormon Hymnody: Kirtland Roots and Evolutionary Branches," *Journal of Mormon History* 32.1 (Spring 2006), 146–49.

30. "Preface," in Emma Smith, ed., *A Collection of Sacred Hymns for the Church of the Latter Day Saints* (Kirtland, OH: F. G. Williams, 1835), 4–5. See hymns on pp. 12, 18, and 24.

31. Michael Hicks, *Mormonism and Music: A History* (Urbana: University of Illinois Press, 1989), 20.

32. Smith, *Collection of Sacred Hymns*, 111–13.

33. Amanda Barnes Smith, in Tullidge, *Women of Mormondom*, 129–31.

34. Smith, *Collection of Sacred Hymns*, 75–81.

35. Emmeline B. Wells, "'Eliza Roxie Snow Smith': A Tribute of Affection," *Woman's Exponent* 16 (Dec. 15, 1887): 109.

36. Eliza R. Snow, "Sacramental Hymn [How Great the Wisdom and the Love]," *Sacred Hymns and Spiritual Songs for The Church of Jesus Christ of Latter-day Saints* (Salt Lake City: Deseret News, 1871), 401–2.

37. See, for example, Eliza R. Snow, "Sacramental Hymn" [Again we meet around the board], *Millennial Star* (June 13, 1871); Snow, "Sacramental Hymn [How great the wisdom and the love]," *Sacred Hymns*; "Hymn [Behold the great Redeemer die]," *Sacred Hymns*, 400–401.

38. Smith, *Collection of Sacred Hymns*, 6–7.

39. Nancy A. Tracy, "Diary of Nancy Naomi Alexander Tracy," typescript, 7–8, Nancy Alexander Tracy, autobiography, 1885, holograph, Harold B. Lee Library, Brigham Young University, Provo, UT; see also Johnson and Reeder, *Witness of Women*, 185.

40. Webster, *An American Dictionary*, "elect," n.p.

41. Kimball, "Early Relief Society Reminiscence."

42. Nauvoo Female Relief Society, minute book, 1842–1844, March 17, 1842, 13, CHL; see also Derr et al., *First Fifty Years of Relief Society*, 36.

43. Eliza R. Snow, "An Address," *Woman's Exponent* 2.8 (Sept. 15, 1873): 62–63, Derr et al., *First Fifty Years*, 384. See also Eliza R. Snow, "Female Relief Society," *Deseret News* (Apr. 22, 1868), 1; Derr et al., *First Fifty Years*, 271.

44. Webster, *American Dictionary*, "office," "comfort," n.p.

45. Nauvoo Female Relief Society, minute book, March 24, 1842, 15, 19–20; Apr. 14, 1842, 27; Derr et al., *First Fifty Years*, 38, 41, 48.

46. Nauvoo Female Relief Society, minute book, June 16, 1843, 88; July 7, 1843, 92; Derr et al., *First Fifty Years*, 100, 102.

47. Nauvoo Female Relief Society, minute book, Apr. 28, 1842, 38; Derr et al., *First Fifty Years*, 57.

48. Nauvoo Female Relief Society, minute book, Mar. 24, 1842, 18; Derr et al., *First Fifty Years*, 40.

49. Nauvoo Female Relief Society, minute book, Apr. 19, 1842, 29–32; Derr et al., *First Fifty Years*, 49–52.

50. Nauvoo Female Relief Society, minute book, June 9, 1842, 62; Derr et al., *First Fifty Years*, 79.

51. Nauvoo Female Relief Society, minute book, Mar. 30, 1842, 21; Derr et al., *First Fifty Years*, 43.

52. Nauvoo Female Relief Society, minute book, Apr. 28, 1842, 38–39; Derr et al., *First Fifty Years*, 58–59.

53. Weber Stake Relief Society Minutes, vol. 1, May 9, 1879, 55–56, CHL, emphasis original.

54. Weber Stake Young Women Minutes, June 9, 1881, CHL; Santaquin Ward, Utah Stake, Relief Society Minutes, vol. 3, July 1, 1875, CHL.

55. Weber Stake Young Women Minutes, Sept. 9, 1881; Weber Stake Young Women Minutes, Mar. 14, 1884.

56. Nauvoo Female Relief Society, minute book, 1842–1844, May 27, 1842, 57–58, CHL.

57. Joseph Smith, Journal, Book 3, July 15, 1843–February 29, 1844, September 28, 1843, in Andrew H. Hedges, Alex D. Smith, and Brent M. Rogers, eds., *The Joseph Smith Papers: Journals*. Volume 3 (Salt Lake City: Church Historian's Press, 2015), 104; "endowment, n.", Oxford Dictionary of English (Oxford: Oxford University Press).

58. Wilford Woodruff, journal, 1833–1898, December 23, 1843, CHL; Bathsheba W. Smith, Deposition, 8th Circuit Court Testimony, 1892, CHL.

59. Mercy Fielding Thompson, "Recollections of the Prophet Joseph Smith," *Juvenile Instructor* 27.13 (July 1, 1892): 400.

60. Bathsheba W. Smith, "Pioneer Stake," *Woman's Exponent* 34.2–3 (July/Aug. 1905):14.

61. Carol Cornwall Madsen, "Mormon Women and the Temple: Toward a New Understanding," in *Sisters in Spirit: Mormon Women in Historical and Cultural Perspective*, edited by Maureen Ursenbach Beecher and Lavina Fielding Anderson (Urbana: University of Illinois Press, 1987), 88.

62. See Stapley, *The Power of Godliness*, 26, 29, 84.

63. Andrew F. Ehat, "Joseph Smith's Introduction of Temple Ordinances and the 1844 Mormon Succession Question," master's thesis, Brigham Young University, Provo, UT, 1982, 63.

64. Richard L. Bushman, *Joseph Smith: Rough Stone Rolling* (New York: Alfred A. Knopf, 2006), 439–40.

65. M. Elizabeth Little, "Kanab Relief Society," *Woman's Exponent* 9.21 (Apr. 1, 1881), 165; see also Maureen Ursenbach Beecher, "The Eliza Enigma," *Dialogue*: 11.1 (Spring

1978), 38; Linda King Newell, "The Historical Relationship of Mormon Women and Priesthood," in *Women and Authority: Re-emerging Mormon Feminism*, edited by Maxine Hanks (Salt Lake City: Signature Books, 1992), 23–48.

66. For example, see Big Cottonwood Ward, Granite Stake, Relief Society Minutes, vol. 1, July 7, 1869, 59–61; Lehi Ward, Alpine Stake, Relief Society Minutes, vol. 1, Oct. 27, 1869, 26–29; Payson Ward, Utah Stake, vol. 1, Sept. 9, 1871, 110, all sources CHL.

67. See Jill C. Mulvay Derr, "Eliza R. Snow and The Woman Question," *BYU Studies* 16.2 (Apr. 1976): 259; Beecher, "The Eliza Enigma," 41; Boyd Jay Petersen, "'Redeemed from the Curse Placed Upon Her': Dialogic Discourse on Eve in the *Woman's Exponent*," *Journal of Mormon History* 40.1 (Winter 2014): 135–74.

68. Eliza R. Snow, "An Address," 63; Derr et al., *First Fifty Years of Relief Society*, 388.

69. Lehi Ward, Relief Society Minutes, vol. 1, Oct. 27, 1869, 26–29, CHL. See Ryan G. Tobler, "'Saviors on Mount Zion': Mormon Sacramentalism, Mortality, and the Baptism for the Dead," *Journal of Mormon History* 39.4 (Fall 2013): 182–238.

70. Joseph Smith, Discourse, March 27, 1842, Nauvoo, Illinois, the Joseph Smith Papers Online, accessed May 15, 2023, https://www.josephsmithpapers.org/paper-summary/discourse-27-march-1842/1. Although Joseph Smith had preached the doctrine of baptism for the dead in August 1840 and then again in October 1840, the ordinance was not practiced until 1842.

71. Jane Neyman, "Statements," Nov. 29, 1854, Joseph Smith History Documents, CHL.

72. Jill Mulvay Derr, *Mrs. Smith Goes to Washington: Eliza R. Snow Smith's Visit to Southern Utah*, Juanita Brooks Lecture Series, pamphlet (St. George, UT: Dixie State University Press, 2004), 22–23.

73. Esther, "Celestial Marriage, Opening a New Era," *Woman's Exponent* 6.11 (Nov. 1, 1877), 83.

74. Elmina S. Taylor, *Biographical Sketch*, January 1881, CHL.

75. Lydia Ann Wells, *Papers*, March 28, 1881, CHL, 2.

76. Joseph Fielding Smith, *Life of Joseph F. Smith* (Salt Lake City: Deseret News Press, 1938), 4.

PART II

Theological Explorations

CHAPTER 8

Notes on Life, Grace, and Atonement

ADAM S. MILLER

Originally published in *Rube Goldberg Machines: Essays in Mormon Theology* (Greg Kofford Books, 2012), 3–20. Original paginations appear in square brackets.

1. The King James Version of the New Testament uses the English word "atonement" only once. In Romans 5:11, it renders the Greek word *katallagē*: "And not only so, but we also joy in God through our Lord Jesus Christ, by whom we have now received the atonement." Though *katallagē* occurs elsewhere in the New Testament, it is translated as atonement only in this passage. Here, the word means reconciliation. More broadly, *katallagē* is perhaps related to the English word "catalyst,"[1] and, at root, it means to change or exchange, as in to reconcile estranged parties by precipitating a change from enmity to friendship.[2]
2. The LDS Bible Dictionary entry on "atonement" reads, in part, like this: "The word describes the setting 'at one' of those who have been estranged, and denotes the reconciliation of man to God. Sin is the cause of the estrangement, and therefore the purpose of the atonement is to correct or overcome the consequences of sin." In this way, the English word atonement is felicitous. To atone is to catalyze a reconciliation that sets things "at-one" with each other. In particular, the atonement sets humans at-one with God. Here, Jesus, as the Christ, is the catalyst for this gathering in one.
3. Christ: a title that refers to Jesus's role as the one who catalyzes atonement.
4. In Mormonism, Christ's work of atonement is generally seen as operating on two related but distinct planes. I propose that, as a basic schema, we should see it as working on at least three. Traditionally,

Christ's atonement: (1) gathers up and reunites human bodies with human spirits through the resurrection, and (2) reunites or reconciles human beings with God. This is sound Biblical doctrine. But in light of Joseph Smith's revelations, [4] it seems essential to see the atonement as being at work on at least one additional plane: Christ catalyzes not only the reunion of bodies with spirits and humans with God but, additionally, he gathers and seals husbands to wives and parents to children. Christ's work will not end until the whole human family has been gathered together as "one."

5. Resurrection: a name for how Christ's atonement catalyzes the body.
6. Repentance: a name for how Christ's atonement catalyzes an individual's reunion with the grace of God.
7. Gathering: a name for how Christ's atonement macro-catalyzes the sealing of human families (and, in the end, the whole human family) as one great family.
8. Christ's atonement: that which catalyzes the life of the body (resurrection), the life of the soul (repentance), and the life of the family (gathering).
9. Christ's atonement: the marrow in life's bone.
10. "I am come that they might have life, and that they might have it more abundantly" (John 10:10).
11. Discussions of atonement should begin with and lead back to life. Not life in the abstract, but life as it is lived in the everyday. Life with its damp, earthy smell, its messy embeddedness, its sticky embodiment. Life with all of its breathing, sleeping, speaking, eating, defecating, building, feeling, figuring, copulating, and gesturing.
12. A common feature at work in all of this living is that *things are given and things are received*. Breath, rest, words, food, excrement, handiwork, sensations, ideas, bodies, and intentions—each of them, the very stuff of life, are given and each of them are received. Life is this giving.
13. A guiding axiom: life is givenness.
14. A theological version of this axiom: life is grace.
15. Grace names what comes as a *gift*. In short, grace names what is given. Or, more precisely: grace names, as Jean-Luc Marion puts it, the *givenness* of whatever is given and received.[3]
[5] 16. Givenness names the giving and receiving that constitute life. It names our interdependence. It names a dynamic process of exchange, of giving and receiving, acceptance and conversion, that is always already dependent on things outside of itself. Here, to be alive, to give and receive, is to be in an open relation of interdependence with the world for food, air, words, materials, sensations, companionship.
17. Should we be surprised to find life itself defined in terms of exchange (*katallagē*)?

18. The primary difficulty faced in approaching life in terms of grace is that grace so easily slips the knot of our attention. Our preoccupation with w*hat* is given and received so easily eclipses any awareness of its having been given, of its *givenness*. How easy it is to receive a gift from someone and, in light of its heft, shine, and appeal, forget that it is a gift. How difficult it is to keep its giftedness at the forefront of our attention.
19. Addressing ourselves to the givenness of life (and not just to what is given), will require a kind of focused attention that we don't generally employ. We will have to attend to the immediacy of life with a kind of awareness that we rarely bring to bear. We will have to shift down a few gears, leave off the gas, and be patient enough to linger with the givenness of the present moment. If we are racing off to somewhere else, we will see only what is given and its givenness will fail to appear.
20. In Matthew, Jesus gives clear instructions on *how* to attend to the givenness of life in its immediacy:

    > Therefore I say unto you, Take no thought for your life, what ye shall eat, or what ye shall drink; nor yet for your body, what ye shall put on. Is not the life more than meat, and the body than raiment? Behold the fowls of the air: for they sow not, neither do they reap, nor gather into barns; yet your heavenly Father feedeth them. Are ye not much better than they? Which of you by taking thought can add one cubit unto his stature? And why take ye thought for raiment? Consider the lilies of the field, how they grow; they toil not, neither do they spin: And yet I say unto you, That even Solomon in all his glory was not arrayed like one of these. Wherefore, if God so clothe the grass of the field, which to day is, and to morrow is cast into the oven, shall he not [6] much more clothe you, O ye of little faith? Therefore take no thought, saying, What shall we eat? or, What shall we drink? or, Wherewithal shall we be clothed? (For after all these things do the Gentiles seek:) for your heavenly Father knoweth that ye have need of all these things. But seek ye first the kingdom of God, and his righteousness; and all these things shall be added unto you. Take therefore no thought for the morrow: for the morrow shall take thought for the things of itself. Sufficient unto the day is the evil thereof (Matt 6:25–34).

21. A formula for attending to the givenness of life: take no thought for tomorrow but attend to the unconditional character of the present moment.
22. To be catalyzed by the atonement: to see and enter the kingdom of God as it is manifest in the grace of whatever is given in the present moment.

23. The gospel: a promise that joy does not depend on what is given but on its givenness.
24. With respect to grace or givenness everyday language tends to fail. It tends to fail because everyday language focuses our attention on the "what" of whatever is given rather than on its givenness. For the sake of grace, I propose that we distinguish between two ways of talking. One way of talking (our everyday way), focuses on the *conditional* nature of whatever is given. The other way of talking focuses on the *unconditional* givenness of whatever is given.
25. Where our everyday way of talking (about religion or anything else) emphasizes the conditional, *sequential* nature of life, this other way of talking emphasizes the absolute or *nonsequential* character of life's present givenness. In order to approach the atonement in terms of life and in order to approach life in terms of givenness, it is necessary (at least initially) to bracket sequential discourse in favor of a nonsequential approach.
26. What is the difference between a sequential approach to life and a nonsequential one? Where sequential theologies are primarily *mythological*, nonsequential theologies are not.

[7] 27. What do I mean by mythological? By mythological I have two things in mind. First, I have in mind the original meaning of the Greek word *mythos*. In Greek, mythos simply means something like "story" or "narrative explanation." In this sense, to say that a sequential theology is mythological is just to say that it foregrounds the sequential narration of a series of events. Here, sequence means story.
28. Sequential theology also tends to be mythological in that the scope of its temporal extension often exceeds the bounds of our present, mortal experience. As a result, these narrative sequences tend to depend heavily on symbolic or anticipatory references that are significantly lacking in presently available content. In this sense, sequential theologies also tend to be mythological in that they rely on references to what is *not* given. Let's say: a theology that is grounded in what is not presently given is mythological.
29. What, then, is nonsequential theology? A nonsequential theology would be occupied with the givenness of what *is* presently given, rather than with the place of the given in the arc of a larger temporal sequence. In this sense, it would differ from a sequential theology precisely in that it would be non-mythological. Rather than reading key theological ideas in terms of an overarching, cosmic narrative headed toward some particular end, a nonsequential theology would read them in light of the key features of our present lived experience of the world.

30. An additional note about the weakness of a sequential approach. Sequential theologies, as sequential, tend to be biased in favor of works in a way that obscures grace. Why? Sequential theologies, due to their temporal structures, tend to highlight the importance of projects. If I want to accomplish a certain end, then I'll need to do a certain amount of work. The work itself is sequential and our relation to the end or outcome at which the work aims is also ordered in terms of a "*first* works, *then* outcome" sequence. In order to get result A, I must first do X then Y then Z. In this sense, sequential or mythological theologies are built on the foundation of a *conditional* works/outcome understanding of objects and events that tends to subordinate and instrumentalize the work as a means to an end. This sequential instrumentalization of what is given as a means to an end occludes the *unconditional* character of grace and givenness.

[8] 31. Ironically, sequential approaches to work tend to also obscure the unconditional worth of work itself. To the extent that work is instrumentalized as a means to an end, its value is conditioned by that end. Work, in and of itself, is devalued. In order to take work seriously, a theology would have to uncouple work from its outcomes and consider it nonsequentially. That is to say, in order to take work seriously *as work*, we would have to acknowledge its unconditional givenness. We would have to see work *as* a grace.

32. Even when sequential theologies do take up the question of grace, such theologies tend to read grace as a kind of supplement that is useful because it does the *work* that our normal works cannot do. Say I'm trying to get to heaven (i.e., I'm trying to go from where I am now, point A, to someplace that comes later in the sequence, point B), but I'm a sinner and my works aren't sufficient. Grace, on this model, is a name for what does for me the work that I'm unable to do and, thus, allows the sequence to reach the desired end. Even when grace is valorized or prioritized in a sequential theology, it is not prioritized as such but only as a modulation of work.

33. In relation to sequence, grace always gets described as a special *kind* of work.

34. This difficulty coincides with the primary problem faced by all of the recent (but welcome) work that has been done on grace among Mormons by writers like Stephen Robinson and Robert Millet. For instance, Robinson's famous "parable of the bicycle,"[4] despite its explicit valorization of grace, is a strongly sequential bit of theology that valorizes grace precisely *as* a special kind of work. The little girl, wanting a particular outcome (the acquisition of a bicycle) and finding herself unable to reach it with her own bit of change, is saved by a father whose earning power is far in excess of her own. Whatever the

merits of this story (and the parable is not without them), it clearly reads grace from the instrumentalizing perspective of work itself. Here, grace is a means to a noble end, *but a means nonetheless*. To this degree, it leaves grace, as an unconditioned end in itself (i.e., as givenness), untouched.

35. From a nonsequential perspective, grace is not a kind of conditional supplement to the present moment that takes us to some other [9] place we would rather be. Rather, grace *is* the unconditional fullness of the present moment.

36. Grace is the substance of life itself.

37. We might also mark the difference between sequential and nonsequential approaches in terms of a distinction between foreground and background. Our awareness of the world typically unfolds as the interplay between a given focal point (or foreground) and a withdrawn periphery (or background). In most experiences, something will *take* center stage and something else will *be* the stage.

38. In terms of this foreground/background distinction we might say that sequential thinking emphasizes how the present moment is conditionally embedded in a larger temporal sequence of past, present, and future events. In sequential thinking, the present moment withdraws and is overshadowed by our concern for the past and the future. Nonsequential thinking, on the other hand, is a kind of attention that foregrounds an awareness of the present moment as unconditionally present. Here, a strong degree of present moment awareness narrowly focuses our attention in such a way as to allow the sequential connection of the present to its own past and future to significantly withdraw into the background.

39. Thesis: the givenness of life (and, with it, the grace of Christ's atonement) appears to the degree that the absolute character of the present moment is foregrounded as such.

40. Or, the givenness of life (and, with it, the grace of Christ's atonement) appears to the degree that the present moment is received as unconditionally imposed without regard to how one arrived there or where one is going. The atonement, as what gives life, is what calls us back to the living grace of the present moment.

41. The present moment is absolute or unconditioned because, regardless of its place in a larger sequence, it is—right now—irreparably whatever it is.

42. Givenness: the irreparability of *this* present moment.

[10] 43. Life is never given in either the past or the future. Rather, life is forever and always and only given in the present.

44. Sequence is seductive. To the degree that past or future events dominate our attention and cause the richness of the present moment to

withdraw into the background of our lived experience, we die and become enemies of the kingdom of God. In this sense, we die a thousand deaths every day. Failing to be fully present, we fail to be at-one with our bodies, with God, and with the people around us. Failing to be present, we suffer that triple death of death, sin, and scattering. Only grace (i.e., the givenness of the present moment) can save us from this fate.

45. Nothing could be more natural than being seduced by sequence. Indeed, the death induced by this seduction is what defines the "natural" man as such. The natural man, King Benjamin tells his people, is a man in revolt, an enemy who refuses the present, a fugitive who fails to receive what is given or give what is required.

> The natural man is an enemy to God, and has been from the fall of Adam, and will be, forever and ever, unless he yields to the enticing of the Holy Spirit, and putteth off the natural man and becometh a saint through the atonement of Christ the Lord, and becometh as a child, submissive, meek, humble, patient, full of love, willing to submit to all things which the Lord seeth fit to inflict upon him, even as a child doth submit to his father. (Mos 3:19)

46. The natural man is an enemy to the present moment and will be forever and ever unless he yields to the enticing of life and becomes as a child, submissive, receptive, humble, patient, full of love, willing to submit to all things which life, in the present moment, sees fit to inflict upon him.
47. It is the absolute character of givenness that chafes us so. The present moment, so irreparably and unconditionally given, brings the full weight of life to bear upon us. Givenness gives without consulting us, without condition, without recourse. We suffer the imposition of its grace with an unavoidable passivity. In opening our hands to receive what it offers and give what it requires, we must confess our dependence, our insufficiency, our lack of autonomy. But we grit our teeth at the shame of it, refuse to suffer the grace of it, and seek refuge from the present moment in the conditional character of sequence. We cower [11] before the absolute, failing to recognize its image in our countenances, and hide behind a fragile veil of fantasies, memories, and projected improvements. We withdraw from the present, abandon life, give ourselves wholly to the past or future, and die.
48. Sin: a refusal of life.
49. Sin: a refusal of givenness.
50. Sin: a refusal of grace.
51. Sin: a refusal of the present moment.
52. Sin: death.

53. Grace is a name for that which we suffer. It is because we suffer it that we refuse it. In refusing it we dream of something other than life—i.e., we dream of death.
54. In sin, we come unplugged. When we refuse the givenness of life and withdraw from the present moment, we're left to wander the world undead. Zombielike, we wander from one moment to the next with no other goal than to get somewhere else, be someone else, see something else—anywhere, anyone, anything other than what is given here and now. We're busy. We've got goals and projects. We've got plans. We've got fantasies. We've got daydreams. We've got regrets and memories. We've got opinions. We've got distractions. We've got games and songs and movies and a thousand TV shows. We've got anything and everything other than a firsthand awareness of our own lived experience of the present moment.
55. If we are not capable of being where we are right now, we will not be capable of being fully present when we arrive at some ostensibly more desirable destination later on. Thus unplugged, what good would heaven be?
56. The zombie life of sin sets us wandering away from the present moment because it sifts everything through a screen of preference that inevitably filters out the absolute givenness of life itself. Spiritually undead, we see things only in terms of our own (often legitimate) preferences. Undead, we see things only in terms of our selves. How will this benefit me? How will this harm me? How might this current situation [12] be leveraged for my own profit? If something doesn't show up as being to my advantage, then typically it doesn't show up at all. Absent the appearance of what fails to comport with my preferences, the fountain of life is squeezed back to a trickle.
57. With respect to grace, the *legitimacy* of my preferences for pleasant or productive things is a secondary issue at best. Grace is not concerned with preferences, legitimate or not. Grace, in its prodigality, is relentlessly and single-mindedly concerned with just one thing: the givenness of *whatever* is given, regardless of how such things may or may not comport with my preferences.
58. Grace, as unconditional, is indifferent to the conditions set by my preferences—even my legitimate ones.
59. Sin refuses givenness (and, thus, life) by screening experience in terms of its perceived desirability. Some things are reflexively marked as desirable and so we hunger for them and fantasize about them. Some things are reflexively marked as undesirable and so we flee from them and worry over them. Some things are reflexively marked as neither, and so, we ignore them.
60. Sin refuses the *unconditional* givenness of life by imposing its own *conditions*.

61. The results are predictable. Striving after the gnat of pleasure, straining away from the sting of pain, we ignore the bulk of life and marvel at our own morbidity. Failing to be where we are, to receive what is given, to *feel* what we are feeling, we fantasize instead about what has not come, fret over what has already passed, and are bored to tears by the grace of what is actually present.
62. Fantasy, fear, and boredom: the hallmarks of sin.
63. Boredom: *the* hallmark of sin?
64. Seen nonsequentially, grace is not what insures a desirable outcome by restricting our experience to feeling only good and pleasant things. (The heavens themselves weep, after all.) Rather, grace *is* feeling. Here, the choice is not between feeling good things or feeling bad things. The choice is more fundamental: *it is between feeling and not feeling*. We can refuse to feel what we want to avoid only at the cost of feeling itself.

[13] 65. Sequential and nonsequential approaches are oriented by different root values. A sequential, works-based approach, oriented by the acquisition of some projected end or outcome, sees everything as conditioned by the end it is pursuing. That which conduces to the desired end is good and that which does not is evil. For a nonsequential approach, in which the present moment is foregrounded as absolute regardless of its relation to the larger sequence, everything is oriented instead by the difference between life and death.
66. Good and evil are the root values of a mythological, works-based, sequential approach. Life and death are the root values of a nonsequential approach.
67. There is nothing wrong with sequence. There is nothing wrong with rightly and legitimately distinguishing between good and evil. There is nothing wrong with wanting to promote joy and reduce suffering. But it is a question of what must come first, of what gets foregrounded. If good and evil are foregrounded (however legitimately) and used as a screen for sifting and judging the givenness of life, then we will have neither life, nor good, nor evil, but only death. Only a fearless and faithful submission to the givenness of the present moment in its entirety opens the way to a world in which goodness can *live*.
68. Sin: judging life by the standard of goodness.
69. Atonement: catalyzing goodness through a reception of life.
70. Jesus's call to suspend judgment—"Judge not that ye be not judged" (Matt 7:1)—is a call to suspend preference in favor of the absolute givenness of the present moment. It is a call to suspend sequence in favor of the nonsequential, good and evil in favor of life. In Matthew's account, this call to suspend judgment immediately follows the closing verses of chapter 6 where we are told to "take therefore

no thought for the morrow: for the morrow shall take thought for the things of itself" (6:34). Only this suspension of judgment and sequence can give life room to blossom in the present moment.

71. Jesus catalyzes atonement by modeling it. He gives life by receiving it. It is his fearless and faithful submission *to the entirety* of the present moment, regardless of his preferences, that opens the way to a world in which goodness can live.

[14] 72. When the resurrected Christ finally appears to his disciples in the New World, he greets them with these words:

> I am the light and the life of the world; and I have drunk out of that bitter cup which the Father hath given me, and have glorified the Father in taking upon me the sins of the world, in which I have suffered the will of the Father in all things from the beginning (3 Ne 11:11).

Here, light, life, suffering, bitterness, and glory all coincide in Christ's unremitting acceptance of *everything* willed by the Father.

73. Sequentially, Christ's claim to *be* "the life of the world" is easily taken as a metaphysical claim about his being the conditional cause of the world's creation. However, nonsequentially, we might more productively read this as a claim that Christ has conquered death and sin by wholly receiving the unconditional givenness of the living, present moment as such. Read nonsequentially, Christ's claim is one of identification rather than causation. Because he refused to withdraw from the absolute fullness of the present moment and hide in the undead vagaries of fantasy, memory, or distraction, Christ is filled with life, grace, and truth.

74. Christ's prayer in the Garden of Gethsemane is the focal point of his atoning work. As Matthew recounts it, on the eve of his crucifixion, Christ retired to the Garden of Gethsemane. There, in the darkness, a little distance from his disciples, he "fell on his face, and prayed, saying, O my Father, if it be possible, let this cup pass from me: nevertheless not as I will, but as thou wilt" (Matt 26:39). The key word in this account is the adverb rendered in the King James Version as "nevertheless" (a translation of the Greek word *plēn*). This "nevertheless" is crucial because it inserts a gap, a space, between Christ's legitimate preference for what is good rather than harmful (i.e., a space between his judgments) and his unconditional reception of the present moment. It allows him to receive the givenness of whatever is given (i.e., whatever may be the will of his Father) without first filtering it through a screen of preferences and judgments.

75. "Let this cup pass from me: *nevertheless...*"

76. The cup that Christ must drink is life itself and, even if bitter, he will choose to drink all of it before he chooses to be undead. His commitment to life is absolute.

[15] 77. Christ's "nevertheless" privileges the unconditional character of the present moment without regard to where that moment came from or where it is going. His nevertheless pries open a space between the present moment and its place in the sequence of events. This space is givenness. It is grace. It is freedom.

78. Christ's nevertheless *is* life.

79. Say that, in the present moment, something is given that I do not want, that I would prefer not to receive. I become sick, I lose my job, I experience something humiliating, a loved one passes. A sinful response to what is given would involve my withdrawal from this difficult present moment. As a natural man, I would naturally take refuge from the difficulty in fantasy, memories, distractions, blame, and complaints (i.e., in sequence). However, to withdraw in this way would be sinful regardless of whether I have a legitimate preference for what is good rather harmful. Whatever my preferences, the present is imposed unconditionally, absolutely, and to flee its givenness, even on legitimate grounds, is to choose the path of the undead rather than the path of life.

80. The key to grace is Christ's nevertheless. If what is given is not preferable or desirable, I must *nevertheless* receive it as it is given, as *whatever* kind of grace it may be.

81. Say that, in the present moment, something is given that I *do* want. I may have good health, find a better job, see the recovery of a loved one. Here, the same holds as in the previous example. If I selectively *receive* (rather than selectively *reject* as in the previous example), I will still have chosen the path of the undead rather than the path of life. The screen of preference is just as ruinous, just as deadening, when it comes to things that I do want as when it comes to things that I do not. The desirable must be welcomed in precisely the same way as what is undesirable: it must be received with the equanimity of a nevertheless that allows it to appear as what it is, as whatever kind of grace it may be. Never more, never less.

82. The gospel: a promise that joy does not depend on what is given but on its givenness.

83. Nevertheless: that which unlocks givenness.

[16] 84. Nevertheless: that which catalyzes, with open hands, the give and take of life.

85. Nevertheless: that which recognizes in the absolute character of the present moment its own countenance.

86. Nevertheless: that which, no matter what is given, is never the less.

87. Nevertheless: atonement.
88. A new parable of the bicycle. A small girl wants a bicycle that she does not have. "I do not have what I would prefer," she thinks to herself. "*Nevertheless* my joy does not depend on *what* is given but on my reception of its unconditional givenness."
89. A second new parable of the bicycle. As a result of fortunate circumstances, a small girl *gets* precisely the bicycle she wants. "I have exactly what I would prefer," she thinks to herself. "Nevertheless, my joy *still* does not depend on *what* is given but on my reception of its unconditional givenness in the immediacy of *this* present moment."
90. Superimposing our judgments on the present moment, selectively grasping after, fending off, or ignoring what is given, we magnify our suffering. The screen of preference inserts into the present moment a self-escalating feedback loop of craving and repulsion. Here, life is relentlessly looped out beyond itself and reflected back to itself only through the vagaries of sequence, only through the prism of our desires and fears for the past and future.
91. Judging, we never trust what is given to show itself as what it is and, instead, always assume that its truth could only appear in relation to our *own* desires.
92. Once our attention has shifted away from the work of receiving the givenness of whatever is given and toward judging the given, then we've come ungrounded and unplugged. The truth, together with the present moment, will withdraw, and all of our fears and anxieties will grow, unchecked by truth, with an unsustainable compounding of interest. Nothing is so bad that the self-escalating loop of our own judgments cannot make it worse. Nothing is so good that the self-grasping loop of our own judgments cannot ruin its goodness.
[17] 93. Though similar in function and result, my screen of preferences is not identical to yours. The particulars of my preferences depend on the situations in which they took shape, on the materials of time, place, and circumstance out of which they were woven. Above all, the particulars of my screen were shaped by my relationships with those closest to me in my earliest years: my parents and family.
94. By way of a thousand copies, inversions, and emendations, desires are routed, wired, and rewired by these family relationships around specific objects, goals, and projects and then knotted into unique patterns of preference. These tangled and codependent knots of familial fears and desires are what we use to screen and judge our experience of the world.
95. The fear, craving, and ignorance that characterize sin are responsive, mimetic, and contagious.
96. My screen of preference, in its particularity, is woven from these tangled, familial threads. The imposition of this screen of prefer-

ences is what separates me from the grace of this present moment. Separated from the grace of this present moment, I come unplugged from my own lived experience of this world, this life, and this body. Unplugged from my own life and body, I die.

97. Or, again: my separation from my own body is the result of my separation from the present moment. This separation from the grace of the present moment is sin. Sin results when I attempt to screen what is given on the basis of my preferences. The particulars of my preferences are profoundly shaped by my relationships with my parents and family.

98. Pull the thread of sin and both family and body inevitably come with it.

99. To address the unconditional character of the present moment is to address the nature of my relationships with my parents and family. To lay aside the screen of judgment and preference, in favor of life, is to set myself the task of unknotting the threads of fear and desire that have prevented me from unconditionally embracing my family and my family from unconditionally embracing me.

100. To embrace one's family: to embrace one's dependent origination.

[18] 101. To embrace one's dependent origination: to *willingly* suffer the grace of life as something that we cannot master or repay.

102. In Section 128 of the Doctrine and Covenants, Joseph Smith underscores this essential link between personal and familial redemption:

> It is sufficient to know, in this case, that the earth will be smitten with a curse unless there is a welding link of some kind or other between the fathers and the children, upon some subject or other—and behold what is that subject? It is the baptism for the dead. For we without them cannot be made perfect; neither can they without us be made perfect. Neither can they nor we be made perfect without those who have died in the gospel also; for it is necessary in the ushering in of the dispensation of the fulness of times, which dispensation is now beginning to usher in, that a whole and complete and perfect union, and welding together of dispensations, and keys, and powers, and glories should take place, and be revealed from the days of Adam even to the present time (D&C 128:18).

103. With this complex account of atonement, Mormonism makes plain what is otherwise left implicit: liberation from the bonds of sin cannot be disentangled from the work of sorting out our family relationships. The screen of preference upon which sin depends is forged in family fires and must be addressed in precisely that context. We cannot be saved from sin and death without our families, nor they without us.

104. The welding link that ushers in a whole and complete and perfect

union, a welding together of bodies, hearts, and families: Christ's infinitely atoning, catalyzing "nevertheless."

105. Reconciliation with one's family: an absolutely integral element of *any and all* salvation from one's own sinfulness.
106. Reconciliation with one's body, with God's grace, and with one's family is a difficult and acute affair. The unconditional character of the present moment purifies our hearts—but only with a baptism of fire. As F. Enzio Busche beautifully describes it:

> [If we are] enlightened by the Spirit of truth, we will then be able to pray for the increased ability to endure truth and not to be made angry by it (see 2 Ne 28:28). In the depth of such a prayer, we may [19] finally be led to that lonesome place where we suddenly see ourselves naked in all soberness. Gone are all the little lies of self-defense. We see ourselves in our vanities and false hopes for carnal security. We are shocked to see our many deficiencies, our lack of gratitude for the smallest things. We are now at that sacred place that seemingly only a few have courage to enter, because this is that horrible place of unquenchable pain in fire and burning. . . . This is the place where suddenly the atonement of Christ is understood and embraced. . . . With this fulfillment of love in our hearts, we will never be happy anymore just by being ourselves or living our own lives. We will not be satisfied until we have surrendered our lives into the arms of the loving Christ, and until He has become the doer of all our deeds and He has become the speaker of all our words.[5]

107. That place of unquenchable fire and burning: the present moment.
108. That place of unquenchable fire and burning: life.
109. That place of unquenchable fire and burning: atonement.
110. Lay down the burden of judgment and preference. Lay aside your defensive goals, projects, and explanations. Stand in the fire of the present moment, just as you are, receiving it just as it is, as whatever kind of grace it may actually and unconditionally be. Lay aside sin and *live*.
111. The first and most pronounced mark of one's unconditional return to the present moment: a baptism of fire in which one's body is once again felt, lived, and alive.
112. To foreground the present moment is, first and foremost, to foreground the depth, breadth, and complexity of our embodiment, our sensations, our groundedness in the flesh. It is to feel the breath in one's lungs, the blood in one's veins, the light in one's eyes, the rushing of a mighty wind in one's ears. As Parley Pratt puts it:

> Spirit adapts itself to all these organs or attributes. It quickens all the intellectual faculties, increases, enlarges, expands and purifies

all the natural passions and affections; and adapts them, by the gift of wisdom, to their lawful use. It inspires, develops, cultivates and matures all the fine toned sympathies, joys, tastes, kindred feelings and [20] affections of our nature. It inspires virtue, kindness, goodness, tenderness, gentleness and charity. It develops beauty of person, form and features. It tends to health, vigour, animation and social feeling. It develops and invigorates all the faculties of the physical and intellectual man. It strengthens, invigorates, and gives tone to the nerves. In short, it is, as it were, marrow to the bone, joy to the heart, light to the eyes, music to the ears, and life to the whole being.[6]

113. This Spirit-worked reunion with one's body in the everlasting fire of the present moment is the essence of resurrection.
114. Resurrection: a name for how Christ's atonement catalyzes the body.
115. Repentance: a name for how Christ's atonement catalyzes an individual's reunion with the grace of God.
116. Gathering: a name for how Christ's atonement macro-catalyzes the sealing of human families (and, in the end, the whole human family) as a family.
117. There is no repentance without resurrection. There is no resurrection without gathering. There is no gathering without repentance.
118. Atonement: a name for how the resurrection of my body, my reunion with the grace of God, and the sealing of my family all coincide as *one* in the absolute givenness of this present moment.

Notes

1. Technically, "catalyst" is a Latinized form of the Greek verb *katalyō*, meaning "to dissolve" or "to break down."

2. See Walter Bauer, "katallassō," *A Greek-English Lexicon of the New Testament and Other Early Christian Literature*, edited by Frederick William Danker, translated by William F. Arndt, F. Wilbur Gingrich, and F. W. Danker, 3rd edition (Chicago: University of Chicago Press, 2000), 521; See the discussion of the term in chapter 2, Eric D. Huntsman, "Latter-day Saints and Atonement in the New Testament," and chapter 4, Nicholas J. Frederick, "'Atonement' in the Book of Mormon," above.

3. Cf. Jean-Luc Marion, *Being and Givenness*, translated by Jeffrey L. Kosky (Stanford: Stanford University Press, 2002), 7–70.

4. Stephen E. Robinson, *Believing Christ: The Parable of the Bicycle and Other Good News* (Salt Lake City: Deseret Book, 1992), 30–34.

5. F. Enzio Busche, "Truth is the Issue," *Ensign* (Nov. 1993): 25–26.

6. Parley P. Pratt, *Key to the Science of Theology* (Liverpool: F. D. Richards, 1855), 98–99.

CHAPTER 9

Atonement and Retributive Justice

FIONA GIVENS

In the eschatology of The Church of Jesus Christ of Latter-day Saints (hereafter Latter-day Saint Church), the consummation of the Godhead's grand design for the universe occurs in a moving scene at once viscerally vivid and powerfully symbolic: "We will receive them into our bosom and they shall see us; and we will fall upon their necks and they shall fall upon our necks, and we will kiss each other; And there shall be mine abode, and it shall be Zion, which shall come forth out of all the creations which I have made" (Moses 7:63–64). This moment of climactic (re)unification captures the ultimate achievement for which Christ labors: a community fully integrated in love and harmony, bound to each other and to their God, after a harrowing but educative journey through mortality. According to the sacred texts of the Latter-day Saint Church, Zion is the goal toward which humankind, in collaboration with the Godhead, is striving. All humanity—having been battered and bruised psychologically, emotionally, and physically during their mortal sojourn—are made whole through the atonement. Zion is the concrete manifestation of a universal at-one-ment eventuating in a new world, immersed in the light of the Holy Spirit.

This vision of at-one-ment, culminating in Zion, is one of the key interventions of Restoration teachings. The Latter-day Saint faith sees itself as a divinely directed "restoration" predicated on repairing a conceived misdirection in early Christianity tantamount to a "great apostasy." As part of this restoration, Latter-day Saint theology promulgates a thoroughgoing revisioning of the atonement of Jesus Christ, the paramount doctrine of that Christian tradition. The scene from Enoch's vision (Moses 7:63–64) intimates a powerful and potentially novel conception of atonement as a comprehensive and universal project of reconciliation and healing. This theology has rich implications for how Latter-day Saint practitioners can enact these understandings of woundedness and healing in our social and political systems—including, as I will suggest, in Latter-day Saint attitudes toward contemporary penal practices.

However, as I hope to show in the pages following, a Restoration project begun so auspiciously has yet to break completely from atonement theologies that undergird much of the Western Christian tradition and fulfill this radical potential. I propose to do this by making two arguments in particular. First, that, starting with Tertullian, a legalistic view of salvation infiltrated and soon dominated Western atonement theology, evident not only in the theological language of sin and retributive punishment but strikingly manifest in penal codes and practices as well. And second, that Restoration teachings (and etymological insights) provide the means of a different conception, shifting from sin and retribution to woundedness and healing as the polarities that atonement might be reconceived to address. When these teachings are allied with the proliferating strands in contemporary theology and science attuned to suffering and trauma, Latter-day Saints can more effectively embody them in social and political institutions that often feature the most wounded among us.

Origins of Retributive Justice

The relationship between theologies of atonement and penal practice are tightly intertwined in Western Christian culture. One of the most dominant and enduring versions of atonement theory is satisfaction theory. First articulated by Anselm, this model stipulates that human sin offended "the honor of God and brought disharmony and injustice into the universe" and required a "debt payment . . . to restore God's honor or to restore order and justice in the universe." As J. Denny Weaver explains, the "voluntary death of Jesus paid or satisfied a debt to God's honor that sinful humans had no way of paying themselves."[1] In his book, *God's Just Vengeance*, Timothy Gorringe asserts that the penal system in England, for example, has its roots in this especially virulent version of atonement theology, which "provided one of the subtlest and most profound of . . . justifications, not only for hanging but for retributive punishment in general."[2] More specifically, he argues that the "connection of satisfaction theory with the retributive justice theory of punishment was a commonplace of late nineteenth-century theology. . . . In fact, satisfaction theory emerged in the eleventh century, at exactly the time as the criminal law took shape."[3] Satisfaction theory, in other words, finds its penal equivalent in retributive justice.

Retributive justice became central to North American Protestantism after the Reformation. As Diarmaid MacCulloch writes, "One of the most important consequences of the European Reformation was the export of a militant form of English Protestantism to North America,"[4] of which retributive justice was an element. As late as the nineteenth century, theologian William Paley explicitly linked the divine infliction of pain to the satisfaction of justice: "By the satisfaction of justice, I mean the retribution of so much pain for so much guilt; which . . . we expect at the hand of God, and which we are accustomed to consider as the order of things that . . . justice dictates and requires."[5] The philosopher Friedrich Nietzsche's analysis of the psychology behind such versions of justice—even or especially in the Christian version—seems accurate: "Every injury has its *equivalent* and can actually be paid back, even if only through the *pain* of the culprit. . . . To what extent can suffering balance debts of guilt? To the extent that to *make* suffer was in the highest degree pleasurable [emphases original]."[6] Therefore, Christ's suffering provides the satisfaction necessary to zero out the sum total of human offense, resulting in a state of equilibrium. Not only is the suffering and crucifixion of Christ necessary to repair the damage initiated by Adam's sinful fall, satisfaction theology emphasizes that only the punishment inflicted upon the innocent Christ at the behest of the Father can assuage his anger toward Adam and Eve and their subsequent human family.

The roots of atonement theology based on retributive justice are traceable to the writings of Tertullian (c.155–240? CE), the theologian from Carthage, a Roman province of Africa. A lawyer by profession, Tertullian created a legal framework for atonement theology. Framing atonement theology in the context of Roman law was a substantiative shift from the doctrine's earlier articulation among the Greek patristic fathers. Irenaeus (c. 120/140–c. 200/203), for example, suggested that atonement was educative rather than punitive—the movement from paradise to earth being a step closer to the divine life rather than a fall away from the Godhead, with eventual divinization to follow. These Fathers (including, among others, Origen, Gregory of Nyssa, and his sister, Macrina) regarded the statement in Genesis 3:22 rather more literally than did subsequent theologians: "They have become as one of us, knowing good and evil." Irenaeus declared that "Man has received the knowledge of good and evil . . . Wherefore he has . . . had a two-fold experience, possessing knowledge of both kinds, that with discipline he may make choice of the better things. But how, if he had had no knowledge of the contrary, could he have had instruction in that which is good? . . . How, then, shall he be a God, who has not as yet been made a man?"[7] Origen, a few decades later, had an equivalent view of morality as necessarily entailing the experience of good and evil: "You could not have reached the palm-groves unless you had experienced the harsh trials; you could not have reached the gentle springs without first having to overcome sadness and difficulties."[8] The view of humans as incomplete creations, like children "brought into being with all the imperfections endemic in human nature but with the prospect of development as part of God's creative plan," found "many supporters" in the early Christian centuries, notes B. R. Rees.[9]

In contrast to the emphasis among Greek patristic fathers on the educative repercussions of the fall and the moral development made possible by Christ's atonement, Christians influenced by Roman law interpreted the fall and atonement chiefly in penal terms. In his survey of Christian doctrines of atonement, the early twentieth-century Anglican theologian Hastings Rashdall described this influence in severe but illuminating terms: "It is hardly possible," he writes, "to exaggerate the importance of the effects exercised upon the development of theology [in] that the Greek Fathers had been trained in the schools of Greek philosophy, while education of the Latins had been for the most part an education in Roman law."[10] As a result, the "whole conception of religion—of God, of duty, and of salvation—is poisoned by the substitution of legal for moral conceptions. Morality is for [Tertullian], as for no previous Christian writer, a doing of the will of God . . . because an autocratic Deity commands it. . . . God is represented almost entirely as a criminal judge . . . Fear becomes the prevailing religious motive."[11]

With Tertullian, then, began the legalism which undergirds Western atonement theology—or what Nikolai Berdyaev refers to as "the forensic interpretation of Christianity."[12] The legacy of such a reading for the Christian West is prominent and pervasive. It has been noted that "the God in whom we choose to believe impacts human behaviour . . . [Consequently] those who believe in a God of wrath become wrathful with others."[13] This relationship between the perception of God's nature and of our relationships with each other is particularly salient in the retributive penal culture of North America.

Justice and Atonement in North America

Of the major Reformers, John Calvin's theory of retributive atonement exerted the greatest influence in the United States. Moving beyond Anselm's satisfaction theory of atonement in which Christ's sacrifice restores God's honor, Calvin develops a penal substitution theory first intimated by Justin Martyr and Tertullian. In Calvin's version, Christ pays the punishment for humankind's desertion by inserting himself between God's wrath and the fallen creation. God's anger is thereby propitiated. "By his sacrifice," in Calvin's words, Jesus "appeased the divine anger; by his blood washed away our stains; by his cross, bore our curse; and by his death, made satisfaction for us."[14] The influential John Milton describes Christ's atoning sacrifice in terms that are more poetic but equally as troubling. To God, the Father, Jesus offers intercession for humankind:

> Behold me then, me for him, life for life / I offer, on me let thine anger fall; / Account me man; I for his sake will leave Thy bosom, this glory next to thee /

> Freely put off... and for him lastly die... on me let Death wreck all his rage /... and return... to see thy face, wherein no cloud / Of anger shall remain, ... wrath shall be no more.[15]

While satisfaction atonement differs from penal substitutionary atonement, retribution is fundamental to both ideas. Through Adam and Eve's rebellion, Calvin argues that every descendant is born "tainted with the contagion of sin. ... Before we behold the light of the sun we are in God's sight defiled and polluted,"[16] "iniquity is an abomination to the Master under whom we live," and "those who, by wicked lives, provoke his anger, will not escape his vengeance."[17] God's vengeance, in Calvin's eyes, was often implemented by capital punishment—decreed by civil officials but under the guidance of proper ministers. As it is virtually impossible to know, with any degree of certainty, whom will be elected and whom will be damned, humankind is left to pass through mortality in terror like "a poor criminal with a rope around his neck."[18] For example, an acquaintance, Michael Servetus, was burned slowly at the stake after Calvin instigated charges against him for heresy, which Calvin justified in these terms: "Servetus... suffered the penalty due to his heresies... And what crime was it of mine if our Council, at my exhortation, indeed, but in conformity with the opinion of several Churches, took vengeance on his execrable blasphemies?"[19] In Calvin's Geneva, instances of capital punishment were recorded for homicide, witchcraft, theft, and sodomy, among other crimes.[20] In justifying the capital punishment of murderers, he argued that despite scriptural injunctions against killing, the "Lawgiver himself puts the sword into the hands of his [civil] ministers" to "execute [His] judgments."[21] And if criminals escape their civil punishment, he notes in another exegetical passage, "God sends executioners from other quarters."[22]

The "immensely influential" criminal metaphors encountered in Calvin's atonement theology and penal policies reveal a congruence of retributive conceptions in both his doctrine and Western Christian conceptions of damnation.[23] In the early Republic, revival sermons were replete with depictions of the evils of sin, and the fires of everlasting hell, in an attempt to frighten the populace into conversion and rebaptism. The most famous of these is, of course, Jonathan Edwards's oft-quoted sermon, "Sinners in the Hands of an Angry God," which he gave on a number of occasions to a rising cacophony of fearful cries throughout the congregation. This and similar sermons of itinerant revivalists employed fear as a motivator for religious reformation. Edwards's uncle was so frightened at the awful prospect of his imminent damnation that, following a revival in Northampton, he committed suicide in order to preempt his judgment. His nephew castigated his anxiety-ridden listeners with variants of the following: "[How] awful it is to be left behind on [the day of Redemption] to see so many feasting, while you are pining and perishing!"[24] Although Calvinism dominated the theological tradition in the United States, it was not without its opponents. Thomas Jefferson was one voice decrying this fear-instigating rhetoric. "It would be more pardonable," he declared, "to believe in no god at all, than to blaspheme him by the atrocious attributes of Calvin."[25]

Despite a backlash from other religious and philosophical quarters, this legacy of vengeful justice survives into the modern era. Marie Gottschalk argues that early colonists, Puritans in particular, "made virtually no distinction between sin and crime," establishing a penal justice system "that was in many ways another arm of religious authority."[26] As a result, a "narrow conception of retribution has become a central feature" of the American penal system with "mercy, forgiveness, and redemption" omitted.[27] While most Americans are aware of Alexis de Tocqueville and Gustave de Beaumont's praise for American democracy, few know of their criticisms of the American penal system. Both men wrote: "While society in the United States gives the example of the most extended liberty, the prisons of the same country offer the spectacle of the most complete despotism."[28] These trends were reinforced by nineteenth-century evangelical attitudes toward sin and punishment. "It is no accident," argues Timothy Gorringe, "that the new retributivism of current penal policy has gone along with the rise of Christian Fundamentalism, especially in the United States. Many of the arguments advanced in favor of it resemble those of evangelical Christians in the nineteenth century who believed that prisons ought to be places where criminals made atonement."[29] As a result, Gottschalk writes that the American penal system continues "long on degradation and short on mercy."[30]

This legacy is manifest in the distinctive features of the current U.S. carceral state: "the sheer size of its prison and jail population; its reliance on harsh degrading sanctions; and the persistence and centrality of the death penalty, the continuation of which is a key feature of the US carceral state."[31] Indeed, the United States leads the world in the number of adults incarcerated behind bars. Approximately seven million people "are under the supervision of the correctional system, including jail, prison, parole, probation, and other community service sanctions."[32] The number of people affected by the U.S. carceral state runs into the tens of millions. According to a former prison guard, if "there had to be a hell to house and punish evildoers after death," then prisons were needed to punish evildoers in life.[33] From its inception in the early Republic, America's criminal justice system has operated in imitation of God's retributive justice.

Latter-day Saint Tensions

Teachings and scripture of the Latter-day Saint Church manifest the influence of the legalistic atonement culture described above, while also containing the seeds of an alternate conception of justice and atonement. This is particularly evident in the first two presidencies of the Church under Joseph Smith and subsequently Brigham Young, which spanned a range of views on justice, atonement, retribution, and penal practices.

While in earlier years, Joseph Smith propounded traditional views of retributive justice,[34] by the time of his presidential platform of 1844, he had shifted toward rehabilitative reform: "Let us be one great family, and let there be a universal peace. Abolish the cruel custom of prisons (except certain cases), penitentiaries, courts-martial for desertion; and let reason and friendship reign over the ruins of ignorance and barbarity." Criminals, he argued, should be compassionately reformed, not damned; in the rare occasions where imprisonment was necessary, they should be a site of rehabilitation rather than punishment:

> Petition your state legislatures to pardon every convict in their several penitentiaries; blessing them as they go, and saying to them in the name of the Lord, *go thy way and sin no more*. Advise your legislators . . . to make the penalty applicable to work upon roads, public works, or any place where the culprit can be taught more wisdom and more virtue; And become more enlightened. Rigor and seclusion will never do as much to reform the propensities of man, as reason and friendship. Murder only can claim confinement or death. Let the Penitentiaries be turned into seminaries of learning, where intelligence, like the angels of heaven, would banish such fragments of barbarism: Imprisonment for debt is a meaner practice than the savage tolerates with all his ferocity. *Amor vincit omnia*. Love conquers all.[35]

Despite his exception for murderers, Joseph Smith's general confidence in the perfectible nature of mankind, when tutored by love and reason, was informed by a radical atonement theology of reconciliation and co-participation.

However, other Latter-day Saint teachings and scriptural passages bears the imprint of penal substitution theology. One prominent example, found in the Doctrine and Covenants, portrays the Son of God assuming a role very similar to that of the Christ of John Milton's *Paradise Lost*, inserting himself between his wrathful, vengeful Father and humankind. He pleads with his Father to "spare these my brethren" and to accept his suffering in lieu of theirs (D&C 45:3–5). Such attitudes are expressed in the Criminal Code of the State of Deseret. Published in 1851, under Young's leadership, the Criminal Code decreed that "when any person shall be found guilty of murder, under any of the preceding sections of this ordinance, and sent[enc]ed to die, he, she or they shall suffer death by being shot, hung or beheaded." The Criminal Code was informed by Young's infamous theology of "blood atonement" relegating penal substitution to a human rather than divine offering. While this idea exempts Christ from the responsibility for the lion's share of the atonement, it does leave humanity with its burden, thus seriously limiting the power and scope of the Divine to redeem.

> There are sins that men commit for which they cannot receive forgiveness in this world, or in that which is to come, and if they had their eyes open to see their true condition, they would be perfectly willing to have their blood spilt upon the ground, that the smoke thereof might ascend to heaven as an offering for their sins; and the smoking incense would atone for their sins, whereas, if such is not the case, they will stick to them and remain upon them in the spirit world.[36]

Blood atonement has long since been abandoned in the Latter-day tradition but some modern voices in the Latter-day Saint Church continued to affirm capital punishment as a necessary penalty for some sins. Bruce R. McConkie, in his *Mormon Doctrine*, declared that the practice was appropriately authorized by the state. In addition, quoting Leviticus 20:10, he lamented that "modern governments do not take the life of an adulterer . . . all of which is further evidence of the direful apostasy that prevails among . . . Christians," including his own religious tradition.[37] The Latter-day Saint Church ceased publishing *Mormon Doctrine* in 2010. However, as late as the 1970s, church and civic leaders publicly endorsed the continuation of capital punishment in *Church News* editorials and publications, and the 1992 *Encyclopedia of Mormonism* (semi-authoritatively) states, "capital punishment is viewed in the doctrines of the Church to be an appropriate penalty for murder."[38]

Only in more recent years has the Church moved from its pro–capital punishment position to one of neutrality. The Catholic and some non-evangelical Protestant churches officially oppose capital punishment, although their congregations incline toward support.[39] Why are American Latter-day Saints even more vulnerable to lingering modes of retributive thinking than their fellow non-evangelical Christians? A full explication is beyond the scope of this present analysis, though it undoubtedly would include the unflagging devotion of the Latter-day Saint community to the Old Testament, and a general alignment with evangelical conservative politics traceable to the social and sexual revolution of the sixties.[40] While the language of substitution is part of the Latter-day Saint canon, so are bases for an understanding of atonement more in line with some of the Patristic Fathers. This "restored" conception of atonement might, in turn, reshape much of Latter-day Saint religious language and, perhaps, some of its social and political commitments.

Latter-day Saint atonement theology comprises both historical and scriptural foundations to follow in the path of Victor Hugo, who asks the pertinent question: "Can the man created good by God be rendered wicked by man? Can the soul be completely made over by fate, and become evil, fate being evil? ... Is there [not] in every soul ... a first spark, a divine element, incorruptible in this world, immortal in the other, which good can develop, fan, ignite, and make to glow with splendour?"[41] Consistent with the sentiment behind his queries, the Latter-day Saint tradition is in a strong position to move in the direction being advocated by a growing number of religious voices—supported by developments in neuroscience and in the therapeutic sciences.

Contemporary Theological and Scientific Shifts

In recent years there has been a proliferation of books tackling anew the subject of atonement, several of which call for an entirely new approach. There is widespread agreement that explanations of atonement theology "along the lines of compensation (or satisfaction) ... traceable to St. Anselm, are now untenable."[42] According to Michael Winter, "the Christian doctrine of liberation centered upon the crucifixion is an insuperable barrier to belief in the kind of God who would require such a process to take place in his honor."[43] Some influential early Christian writers did not primarily associate the Eucharist with the crucifixion, the death of Christ or with retributive justice. The Eucharist bread, sanctified by the descent and overshadowing of the Holy Spirit, was considered to have the power to heal one from death and initiate resurrection. Ignatius, for instance, called the Eucharist the "medicine of immortality, and the antidote which prevents us from dying." It was an ordinance pointing to our eventual "divinization or deification."[44]

For many early Christians Incarnation and Resurrection formed the basis for the incipient gospel message. Death simply provided the bridge between the two. It was the Western Church, not the Eastern, that emphasized the universal death in Adam over against the universal life in Christ. Winter argues convincingly that the original atonement narrative as propounded by the Greek Church Fathers "has been distorted ... by an almost exclusive connection between the crucifixion and the atonement."[45] David Bentley Hart makes the same point in his latest work.[46]

In recent decades, the paradigm of universal sin and atonement hinging on the crucifixion has been challenged to move in the direction of universal woundedness and healing. Rita Nakashima Brock is one of the scholars who have become deeply committed to this shift. In her opinion, "Christianity is afflicted with a hierarchical view of power that undercuts its understanding of love in its fullest incarnation—that we are all part of one another."[47] Richard

Rohr and David Bentley Hart are two of a burgeoning number of theologians who are propounding that humankind is essentially wounded, not sinful, and that Christ's mission is not one of limited salvation but of universal healing.[48] In his best-selling book, *Just Mercy: A Story of Justice and Redemption,* Bryan Stevenson discusses the prevalence of brain disease among the incarcerated. He writes: "Today, over 50 percent of prison and jail inmates in the United States have a diagnosed mental illness, a rate nearly five times greater than that of the general population. Nearly one in five prison and jail inmates has a serious mental illness." [49]

Womanist and feminist scholars, particularly, are moving away from the rhetoric of "sin and salvation" to one of "woundedness and healing" and are promoting an atonement of healing from wounds either inherited or incurred during one's lifetime. Shelly Rambo asserts that that trauma is a universal condition that "poses deep challenges to theology in terms of the radicality of suffering. It exposes the impossibility of professing Christian claims—[of] God's presence and of human goodness."[50] The increased understanding of the causes and effects of trauma should "constitute the hermeneutical lens through which an alternative theological vision . . . emerges": one of "healing and redemption."[51] This new understanding would disrupt traditional readings of the crucifixion's relationship to atonement. Joanne Carlson Brown and Rebecca Parker, for example, reject categorically the centrality of the cross to atonement theology, calling the theology abusive because it glorifies suffering. They write, "the image of God the father demanding and carrying out the suffering and death of his own son has sustained a culture of abuse and led to the abandonment of victims of abuse and oppression. Until this image is shattered it will be . . . impossible to create a just society."[52] In order to change our social and political systems, they argue, we need to amend the theological principles underlying them.

The advances being made in neuroscience have become an unexpected ally in a movement away from a religious paradigm of sin and punishment to one of woundedness and healing. The author and psychiatrist Dr. Bessel van der Kolk opines that one does not need to be a veteran to experience trauma. "Trauma happens to us, our friends, our families, and our neighbors."[53] He argues that much of the behavior we see as deviant, unhealthy, or in any way disruptive or criminal can be traced back to trauma experienced by that person at some point in her or his life. Hart also suggests that woundedness or trauma, and not intentional aberrance, is at the root of deviant behavior:

> The character of even the very worst among us is in part the product of external contingencies, and somewhere in the history of every soul there are moments when a better way was missed by mischance, or by malign interventions from without, or by disorders of the mind within, rather than by intentional perver-

sity on the soul's own part.... No-one could ever fulfil the criteria necessary justly to damn himself or herself to perpetual misery... There is no such thing as perfect freedom in this life, or perfect understanding... There are always extenuating circumstances.[54]

Hart's assertion could be put more simply in Thomas Traherne's poetic formulation: "No man can sin that... seeth the beauty of God's face because no man can sin against his own happiness."[55]

As neuroscience continues to advance, increasing numbers of people with extenuating circumstances join those who are recognized as needing healing in lieu of retributive punishment. A growing number of neuroscientists suggest that, in many cases, trauma is to be found at the root of most antisocial behavior. These include individuals whose ability to control aggression due to brain tumors or other inhibitors is hampered, as well as patients with dementia and football players suffering Chronic Traumatic Encephalopathy (CTE). Neuroscientist Dr. Kent Kiehl has employed fMRI (functional magnetic resonance imaging) to scan the brains of over one thousand inmates. He concludes that "brains of psychopaths tend to show distinct defects in the paralimbic system, a network of brain regions important for memory and regulating emotion."[56]

Robert Gur, director of the Brain Behavior Center at the University of Pennsylvania propounds: "The brain doesn't lie. If there is tissue missing from your brain, there is no way you could have manufactured it for the purpose of [a] trial."[57] Additionally, Owen D. Jones has stated what has now become accepted fact among neuroscientists: the "areas of the brain that regulate judgment and self-control are... not fully mature in young adults, rendering behavior more impulsive... in emotionally-charged contexts."[58] If these views are accurate, then a neuroscientific understanding of human agency might well "supplant our cherished commonsense notions of free will, agency, and responsibility, which ground our legal practice of blame and punishment."[59]

In short, the increasing advances being made in neuroscience threaten to undermine the bases for linking atonement to retributive justice, which undergird the U.S. penal system. What the advances in neuroscience suggest is that brokenness, not sinfulness, is our primary condition; healing from trauma is what is needed.[60] Deanna Thompson says it most simply: "All of our lives bear the marks of suffering."[61] Toni Morrison's writings are poignant meditations on this truth: "cycles of violence play out across generations. The wounds do not simply go away."[62] Rambo argues that trauma "persists in symptoms that live on in the body, in the intrusive fragments of memory that return. It persists in symptoms that live on in communities."[63]

The immense gap between traditional notions of sin and punishment and current understandings of human suffering is a source of spiritual and psychological distress. Rambo's assertion that trauma has "not as yet been adequately addressed either in our homes, our churches, or our religious communities,"[64] is informed by the experience of Paul Womack, a three-tour U.S. veteran who stated that his "deepest experiences remain untouched by the practices and teachings of the Christian faith. They are met with theological silence."[65] The inadequacy of traditional theologies in healing and rehabilitating those who have caused or been afflicted by trauma and pain, or both, can be uniquely met by Latter-day Saint understandings of atonement enriched by new insights from contemporary science and theology.

A New Model?

Serene Jones states: "I [have] come to see that when one becomes aware of the extensive wounds that events of overwhelming violence can inflict on the souls, bodies, and psyches of people, one's understanding of what human beings are and what they can do changes." The shift in our understanding of the human condition as one inextricably bound to suffering necessitates a theology that seeks first and foremost to repair and heal that condition, rather than justify it. This calls for a different language altogether: as Jones continues: "It is hard to think of a task more central to theology than [that of] finding the language to speak grace in a form that allows it to come toward humanity in ways as gentle as they are powerful."[66] Nowhere is this need more critical than in atonement theology in particular, where images and language of retributive justice can threaten to overwhelm grace and forgiveness.

This does not necessarily require invention or revolution, but restoration and return. By disentangling Christianity from its Augustinian influences and returning to a New Testament model, the template for a reparative, reconciliatory Christianity reemerges. Krister Stendahl argues that modern theological conceptions about sinfulness are in fact Augustinian, rather than genuine expressions of New Testament Christianity:

> The point where Paul's experience intersects with his ... understanding of the faith, furthermore, is not "sin" with its correlate "forgiveness." It is rather when Paul speaks about his weakness that we feel his deeply personal pain. Once more we find something surprisingly different from the Christian language that most of us take for granted: it seems that Paul never felt guilt in the face of this weakness—pain, yes, but not guilt. It is not in the drama of the saving of Paul the sinner, but it is in the drama of Paul's coming to grips with what he calls his "weakness" that we find the most experiential level of Paul's theology.[67]

When the focus is on Paul's weakness and suffering, rather than his sin or guilt, an entirely different theology takes shape—one that David Bentley Hart has argued is in fact truer to Paul's original language in Romans. "Paul speaks of

... sin as a kind of contagion, a disease with which all are born; but never as an inherited condition of criminal culpability."[68]

Indeed, biblical scholarship, in recent decades, has begun to move in this direction. While the conventional reading of the Hebrew word for atone, *kpr*, is "to cover" sin, Mary Douglas notes that *kpr* can also mean to "to repair a hole, cure a sickness, mend a rift, make good a torn or broken covering.... [In the Hebrew consciousness] atonement [did] not mean covering a sin so as to hide it from the sight of God; it means making good an outer layer which has rotted or been pierced."[69] To heal, in other words. Another English scholar agrees, suggesting that the term "has to mean restore, recreate, or heal," and argues that for the Hebrews, atonement was "the rite of healing."[70]

The Greek New Testament, in fact, warrants a reappraisal of the way in which sin and salvation came to displace attention to trauma and healing. Trauma, as a near universal condition, is perhaps but a modern diagnosis for what scripture calls pain, affliction—and may include sin in the whole galaxy of infirmities that Christ came to heal. The usage of the Greek term *sōzō* (to heal) in story in Luke 7 of the woman "who loved much" is particularly instructive in this regard. She appears in the New Testament narrative as the woman anointing the feet of the Christ with ointment from an alabaster box. She is, according to the story in Luke, a woman who "sinned much." And yet, Jesus speaks to her the identical Greek words he spoke to the blind man and to the ailing woman in the stories of Matthew and Mark: *hē pistis sou sesōken se*, or "your faith has healed you."[71] *Sōzō*, the root of *sesōken*, is the same word in identical phrases used by Matthew and Mark, but in this scene the affliction is explicitly sin not physical malady.

The import is unambiguous: Christ sees before him a woman wounded by her past and in need of healing, though the trauma is manifest in this case as spiritual rather than corporeal. This fact is muddied by the translator's choice to diverge from the language in Matthew and Mark, and have Christ say the woman is "saved" rather than "healed" by her faith. While the Greek word *sōzō* may be translated in many instances as save, the prism of William Tyndale (principal translator of the King James Bible) appears to have predisposed him to such a rendition, when the context so clearly favors "heal." As Tyndale's biographer notes, he embraced the Reformationist paradigm of humankind as sinners with "horrible damnation and ... the fearful sentence and judgment of God looming."[72]

In the Book of Mormon, also, we find an affirmation of sin as a variety of trauma in need of healing. In his appearance to the Nephite people, Christ explicitly refers to a sinful condition as in need of healing ("repent of your sins ... that I may heal you," 3 Ne 9:13). Other passages in the Book of Mormon suggest that Christ came with the intent to heal and to release humanity from a wide range of afflictions:

> And he shall go forth, suffering pains and afflictions and temptations of every kind; and this that the word might be fulfilled which saith he will take upon him the pains and the sicknesses of his people. And he will take upon him death, that he may loose the bands of death which bind his people; and he will take upon him their infirmities, that his bowels may be filled with mercy, according to the flesh, that he may know according to the flesh how to succor his people according to their infirmities (Alma 7:11–12).

This description of Christ's ministry and atonement makes no mention of sin, justification, or guilt. The emphasis on Christ freeing and healing people from their pain, in part through an empathic experience of humanity's suffering, is free from the Augustinian distortions.

This broader cultural and pastoral shift toward healing woundedness is manifest in current Latter-day Saint discourse. Sermons delivered at Latter-day Saint biannual conferences refer increasingly to atonement as a rite of healing: "The Good Shepherd . . . views disease in His sheep as a condition that needs treatment care, and compassion [and He] promised healing," said Elder Dale Renlund.[73] In fact, growing attention to this condition on the part of the LDS leadership is evident in the fact that in the past decade, the frequency of the term "heal" with reference to Christ's redemptive role has increased fivefold in General Conference talks directed primarily to Latter-day Saints.[74]

From its earliest days, Latter-day Saint teachings have regularly diverged from the traditional theological framework of original sin and culpability. Together, these teachings form a constellation of ontological and eschatological principles that emphasize potential and progress over punishment. For example, Restoration scripture states sin is not a heritable or baseline condition: "Children are whole from the foundation of the world" (Moses 6:54; A of F 2). Additionally, a revelation to Joseph Smith describing judgment resituates the determining factor on our capacity to "receive" heaven over divine retribution for unworthiness: each person shall enjoy precisely that condition which s/he is "willing to receive" (D&C 88:32). More recently, Elder Jeffrey Holland emphatically denied any punitive aspect to God's actions: "God does not now nor will He ever do to you a destructive, malicious, unfair thing—ever. It is not in what Peter called 'the divine nature' to even be able to do so."[75] This unequivocal rejection of a God who inflicts pain to execute his will is perhaps the clearest example of disentangling of Latter-day Saint teachings from Augustinian-inflected Protestant influence and pushing forward a theology of divinely collaborative growth and healing.

Latter-day Saint perspectives on atonement are additive as well as corrective. The emphasis on Zion, as indicated in the introduction, refashions atonement with an emphasis on the "at-one-ing" of the entire human family. Zion-building, in this light, is an invitation in which humanity is to participate in Christ's healing work of at-one-ing. Heaven, as Joseph Smith taught, is not a matter of reward or position or place, but a particular kind of sociability (D&C 130:2). Christ's atonement mends the fractures that divide self from self and self from the other. Zion is the perfect culmination of Latter-day Saint atonement theology, which comprises the absolute harmony of human relationships that is a result of Christ's capacity "to mend a fractured reality."[76] The message of the gospel of The Church of Jesus Christ of Latter-day Saints, as articulated in temple work for the deceased, is that humanity has been invited to collaborate with Christ to build Zion through the revivification of all relationships, past and present.

This invitation to collaborate with God in universal healing and restoration extends to people of good will everywhere. Theodore M. Burton (1970–1989), an Assistant to the Twelve and later a member of the Seventy, reminded members of The Church of Jesus Christ of Latter-Day Saints in a 1974 Church Conference: "We are part of a total community . . . we are all members of one family, for God hath made of one blood all nations" (Acts 17:26).[77] The work of atonement is intended to bring about the healing of the entire human family. The building of Zion is a global enterprise and all are invited to be co-participants with the Godhead in its construction. Indeed, Latter-day Saint sacred texts suggest that atonement cannot be accomplished without humanity's collaboration.

The most emphatic invitation to participate in that grand design is articulated in the ordinance of adoption into the heavenly family—otherwise known as baptism. At this most appropriate moment of covenant making, Latter-day Saints commit to join with Christ in the enterprise of atonement or healing, the primary purpose of which is to erect, edify, and constitute a community of love. Alma's language in Mosiah 18 is a powerful articulation of what humankind's primary activity should be as converts are invited to enter into three covenants: First to bear one another's burdens, that they may be light," second to "mourn with those that mourn," and third to "comfort those that stand in need of comfort." (Mos 18:8–9).

By alluding to the primary activity of each member of the Godhead, disciples are invited into the collaborative project of the Godhead. The God who "bears" humanity's burdens throughout his life, into Gethsemane and onto Golgotha, is God, the Christ. The God who mourns in empathy of the grief, despair, and sorrow experienced by each and every child evokes the weeping God the Father witnessed by Enoch. And the God who comforts the children when they stand in need of comfort is God, bearing the name "The Comforter"—the Holy Spirit (John 14:26–27). This is not to say that members of The Church of Jesus Christ of Latter-day Saints are the only ones invited into this particular collaborative activity with divinity. God has many names, and diverse ways of co-participating in his work abound.

If Zion comprises all members of the human family, then the entire human family is necessary to complete the project of universal healing. "We ought to have the building up of Zion as our greatest object" Joseph Smith urged the fledgling church.[78] As the Russian theologian Vladimir Solovyov similarly argued, "Mankind has to co-operate with God in this work, for otherwise there cannot be a complete oneing of God with his creatures and a full expression of the meaning of existence."[79] Atonement theologies are often mired in a rhetoric of violence and retributive justice. Contemporary voices increasingly agree with the Russian theologian Nikolai Berdyaev, who wrote decades ago that "the legal interpretation of Christianity and redemption" is "degrading both to God and man."[80] The Latter-day Saint tradition has often been complicit in importing retributive justice into human and divine realms alike; however, Latter-day Saint teachings envision a universal Zion and a universally healing atonement; it is past time to move in those directions.

Notes

1. J. Denny Weaver, *The Nonviolent Atonement*, 2nd ed., (Grand Rapids, MI: William B. Eerdmans Publishing Company, 2011), 17, 3.

2. Timothy Gorringe, *God's Just Vengeance* (New York: Cambridge University Press, 1996), 6–7, 12.

3. Gorringe, *God's Just Vengeance*, 22.

4. Diarmaid MacCulloch, *The Reformation* (New York: Viking, 2004), xxii.

5. William Paley, *Works* (London: Longman, 1838), 3:298–99.

6. Friedrich Nietzsche, *The Genealogy of Morals*, translated by Walter Kauffman (New York: Vintage, 1989), 63, 65.

7. Irenaeus, *Against Heresies*, 4.39.6, in *The Ante-Nicene Fathers,* edited by Alexander Roberts and James Donaldson (Grand Rapids, MI: Eerdmans, 1977), 1:457; see also Moses 5:11.

8. Origen, *Homilies on Numbers* 27.11, in Antonia Tripolitis, *Doctrine of the Soul in the Thought of Plotinus and Origen* (Roslyn Heights, NY: Libra, 1977), 126.

9. B. R. Rees, *Pelagius: Life and Letters* (Woodbridge, UK: Boydell Press, 1991), 57.

10. Hastings Rashdall, *The Idea of Atonement in Christian Theology* (London: MacMillan, 1925), 248–49.

11. Rashdall, *Idea of Atonement,* 253–54.

12. Nikolai Berdyaev, *Truth and Revelation* (London: Geoffrey Bles, 1953), 56.

13. Joan Chittester, *In Search of Belief* (Liguori, MO: Liguori, 1999), 20–21, 22.

14. John Calvin, "Reply to Sadoleto," in *A Reformation Debate*, edited by John C. Olin (Grand Rapids, MI: Baker, 2002), 66.

15. John Milton, *Paradise Lost* in *The Complete Poetry and Essential Prose of John Milton*, edited by William Kerrigan, John Rumrich, and Stephen M. Fallon (New York: The Modern Library, 2007), 3:236–41; 261–64.

16. John Calvin, *Institutes of the Christian Religion*, translated by Henry Beveridge (Peabody, MA: Hendrickson, 2008), 2.1.5, 150.

17. Calvin, *Institutes*, 3.2.26.

18. John Calvin, *Sermons on Genesis 1–11*, translated by Rob Roy MacGregor (East Peoria, IL: Banner of Truth Trust, 2009), 260.

19. Philip Schaff, *History of the Christian Church*, "The Servetus Literature," reply to Baudouin, vol. 8, ch. 16 §136, 1562; *Responsio ad Balduini Convicia, Opera*, IX.575.

20. E. William Monter, "Crime and Punishment in Calvin's Geneva, 1562," in *Articles on Calvin and Calvinism: Volume 3: Calvin's Work in Geneva*, edited by Richard C. Gamble (New York: Garland Publishing, Inc., 1992), 272.

21. Calvin, *Institutes of the Christian Religion*, 6.21.20

22. John Calvin, "Bible Commentaries: Genesis 9" in *Calvin's Commentary on the Bible*, StudyLight.org., accessed March 29, 2023, https://www.studylight.org/commentaries/eng/cal/genesis-9.html.

23. David Bentley Hart, *That All Shall Be Saved: Heaven, Hell, and Universal Salvation* (New Haven: Yale University Press, 2019), 77.

24. Kathryn Gin Lum, *Damned Nation: Hell in America from the Revolution to Reconstruction* (Oxford: Oxford University Press, 2014), 16.

25. H. A. Washington, ed., *Thomas Jefferson: Inaugural Addresses*, (Washington, DC: Taylor & Maury 1854), 8:165.

26. Marie Gottschalk, *The Prison and Gallows: The Politics of Mass Incarceration in America* (Cambridge: Cambridge University Press, 2006), 47.

27. Marie Gottschalk, *Caught: The Prison State and the Lockdown of American Politics* (Princeton: Princeton University Press, 2015), 186.

28. Gustave de Beaumont and Alexis de Tocqueville, *On the Penitentiary System*, quoted in Gottschalk, *Caught*, 241.

29. Gorringe, *God's Just Vengeance*, 29.

30. Gottschalk, *Prison and the Gallows*, 16.

31. Gottschalk, *Prison and the Gallows*, 1, 22.

32. Gottschalk, *Prison and Gallows*, 1.

33. Lum, *Damned Nation*, 234

34. See Martin Gardner, "Mormonism and Capital Punishment: A Doctrinal Perspective, Past and Present," *Dialogue* 12 (1979): 9–26. For example, in an 1843 debate with George A. Smith (who originally opposed capital punishment, before changing his mind), Joseph Smith said: "In debate, George A. Smith said imprisonment was better than hanging. I replied, I was opposed to hanging, even if a man kills another, I will shoot him, or cut off his head, spill his blood on the ground, and let the smoke thereof ascend up to God; and if ever I have the privilege of making a law on that subject, I will have it so" (10).

35. *General Smith's Views of the Powers and Policy of the Government of the United States*, circa January 26–February 7, 1844, in *Documents, Volume 14: 1 January–15 May 1844*, edited by Alex D. Smith, Adam H. Petty, Jessica M. Nelson, and Spencer W. McBride, vol. 14 in the Documents series of *The Joseph Smith Papers*, 9.

36. Brigham Young, *Complete Discourses*, edited by Richard S. Van Wagoner (Salt Lake City: Smith-Petit Foundation, 2009), 2:1169.

37. Bruce R. McConkie, *Mormon Doctrine* (Salt Lake City: Bookcraft, 1958), 104.

38. Stuart W. Hinckley, "Capital Punishment," in *Encyclopedia of Mormonism*, edited by Daniel H. Ludlow (New York: Macmillan, 1992), 1:255.

39. Michael Lipka, "Some Major U.S. Religious Groups Differ from Their Members on the Death Penalty," Pew Research Center, July 13, 2015, https://www.pewresearch.org/fact-tank/2015/07/13/some-major-u-s-religious-groups-differ-from-their-members-on-the-death-penalty/.

40. See Gardner, "Mormonism and Capital Punishment," for a fuller exploration of this topic.

41. Victor Hugo, *Les Misérables*: *Fantine*, 30 vols. (New York: The Century Co., 1906), 1:106.

42. Michael Winter, *The Atonement: Problems in Theology* (London: Geoffrey Chapman, 1995), vii.

43. Winter, *The Atonement*, 7.

44. Ignatius, *Letter to Ephesians*, 20, in Roger E. Olson, *The Story of Christian Theology* (Downers Grove, IL: InterVarsity, 1999), 48.

45. Winter, *The Atonement*, 54.

46. See numerous iterations of this differing emphasis in David Bentley Hart, *That All Shall Be Saved: Heaven, Hell, and Universal Salvation* (New Haven: Yale University Press, 2019).

47. Rita Nakashima Brock, *Journeys by Heart: A Christology of Erotic Power* (New York: Crossroad, 1988), 49.

48. See Richard Rohr, *The Universal Christ: How a Forgotten Reality Can Change Everything We See, Hope For, and Believe* (New York: Convergent, 2019); Hart, *That All Shall Be Saved*, esp. 357.

49. Bryan Stevenson, *Just Mercy: A Story of Justice and Redemption* (New York: Spiegel & Grau, 2014), 188.

50. Shelly Rambo, *Spirit and Trauma: A Theology of Remaining* (Louisville: Westminster John Knox, 2010), 10.

51. Rambo, *Spirit and Trauma*, 11.

52. Joanne Carlson Brown and Rebecca Parker, "For God So Loved the World?" in *Christianity, Patriarchy, and Abuse: A Feminist Critique*, edited by Joanne Carlson Brown and Carol R. Bohn (New York: Pilgrim, 1989), 9.

53. Bessel van der Kolk, *The Body Keeps the Score: Brain, Mind, and Body in the Healing of Trauma* (New York: Penguin Books, 2015), 1.

54. Hart, *That All Should be Saved*, 38–39.

55. Thomas Traherne, *Selected Writings,* edited by Dick Davis (Manchester: Carcanet, 1980), 84.

56. Virginia Hughes, "Science in Court: Head Case," *Nature* 464 (2010): 340–42.

57. Hughes, "Science in Court," 6.

58. Alexandra O. Cohen et al., "When Is an Adolescent an Adult? Assessing Cognitive Control in Emotional and Nonemotional Contexts," *Psychological Science* 27 (2016): 549, https://journals.sagepub.com/doi/abs/10.1177/0956797615627625.

59. William Hirstein, Katrina L. Sifferd, and Tyler K. Fagan, *Responsible Brains: Neuroscience, Law, and Human Culpability* (Cambridge, MA: MIT Press, 2018), 9–10.

60. Van der Kolk, *Body Keeps the Score*, 1.

61. Deanna A. Thompson, "Faith in a Traumatized World," lecture given at Brigham Young University, Feb. 13, 2020.

62. Shelly Rambo, "How Christian Theology and Practice Are Being Shaped by Trauma Studies: Talking about God in the Face of Wounds that Won't Go Away," *The Christian Century* 136.24 (Nov. 1, 2019), 2.

63. Rambo, *Spirit and Trauma*, 2.

64. Ibid.

65. Ibid.

66. Serene Jones, *Trauma and Grace: Theology in a Ruptured World* (Louisville, KY: Westminster John Knox, 2009), xxii, 11.

67. Krister Stendahl, *Paul Among Jews and Gentiles* (Philadelphia: Fortress, 1979), 40–41, 85.

68. David Bentley Hart, *The New Testament: A Translation* (New Haven: Yale University Press, 2017), 296–97.

69. Mary Douglas, "Atonement in Leviticus," *Jewish Studies Quarterly* 1 (1993–94): 117–18.

70. Margaret Barker, "Atonement: The Rite of Healing," *Scottish Journal of Theology* 49.1 (Feb. 1996): 1–20.

71. See Matt 9:22 and Mark 10:52.

72. David Daniell, *William Tyndale: A Biography* (New Haven: Yale University Press, 2001), 165.

73. Dale G. Renlund, "Our Good Shepherd," *Ensign* (May 2017): 30.

74. This figure can be ascertained by a simple word search of the database found at the LDS General Conference Corpus, https://www.lds-general-conference.org/.

75. Jeffrey R. Holland, "A Saint through the Atonement of Christ the Lord," *BYU Speeches* (Provo, UT: Brigham Young University, January 18, 2022), 2.

76. Philip Barlow, "To Mend a Fractured Reality: Joseph Smith's Project," *Journal of Mormon History* 38.3 (Summer 2012): 28–50.

77. Theodore M. Burton, "Blessed are the Peacemakers," *Ensign* 4 (Nov. 1974): 54.

78. Andrew F. Ehat and Lyndon W. Cook, eds., *Words of Joseph Smith* (Orem, UT: Grandin, 1991), 11.

79. As quoted in Stephen Finlan, *Problems with Atonement: The Origins of, and Controversy about, the Atonement Doctrine* (Collegeville, MN: Liturgical Press, 2005), 123.

80. Nikolai Berdyaev, *The Divine and the Human* (London: Geoffrey Bles, 1949), 2.

CHAPTER 10

Relational Atonement
Groundwork

BENJAMIN KEOGH

Atonement, when broken into its constituent parts—at-one-ment—speaks out the end toward which it is aimed.[1] It also implies the reason for its own necessity. Adaptation in the sixteenth century for explicitly theological purposes ties it to God, and thereby to God's creating. There, with humanity introduced as God's image and creation declared good, certain kinds of relationships were conveyed. Primordially, these included relations between (1) God and humans, (2) God and the nonhuman creation, (3) humans and humans, (4) humans and the nonhuman creation, and (5) individual humans and themselves. In the beginning all was in right relation with all. For humanity this included responding to God's love with love and mirroring God's creative care over creation. In the Fall a dislocation in each of these relations is expressed. In atonement, relocation in right relation is communicated.

As all accounts of atonement have some form of reconciliation in view each is, at least nominally, relational. While this is true of their intent, when the images of atonement's outworking are surveyed, the waters muddy and questions are raised. How does the death of an innocent reconcile the guilty? Can violence right wrong relationships? Does the mechanism communicate the intent? This last question is particularly important. If it does not, to what extent can the account be considered relational? Is it a case of the ends justifying the means? Or must the means be in concert with their end? It is the contention of this chapter that they must. If creation and the Fall are understood to be expressions of the centrality of relation to God's nature, then as the solution to the negative consequences of the Fall, and the process by which God's positive intents in creation are fulfilled, atonement must be in continuity.

Atonement's ties to God and creation are an interpretive key. One's conception of God informs one's conception of creation and atonement so extensively that it has been suggested that an account of atonement will "stand or fall with the adequacy of its understanding of God's nature and action in the world" in its relation with humanity.[2] Engaging Latter-day Saint scripture and contemporary theological discourse, this chapter investigates the portrayal of God's relational nature in the raising of Lazarus, and explores what that nature means for accounts of creation, fall, and atonement. While no new account of atonement will be provided, groundwork for such an account will be laid.

Lazarus and the Relational God

In developing a relational theology of creation biblical theologian Terence Fretheim identified five characteristics of the God-human relation. These are:

1. God is not the only one who has something important to say.
2. God is not the only one who has something important to do and the power with which to do it.
3. God is genuinely affected by what happens to the relationship.
4. The human will can stand over against the will of God.
5. The future is not all blocked out . . . the people of God are capable of shaping the future in various ways, [including] the future of God.[3]

Together these suggest the relationship between God and humans is characterized "by risk, sacrifice, commitment, limitation, change, power-sharing, and the ability of both parties to shape the future, even God's future."[4] For this, Fretheim makes a convincing case.[5] Elsewhere, German theologian Christoph Schwöbel has argued persuasively that questions of creation cannot be separated from questions of the nature of the Creator, and that together they imply "the task of relating [these] to statements about God reconciling the world."[6] It is to this task we turn now: are Fretheim's propositions identifiable in accounts of atonement?

The story of Lazarus (John 11:1–46) begins with Jesus receiving word that his friend is sick. Jesus then remains where he is for two days before announcing to his disciples that Lazarus is asleep and the time has come to wake him. In the face of their misunderstanding he more plainly states, "Lazarus is dead." Upon arriving in Bethany he meets Martha, weeps with Mary, and travels to the tomb where the dead man is brought back to life. Narratively, the story plays multiple roles in John's Gospel: as the concluding sign it provides the strongest witness of Jesus as the resurrection and the life; as a transition it directs the reader toward Jesus's forthcoming passion and seals his fate; and as the central scene it prophetically enacts the meaning of an incarnate Christ. In these ways the story is significantly intertwined with John's account of atonement. Within it, Fretheim's five characteristics will be explored.

1. God is not the only one who has something important to say

Throughout John's narrative four voices direct eight contributions toward Jesus. Two are particularly striking. First, from Mary and Martha—"he whom thou lovest is sick" (11:3). Jesus's public ministry appears to close with chapter 10 as he retreats "across the Jordan" (10:40). There he abides, seemingly in preparation for the final confrontation that will lead to his death—until he is sent word. While he leaves in his own time and provides his own reasons, the message is the initiating factor. Thus, the in-text transition "from a God-like Jesus who is distant [from where he is needed] to one who sets out to become involved," is not quite as one-time Dominican priest Thomas Brodie suggests.[7] The sisters draw God back into the fray.

By the midpoint of the scene the once-distant Jesus is in the thick of human things. The "Lord" (11:3, 34) has become "this man" (11:37), the "I am" (11:25) weeping as one among many (11:33, 35). The immediate cause of his weeping is the response to his asking where Lazarus was laid: "Come and see" (11:34). Uttered three times in John's Gospel, the first two—by Jesus, then Philip, also in response to questions (John 1:38–39, 46)—produced human declarations of faith in Jesus as the one sent from God (John 1:41, 49). This third, addressed to Jesus by a human community in response to *his* question, draws out his most human response. If a word from the sisters draws God back into the fray, these revealed the humanity of his Incarnation. God is not the only one with something important to say.

2. God is not the only one who has something important to do and the power with which to do it

Of the things done in the story of Lazarus by people other than Jesus, three are most striking. First, "many of the Jews came ... to comfort" (John 11:19) and weep (11:33) with the bereaved sisters. In the Book of Mormon, burden-bearing joins comforting and mourning to form a holy trinity of actions that give witness to a covenant-keeping community. These, as Latter-day Saint scholar Fiona Givens has pointed out, mirror in human form the work of the godhead.[8] Or, expressed more pointedly, in performing these actions the earthly covenant community embodies—(re-)incarnates—the heavenly godhead. Together, the second—removing the stone—and third—removing the grave clothes—portray another aspect of a covenant-keeping community performing the work of the godhead. While Jesus performs the miracle, the actions of the community are likewise salvific; without them, Lazarus is still bound in the tomb. Salvation, on this reading, is tripartite, involving Christ, the community, and ourselves.

To this we will return, noting for now that God is not the only one who has something important to do.

3. God is genuinely affected by what happens to the relationship

In the initiating message Lazarus is referred to by his relationship with Jesus, not his name: "he whom thou lovest" (John 11:3). There is no direct request for healing. Rather, the sisters' expectation seems to be that Jesus's emotional investment in the relationship will move him to provide it. When he later sets off he again invokes relationship, suggesting the sisters' expectation was correct, at least in part: "Our friend Lazarus sleepeth; but I go that I may wake him" (11:11).[9] If this is suggestive, the encounter with Mary and the Jews before reaching the tomb is declarative: "When Jesus . . . saw [the] weeping . . . he groaned in the spirit, and was troubled" (11:33). While there is some debate over what exactly this groaning entailed, the cause is clear. What happens to the relationship genuinely affects God.

4. The human will can stand over against the will of God

This fourth proposition can be demonstrated straightforwardly by two incidents toward the end of the narrative. In the first, Jesus's initial command to remove the stone is opposed (John 11:39). In the second, despite Jesus's prayer that "they may believe" (11:42), the watching Jews have contrasting reactions: "many . . . believed . . . But some . . . went their ways to the Pharisees" (11:45–46). That the command was opposed and that not all believed suggests the human will can stand over against the will of God.

5. The future is not all blocked out . . . the people of God are capable of shaping the future in various ways, [including] the future of God

As in the healings portrayed in chapters 5 and 9 of John, the raising of Lazarus involves what Brodie terms a "triple command." In 5 and 9 "the life giving commands follow each other immediately"; at the tomb they "must wait upon the development of faith."[10] The interludes are instructive. Between the giving and fulfilling of the first command Martha's faith needs strengthening: "Said I not unto thee, that if thou wouldest believe, thou shouldest see the glory of God?" (11:40). Between the fulfilling of the first and the giving of the second there is a prayer: "that they may believe" (11:42). Martha believes, the stone is removed, Lazarus is raised, yet not all believe. The responses to the commands are similarly instructive. To the first there is opposition (11:39), to the second immediate fulfillment (11:43–44), and to the third none was recorded. Three commands with three different responses suggests an open future. Of the three, the third is the most intriguing. The lack of recorded response leaves open the possibility of a variety of responses. For John Suggit, a New Testament scholar, it suggests the writer "intends the reader to understand that salvation *depends* on the obedience of the community as well as on the call of Christ."[11] For Brodie, "What is essential" in the scene as a whole, "is that however much Jesus is presented as Creator-like, the bringing of life *depends* also on human activity and interaction."[12] Dependence upon a human community suggests that community is capable of shaping the future in various ways.

That Fretheim's conception of the God-human relation is discernible in the story of Lazarus suggests a certain kind of continuity in God as a relational being. The balance of this chapter will examine what that continuity might mean for the interpretation of God's work.

Creation

Perhaps the most useful starting point when discussing creation is to make clear what is meant. In scripture, to talk of creation is to talk primarily in theological terms. It is, as Fretheim puts it, "to state that the cosmos does not simply exist; it was *created* by God."[13] To talk about creation is, then, to stake a particular set of claims. These include both beginning and bringing about. Thus, creation implies not only nonexistence before existence, but existence at the agency of another. Together these suggest a distinction between the creator and the thing created: the creator precedes the thing created, being necessarily prior, while the created is necessarily dependent—without its creator, it could never be.[14] In this way, "the doctrine of creation properly refers to *the totality of God's relations to everything that is not God*."[15] As such, relation is at the core of the doctrine of creation and a theology of creation is primarily an explication of that relation. When understood this way it becomes clear that accounts of creation are much more proclamations of the manner in which God relates to that which is not God than they are explanations for how that which is not God came to be. If this is correct, then the manner of God's relating must be detectable in an account of creation. After examining the Genesis account, accounts produced by Joseph Smith and canonized in the books of Moses and Abraham will be read in that light.[16]

Genesis 1–2

A doctrine of creation assumes, according to the American theologian Robert Jenson, "absolute difference between Creator and creature [as] an automatic qualification."[17] However, as the account in Genesis does not define God explicitly there is variation in how this "absolute difference" is cashed out relationally. Traditionally the image suggested is one of a "God in absolute control of the developing creation, working independently and unilaterally."[18] On this basis there has been a tendency to conceive God's sovereignty as cold and distant, or as utterly determinative. In contrast to this Fretheim's reading of Genesis 1–2 finds a God who is involved and involving, and whose "approach to creation is communal and relational."[19] Over the course of these two chapters he identifies eleven modes of creation and twenty images of God as creator. Together, he asserts, they "provide a more relational model of creation." Two of these images—"God as speaker" and "God as consultant of others"—will be examined here.[20]

In the first chapter of Genesis the speech acts of God are described in three different ways—(1) as God speaking, "God said"; (2) as God naming, "God called"; and (3) as God blessing, "God blessed"—and take seven different forms.[21] This alone suggests that any interpretation holding creation by speech demonstrates the absolute sovereignty of God takes too narrow a view. A closer look at the different forms confirms this. Most tellingly, of the seven creative speech acts (vv. 3, 6, 11, 14, 20, 24, and 26), only three (vv. 3, 6, and 14) depict God creating something independently. These three—the initial breaking of creative light on day one (v. 3), the firmament on day two (v. 6), and the lights "in the firmament of heaven" on day four (v. 14)—appear from the text to be *ex nihilo* creations. With one of these—the greater and lesser lights—God shares power. It is they, not God, who will "rule over the day and over the night" (v. 16). God, paradoxically, shares rather than hoards sovereignty. In the other four, God invites participation: twice from the earth ("Let the earth bring forth," v. 11 and 24), and once each from the waters ("Let the waters bring forth," v. 20), and the divine council ("Let us make," v. 26). These invitations, it appears, are all made to entities that existed *before* the beginning.[22] These creative speech acts reveal a God who relates to the world in at least two ways: by (1) performing necessary acts that no other can do—creating light, firmament, and lights; and (2) inviting participation from others wherever possible. Here, as biblical scholar Susan Brayford points out, it is important to note that these participative involvements are of different kinds: "Whereas the earth was able to produce vegetation on its own, it seemingly lacks the power to bring forth living beings." So too the waters, "without God's involvement."[23] This second way of relating, then, invites participation through acts that can be completed both with and without God's assistance. While "God alone" has "sovereign, effortless, creative power," by inviting others to participate to the maximal degree possible God vitalizes their contribution.[24]

God's other speech acts also have relational implications. The act of ordering (v. 9) brings the water together in such a way that space is made for the dry land. The two now coexist side by side, the waters no longer dominating the land in smothering dominion. The acts of naming—Day, Night (v. 5), Heaven (v. 8), and Earth (v. 10)—have a familiarizing effect. This is particularly so, Brodie suggests, in the case of Night, where naming has the effect of "demystifying" darkness, making it less threatening. Through naming God makes the world "essentially friendly."[25] Likewise, the act of blessing not only demonstrates God's care for creation, but also, through the blessing's content, God's trust in it.

For Fretheim, God's speaking "means that creation is not an accident." Rather, "it is a deliberate act of divine will."[26] God's creating is both intentional and careful. Together these suggest something of the manner of God's creating—it is planned, methodical, and thought through. There is no rush in God. God spoke: "Let there be light" (v. 3); and observed: "And God saw the light" (v. 4). God is not one to send out words without thought for consequence, or sense of responsibility. Having spoken the word, God watched for its effect. In so doing God not only saw the light; God saw "that it was good" (v. 4). God's intention and care in creation also suggest the kind of posture God adopts toward that which is not God. As Fretheim observes, "use of the jussive 'let'" throughout the narrative "means that God's speaking does not function as an imperative, it leaves room for creaturely response," meaning, "the receptor of the word is important in the shaping of the creative order."[27] God's relational posture is one of invitation and collaboration, not coercion.

This collaborative impulse is evident in the "let us make" of 1:26.[28] With space left for consultation humanity's creation is "the result of a dialogical act." While God "takes the initiative" the "participation" of the divine council is "genuine" and the "product of their creative work"—humanity—is understood "to be in the image of all involved."[29] In David Bentley Hart's reading of Gregory of Nyssa (c. 335–395), humanity as the image of God refers to the "full community of all humanity" whose reflection of "the divine likeness and the divine beauty" occurs only in "the concrete solidarity of all persons in that complete community that is, alone, the true image of God."[30] The emergent image is one in which a collaborative divine community above is mirrored in a collaborative human community below. Read this way, Claus Westermann's statement that "humans are created in such a way that their very existence is intended to be their relationship to God" takes on new meaning.[31] Not only is humanity to be defined by its relationship to God, humans are to relate to others like God does. Thus, from the beginning God's creational intentions were deeply relational. While these creational intentions demarcate the absolute otherness of God from that which God is not, by inviting that which God is not to do what God does—namely, participate in creation—God transcends that otherness from the beginning.

Moses 2 and Abraham 4

Along with the accounts in Genesis, Latter-day Saints accept accounts in Moses and Abraham as authoritative. These essentially replicate the text of Genesis with some subtle and significant differences. The acceptance of three similar but varying accounts should give reason for pause. If accounts of creation are proclamations of the manner in which God relates to that which is not God, why authorize multiplicity? Perhaps the beginnings of an answer may be found in the work that such authorization does toward the legitimizing of difference. It may be that a single proclamation, which defines humanity's relations with God and each other, might produce a stifling orthodoxy that works to subvert God's intentions for creation. Humanity in the image of God was to be fruitful and multiply—with all the diversity such multiplication brings—or homogenize. As God pronounced more than one way of creating good, so too there is more than one way to properly relate to God, and each other. This, at least, is one implication of multiple authorized accounts.

Turning to the texts themselves—what, if anything, do they contribute to a relational understanding of creation? Here the first thing to note is that, unlike Genesis, the Book of Mormon's creation accounts are not the first thing the reader encounters. Rather, readers are met with increasing amounts of preamble. In Moses the creation account comes in chapter 2, in Abraham it is chapter 4. Both are presented as direct revelations, and both are preceded by a personal encounter with God. However, within that similarity there are significant differences. This is evident in the nature of the revelations themselves: Moses "discerned ... by the Spirit of God" (Moses 1:28); Abraham "saw" in "the Urim and Thummim" (Abr 3:1–2). Further, it appears Moses's encounter was initiated by God—"Moses was caught up into an exceedingly high mountain" (Moses 1:1); and Abraham's, by Abraham—"I sought for mine appointment" (Abr 1:4).[32] To each, God was introduced by name—to Moses, "Endless is my name" (Moses 1:3), to Abraham, "my name is Jehovah" (Abr 1:16); to each a relationship with God was described—to Moses, "thou art my son" (Moses 1:4), and to Abraham, "I will take thee, to put upon thee my name" (Abr 1:18). Both were also invited to join in God's work of salvation—Moses to "deliver [God's] people" (Moses 1:26), and Abraham to make "[God's] name ... known in the earth forever" (Abr. 1:19)—in each case, variation. Finally, the accounts of creation themselves are both directly preceded by statements from God regarding creation's ultimate end—"immortality and eternal life" to Moses (Moses 1:39), and "glory added upon [the] heads" of those "who keep their second estate" to Abraham (Abr 3:26).

Although much could be said about these individually, a word or two on them collectively will suffice. Strikingly, in both cases the creation accounts emerge from an intensely relational place. Presented as revelations, both Moses and Abraham are appointed a work. Thus, while the revelations have a commissioning quality, their bulk—which includes the creation accounts—situate Moses and Abraham, and their work, in relation to God and God's work. Rather than an astronomy lesson, the point of Abraham's tour of the cosmos seems to be relational. As God multiplied the stars (Abr 3:12), God will multiply Abraham (Abr 3:14). As proximity to God conferred greatness upon the stars (Abr 3:3, 16), so glory upon humanity (Abr 3:25–26). As God set the stars in order (Abr 3:3, 12), so Abraham is commissioned to disrupt the order of humanity (Abr 1:19; 3:15, 23–26). Abraham is called to restore God's place in their midst. This situating of human work in relation to the divine primes the reader to read the creation account as a situating of God's work in relation to God's creations. That the accounts in Moses and Abraham do so through the sustained diversity of their similarities emphasizes both the collectivity and individuality of humanity. While humanity is only truly the image of God in its totality, like a multifaceted diamond each human refracts and relates to the image in its own way.

Variations in the accounts themselves yield similar insights. Appearing fifty-two times in thirty-one verses, the account in Moses is littered with the first-person pronoun, "I." In contrast, it does not appear in either Genesis or Abraham. In Moses, each "I" is uttered by, and refers to, God. Individually they emphasize the utter otherness of God to humanity. Collectively, they underscore God's relational nature. To the former, two statements, one from the beginning of the account—"I created the heaven, and the earth upon which thou standest" (Moses 2:1)—and one from its end—"I grant life" (Moses 2:30). Previously, Moses encountered God and came away "know[ing]" that in comparison to God, humanity was "nothing" (Moses 1:10); now, he is shown the fact concretely. And yet, "the Lord spake unto *Moses*, saying: Behold, I reveal unto *you*" (Moses 2:1). Framed as a personal interaction, the repetition of "I" (thirty times in the first twelve verses) works to heighten the sense of intimacy. God, in transcendent otherness, is the provision, pattern, and precedent of human relating.

Not only are these creation accounts interconnected, but when read together they demonstrate the interconnectedness of God and creation. While their authorized existence in the Latter-day Saint canon performs work toward the legitimizing of difference, reading them, either individually or together, points toward a relational God—one intricately bound up with that which is not God.

Fall

As Fretheim has it, this "divine way of creating" reveals "a divine vulnerability." Said differently, "involving those who are not God" gives space "for the activity of finite creatures" bringing with it "all of the attendant risks in allowing creatures to be themselves."[33] Elsewhere, Avivah Gottlieb Zornberg, a contemporary Torah scholar, terms these risks "new possibilities" and "new hazards."[34] The possibility of relationship entails the possibility of alienation, of opposition, and of conflict. This means the choice to create necessitates at least the ceding of some power, and the giving away of some control. To take a relational stance is to accept the possibility of right *and* wrong relations, with their attendant consequences. If accounts of creation are primarily proclamations of the manner in which God relates to that which is not God, then accounts of the Fall can be read as explanations for why things are the way they are.[35]

Read this way, the issue at the heart of accounts of the Fall is the rejection of relationship. Along these lines, Zornberg suggests trouble came not from defiance of God's laws, but from the "abandonment of a difficult posture."[36] Relationship—with the messiness of speaking, of struggling, and of reckoning—is hard—even with God. Before partaking of the fruit, Adam "could hear God speaking and stand on his legs . . . he could withstand it." After, "he hides." This hiding is imagined as a "shrinking," a "pretending *not to be*," an attempted removal of presence.[37] Eating the fruit was not the problem, per se; the problem was Adam's and Eve's inability to endure in the relationship. Eating the fruit was an escape.

Eating the fruit, however, not only signaled a rejection of relationship with God, but also with others. Indeed, one strand of Hegelian thought suggests that the recognition of an other is a prerequisite for self-consciousness. This recognition, for the newly conscious, recognized self, presents a choice: acceptance or rejection of mutual dependence. Rejection is an exercise in egoism and becoming a "being-for-myself" while "rendering the other a being-for-*me*."[38] Acceptance enters the self into a relationship aimed at the unification of opposites, seeking the eradication of dominance—not difference—of one by the other. This is the situation that plays out in Genesis. Adam's comprehension of himself as a self corresponds to his comprehending Eve as an other, a self distinct from his own. Up until that point, Adam's lack of awareness of his own self extended to the removal of a part of that self without his apprehension.

Comprehending Eve, however, he not only recognized her flesh, but his own. Now, faced with a choice, he chose mutual dependence: the two flesh "shall be one" (Gen 2:24). Entering into a relationship aimed at the unification of opposites, neither Man nor Woman was shamed, because neither sought to dominate the other. Yet, after eating the fruit, a pronouncement: "thy husband . . . shall rule over thee" (Gen 3:16). "Relationships," Brodie observed, "from now on will involve pain."[39] This, it seems clear, is a reflection of the relationship's changed status because of its rejection, not a description of the relationship's natural order.[40] Humanity has traded unity and relationship for domination and alienation. Rejecting the proffered relation with God, misrelation with each other ensues. Right relation with others, it seems, is impossible without right relation with God.[41]

The natural end of such a trade is played out in the very next story. Cain, faced with the otherness of Abel, refused relationship and declined to be his brother's keeper. A slave to his ego, and seeking domination, "Cain rose up" and slew his brother (Gen 4:8). Humans, Kant observed, don't have to be bad in order to corrupt each other; "it suffices that they are there."[42] Then, when left unchecked, an "unjust desire to acquire superiority for oneself over others" results in "a maximum of evil."[43] Such, it would appear, is the risk of community.

In this way, "the essence of sin," as Wheeler terms it, "is eminently personal."[44] Enacted in relation, it has consequences for both relations and selves, resulting in disordered relations populated by deformed selves incapable of setting things right, or even seeing things right. This is the situation that greets us in the opening chapters of the Book of Mormon. These too can be read as a fall narrative, albeit taking a quite different form from that in Genesis.[45] The book begins with a vision in Jerusalem and very quickly thereafter a family fleeing into the wilderness (1 Ne 2:4). It is noticeable that the family left together, as a group, without any hint of division. This lasted three days (1 Ne 2:6) before the revelation that none of the sons believed the visions of their father. For Laman and Lemuel, unbelief bred complaint, and belief never materialized (1 Ne 2:11–13); for Nephi and Sam, turning to God meant that it did (1 Ne 2:16–17). Having left as one, the family was quickly divided in its beliefs (1 Ne 2:18). Later, Sariah complained, using the same language as Laman and Lemuel before expressing her own belief (1 Ne 5:2–3, 8). Soon, Lehi dreamed about a fruit tree (1 Ne 8). Eating the fruit filled Lehi with joy and he searched for his family. Finding Sariah, Nephi, and Sam some way off at the head of a river, standing "as if they knew not whither they should go" (1 Ne 8:14), Lehi called them to him. They traveled uneventfully to the tree and partook of the fruit. Next, looking for Laman and Lemuel, Lehi found them in the same spot, "but they would not come" (1 Ne 8:18). From this moment the dream drastically changed as mists, rods, and concourses of people not only complicated the way to the tree, but also the experience at the tree.

That Lehi looks twice is notable. Perhaps, however, this is the point. This twice looking and twice issuing suggests Lehi had internalized the division, dividing his sons in *his* dream as they had divided themselves in their lives. Thus, the Genesis narrative suggests that wrong relations with God complicates relations with others—this, that wrong relations with others complicates relations with God.[46] The narrative of the book bears this out. In Lehi's exhorting only one side (1 Ne 8:37), when on both sides of the brothers' divided relations with God and each other are severely compromised, the incapability of those involved in disordered relations to set or see them right is demonstrated—even when they are seers. This divided relational state is perpetuated for hundreds of years—despite the efforts of multiple seers—until the people directly encounter the resurrected Jesus. However, once division resurfaces, Kant's "maximum of evil" ensues.

A relational understanding of creation asserts relationships were established between God and humans "such that [human] decisions about the creation truly count."[47] As the feminist biblical scholar Phyllis Trible puts it, in committing to a meaningful relationship in which the contributions and decisions of both parties mean something, God "forfeits the right to reverse human decisions."[48] Their decisions have meaningful consequences. In suggesting that the relational consequences of rejecting relationship see "relationships at every level fall[ing] apart" accounts of the Fall attempt to explain the lived reality of human existence.[49] For Zornberg, rejection is a result of human consciousness. While vital to Hegelian self-awareness, too often a move toward domination is favored over mutual dependence. Sin, as manifest in the failure of relationships, stunts our capacity for right relation, leading humans to construct their own reality. In so doing, "the whole creation story is subtly undermined," and "what remains is a world that *is not really there*,"[50] a counterfeit image in need of redemption. What is needed is an atonement that actualizes God's original purpose for creation.

Atonement

Like Lazarus, bound and dead in his tomb, humanity cannot resolve its own predicament. Division from God perpetuates division with others, which perpetuates division from God. As with Lazarus, something new is required. For both, the solution is found in the scandal of the incarnation. For our purposes, this hypostatic union—the indwelling in the person of Jesus the fullness of both humanity and divinity—has two particularly significant implications: first, that the righting of relations truly matters to God; and second, that right relation is not only possible, it is integral to the fulfillment of God's purposes in creation. Each will be explored in turn.

On relations mattering to God

The third of Fretheim's five characteristics of the God-human relation states that God is genuinely affected by what happens to the relationship. While one may take issue with Wheeler's terms when he writes of God being "enriched" or "diminished" in relationship, it is harder to argue against "the divine passion, the responsiveness, the joy over repentant sinners and the grief over the rebellious and impenitent" as the repeated "testimony of scripture."[51] Doing so, in many instances, requires reading against the grain of their plain meaning that portrays a God deeply involved in, and genuinely affected by, the relationship. Perhaps this is best exemplified in the Incarnation. In assuming humanity, God's involvement became absolute. In Jesus's life, ministry, and passion, the relationship's importance is made clear. The Incarnation finds consummation in atonement, and both are for the sake of relationship. As the Evangelist expresses it: "God so loved the world that he gave his only begotten Son" (John 3:16).

Too often, however, this statement floats in the consciousness of Christians shorn of its context: Jesus's encounter with Nicodemus. A statement from Nicodemus—"we know that thou art a teacher come from God" (John 3:2)—initiates the interaction, implying "the *one* question" the Jerusalem establishment must "put to Jesus," that is, "the question of *salvation*."[52] If that is not immediately clear from the statement itself, it becomes startlingly so with Jesus's response: humanity in its current condition cannot be saved.[53] When read through the prism of a relational fall, the problem of our orientation in relationship is thrown into sharp relief: when relations are disordered, salvation is impossible. Jesus's use of birth imagery underscores this. Birth, as Bultmann observes, suggests "origin."[54] Together with the language of "except" and "cannot" (John 3:3, 5), this works to reveal the relational brokenness of humanity. As birth entails not just a bringing about of existence, but a bringing about in relation, Jesus here rejects the whole foundation of human relations.[55] Both humans and their entire relational matrix need to be reborn. And yet, as Dutch theologian Hermann Ridderbos reminds us, as "the Word" Jesus "did not come to a world that was foreign to him." He had made it. The distinction between flesh and spirit then (John 3:6) is contained in "the creatureliness and dependence of humanity in relation to God as Spirit, Source, and Ruler of all of life." Thus, spirit as God is here contrasted with flesh as "the radical disturbance that has arisen in [our] existence as a result of the self-direction that has brought us into a position of estrangement from God."[56] Having exchanged flesh that originated in image for a counterfeit, participation in God's kingdom—in life as God intended—requires rebirth, a re-creation bringing a radical re-origination and with it the relational reorientation that comes with new existence. As creation and birth are works of others that define us relationally as creature and child, so too is re-creation and its relational redefining as new creatures in, and children of, Christ (2 Cor 5:17; Moses 5:7). Each is a grace to be received as a gift.

In this way the incarnation is a reorienting event. Jesus, as Christ, not only exemplified "the optimal divine-human relationship," he embodied it.[57] It was the harmonic fusion in his body of the human and the divine that introduced the world to the possibility of relational harmony. His submission to the decay and disorder of death revealed the extent of his investment in making it available. For the Evangelist, it is this—the humanity of Jesus, as expressed in his life and death—that is *the* essential eschatological event. While humans are incapable of bringing about salvation, and their ongoing state of disrelation makes it impossible, the Incarnation holds open its possibility. In the exaltation of the Son of man, salvation is made available. The resurrection and ascension of the risen Lord is the determinative thing. Yet, resurrection and ascension, too, have necessary preconditions: descent (John 3:13), and death (John 3:14). The redemption of human relations requires God's complete participation in them and, therefore, in all the conditions of human mortality.

Alma, in the Book of Mormon, makes this same point: "the Son of God" he preached, "suffereth according to the flesh that he might take upon him the sins of his people," and this despite the Spirit's knowing "all things" (Alma 7:13). Here, the Son of God's human experience appears to trump his divine knowledge. It is his suffering as "flesh" that facilitates his taking upon himself "the sins of his people." When "flesh" is understood as estrangement and sin as "eminently personal" then the reality of disordered relations as the root cause of human suffering is exposed.[58] It is this that the Son of God takes upon himself. Having been "born of Mary" (Alma 7:10) Alma notes, "he shall go forth suffering" (Alma 7:11). Mortal birth through a human mother incarnates God in the midst of the brokenness of human relations. From Herod's slaughter of the innocents to the desolation of his passion, his life was marred by their extremes from beginning to end. Indeed, R. Alan Culpepper, an American scholar of the New Testament, has traced through Mark's Gospel Jesus's gradual abandonment, culminating with the cry of dereliction.[59] In his own desolating end the ultimate end of broken relations is revealed. To the cry itself William Lane notes, "Various expedients have been adopted to cushion the offense." For him, they all "bear the marks of special pleading and are unsatisfactory." Instead, he argues, in its expression of "the unfathomable pain of real abandonment by the Father," the "sharp edge of this word must not be blunted."[60] Having been progressively deserted by humanity, Jesus was finally forsaken by

God and in the horror of that separation encountered the agony of desolation and alienation in its fullness.

In participating completely in human relations Jesus experienced the full ramifications of their disintegration and provided a way for humanity's escape. This rebirth not only reorients humans relationally, it makes generally available the relational possibilities of the Incarnation. God embraced—to the fullest extent—the humiliation of disordered human relations, in order to make available—to the fullest extent—human participation in the divine relation.

On right relations and the fulfilling of God's Purposes

If sin is relational, then atonement for sin must entail the at-one-ment of all broken relationships.[61] However, despite the historical passion of Jesus two thousand years ago, it is clear relations are not "at-one'd." Humanity's problems continue to proliferate, from the interpersonal to the international. Where does this leave an account of atonement? Perhaps with this observation from Oxford systematic theologian Paul Fiddes: "there is a great deal of difference," he writes, "in believing that God 'saves' through Christ, and believing that we simply claim the benefits of a salvation that has already happened, a deal that has already been concluded."[62] The first suggests a process that is ongoing and transformative in the present; the second, an event that is done and transactional with the past. Approaching atonement relationally favors the first: the continuing phenomenon of disordered relationships necessitates atonement be a continuing phenomenon. To be effective, salvation must perpetually occur right here, right now, as relationships do. Accepting this has implications for what it means to understand Jesus, as Christ, to be the Savior of the world.

For salvation to be perpetual—as the continuing state of one being or as an ever-present possibility for generations of beings—atonement must be infinite. To describe the atonement as infinite, then, is not to make a statement about either the quantity or the quality of Jesus's suffering. This is observed most basically in the passion's finite duration. And, while the suffering of others plays a complex role in the righting of wrong relations, Amulek is emphatic that as a strategy for atonement it is unjust and ineffectual. Atonement cannot work that way (Alma 34:11). Violence cannot redeem violence and the suffering caused by disordered relations does not set them at one. Instead, Amulek argues for "an infinite atonement" (Alma 34:12), because of the "hardened," "fallen," and "lost" state of *all* humanity in which the unavoidable outcome is their perishing (Alma 34:9). Here Amulek sets up a contrast between humanity's complete loss and its complete salvation. Appealing to the law of Moses, Amulek suggests the ultimate end of atonement is the cessation of bloodshed (Alma 34:13). While initially the immediate context of sacrifice and the law of Moses seems to connect atonement with ritual slaughter, Jesus's own summation of the law points beyond this: "Thou shalt love the Lord thy God with all thy heart, and with all thy soul, and with all thy mind," and "Thou shalt love thy neighbour as thyself" (Matt 22:37, 39). It is on these Jesus hangs the law. For it to "be all fulfilled" (Alma 34:13) bloodshed must completely cease. All relations between all persons must be healed. *This* is "the whole meaning of the law" (Alma 34:14). It is this possibility and the sustaining of its reality that makes atonement infinite.

In this way an invocation of infinite atonement asserts the redemption of all individuals *and* the totality of their relations. Claiming Jesus as Savior of the world affirms his ability to save all in the world—regardless of social location, class, race, ethnicity, sexuality, or religion—and to do so in community. This variety suggests a one-size-fits-all theory of atonement will not do, and neither will a pro forma Jesus. Atonement must embrace multiplicity and Jesus must have many faces.[63] "Jesus Christ, yesterday, today, and tomorrow," writes Ghanaian theologian Mercy Amba Oduyoye, "requires that each generation declare its faith in relation to its today."[64] Put another way: if Jesus of Nazareth is to be the Christ of all people, at all times, and in all places, then he must be relatable to, and identifiable as, the Christ, in all places, at all times, to all people. This is a Christological necessity. As Cameroonian Catholic thinker Thérèsa Souga suggests: "There can be no understanding of Jesus Christ outside of the situation in which we seek to understand ourselves."[65] It is from these situations that one must declare faith, and it is in these situations that salvation must occur.

To this, the Book of Mormon lends credence. After Lehi's dream comes Nephi's vision. If Lehi's dream articulates the problem of divided relations, Nephi's vision suggests the solution. Yet it does so in a puzzling way. After Nephi's confession of belief, the vision proper is introduced with the promise of a sign: After seeing the tree he shall "behold a man descending out of heaven" (1 Ne 11:7). While he is told what the sign will be, he is not told what it means, and upon seeing the tree he does not immediately see the sign.[66] Rather, he sees the birth, ministry, and death of Jesus. Curiously he does not see the resurrection. Instead, he sees the tumultuous history of his own people, as disordered relations give rise to wars and bloodshed. Then, with his society on the brink, "[he] saw the heavens open, and the Lamb of God descending out of heaven" (1 Ne 12:6). The sign was given and "three generations pass away in righteousness" (1 Ne 12:11). That Nephi does not see the resurrection is suggestive, as is the location of the sign in the vision's narrative. Death at Jerusalem followed by descending—*alive*—amongst Nephi's descendants has the effect of placing the resurrection there, amongst them. As the "completion" of "the atoning work of God" Fiddes "maintain[s] the resurrection [as] a historical event" is "essential" because of its "challenge to the way the world is" and its testimony "of a God who is free to do new things."[67] Nephi's vision takes a step beyond. The resurrection it proclaims must be experienced in one's own context. When it is, the way the world is changes.

The contextual nature of this experience implies the continued expansion of "what it means for the risen Christ to be Saviour of the world today."[68] As the multiplicity of creation accounts legitimizes difference, so multiplicity in accounts of atonement validates it, first, by disclosing the particularity inherent in universal salvation, and second, by hinting toward its ultimate end: sacralized right relation. These relations include those between God and humanity and humanity amongst themselves. Use of "selves" here is important. Homogenization is not a byproduct of reconciliation. Right relations harmonize individuality rather than flatten difference. The saved community is, necessarily, a diverse community. However, it must also be a *saving* community. As the story of Lazarus suggests, salvation is tripartite, involving Christ, the community, and ourselves. This seems to be the position advocated by Jesus in his visit to the Nephites. There he commanded the community not to "cast [people] out." Rather, they should "continue to minister; for ye do know not but what they will return and repent . . . and I shall heal them, and ye shall be the means of bringing salvation unto them." Again the three, in strikingly similar terms to those enacted in raising Lazarus: they will return, I will heal, and *you* will be the means of salvation. Yet, there is in those words of Jesus one further astonishing implication—not only does the community participate in the salvific process, but their participation enables the full expression of Christ's own. In the Incarnation, humanity and divinity is harmonized in the person of Christ, and salvation is catalyzed. Atonement makes that same union available to Christ's body—his community—and when it is replicated, salvation is actualized.

Conclusion

"Theories of atonement are," in Fiddes words, "conceptual tools with which we try to grasp a mystery in the divine-human relationship."[69] This chapter has attempted some work toward expanding the tool kit. While a fully systematic account has not been presented, suggestive groundwork has been laid. Taking relation seriously as the core of God's being and purpose in creation has ramifications for understanding atonement. The personal nature of sin requires the personal response of an incarnate God making generally available the relational possibilities embodied in the incarnation, while suggesting atonement is an ongoing phenomenon. As in creation, atonement involves necessary acts by God that none other can do *and* the community's participation. God's relational posture is unremittingly collaborative, and this is reflected in the redeemed community. "And the Lord called his *people* Zion," the scripture attests, "because *they* were of one heart and one mind" (Moses 7:18, emphasis mine). Zion is always a people, never a person; always a they, never an I; always a multiplicity, never a singularity. It not only exists in community, it depends upon it. Zion, it is clear, is right relations. And so too is salvation.

In Memoriam Terence E. Fretheim (1936–2020)[70]

Notes

1. The ubiquitousness of this "insight" in Latter-day Saint spaces may stem from its use by James E. Talmage in his wildly influential *Jesus the Christ*. Despite its proliferation in talks, articles, and books—and Talmage's terming it a "basal thought,"—its implications have yet to be fully plumbed. This chapter is a gesture in that direction. See James E. Talmage, *Jesus the Christ*, 17th ed. (Salt Lake City: Deseret Book, 1948), 21.

2. David L. Wheeler, *A Relational View of the Atonement: Prolegomenon to a Reconstruction of the Doctrine* (New York: Peter Lang: 1989), 109.

3. Terence E. Fretheim, *God and World in the Old Testament: A Relational Theology of Creation* (Nashville, TN: Abingdon, 2005), 21–22. In his last book, Fretheim added five more characteristics: God will be absolutely faithful to the commitments God has made; God is concerned about our entire selves; God will be present with God's creatures at all times and in all places; God will be active in the life of the world; God recognizes the need for a healthy "space" between those who are in relationship. See Terence E. Fretheim, *God So Enters into Relationships That . . . : A Biblical View* (Minneapolis: Fortress Press, 2020).

4. Michael J. Chan and Brent A. Strawn, eds., *What Kind of God: Collected Essays of Terence E. Fretheim* (Winona Lake, IN: Eisenbrauns, 2015), 4.

5. See Fretheim's *God and World in the Old Testament* for its most comprehensive expression.

6. Christoph Schwöbel, "God, Creation, and the Christian Community: The Dogmatic Basis of a Christian Ethic of Createdness," in *The Doctrine of Creation: Essays in Dogmatics, History and Philosophy,* edited by Colin E. Gunton (New York: T&T Clark, 2004), 154.

7. Thomas L. Brodie, *The Gospel According to John: A Literary and Theological Commentary* (New York: Oxford University Press, 1983), 385.

8. See Moses 18:8–10 in the Book of Mormon, and Givens's discussion of a weeping God, a burden-bearing Christ, and a comforting Spirit in Fiona and Terryl Givens, *All Things New: Rethinking Sin to Salvation and Everything in Between* (Meridian, ID: Faith Matters Publishing, 2020).

9. "At least in part" because Jesus initially responds the sickness is "for the glory of God" (John 11:4). However, given the story's thoroughly relational setting, the invocation of relationship when they do set out, the involvement of the community in the raising, and the suggestion of a symbolic depiction of Jesus's journey to resurrection

which gives life to believers, it may be that the two are one: God is glorified by the setting right of relationships.

10. Brodie, *Gospel according to John*, 397. Compare John 5:8, "Rise, take ... walk," and 9:7, "Go, wash ... Siloam," with 11:39, "Take ye away the stone"; 11:43, "Lazarus come forth"; and 11:44, "Loose him and let him go."

11. John N. Suggit, "The Raising of Lazarus," *The Expository Times* 95.4 (1984): 107, (emphasis mine).

12. Brodie, *Gospel according to John*, 398 (emphasis mine).

13. Fretheim, *God and World in the Old Testament*, 4 (emphasis in original).

14. As Norman Pittenger has it, "Man is a dependent being. He does not explain himself; he did not bring himself into existence; if he has any significance at all it is a significance that must be found in his relationship as a being dependent on that which is not man." See W. Norman Pittenger, *The Christian Understanding of Human Nature* (Philadelphia: Westminster, 1964), 21. By constitutional necessity, humanity is absolutely relational.

15. Ian A. McFarland, *Creation and Humanity: The Sources of Christian Theology* (Louisville: Westminster John Knox, 2009), xiii.

16. To refer to a Genesis account, singular, goes against the grain of much biblical scholarship showing the probability of chapters 1 and 2 being separate accounts. I do so here not to stake a position against that, but in recognition of the fact that the final text is written so they are read together.

17. Robert W. Jenson, "Aspects of a Doctrine of Creation" in Gunton, *The Doctrine of Creation*, 17. This "absolute difference" was in many ways the impetus for the traditional understanding of an *ex nihilo* creation. Settled in the second century, this teaching was spurred by a desire to protect God's sovereignty. "Nothing" it was advanced, "can be co-eternal with the one God." Matter cannot be "unoriginate and coexistent" because then, (1) it must needs be considered divine, and (2) God could not be declared the creator of everything. See David Fergusson, "Creation," in *The Oxford Handbook of Systematic Theology*, edited by John Webster, Kathryn Tanner, and Iain Torrance (New York: Oxford University Press, 2007), 79–80.

18. Terence E. Fretheim, "Preaching Creation: Genesis 1–2," *Word and World* 29 (2009): 77.

19. Terence E. Fretheim, *Creation Untamed: The Bible, God, and Natural Disasters* (Grand Rapids, MI: Baker Academic, 2010), 66.

20. Fretheim, *God and World in the Old Testament*, 36, 37, 42. For modes of creation, see 34–36; for images of God as creator see 36–48.

21. "God said" occurs ten times, in verses 3, 6, 9, 11, 14, 20, 24, 26, 28, and 29; "God called" occurs three times, in verses 5, 8, and 10; and "God blessed" occurs twice, in verses 22 and 28. The eight forms of speech acts are: (1) creating, vv. 3, 6, 14; (2) naming, vv. 5, 8, 10; (3) ordering, v. 9; (4) participation in creation, vv. 11, 20, 24, 26; (5) blessing, vv. 22, 2; (6) commissioning, v. 28; and (7) sharing power, vv. 28, 29.

22. Given the relational implications for one's understanding of God, it is significant and worth emphasizing that Genesis 1 appears to portray God as both creating from nothing *and* from existing materials.

23. Susan Brayford, *Genesis* (Leiden, Netherlands: Brill, 2007), 220.

24. David W. Cotter, *Genesis* (Collegeville, MN: Liturgical Press, 2003), 4. Here Cotter notes that God's aloneness in this creative "prerogative" is conveyed by "the initiatory verb *bārā'*" referring solely to God.

25. Thomas L. Brodie, *Genesis as Dialogue: A Literary, Historical, and Theological Commentary* (New York: Oxford University Press, 2001), 134.

26. Fretheim, *God and World in the Old Testament*, 37.

27. Fretheim, *God and World in the Old Testament*, 38.

28. The reference to "us" here "is commonly understood to be a reference to divine or semi-divine beings of the heavenly realm or divine council/ assembly (see 1 Kgs 22:19; Job 38:7; Ps 8:5–6; Isa 6:1–8; Jer 23:18–23)" (Fretheim, *God and World*, 42).

29. Fretheim, *God and World in the Old Testament*, 42.

30. David Bentley Hart, *That All Shall be Saved: Heaven, Hell, and Universal Salvation* (New Haven: Yale University Press, 2019), 141, 143.

31. Claus Westermann, *Genesis 1–11: A Commentary*, translated by John J. Scullion (Minneapolis: Augsburg, 1984), 158.

32. See also Abr 1:15, "I lifted up my voice unto the Lord my God, and the Lord hearkened," and 1:16, "I have heard thee, and have come down."

33. Fretheim, *God and World in the Old Testament*, 38.

34. Avivah Gottlieb Zornberg, *The Beginning of Desire: Reflections on Genesis* (New York: Schocken Books, 2011), 4.

35. "Explanation" here does not mean historical report. Rather, "explanation" signals an attempt to understand and portray the human predicament. As Karl Barth frames it, "Adam is the truth concerning us as it is known to God and told to us." See Karl Barth, *Church Dogmatics*, IV/1 (Edinburgh: T&T Clark, 1956), 509.

36. Zornberg, *Beginning of Desire*, 24.

37. Zornberg, *Beginning of Desire*, 23 (emphasis in original).

38. Todd DuBose, "Lordship, Bondage, and the Formation of 'Homo Religiosus,'" *Journal of Religion and Health*, 39.3 (2000): 218, emphasis in original.

39. Brodie, *Genesis as Dialogue*, 142.

40. Fretheim terms this God's "*announcement* of what the sinful deeds have wrought" commenting that "it is especially remarkable that the 'rule' of the man over the woman is seen as a consequence of sin; hence it stands over against God's creational intention." See Fretheim, *God and World in the Old Testament*, 76.

41. While the focus here is on the God-human relation, it is important, as Fretheim points out, "to see that this text does not simply speak of the effects of sin in terms of a breakdown of the God-human relationship; all creatures are caught up in the snowballing effects of human sinfulness, becoming creation-wide in its scope" meaning there is now "dissonance in every relationship, between humans, humans and God, humans and animals, humans and the earth, and within the self"—hence the need for atonement that is similarly creation-wide in its scope. See Fretheim, *God and World in the Old Testament*, 73, 75.

42. Immanuel Kant, quoted in *Religion within the Boundaries of Mere Reason and*

Other Writings, edited by Allen Wood and George di Giovanni (Cambridge: Cambridge University Press, 2016), 105.

43. Kant, quoted in Wood and Di Giovanni, *Religion within the Boundaries of Mere Reason*, 51.

44. Wheeler, *Relational View of the Atonement*, 191.

45. Joseph Spencer influences characterization of this as a fall narrative. He has argued convincingly for a four-part structure to the two books that open the Book of Mormon of creation, fall, atonement, and veil. While he places the Fall section later, after the brothers physically separate, as I read Lehi's dream that moment finds it foreshadowing in 1 Ne 8. For Spencer's four-part structuring see Joseph M. Spencer, *An Other Testament:* (Provo, UT: Neal A Maxwell Institute for Religious Scholarship, 2016), 33–68.

46. For a much fuller outworking of this relational reading of the dream see my chapter, "Lehi and His Dream: A Relational Reading," in *Re-Visioning the Dream: Interpreting 1 Nephi 8*, edited by Benjamin Keogh, Joseph M. Spencer, and Jennifer Champoux (Provo, UT: Neal A. Maxwell Institute for Religious Scholarship, forthcoming).

47. Fretheim, *God and World in the Old Testament*, 59.

48. Phyllis Trible, *God and the Rhetoric of Sexuality* (Philadelphia: Fortress Press, 1986), 93.

49. Fretheim, *God and World in the Old Testament*, 71.

50. Zornberg, *Beginning of Desire*, 26 (emphasis in original).

51. Wheeler, *Relational View of the Atonement*, 196–97.

52. Rudolf Bultmann, *The Gospel of John: A Commentary*, translated by G. R. Beasley-Murray, R. W. N. Hoare, and J. K. Riches (Philadelphia: Westminster, 1971), 134.

53. Jesus's first two statements are variations of the same construction: "*except*" for rebirth, humanity "*cannot*" participate in the "kingdom of God" (John 3:3, 5, emphasis mine). Ridderbos points out that "see" in verse 3 should be understood as "permitted to share in," or "have personal experience of, participate in," aligning it more fully with verse 5's "enter" than it may initially appear in English. See Herman Ridderbos, *Gospel of John: A Theological Commentary*, translated by John Vriend (Grand Rapids, MI: William B. Eerdmans, 1997), 125.

54. Bultmann, *Gospel of John*, 137.

55. In a similar way this can also be seen in his asking and answering whom his mother and brethren were. See Matt 12:47–50; Mark 3:32–35; and Luke 8:19–21.

56. Ridderbos, *Gospel of John*, 131.

57. Wheeler, *Relational View of the Atonement*, 209.

58. Wheeler, *Relational View of the Atonement*, 191.

59. Culpepper mentions the plotting of his death by religious and political leaders, "early on," the misunderstanding of his ministry by his family and disciples, his rejection in his hometown, his betrayal by Judas, denial by Peter, and desertion by others, and his abuse at the hands of crowds, soldiers, Pilate, and crucified thieves. See R. Alan Culpepper, *Mark* (Macon, GA: Smyth & Helwys, 2007), 558–59.

60. William L. Lane, *The Gospel of Mark* (Grand Rapids: William B. Eerdmans, 1974), 572–73.

61. As noted above and despite the glancing focus here, this reconciliation must reach beyond the human creation to include the healing of estrangements with the nonhuman creation as well.

62. Paul S. Fiddes, *Past Event and Present Salvation: The Christian Idea of Atonement* (London: Darton, Longman and Todd, 1989), 14.

63. For an introduction to the plurality of legitimate Christologies from around the globe, see Volker Kuster, *The Many Faces of Jesus Christ: Intercultural Christology* (New York: Orbis Books, 2001), and Veli-Matti Kärkkäinen, *Christology: A Global Introduction* (Grand Rapids, MI: Baker Academic, 2016); for the plurality of Christologies detectable in the New Testament, see Raymond E. Brown, *An Introduction to New Testament Christology* (Mahwah, NJ: Paulist, 2004), or Thomas P. Rausch, *Who Is Jesus? An Introduction to Christology* (Collegeville, MN: Liturgical Press, 2003); for the plurality of Christologies throughout history, see Gerald O'Collins, *Christology: A Biblical, Historical, and Systematic Study of Jesus* (New York: Oxford University Press, 2009), Elizabeth A. Johnson, *Consider Jesus: Waves of Renewal in Christology* (New York: Crossroad, 2000), and Jaroslav Pelikan, *Jesus Through the Centuries: His Place in the History of Culture* (New Haven: Yale University Press, 1999).

64. Mercy Amba Oduyoye, "Jesus Christ," in *The Cambridge Companion to Feminist Theology*, edited by Susan F. Parsons (Cambridge: Cambridge University Press, 2004), 151.

65. Thérèsa Souga, "The Christ-Event from the Viewpoint of African Women: A Catholic Perspective," in *Passion and Compassion: Third World Women Doing Theology*, edited by Virginia Fabella and Mercy Amba Oduyoye (Maryknoll: Orbis Books, 1990), 21.

66. Joseph Spencer points out the curiosity of the sign's delay and provides his own reading in Joseph M. Spencer, *1st Nephi: A Brief Theological Introduction*, (Provo, UT: Neal A. Maxwell Institute for Religious Scholarship, 2020).

67. Fiddes, *Past Event and Present Salvation*, 40–41.

68. Fiddes, *Past Event and Present Salvation*, 38.

69. Fiddes, *Past Event and Present Salvation*, 28.

70. Terence Fretheim is one of the most prolific and influential biblical theologians of recent times. His writings have impacted my own thinking immensely. As I was preparing the final draft of this piece he passed away, on November 16, 2020. For that reason, and in his memory, I dedicate this to him.

CHAPTER 11

One Prophet's Vision of a Nonviolent Atonement

The Book of Mormon as Theological Resource

JOSEPH M. SPENCER

Sifting the historical evidence, Terryl Givens states that "two conclusions are possible" regarding early Latter-day Saint reflection on the Christian idea of atonement. Either "the atonement was not central to Mormon thought in the church's formative years," he says, or "atonement theory was absolutely central, but largely adopted without comment from contemporary Christian usage."[1] Given the prevalence of atonement theology in the Book of Mormon, the publication of which launched the Latter-day Saint movement, the second possibility appears most likely. That is, it seems probable that nineteenth-century Latter-day Saints were in fact "distracted by the need to elaborate and defend [their] points of radical difference" and so were "slower to fully explore and articulate the doctrine on which all else depends."[2] They certainly seem to have only found in the Book of Mormon "the same terminology" used and "the same views" held by "early nineteenth-century evangelicals," to use Charles Harrell's words.[3]

On closer inspection, however, the Book of Mormon proves a rich and robust source for theologizing about Christian atonement. It has been used in recent decades to articulate potential problems with traditional notions of penal substitution, to argue for a concept of grace that outstrips human salvation, to assess the merits of an incarnational "compassion" view of atonement, and to debate Latter-day Saint commitments to robust notions of a justice that is binding on God.[4] To this point, however, the Book of Mormon has been more of a resource than a direct object of theological reflection. That is, Latter-day Saint theologians interested in thinking Christian atonement have used the Book of Mormon as an authoritative source, but there has been less interest in asking how the Book of Mormon itself might be said to participate directly in debates about the meaning of atonement.

The Book of Mormon presents itself as a narrative history, not as a doctrinal manual. It should therefore not be expected to present a consistent view on any particular theological idea or question. This means, at the very least, that it might be better read as something *other than* a collection of authoritative or "correct" positions on atonement theology, despite the fact that the book presents all such positions as ones taken by prophetically gifted individuals. The Book of Mormon is or can be read as, instead, a long and complex story about how changing historical circumstances give believers to reflect in changing ways on Christian atonement.[5] My aim in this paper is to show just how fruitful this sort of approach might be for theological reflection, as much for traditional Latter-day Saint theologians committed to the divinity of the Book of Mormon as for interested theologians from outside the Latter-day Saint tradition. I will consider just one short stretch of the Book of Mormon, working to show how it sets up a complex contrast between two dramatically different ways of reflecting on Christian atonement, and then relate these two different styles of theologizing within a larger investigation of the relationship between religious belief and political power.[6]

I will argue that there lies at the heart of these two rival Book of Mormon visions of Christian atonement—each nested within a rival conception of the relevance of the state to Christianity—a subtle question of whether it is right to focus atonement talk at all on the blood of Jesus Christ. Is the violent imagery of sacrifice a help or a hindrance in creating a community of believers that might "stand as witnesses of God at all times and in all things and in all places" (Mos 18:8)?[7] Obviously, theologians at various times in Christian history have provided answers to that question for reasons they have made clear. The Book of Mormon adds to that protracted historical conversation not by inserting yet another answer with yet another set of reasons to defend it, but rather by showing the difficulty of answering the question straightforwardly. This it accomplishes through the telling of a rich and interesting story.

The Shape of Book of Mormon Political Theology

Like the Bible, the Book of Mormon is made up of books that generally bear the names of major characters or key prophetic figures. The theological question regarding atonement I will track here finds its context in the book of Mosiah, named for a king over the Book of Mormon's chief protagonists, the Nephites.[8] The book of Mosiah covers a period when the Nephites are settled principally in the land of Zarahemla (having abandoned their original geographical setting, the land of Nephi) and live under the governmental form of monarchy. The book ends when the Nephites willingly give up monarchy to be governed by a system of judges, expressing their collective anxiety "that every man should have an equal chance throughout all the land" (Mos 29:38). The book of Mosiah is thus in some sense the Book of Mormon's "book of kings," a sustained reflection on the institution of monarchy (or any strongly centralized state without an established commitment to the rule of law). One scholar points out the relatively obvious: "The book is an extended treatise on good and bad government."[9] At the book's heart is a comparison between two extreme figures—the righteous King Benjamin and the wicked King Noah.

Benjamin and Noah are not strict contemporaries in the Book of Mormon. Each, however, is the second figure in parallel Nephite dynasties that consist of three kings each, one ruling in the new Nephite land of Zarahemla and the other in a Nephite colony established temporarily and precariously among the Nephites' enemies, the Lamanites, in their abandoned former land of Nephi. The text draws attention to contrasting parallels between the two royal figures.[10] In a long address to his people at the end of his life, Benjamin claims that he has "not sought gold, nor silver, nor no manner of riches" from his people (Mos 2:12), while the narrator points out that Noah "laid a tax of one fifth part of all [his people] possessed: a fifth part of their gold, and of their silver" (11:3). Benjamin tells his people that he has "labored" to serve them, encouraging them "to labor to serve one another" (2:14, 18), but the narrator explains that Noah's people were forced to "labor exceedingly to support iniquity," the excesses of their king and his priests (11:6). Benjamin warns his people directly to "beware, lest there shall arise contentions among you" (2:32), while Noah's son reports to his people later that, under Noah, "there arose contentions among them, even so much that they did shed blood among themselves" (7:25). Both kings are described as building towers next to their temples, but for dramatically different purposes: Benjamin in order to ensure that his people "might hear the words which he should speak unto them" in a discourse about the coming Messiah (2:7), but Noah in order to "stand upon the top thereof and overlook . . . all the land round about" in acts of surveillance (11:12).

Contrasting parallels between the two kings pile up, but the most important of them concerns the fact that both are visited by a divine messenger with a strikingly similar message to which each has to decide how to react.[11] The message is, in both cases, that "God himself shall come down among the children of men and shall redeem his people" (Mos 15:1).[12] As the future tense of this prediction makes perfectly clear, these words come to the two respective kings in the pre-Christian era—more than a century before the birth of Jesus of Nazareth, according to the Book of Mormon's internal chronology. The message comes to Benjamin through a personal visit from an unnamed angel, but to Noah through the arrival among his people of a prophet named Abinadi.

Benjamin, the obviously exemplary king, not only responds positively to the angelic word at a personal level; he also arranges for his whole people to hear the angel's words, delivered to them at a kind of national assembly focused on "sacrifice and burnt offerings" mandated by "the law of Moses" (2:3).[13] When the gathered crowd is too large for Benjamin to be heard, the text reports, "he caused that the words which he spake should be written and sent forth among those that were not under the sound of his voice, that they might also receive his words" (2:8). Noah, by contrast, responds in a wholly negative fashion to the prophet that comes among his people, having him brought in for a trial—at the conclusion of which the prophet, Abinadi, dies for his testimony (see 17:6–8). The prophet's words are written and circulated, like those of the angel who visits Benjamin, but this happens against Noah's wishes, undertaken by a rogue priest named Alma, who writes an account of the trial while in hiding and then goes about "privately among the people . . . to teach the words of Abinadi" (18:1).

The carefully constructed book of Mosiah thus sets side by side two parallel but contrasting accounts of Christian teaching in a pre-Christian context. In both accounts, the message is largely the same—that God would come down in the flesh to redeem his people. What happens among believers in the two stories, however, differs substantially in their respective contexts. Where a good and righteous king sits in power, he receives and passes along that message with stark clarity, even taking care to produce a written account of the divine word so that all of his people have an opportunity to know it. And the result of Benjamin's efforts with the angel's words is the voluntary establishment of a covenant commitment to the Christian message among the whole of his people. As the text reports the aftermath of Benjamin's speech: "There was not one soul—except it were little children—but what had entered into the covenant and had taken upon them the name of Christ" (Mos 6:2). A much less impressive situation obtains in the otherwise parallel situation where a corrupt and wicked king rules. Noah has the (unfortunately mortal) messenger who comes among his people killed, and so the prophet Abinadi's words circulate, even in written form, only among a few of those under Noah's reign. The sharing of Abinadi's words has to be done "privately, that it might not come to the knowledge of the king," and those who believe it gather in secret only "in the borders of the land" (18:3–4). There, Alma's preaching of Abinadi's words has some success, and "two hundred and four souls" make a covenant like that of Benjamin's people (18:16). This group soon swells its numbers to "about four hundred and fifty souls" (18:35). This might sound impressive, but it is dramatically less spectacular than the nationwide covenant made by Benjamin's people in the parallel story, and Alma's new "church" (18:17) is forced into the wilderness to avoid a raid by Noah's military forces.[14]

These further details show that the book of Mosiah should not be read as a reflection alone on the simple question of good and bad government, righteous and wicked kings. Rather, it seems to be what happens when divinely sent messengers come with a prophetic word about Christ to strikingly different rulers. Where a righteous king rules, the word about Christ reaches the people—in fact, reaches them so forcefully that literally all of them enroll as Christian believers. Where a wicked king rules, the word about Christ is nearly silenced, progressing only in the shadows where a few believers find space for private expression of their Christian belief. In Zarahemla, then, the reader finds an exploration of a kind of total fusion of (good Christian) religion and (monarchical state) power, but in the land of Nephi the reader finds an exploration of a total separation of these spheres.[15] This way of summarizing the book of Mosiah, however, is still overly simplistic, because the book does not reflect simply on the short-term consequences of what happens in Benjamin's and Noah's respective regimes. It continues the story to the end, and surprising turns of event dramatically complicate any straightforward moral. One might of course read the first half of the book of Mosiah and conclude that kings like Benjamin make for great Christian nations and kings like Noah force marginalized Christians into situations of oppression. The second half of the book, however, points in rather different directions.

As the book of Mosiah continues, the parallel Nephite dynasties merge once more. The colony in the land of Nephi, where Noah has reigned, eventually abandons its colonizing project and returns to the main Nephite body in Zarahemla. Also returning to Zarahemla at the same time is Alma's church in the wilderness. Consequently, where the earlier parts of the book of Mosiah keep the two experiments regarding religion and the state quite separate, the last part of the book raises questions about what happens when the two experiments merge, or at least come directly into contact. Although the last king over the colony gives up any claim to kingship upon arrival in Zarahemla, Alma does not cede his position as high priest over his newly formed church—this despite the fact that the kingdom in Zarahemla has its own religious infrastructure, including priests serving with its sacral king (see Mos 27:1; 6:3).[16] Thus, as the generation alive during Benjamin's and Noah's parallel reigns passes and a "rising generation" takes its place in a newly reunited land of Zarahemla (26:1), the question of the long-term efficacy of the two experiments becomes pressing. Does either have the makings of something genuinely stable, prepared to last?

The text makes perfectly clear that Benjamin's national Christian covenant does not last. "Now," it reports, "it came to pass that there was many of the rising generation that could not understand the words of King Benjamin—being little children at the time he spake unto his people—and they did not believe the tradition of their fathers. They did not believe what had been said concerning the resurrection of the dead, neither did they believe concerning the coming of Christ" (Mos 26:1–2). Despite Benjamin's openness to the angelic word, despite his willingness to make it known to everyone in his kingdom, despite his success in provoking his whole people to Christian belief, and despite their universal enactment of a covenant to stay strong "in the faith of that which is to come, which was spoken by the mouth of the angel" (4:11), what Benjamin initiates lasts only a generation. The fusion of Christian religion with state power proves to have—at least in this case—a short shelf life. And Benjamin's son and successor, Mosiah, decides that there is a general lesson (rather than a local aberration) in this. With explicit reference to his father, he says to his people in what turns out to be his own final speech, "If ye could have men for your kings which would do even as my father Benjamin did for this people—I say unto you, if this could always be the case, then it would be expedient that ye should always have kings to rule over you" (29:13). Unfortunately, Mosiah continues, this is not the case. "Because all men are not just," he says, "it is not expedient that ye should have a king or kings to rule over you—for behold how much iniquity doth one wicked king cause to be committed! . . . Yea, remember King Noah, his wickedness and his abominations!" (29:16–17). Mosiah writes up the final report on Benjamin's experiment, and he concludes that the experiment has succeeded only in the short term.

Mosiah provides his summary conclusions regarding the long-term effects of Benjamin's experiment on an important occasion. He gathers his people to hear him, not because an angel has appeared to him, but because he wishes to call for the end of Nephite monarchy as such.[17] The occasion confirms the significance of his words. Despite the apparent potential bound up with a national covenant like the one Benjamin and his people make, it lacks transgenerational stability. Alma's church from the wilderness, however, is a different matter. Although the rising generation that rejects Benjamin's angelic teachings and state-based Christianity also rejects Alma's church ("they would not be baptized," Mos 26:4 reports, "neither would they join the church"), the text suggests that this has to do with their attitude toward Benjamin's program rather than any feelings they have about Alma's church. As time progresses, the text immediately notes, the unbelievers "became more numerous," drawing strength from "dissensions among the brethren" of the church (26:5), but these are (subtly) presented as having their roots in further (Benjamin-like) attempts to wed religion to state power after Mosiah's institution of the reign of the judges.[18] The church itself fares best when pursued and perpetuated as an institution fully independent of the state and its interests. The Book of Mormon, as a result, arguably presses for a vision of Christianity radically divided from state power. It is the vision of Alma's Christian church that prevails, rather than that of Benjamin's Christian kingdom. The church persists through to the arrival of Jesus Christ himself, resurrected, among the Nephites and the Lamanites at the Book of Mormon's climax.

Such, then, might be called the Book of Mormon's conception of political theology. What, however, does political theology have to do with atonement theology? How does the implicit debate in the book of Mosiah regarding ideal religious institutions, or ideal relations between religious belief or practice and state or government power, bear on the value one might or ought to attach to a particular theological conception of Christian atonement? The fact is that, despite certain broad similarities between the teachings of the angel who visits King Benjamin and the teachings of the prophet who visits King Noah, there are deep and important points of contrast between their respective presentations of the meaning of Jesus Christ's suffering and death. And it can be shown that the differences between these are best read as tied to the distinct political visions of Benjamin and Alma.

Two (Political) Theologies of Atonement

From the moment of the angel's words as King Benjamin relays them to his people, the coming Christ is presented as king. The coming figure is, right from the outset, "the Lord Omnipotent, who *reigneth*" (Mos 3:5, emphasis added). His coming to earth the angel further describes with language that suggests traditional biblical enthronement formulas. Thus, his coming is predicted through the announcement of four divine names—"Jesus Christ, the Son of God, the Father of heaven and earth, the Creator of all things from the beginning" (Mos 3:8)—in something like the fashion of the king announced in Isaiah 9:6: "and his name shall be called Wonderful Counsellor, The mighty God, The everlasting Father, The Prince of Peace."[19] Or again, the prediction of Christ's coming employs the traditional biblical identification of matrilineal descent for a king coming to the throne. "And his mother shall be called Mary," the angel predicts through Benjamin (Mos 3:8), just as the books of First and Second Kings report matrilineal descent again and again for those coming to the throne in Israel.[20] The image of Christ in the angel's words, relayed by Benjamin to his people, is thus that of a "heavenly king" (2:19) who "shall come down from heaven among the children of men" (3:5). What does this king do upon arriving among his people, however? He suffers. "And lo," Benjamin quotes the angel, "he shall suffer temptations and pain of body: hunger, thirst, and fatigue—even more than man can suffer except it be unto death!" (3:7). This suffering on the part of God himself, the heavenly king, rejected because his own people "consider him as a man and say that he hath a devil" (3:9), takes a very specific shape in the angel's words: "For behold, blood cometh from every pore, so great shall be his anguish for the wickedness and the abominations of his people" (3:7). Christ is king, here, but he is a king who comes and sheds his blood.

It is not entirely clear what is to be understood by the angel's reference to blood coming from every pore of God enfleshed. Traditional Latter-day Saint commentators tend to point to the Gospel of Luke's description of Jesus's suffering in the Garden of Gethsemane,[21] which says that, as he prayed there prior to his arrest, "his sweat was as it were great drops of blood falling down to the ground" (Luke 22:44). The connection is somewhat tenuous, however. The New Testament text speaks of blood only metaphorically ("as it were"), while the angel quoted by Benjamin speaks of (what certainly appears to be) literal blood, coming from every pore of the suffering Christ.[22] The difference between the two texts can be read as if the Book of Mormon works to make fully material what in the Bible is an immaterial image—thereby setting forth in the Latter-day Saint context what Douglas Davies calls a "proactive Christ."[23] The difference might also, however, suggest that the two texts are actually and ultimately unconnected, with the angel of Benjamin's speech outlining a theology of local or particular relevance, contextualized by the already-emphasized royal context of the speech's delivery and the occasion's emphasis on executing "sacrifice and burnt offerings according to the law of Moses" (Mos 2:3). This second possibility proves not only possible but likely, as further examination reveals.

Certainly, the theme of atoning blood and its complex connection to the law of Moses continues through Benjamin's long quotation of the angel's words. The angel explains at one point that, despite the occasion that has brought Benjamin's hearers together to listen to his words, "the law of Moses availeth nothing except it were through the atonement of [Christ's] blood" (Mos 3:15). This atoning blood, moreover, proves effective for three distinct kinds of person, according to the angel. First, it "atoneth for the sins of those who have fallen by the transgression of Adam who hath died not knowing the will of God concerning them, or who have ignorantly sinned" (3:11). Second, the angel says, "even if it were possible that little children could sin, they could not be saved, but . . . the blood of Christ atoneth for their sins" (3:16). Finally, although "men drinketh damnation to their own souls," if "they humble themselves, and become as little children, and believeth that salvation was, and is, and is to come in and through the atoning blood of Christ, the Lord Omnipotent," they can hope to find salvation (3:18). In short, the effusive blood of God come in the flesh makes atonement for those ignorant of the law—whether because they die too young to know it or because they die never having had an opportunity to learn it—and for those who, knowing the law, repent of their "natural" resistance to it (3:19).

The angel who communicates with Benjamin thus speaks with strikingly bloody words, making constant and consistent reference to Christ's atoning blood. And the text reports that Benjamin's people understood the bloody message well: "They all cried aloud with one voice" after hearing the angel's words, "saying, 'O, have mercy and apply the atoning blood of Christ, that we may receive forgiveness of our sins, and our hearts may be purified!'" (Mos 4:2). The very covenant that binds Benjamin's whole people together in a simultaneously national and Christian bond is, it seems, a bloody one, made in the hopes of retaining a remission of the sins atoned for by the blood of the coming Christ. The people's words, like the angel's, are appropriate to the occasion, uttered in a sacrificial context where, as the reader is clearly meant to imagine, there is copious blood thanks to the performance of the Mosaic rites. The angel's atonement theology is thus a theology of blood, woven directly into the occasion on which his words are transmitted. The suffering one is a king, cast in the image of the one relaying the angel's words, and the suffering has the shape of excessive bleeding (from every pore), cast in the image of the sacrificial rites performed on the occasion of the speech.

Abinadi, the prophet who visits King Noah, speaks in a way strikingly different from the angel who visits Benjamin. Despite numerous important similarities between their doctrines of the coming Christ, for instance, Abinadi generally avoids the royal imagery central to the angel's presentation of God in the flesh.[24] Thus, where the angel speaks of God who will come as "the Lord Omnipotent, who reigneth" (Mos 3:5), the prophet Abinadi speaks instead simply and more humbly of "God himself" (15:1). Moreover, struggling for an image through which to present the "generation" of God in the flesh (15:10), the prophet does not, like the angel, use that of superhuman strength, an ability to suffer more than mortal beings can suffer. Instead, he speaks of "the flesh becoming subject even unto death," coupling this with the filial image of "the will of the son being swallowed up in the will of the father" (15:7). For Abinadi, in short, Christ is a figure of suffering subjection more than a figure of agonistic suffering. That Abinadi stands before an oppressive king as he defends himself might provide a basic motivation for his non-monarchical imagery of the coming Christ. To make the Messiah every bit a king might run the risk of affirming the tyrannical regime the prophet contests. In fact, if there is a specific image in which Abinadi's Christ is cast, it is that of the prophet—that of the very social role that Abinadi himself plays. Explaining a passage from Isaiah to Noah's priests, Abinadi says that "the prophets" are "they which hath published peace, that hath brought good tidings of good, that hath published salvation" (15:13–14). Using the same Isaian language, he then says that Christ is he "that bringeth good tidings, that is the founder of peace—yea, even the Lord who hath redeemed his people, yea, him who hath granted salvation unto his people" (15:18). To the extent that the angel presents Christ to Benjamin's people as if he were something like Benjamin, a king, Abinadi presents Christ to the anti-prophetic priests of Noah's kingdom as if he were something like Abinadi himself, a prophet.

The prophet's teaching regarding the coming Christ differs from the angel's in another key regard: Abinadi says nothing of blood in his depiction of Christ's atoning work.[25] Where there is blood at every juncture of the angel's words, the prophet never mentions blood and in fact seems deliberately to avoid talk of blood. In the course of commenting on the death of Christ, Abinadi takes up Isaiah 53:7, which provides two parallel but deeply distinct lamb or sheep images for the Isaian figure of the suffering servant.[26] The verse speaks on the one hand of one "brought as a lamb to the slaughter," but also on the other hand of one who, "as a sheep before her shearers is dumb, . . . openeth not his mouth."[27] Of these two images, one violent and bloody and the other nonviolent and even idyllic, Abinadi chooses the bloodless one—despite the fact that he uses it to describe the way that Christ "shall be led, crucified, and slain, the flesh becoming subject even unto death" (Mos 15:7). This Christ, Abinadi says, "shall be led—yea, even as Isaiah said: 'as a sheep before the shearer is dumb, so he opened not his mouth'—yea, even so he shall be led" to his death (15:6–7). When presented by the biblical proof text with a potentially bloody and violent image for presenting the atoning death of Jesus Christ, the prophet sent to the oppressive King Noah opts for the pastoral and decidedly bloodless image of a sheep patiently having its wool cut away. The image of Christ is again that of simple submission.

The avoidance of references to blood in the teaching of Abinadi makes contextual sense. He speaks under accusation by a group of priests who claim to "teach the Law of Moses" (Mos 12:28), who, according to the story's narrator, claim that "salvation" comes "by the Law of Moses" (12:32).[28] There is good reason to think that Abinadi's apparently deliberate avoidance of bloody imagery—or even of a lamb's slaughter without direct mention of blood—is meant to direct attention away from the legal system of Noah's priests. The prophet never directly contests the Law of Moses, and he in fact affirms the famed Ten Commandments and claims that Noah's people "should keep the Law of Moses" until the Messiah comes (13:27). He nonetheless claims that the law was given only as an expediency, "a very strict law" for "a stiff-necked people" who needed assistance in remembering "God and their duty towards him" (13:29–30). His final words to the priests are a command about how, "*if* they are to "teach the Law of Moses," they should do so: "*also* teach that it is a shadow of those things which are to come; teach them that redemption cometh through Christ the Lord" (16:14, emphases added). In light of all these details, it is unsurprising that Abinadi quietly (but nevertheless firmly) avoids the language of blood and sacrifice in speaking of the coming Christ.

While Benjamin's people can be simply taught to see in their Mosaic sacrifices so many "signs and wonders and types and shadows . . . concerning [Christ's] coming" (3:14), Noah's people are apparently unprepared to "understand" that "all these things were types of things to come" (13:31–32).

The key differences between the angel's and the prophet's respective teachings regarding the atonement of Jesus Christ in these otherwise parallel preachings are real. The angel emphasizes Christ's pre-mortal royalty and presents his atonement in bloody imagery. The prophet emphasizes Christ's simple submissiveness and presents his atonement in pastoral imagery. Might the distinct presentations of Christ and his atonement be bound up with the respective fates of the two covenantal institutions that grow out of each divine messenger's words? The national covenant made by King Benjamin's people grows out of and cannot be separated from the strongly violent image of the bloody atonement, the extreme and superhuman suffering of heaven's king. Where Christian atonement is thus fused with the mechanisms of state power, the durability and transmissibility of Christian covenant are apparently limited. As Joseph Smith once wrote in a letter scrawled while unjustly imprisoned, "no power or influence can or ought to be *maintained* by virtue" of authoritative office or oppressive dominion, but always and only "by persuasion, by long-suffering, by gentleness and meekness, and by love unfeigned."[29] Despite King Benjamin's many protestations against his own monarchical power, his royal authority rests on his having fought "with the strength of his own arm with the sword of Laban," the Nephite symbol of authority secured by violence (W of M 1:13).[30]

The entirely nonnational covenant made by Alma's people derives, by contrast, from uncompelled trust in Abinadi's nonviolent and non-bloody presentation of Christian atonement.[31] And, it turns out, where Christian atonement is wholly separated out from the mechanisms of state power, the durability and transmissibility of Christian covenant are real and essentially unlimited. Those who bind themselves covenantally to Christ within Alma's church rather than Benjamin's kingdom become convinced—as a later Book of Mormon author writes—that "the preaching of the word had had a greater tendency to lead the people to that which was just . . . than the sword or anything else which had happened unto them" (Alma 31:5).[32] There is good reason to believe that this is a key intentional message, discernible only at a broader level and across the several stories making up the book of Mosiah, for readers of the Book of Mormon. As laudable as Benjamin's attempt may be to work within the machinery of power, and as beautiful as the words of the angel who visits him may be, the institution that lastingly endures in its Christian preaching in the Book of Mormon is the one that has its origins in the emphatically nonviolent atonement talk of the prophet Abinadi.[33]

Conclusion

The larger history of atonement theology in the Christian West has increasingly taught critical theologians that images of and metaphors for atonement tend to reflect the specifically political dimensions of the context in which they arise.[34] The Book of Mormon, it seems, aims to teach this lesson directly to its most careful readers, right within a sacred volume of scripture. The book of Mosiah opens with one depiction of the significance of Christian atonement, one woven with violence and soaked with blood. But it then—particularly in the narrative context of the Book of Mosiah—proceeds to contrast this with a deeply different depiction of the significance of Christian atonement, thoroughly nonviolent and bloodless. As the book proceeds to its close, it tells a story about how the adherents of the second and suggestively nonviolent theological tradition create an institution of realer durability than the adherents of the first and emphatically bloody theological tradition can. In this way, the Book of Mormon resists its readers' penchant for drawing from its pages a supposedly singular and consistent theology (whether of atonement or otherwise), asking them instead to watch for the complex consequences of theological decisions made by its various characters. If one takes this lesson to heart and watches for the story the Book of Mormon tells about theology, it suggests that there is something of greater value—certainly of longer-lasting value—in a committed theological vision of a nonviolent and bloodless Christian atonement.

Notes

1. Terryl L. Givens, *Wrestling the Angel: The Foundations of Mormon Thought: Cosmos, God, Humanity* (New York: Oxford University Press, 2015), 224.

2. Givens, *Wrestling the Angel*, 225.

3. Charles R. Harrell, *"This Is My Doctrine": The Development of Mormon Theology* (Salt Lake City: Greg Kofford Books, 2011), 282–83.

4. Discussions of the issue of justice in this volume include chapter 2, Eric Huntsman, "Latter-day Saints and the Atonement in the New Testament"; chapter 3, Ariel Laughton, "'He Shall Find Satisfaction Through His Knowledge': Atonement in Early Christianity and the Middle Ages"; chapter 4, Nicholas Frederick, "'Atonement' in the Book of Mormon"; and chapter 6, J.B. Haws, "'This Perfect Atonement': Agency, Law, Theosis, and Atonement Theology." See also Terryl L. Givens, *By the Hand of Mormon: The American Scripture that Launched a New World Religion* (New York: Oxford University Press, 2002), 197–208; and Mark D. Ellison, "Beyond Justice: Reading Alma 42 in the Context of Atonement Theories," in *Give Ear to My Words: Text and Context of Alma* 36–42, edited by Kerry M. Hull, Nicholas J. Frederick, and Hank R. Smith (Provo, UT: BYU Religious Studies Center; Salt Lake City: Deseret Book, 2019), 20–49.

5. I have argued elsewhere that the Book of Mormon presents debates within narra-

tives more than it presents stable theological positions. For an argument that it contains such a debate about the nature of reading scripture, see Joseph M. Spencer, *An Other Testament: On Typology*, 2nd ed. (Provo, UT: Neal A. Maxwell Institute for Religious Scholarship, 2016).

6. It is worth differentiating what I undertake in this essay from what Nicholas Frederick undertakes in his survey of atonement theologies within the Book of Mormon earlier in this volume (chapter 4). Frederick skillfully draws out the larger network of distinct approaches to atonement visible throughout the book, in certain cases tying together what the volume presents as historical connections between one Book of Mormon figure's thinking and that of another. In the following pages, however, I not only point to the fact that there are differences between individual voices within the Book of Mormon when it comes to atonement, but also argue that the Book of Mormon is, at the editorial level, directly invested in drawing theological consequences from those differences—and with an astonishing eye to the details of the text. The result, though, is that, where Frederick's project is descriptive, providing a sketch of what the Book of Mormon has to say about atonement generally, my own is in essence prescriptive, outlining the way that the Book of Mormon might—I would say ought—to be used in doing theology.

7. Throughout this paper, I use in-text citations for the Book of Mormon, using standard chapters and verses from the Latter-day Saint tradition. For the base text, I use Royal Skousen, ed., *The Book of Mormon: The Earliest Text* (New Haven: Yale University Press, 2009), although I take the liberty of altering Skousen's proposed punctuation where it seems to me appropriate to do so.

8. The Book of Mormon refers to two kings named Mosiah, the first the grandfather of the other. It is ambiguous whether the first or the second lends his name to the book.

9. Gordon C. Thomasson, "Mosiah: The Complex Symbolism and Symbolic Complex of Kingship in the Book of Mormon," *Journal of Book of Mormon Studies* 2.1 (1993): 24.

10. Grant Hardy has shown that the book of Mosiah, along with other books presented as the work of the author-cum-editor Mormon, does much of its intellectual work by telling parallel stories with instructively contrasting features. See Grant Hardy, *Understanding the Book of Mormon: A Reader's Guide* (New York: Oxford University Press, 2010), 152–79.

11. On the similarities between the two messengers' words, see Spencer, *An Other Testament*, 120–25.

12. This is the wording of the messenger who comes to Noah. The parallel wording of the messenger who comes to Benjamin is this: "With power, the Lord Omnipotent who reigneth—which was and is from all eternity to all eternity—shall come down from heaven among the children of men" (Mos 3:5).

13. Hugh Nibley showed long ago that subtle references in the account suggest that readers are meant to assume that the occasion for Benjamin's announcement of the angel's words was the Israelite Feast of Tabernacles (or Sukkot). For a full elaboration of this possibility, see Terrence L. Szink and John W. Welch, "King Benjamin's Speech in the Context of Ancient Israelite Festivals," in *King Benjamin's Speech: "That Ye May Learn Wisdom,"* edited by John W. Welch and Stephen D. Ricks (Provo, UT: FARMS, 1998), 147–223.

14. The Book of Mormon does not often dwell on clarifying population numbers, but it is instructive that the armies of Noah's father, Zeniff, are presented as having been large enough to have killed "three thousand and forty-three" of their Lamanite enemies "in one day and a night" of battle (Mos 9:18). If the army alone was large enough to produce such casualties, presumably the size of the colony over which Noah rules is meant to be substantial.

15. It is not too strong to say that the situation in the land of Nephi amounts ultimately to a total separation of Christian religion from state power. When Alma's church retreats for safety into the wilderness, Alma finds that his people clamor for him to "be their king" (Mos 23:6). His response is to explain "it is not expedient that [they] should have a king" (23:7) and so to desire that they "trust no man to be a king over [them]" (23:13). Alma thus attempts a stateless (or non-monarchical) religious experiment in the wilderness just outside of Noah's lands.

16. The social-institutional situation in Zarahemla is presented as conflicted from the moment of the arrival of Alma's church there, with difficulties persisting for more than a century. For a good summary treatment of the various constituencies in conflict, see John L. Sorenson, "Religious Groups and Movements among the Nephites, 200–1 B.C.," in *The Disciple as Scholar: Essays on Scripture and the Ancient World in Honor of Richard Lloyd Anderson*, edited by Stephen D. Ricks, Donald W. Parry, and Andrew H. Hedges (Provo, UT: FARMS, 2000), 163–208.

17. Despite differences between Benjamin's and Mosiah's speeches, the book of Mosiah arguably works to connect them in the reader's mind in various ways. See Michaël Ulrich, "King Mosiah's Address," *Journal of Book of Mormon Studies* 28 (2019): 301–9.

18. The text explicitly places these "dissensions" after "the reign of Mosiah" (Mos 26:5), thus within the period covered by the book of Alma, the era of the judges.

19. I use the King James Version here, as the Book of Mormon does, although I eliminate the comma between "wonderful" and "counsellor" in accordance with more recent translations that seek to maintain the fourfold parallelism of the Hebrew original. For some helpful discussion of the traditions behind Isaiah 9:6, see J. J. M. Roberts, *First Isaiah: A Commentary* (Minneapolis: Fortress, 2015), 150–52. For some discussion of the relevance of throne names to Benjamin's speech and its occasion, see Stephen D. Ricks, "Kingship, Coronation, and Covenant in Mosiah 1–6," in *King Benjamin's Speech: "That Ye May Learn Wisdom,"* edited by John W. Welch and Stephen D. Ricks (Provo, UT: FARMS, 1998), 252–53.

20. See 1 Kgs 14:21, 31; 15:2, 10; 22:42; 2 Kgs 8:26; 12:1; 14:2; 15:2, 33; 18:2; 21:1, 19; 22:1; 23:31, 36; 24:8, 18.

21. See Joseph Fielding McConkie and Robert L. Millet, *Doctrinal Commentary on the Book of Mormon, Volume II—Jacob through Mosiah* (Salt Lake City: Bookcraft, 1988), 147; and Monte S. Nyman, *These Records Are True: A Teaching Commentary on Jacob through Mosiah* (Orem, UT: Granite Publishing, 2004), 220. A somewhat less traditional commentator like Brant Gardner notes the possible Gethsemane connection "from our modern perspective" but then argues—as part of a larger case for the antiquity of the Book of Mormon—for an ancient setting among ancient Mesoamerican beliefs regarding blood. See Brant A. Gardner, *Second Witness: Analytical and Contextual Com-*

mentary on the Book of Mormon, Volume Three: Enos through Mosiah (Salt Lake City: Greg Kofford Books, 2007), 151–52.

22. In Luke 22:33–34, as the Greek presents the image, it is unclear whether "as it were great drops of blood falling to the ground" should be taken adjectively, describing the nature of the sweat as bloody, or adverbially, describing how the sweat fell. Significantly, the more concrete and clear image of Mosiah 3:7 is confirmed by another passage of restoration scripture, Doctrine and Covenants 19:18.

23. See Douglas J. Davies, *The Mormon Culture of Salvation: Force, Grace, and Glory* (Burlington, VT: Ashgate, 2000), 46–52. On the general idea that the Book of Mormon reworks the significance of the New Testament's gospels, see Krister Stendahl, "The Sermon on the Mount and Third Nephi," in *Reflections on Mormonism: Judaeo-Christian Parallels*, edited by Truman G. Madsen (Provo, UT: BYU Religious Studies Center, 1978), 139–54; and, more recently and in greater detail, Nicholas J. Frederick, *The Bible, Mormon Scripture, and the Rhetoric of Allusivity* (Madison: Fairleigh Dickinson University Press, 2016).

24. Abinadi does not entirely avoid the language of royalty in speaking of Christ, although it seems significant that he only refers to him as a king in passages where he speaks of the post-resurrection Christ: "the Son reigneth and hath power over the dead" (Mos 15:20). This seems to be Abinadi's gloss on a passage from Isaiah that King Noah's accusing priests ask him to interpret, which includes the phrase "Thy God reigneth!" (Isa 52:7; quoted in Mos 12:21; 15:14).

25. The only reference to blood anywhere in the story of Abinadi comes as he is executed, at which point he warns his accusers that, "if ye slay me, ye will shed innocent blood" (Mos 17:10).

26. As is well known, Isaiah 53 (or, better, Isa 52:13–53:12) contains an extended poetic reflection on a servant figure who suffers for or because of others' evil doings. It is a poem many Jews and Christians have read in messianic terms, albeit with rather different purposes. There are, in both the Jewish and the Christian traditions, other interpretations available as well, with non-messianic readings having become predominant in the era of modern biblical criticism. For a brief sketch of this text's long interpretive history, see John F. A. Sawyer, *Isaiah through the Centuries* (Hoboken, NJ: Wiley Blackwell, 2018), 308–21.

27. Abinadi quotes this verse in its entirety in Mosiah 14:7.

28. It is difficult to know what such a claim means. For very helpful analysis, however, of the place of the Law of Moses in the Book of Mormon, see Avram R. Shannon, "Law of God/God of Law: The Law of Moses in Alma's Teachings to Corianton," in *Give Ear to My Words: Text and Context of Alma 36–42*, edited by Kerry M. Hull, Nicholas J. Frederick, and Hank R. Smith (Provo, UT: BYU Religious Studies Center; Salt Lake City: Deseret Book, 2019), 129–54.

29. Mark Ashurst-McGee et al., eds., *Documents, Volume 6: February 1838–August 1839*, The Joseph Smith Papers (Salt Lake City: Church Historian's Press, 2017), 394. These words have been canonized in the Latter-day Saint tradition as verse 41 of Section 121 of the Doctrine and Covenants. I have followed the documentary source but standardized the punctuation and spelling. I owe this reading of this passage to Patrick

Q. Mason and J. David Pulsipher, *Proclaim Peace: The Restoration's Answer to an Age of Conflict* (Provo, UT: Neal A. Maxwell Institute; Salt Lake City: Deseret Book, 2021), 1–17.

30. I have elsewhere attempted a preliminary reading of the violent story surrounding the sword of Laban. See Joseph M. Spencer, *1st Nephi: A Brief Theological Introduction* (Provo, UT: Neal A. Maxwell Institute for Religious Scholarship, 2020), 66–80. For a survey of Benjamin's paradoxical plea for the undermining of the authority he wields, see Hugh W. Nibley, "Assembly and Atonement," in Welch and Ricks, *King Benjamin's Speech*, 119–45.

31. The son of the Alma who launches the Nephite Christian church later draws a strong contrast between epistemic attitudes toward God that are compelled or uncompelled (see Alma 32). For a theological exposition of the stakes of that later sermon by Alma's son, see Joseph M. Spencer, "Is Not This Real?" *BYU Studies Quarterly* 58.2 (2019): 87–104.

32. This passage has sometimes been read as ironic or as reason for readerly cynicism—see, for example, Hardy, *Understanding the Book of Mormon*, 148–50—but Michael Perry has shown that the longer narrative of the Book of Mormon may be constructed to provide a defense of it, and in terms precisely of long-term durability and transmissibility. See Michael F. Perry, "The Supremacy of the Word: Alma's Mission to the Zoramites and the Conversion of the Lamanites," *Journal of Book of Mormon Studies* 24 (2015): 119–37.

33. One might express nervousness over the possible implication, here, that the angel who comes to Benjamin somehow gets atonement theology wrong. The argument here need have no such implication, however. Through the Book of Mormon's consistent emphasis on the humanness of its authors and contributors, one gains access to the possibility that Benjamin is supposed to have recast the angel's words in terms he knew would speak to his own people. Or again, through the Book of Mormon's equally consistent idea that God condescends to speak to human beings in terms they can understand, it may be that Benjamin is supposed to have reported the angel's words accurately, but the angel brought words that are tailored to the understanding and cultural assumptions of Benjamin's people. However one makes sense of the specifics, though, it seems clear that the book of Mosiah is written so as to lead readers to draw conclusions about what kind of atonement talk might do the most durable work. On the Book of Mormon's humanness, so to speak, see Elizabeth Fenton, "Open Canons: Sacred History and American History in The Book of Mormon," *J19: The Journal of Nineteenth-Century Americanists* 1.2 (Fall 2013): 339–61.

34. For a useful study of this phenomenon, see Adam Kotsko, *The Politics of Redemption: The Social Logic of Salvation* (New York: Bloomsbury, 2010).

CHAPTER 12

Enveloping Grace

DEIDRE NICOLE GREEN

Several essays in this volume have addressed the issue of violence in traditional understandings of Christian atonement, as well as the challenging view of God that accompanies ransom, satisfaction, and penal substitution theories.[1] In this essay, I offer a unique conceptualization of atonement in light of Latter-day Saint scripture and the particular needs of women as identified by feminist religious thinkers, including overcoming cultural demands to be inordinately self-giving, that neither endorses violence nor relies on the aforementioned theories. I address the issue in terms of gender because when values and ideals are gendered, it becomes necessary to "center the experience of gender."[2] Although I will refer to women throughout the essay to honor the voices of the feminist writers upon whose work I draw, it is important to note that the issues I discuss may apply to a person of any gender and that reference to gender is not meant to essentialize or reinforce a gender binary but rather to contextualize the discussion in a shared cultural history in which gendered designations have been socialized and metaphorized in a web of cultural inscription.[3] In this essay, I will first argue for a more expansive notion of sin that considers women's lived experience and clarifies the full breadth of what it is that atonement must redeem. Then, I will discuss what redemption might look like, especially for women or anyone who tends toward excessive self-sacrifice, and how it is achieved. Finally, I will look to Latter-day Saint scripture to offer a model of atonement that speaks to women's particular needs in the process of redemption.

Pride, Selflessness, and the Multiformity of Sin

Central to feminist theology is the project of reformulating traditional theological concepts, such as sin, by drawing from the personal experience of women as an authoritative source. Feminist theologians, beginning with Valerie Saiving, seek to define sin in a way that is inclusive of women's lives and that better speaks to the multiformity of sin.[4] This is necessary because Christian scripture and its interpretation have been traditionally shaped by men and is therefore influenced by a male perspective on the world. As a result, pride, which may manifest as domination over others and selfishness, has been identified as the fundamental sin that must be remedied through self-giving love, which is exemplified and epitomized in Christ's atonement, yet this reductive notion of sin fails to encompass all human experience.

By contrast, numerous feminist scholars identify the problem of women's lack of a substantial sense of self and purpose that results from relentless pressure to be "for others." By placing the needs, wants, and material well-being of others before their own, women often shortchange their own fulfillment and fail to realize their own unique desires, goals, and objectives. In so doing, women may experience a loss of the boundaries that define the self, feeling diffuse and dissolved into other people. Christian ethicist Barbara Hilkert Andolsen explains that because women have a tendency to give to others "to such an extent that they lose themselves," they may eventually "squander their distinctive personal abilities" and lose the capacity to "establish a satisfying self-definition" and ultimately "lose the ability to be centered selves."[5] Rather than seeing this as a virtue, feminist theologians argue that this predicament amounts to sin insofar as it keeps women from living up to the divine potential with which they were created. This means that sin is not reducible to pride alone, as the Christian tradition has assumed, but may also appear as a lack of self-development brought about by excessive selflessness. Such a broadened notion of sin resonates with Latter-day Saint teachings, which emphasize service and selflessness, especially as critical aspects of women's roles, while also encouraging the realization of each person's individual mission as part of their divinely given obligation.

This broadened notion of sin further resonates with Latter-day Saint scripture, which teaches that there are diverse ways and means to commit sin, so many that they cannot be numbered (Mos 4:29), clearly pushing against a reductive interpretation of sin. Moreover, Jacob, after censuring the men in his society for their pride, laments that he must speak to them further "concerning a grosser crime." He assures his audience that his "heart would rejoice exceedingly" if it were merely pride for which he needed to condemn them (Jacob 2:22). Strikingly, this grosser crime to which Jacob refers includes the mistreatment of women, grounded in men's failure to regard them as equals and recognize their autonomy (vv. 21–31). Declaring that "the natural man is an enemy to God," the Book of Mormon is clear that the work of the Holy Spirit, as well as the atonement of Jesus Christ, must be more extensive than solely eradicating pride to overcome the effects of the fall and make one a saint. This includes becoming "as a child, submissive, meek, humble, patient, *full of love*" (Mos 3:19, emphasis mine). This love must be directed toward both neighbors and oneself in a balanced way (Matt 22:39), since overemphasizing one over the other leads to sin. If one loves oneself more than others, one is guilty of pride and prone to domination; if one loves others more than oneself, one is guilty of excessive selflessness and prone to subordination. The very dynamic of domination and subordination is, as a form of misrelation, sinful. Each human being needs divine grace to overcome the multifaceted aspects of her sinful nature and become more like Christ. Given the expansive view of sin articulated by Latter-day Saint scripture, in which its forms prove countless, the accompanying notion of the atonement and grace must be correspondingly robust to redeem humans from every form of sin. Regrettably, the expansiveness of the Latter-day Saint notions of both sin and grace gets overlooked when read through the lens of a traditional Christian preoccupation with pride.

Yet, much of the discourse within Latter-day Saint culture has echoed the Augustinian-Lutheran definition of sin as pride that has dominated Christian thought, eclipsing Latter-day Saint resources for formulating sin in more inclusive ways. A familiar and oft-quoted passage of scripture warns that the powers of heaven connected with priesthood withdraw themselves when we "undertake to cover our sins, or to gratify our pride, our vain ambition, or to exercise control or dominion or compulsion upon the souls of the children of men" (D&C 121:37). Although this passage of scripture does not claim to sum up all forms of sin, in practice it is often used that way. Ezra Taft Benson (1899–1994), thirteenth president of the Church, further entrenched an emphasis on pride in a Latter-day Saint view of sin when he declared: "Pride is the universal sin, the great vice."[6] Further noting not only the ubiquity of pride but also its consequences for the ecclesiastical community, Benson asserted: "Pride is the great stumbling block to Zion."[7] Although pride is undoubtedly an impediment to the flourishing of any community, correlatively, an overemphasis on sin as pride obstructs the recognition and remedying of other forms of sin, which hinders the growth of individuals and the entire Latter-day Saint community.[8]

Although Latter-day Saint discourse does not generally describe disparate forms of sin in a way analogous to the feminist scholarship described above, the canon, which deserves primacy, avers that all human beings, both female and male, must be born again and become new creatures. A penitent Alma declares, "Marvel not that all mankind, yea, men *and women*, all nations, kindreds, tongues and people, must be born again; yea, born of God, changed from their carnal and fallen state, to a state of righteousness, being redeemed of God, *becoming* his sons and *daughters*" (Mos 27:25, emphasis mine). Here, scripture highlights that all persons, women and men alike, experience the negative effects of their fallen state and must become new creatures through the atonement. Despite modern cultural discourse that tends to place women on pedestals, scripture is clear that women are not inherently Christ's—they must attain that identity through spiritual rebirth and transformation as men do, yet their trajectory may be different. That scripture stresses the necessity of women's redemption through Christ is striking given that often women are neither discussed nor addressed nearly as often as are men in the Book of Mormon text, which could be erroneously taken to mean that women are less in need of repentance. However, the canon underscores the fact that women, like men, must be reborn and redeemed. Moreover, it does not lump women in with men by referring to all human beings generally; that women and men are listed separately implies that atonement may work differently for women than it does for men due to cultural influences that may shape disparate patterns of sin.

Former Counselor in the General Relief Society Presidency Sheri L. Dew describes such gendered patterns of sin in her writings. She describes a married couple in which the husband exercised a coercive power over others, often by lying and then "lying about lying," while the wife failed to develop herself, seeking to please others so much that she never discovered or cultivated herself. Dew observes that this woman was "so consumed with her desire to be ... well thought of that she never discovered who she really was—rather than who she thought everyone expected her to be." Both partners in this marriage proved themselves to be disingenuous: in Dew's estimation, the wife was lacking in integrity as much as her husband. In making these observations, Dew acknowledges distinctive patterns of sin, naming each as such. Pointing out that because neither spouse was true to herself or himself their love could not grow,[9] she suggests that each form of sin affects not only the individual but bears a communal impact that can only be corrected when each individual chooses to live with integrity. Living with such integrity demands an initial recognition of the various behaviors that work to impede authentic self-expression and authentic relationship as sin rather than as virtue.

The means to such integrity, or wholeness, has been overshadowed within Christian theology since it has been primarily constructed to remedy the behavioral excesses of the *stereotypical* male.[10] A view of sin that ignores the specific ways in which women (and any others who do not comport themselves as a stereotypical male) may stray from a life of integrity both undermines women's selfhood and drives them deeper into sin. This consequence results from the fact that the tradition generally prescribes greater selflessness to overcome sin based on the assumption that pride is the underlying root of all sin. This is clear in the aforementioned passage on what hinders the operation of priesthood; the same passage prescribes love, long-suffering, and gentleness to ensure that priesthood remains efficacious (D&C 121:41). Although these are admirable characteristics, they are intended to remedy the pride and domination listed earlier in the passage—a passage directed at men who are positioned to exercise power over others. The problem arises when love is reductively equated with self-negation, which in turn comes to be viewed as the remedy to *all* sin. If sin is universally understood as pride, which can only be corrected through self-sacrificing love, then a woman who is already prone to excessive selflessness will further stymie her own potential through her attempts at self-correction and be pushed deeper into sin, growing more and more unaware of how to access divine grace and receive redemption.[11]

In addition to their potential for stymieing the experience of redemption, doctrines of sin also powerfully shape selfhood. Explaining how doctrines of sin are connected to an understanding of the self and its development, Reformed theologian Serene Jones depicts religious doctrines as "imaginative landscapes" that individuals "inhabit." Within these landscapes where beliefs, attitudes, and actions take shape, individuals form their identities. Given this notion of doctrine, one must consider how discussion of sin constructs a woman's sense of self. Jones asks, "Who does this doctrine call *her* to become?" Relying upon the thought of John Calvin, Jones asserts that all discussion of sin ought to have the practical purpose of nurturing awareness of God's grace. According to Calvin, knowledge of sin is "grace-dependent" and should always instruct one in the love of God and motivate one to seek God more zealously.[12] This approach emphasizes why it is vital that sinful potential be accurately described for both women and men: articulations of sin inform the most fundamental way that an individual comes to understand herself, and ultimately, awareness of one's own sin is what drives one to use the atonement by seeking for grace, drawing closer to Christ, and striving to become more godly. This final point resonates not only with Latter-day Saint theology but also with feminist religious thought. Philosopher of religion Grace Jantzen argues that since "our fundamental moral obligation is to become divine," theological discourse must "enable that becoming, or else it is ultimately useless."[13] In order for women to develop themselves, it is imperative that they have a "horizon," or an "ideal of wholeness to which [they] aspire."[14] In light of this, discourse on sin and grace ought to inspire women and men alike to become more like deity. To become what God intends for them to be, women must recognize the form that their individual need for grace and redemption takes.

Arguing that males and females alike ought to cultivate all virtues, theologian Rosemary Radford Ruether affirms that women and men are equally theomorphic, claiming that this affirmation opens up the sphere of women's responsibility and authority. Because women and men share equally in the image of God, the full ground of personhood resides in both.[15] For any individual, full personhood includes both the potential for sin and the absolute need for grace. Challenging a Victorian ideal of womanhood in which women are placed on pedestals as men's moral and spiritual superiors, Ruether maintains that neither femininity nor masculinity ought to be viewed as inherently good or evil; instead, both ought to be seen as "problematic potential." Neither a traditional notion of femininity nor masculinity "discloses an innately good human nature, and neither is simply an expression of evil." Instead, both masculinity and femininity, traditionally defined, "represent different types of alienation of humanity from its original potential."[16] Every one of these types of alienation ought to be deemed sin and corrected to reflect an accurate view of reality, ought to allow individuals to attain integrity within themselves, and establish proper relationships to others.

Despite the Latter-day Saint canon's clear assertion that sin manifests in a multiplicity of ways, contemporary Latter-day Saint discourse tends to describe sin in narrow and androcentric terms analogous to those of the larger Christian tradition that feminist theologians critique. In the Latter-day Saint tradition, this tendency lends itself to a view of gender relations in which women are depicted as men's moral and spiritual superiors, a view which often overlooks the struggles that women themselves have with their own sinful natures and their own need for redemption and grace. Rather than being characterized both as fundamentally good and as culpable of sin, Latter-day Saint women are described as elevating their male coreligionists to a higher plane by virtue of their greater inherent godliness and their intrinsic Christlike attributes. Even as it places women on pedestals—going so far as to compare them to being innately like Christ with regard to their sacrificial acts, Latter-day Saint culture often engenders in women a desire to be even more inordinately selfless and self-sacrificing than they already are. In so doing, the culture effectively offers a prescription for women's self-sacrifice through its description of it.

The stimulus toward selflessness comes from women and men alike. Warning young women that after they marry and become mothers they will experience a sharp decline in recognition and accomplishments outside the home, former Young Women General President Susan W. Tanner states that the benefits of supporting others outweigh the costs. "In no other capacity is there more opportunity to serve selflessly as Christ would do by taking care of hundreds of daily physical, emotional, and spiritual needs." She continues, "You will bring the light of the gospel into your homes—not to be seen of others, but to build others."[17] In a similar vein, one apostle declared to the women of the Church: "We men love you for meeting... selfishness with selflessness.... We are deeply grateful for your enduring us as men when we are not at our best because—like God—you love us not only for what we are, but for what we have the power to become."[18] This statement demonstrates that a one-sided view of sin leads to placing women on pedestals, viewing them as inherently more divine, and fails to make clear the ways in which they themselves need to become—including the development of their talents and a divine sense of self, which may require being less indulgent in response to others' selfishness. Appropriate cultivation of her gifts precludes the excessive selflessness that results in an utter loss of a woman's self-definition so that she can be a full and flourishing self.

Moreover, placing women on pedestals negates their full personhood by denying their own sinful states and their own need for the grace that is accessible only through Christ's atonement. Margaret Toscano clarifies this point in her observation that while such laudatory discourse "seems to privilege women on one level as spiritually superior creatures, on another level it deprives women of full moral agency by assuming their nature is mostly good."[19] Insofar as moral agency is the crux of Latter-day Saint thought, depriving women of it undercuts their ability to fully participate in two of the purposes of human life: overcoming sin and growing spiritually through correct moral choices, as well as assisting others through the same process. Furthermore, beyond being patronizing, denying that women are sinful and that they may sin in ways distinct from men can lead to greater sin and alienation in the lives of women because it fails to acknowledge and discourage the behaviors that lead them away from God, their highest selves, and constructive relationships with others. Such denial, then, harms individuals, families, and communities.

To avoid placing women on pedestals, which impedes the work of redemption in their lives, Latter-day Saints ought to better acknowledge that while women have the potential to realize the divine, as do men, this potential remains merely a potential, not an already realized actuality. The natural *woman* may appear to be the new creature that the man seeks to become, but such an appearance does not absolve her of her individual need to become a new creature in ways that remain specific to her. Women's sin may go unrecognized if it is construed as the virtue that men seek to cultivate, yet the "natural" woman must still be overcome and redeemed. Attending to one's potential to become divine can positively help women to amplify their sense of self-worth without negatively encouraging a sinful form of pride. Highlighting Latter-day Saint resources for feminist theology, Janice Allred explains the connection between divine potential and self-esteem: "Self-esteem emphasizes potentialities while self-approval emphasizes actualities."[20] This focus on potential also facilitates the process of becoming godly. For women to fulfill their duty to realize the divine within themselves, they must have an accurate understanding of their sin so that they can chart the course they must traverse between their sinful actuality and the realization of their divine potential.

If, however, women's sinful tendencies are misconstrued as moral virtues, women become alienated from themselves and the means to their redemption. Misconstruing one's self-identity also has negative psychological and emotional effects on the individual. Former counselor in the General Relief Society presidency Chieko N. Okazaki (1926–2011) observes that guilt, anger, and low self-esteem come about when individuals internalize distorted messages about who they are.[21] From a feminist perspective, this distortion of the self and of one's relations is itself a form of sin. As Ruether explains, sin by its very definition is the distortion of right relations, including one's self-relation, and women's sins are often committed against themselves.[22] These self-directed sins are to be recognized as sin, rather than as a sacrifice for the collective gain. These insights illuminate that when a doctrine of sin is defined expansively, there is a greater possibility for it to enhance rather than undermine women's self-realization and relationship to themselves.

Although women and men stand equally in need of divine grace and the redeeming work made possible by Christ, the ways in which they require redemption and grace manifest themselves differently. Paul teaches that "*all* have sinned, and come short of the glory of God" (Rom 3:23, emphasis mine). Making explicit that women need the teachings and grace of Christ as much as men do, apostle John A. Widtsoe (1872–1952) asserts that the "place of woman in the Church is to walk beside the man, not in front of him nor behind him." Explicitly affirming the full equality between women and men within the Church, he states that the gospel was "devised by the Lord for men and women alike."[23] If doctrines of sin, grace, and atonement have been primarily propounded by men within the Latter-day Saint tradition, then it may take further reflection and deeper analysis of the tradition to identify how some unique needs of women fail to be addressed with respect to these doctrines. More nuanced notions of sin can help draw attention to latent resources within Latter-day Saint theology that better acknowledge the full humanity and divine potential in women and men to the benefit of the entire Zion community.

Community Relation and Self-Realization

From a feminist perspective, a discussion of sin, grace, and redemption cannot be separate from a discussion of community because there is "no sin that is not relational."[24] Even self-directed sins prove to be communally detrimental. In other words, one cannot harm one member of one's community (including oneself) without harming the rest, insofar as acts of sin that are seemingly very personal still take place in a systemic and social context.[25] Feminist theologians view sins that are destructive to the self as automatically resulting in negative consequences for others, including God, because they view the self as intrinsically relational—always already in community. On these grounds, they claim community as the site and source of liberation,[26] emphasizing inclusion in the invitation to flourish because "no one will flourish until we all flourish together."[27] Such insights on relationality point to the fact that too *little* attention to the self can be just as damaging to the community as too *much* attention to the self. This is, at least in part, because a lack of development and flourishing in any one individual impoverishes the whole of the talent and joyfulness that could be contributed otherwise.

With an attentiveness to relationality akin to feminist theological perspectives, Latter-day Saint scripture warns people not to commit sin because by so doing they might cause their neighbor to commit sin (Mos 4:28 and 12:29). This points to a clear connectedness among human persons, which precludes the possibility of sin remaining an isolated occurrence. Joseph Smith reechoes this perspective of an inextricable connectedness between persons in his appropriation of the Corinthian body for the Latter-day Saint community. He states that "the ties of friendship ... and brotherhood have indissolubly united us together." This inextricable connection means that a "kindred sympathy runs through the whole body, even the body of Christ ... no one part of the body can be injured without the other parts feeling the pain ... if one member suffer, all the members suffer with it; and if one member rejoice all the rest are honored with it."[28] This robust notion of communal interdependence ought to motivate an articulation of a doctrine of sin that recognizes its diversity and all persons as full moral agents, equally culpable and equally capable of eternal progression so that redemption becomes viable for all.[29]

Part of this recognition, for women, will require taking themselves and their individual selfhood seriously in a way they have not previously. On Daphne Hampson's interpretation, because a woman who has not taken responsibility for herself values herself insufficiently, she has it as her task to become "a differentiated self, a determinate individual, who may say 'I' without feeling guilty."[30] This distinct sense of self is a necessary precondition of experiencing redemption.[31] Given that cultural forces work to attenuate and enervate women's boundaries by engendering within them a proclivity for excessive selflessness, something external both to the self and androcentric culture is required in order to establish this stronger notion of selfhood. To this end, grace and redemption must be reformulated to counter the cultural and sinful tendencies that alienate a woman from full selfhood.

Confirming that grace must be redefined in light of the particular temptation to be self-negating that often confronts women, theologian Anne E. Carr writes that this new conception of grace must be directed toward women's "failure to discover their own personhood and uniqueness rather than finding their whole meaning in the too-easy sacrifice of self for others." According to Carr, when reconceived from a feminist perspective, grace "takes on a wholly different character as the gift of claiming responsibility for one's life, as love of self as well as love of others, as the assumption of healthy power over one's life and circumstances."[32] As feminist scholars point out, this is an area in which women often need to grow. Latter-day Saint scripture encourages human beings to act for themselves (2 Ne 2:16) by employing their divine endowment of agency (Moses 4:3) for which they are ultimately accountable to God (D&C 101:78). The canon underscores human freedom as a divine gift that they are to embrace by choosing to act rather than be acted upon (2 Ne 2:26–27). For women, this may entail reacting less to the needs of others, instead naming their own objectives and setting the limits necessary to bring them to fruition. This is not to say that caring for the material needs of others ought not to be valued but rather that no individual's worth and role should be seen as reducible to such care at the expense of other contributions. Setting boundaries and creating balance in care for others and household tasks encourages the growth of everyone.[33] A constructive notion of grace for women must include a divinely bestowed capacity to *receive* service as well as to *give* it and to acquire boundaries that contain women separately as individuals apart from the needs and desires of others.

To receive grace and redemption and to realize the goal of becoming divine both individually and collectively, women must first know what has impeded the realization of these goods in the past so that they can improve their situation. For many feminist theologians, what women need is a way to understand God that allows them to identify the divine potential within themselves. In order to realize this potential, the atonement must work to hold together an underdefined, amorphous self and constitute it as that which can establish and carry out its own objectives. In a Latter-day Saint context, for the notion of a female deity to fulfill such a need requires that this similarly underdefined concept be fleshed out in ways that are conducive to women's full flourishing.

Women's Divine Potential

Despite the fact that the Latter-day Saint doctrine of a Mother in Heaven has been taught publicly since 1845,[34] was endorsed by the President of the Church as a revelation given to Eliza R. Snow in 1893,[35] and was affirmed in a statement by the First Presidency of the Church in 1909,[36] the concept of Heavenly Mother remains vacuous within the twenty-first century church. Various expositions on the female deity have relegated her to the role of God's wife,[37] pronounced her as the archetype of the ideal homemaker,[38] and cautioned that she is too sacred to be mentioned.[39] These conceptualizations of a divine female effectively undermine women's ability to name and define themselves as anything more than a mere being for others. Nevertheless, some Latter-day Saints have theologized about Heavenly Mother in more agential and egalitarian ways. For example, Susa Young Gates (1856–1933) asserts that "the divine Mother, side by side with the divine Father, [has] the equal sharing of equal rights, privileges and responsibilities."[40] Similarly, in the formulation of nineteenth-century apostle Erastus Snow (1818–1888), female and male parity actually defines deity: "There never was a God, and there never will be in all eternities, except they are made of these two component parts; a man and a woman; the male and the female."[41] Understandings of female deity need to be further developed along these lines in order to offer a pattern or goal to which women might aspire. Shy of such theological development, the tradition runs the risk of projecting the silent and undefined female onto the divine sphere, thereby reinforcing an ideal subversive to the very divine potential that the concept of female deity should reveal and inspire individual women to realize for themselves. Andolsen argues that although traditions affirming a divine female run the risk of being deemed unchristian, the absence of a divine female just as negatively hinders women's development. She observes that without this affirmation "it will be extraordinarily difficult for Christianity to embody in its symbols a belief that women are full human beings and hence are equally capable of serving as symbols of divine power."[42] Latter-day Saint resources not only affirm the reality of a divine female but further offer an understanding of Christian atonement as that which contains a woman as an individual and gives her shape as she progresses toward her own divine potential.

Luce Irigaray, who similarly maintains that women must have a notion of female deity to which they can aspire as a means to self-development,[43] further articulates women's need for a divinely gifted "envelope" to contain them in a coherent whole so that they can find and situate themselves in their own place.[44] According to Irigaray, the first envelope given to a person is the body, which serves as the boundary delineating the individual from other bodies.[45] Allowing men and women alike to be both separate and whole, this corporeal demarcation is especially crucial for women, who tend to become dissolute in response to cultural expectations. Moreover, insofar as her body is a site that may contain another,[46] a woman is vulnerable to excessively permeable boundaries and therefore needs *another* envelope beyond the corporeal one that is inherently hers. Irigaray writes, "Given that her issue is how to trace the limits of place herself so as to be able to situate herself therein and welcome the other there. If she is able to contain, to envelop, she must have her own envelope."[47] This envelope provides self-definition and appropriate boundaries, offering a woman integrity and wholeness as an individual.

Additionally, such a providential envelope would protect a woman from adopting inauthentic forms of envelopment that she might seek in the world in an effort to construct a false or superficial sense of self-identity, including "clothes, make-up and jewellery."[48] These artificial envelopes prevent her from receiving more authentic forms of envelopment and therefore from establishing more genuine forms of selfhood. Irigaray's analysis here suggests that cultural forces that demean women and erode their corporeal boundaries ultimately excoriate them, leaving them amorphous and vulnerable so that they need an enhanced mode of envelopment. Echoing the claim that the divine undoes and prevents worldly forms of inauthenticity, apostle Neal A. Maxwell (1926–2004) holds that "as we come to know to Whom we belong, the other forms of belonging cease to mean very much."[49] Disentangling oneself from counterfeit modes of containment requires each person to recognize the claim that deity has on her. In concluding that when "our minds really catch hold of the significance of Jesus' atonement, the world's hold on us loosens,"[50] Maxwell makes clear that this process requires divine grace.

Jones elaborates upon the foregoing discussion of Irigaray to offer an explicitly feminist theory of grace in a way that incorporates her thought into a reformulation of Lutheran and Calvinist views of justification and sanctification. Because a woman who struggles with excessive selflessness already lacks a skin or envelope that is sufficient to hold her together,[51] she suffers from an ailment distinct from Luther's classical sinner. Rather than committing the sin of maintaining overly rigid boundaries, a woman's brokenness dwells in her lack of self-containment and in her cultural definition in relation to other people. Whereas Luther's classical sinner suffers with an "overabundance of self," a woman experiences alienation from God as a result of her lack of selfhood. Vividly depicting this dilemma, Jones elaborates that woman is "too liquid, she lacks skin to hold her together, to embrace and develop her." Furthermore, the absence of structuring boundaries precludes her from being "an other in relationship to God in faith."[52] Although this woman is not guilty of hubris or the desire to overpower others, she is not in any less need of justification or sanctification. At the same time, Jones argues, justification and sanctification must take radically different forms when they are not aimed at the sins of pride and domination.

Enveloping, and Encircling, Grace

If an underdeveloped woman is presented with the narrative of dissolution and shattering presented by Luther, then she will become further entrenched in sin and alienation rather than redeemed by grace. For this reason, Jones argues that the Reformation doctrine of grace should be reversed for women so that they are first built up and held together as independent subjects prior to judgment. On this alternative trajectory, God "desires to empower and liberate women rather than to break what little self-confidence they have."[53] Characterizing God's relationship to women as essentially edifying, Hampson writes, "Far from undermining our self-integrity and 'shattering' our selves, God becomes the one who allows us to come into being."[54] God's redemptive, gracious influence in the lives of women works to build them up, expanding their vision of who they may become.

Reading Irigaray theologically, Jones theorizes divine grace as that which envelops and thereby contains the multiple and fluid female self and prevents her from being "dissolved into the projects, plans, and desires of others," which would leave her "without a 'skin' to define the integrity of her personhood."[55] God's grace is precisely what offers woman a skin—a divinely gifted envelope—that holds and contains her in a cohesive whole. Insofar as divine grace intends a woman's ultimate flourishing, it provides her with a "skin of her own (and God's) best desires" so that she is "clothed in grace."[56] In this way, a woman is perpetually renewed in her agency, opened up to free relationship with God and others. Grace, then, is that which allows a woman the integrity to be a self and facilitates the fulfillment of her potential through the means of divine envelopment.

This means that Christ's atonement and the grace that it effects must be experienced by women as that which *contains* a woman as a cohesive and authentic self. The Book of Mormon provides the possibility of seeing women's relationship to redemption as unique and categorically distinct from men's relation to redemption. The prophet Jacob specifies that Christ "suffereth the pains of all men, yea, the pains of every living creature, both men, *women*, and children, who belong to the family of Adam" (2 Ne 9:21, emphasis added). Here, Jacob takes care to single out distinct groups of human beings to clarify that Christ has suffered all their pains. This suggests that from Jacob's prophetic perspective, women's pains differ from men's pains significantly enough that they belong to separate categories that are delineated separately, and yet Christ has suffered all of them. Christ knows how to redeem not only the sin of pride and all that grows from it, but also the sin of excessive selflessness and unwillingness to magnify one's God-given potential. Jacob's prophetic witness invites us to search the canon for redemptive imagery informed by women's particular experience of sin.

Although the description of divinely gifted skin or an "envelope of grace" may sound foreign to Latter-day Saints, their scripture provides analogous images depicting Christ's love for human beings. In a revelation to Oliver Cowdery, Christ instructs him to be "faithful and diligent in keeping the commandments of God, and I will *encircle* thee in the arms of my love" (D&C 6:20, emphasis added). Similarly, Lehi, in testifying that the Lord has redeemed his soul, declares: "I have beheld his glory, and I am encircled about eternally in the arms of his love" (2 Ne 1:15). Additionally, Alma describes converts to the church who once had been "encircled about with everlasting darkness and destruction" until their conversion; at that point, they were "encircled about with the matchless bounty of [God's] love" (Alma 26:15). Applying these depictions of divine love encircling an individual to the diffuse, dissolute, and overly selfless woman offers a uniquely Latter-day Saint formulation of grace as Jones envisages it. As women seek to realize their divine potential, magnifying their unique and divinely endowed talents and abilities, they can trust that Christ's embrace encircles them individually and holds them together as whole, coherent selves. As a woman demonstrates her willingness to come unto Christ and become what he has made it possible for her to become, Christ takes the amorphous, diffuse self and embraces it, pulling it together into its true, definite identity that embodies God's fullest intention for her selfhood.

Moreover, the Latter-day Saint canon pushes Irigaray's and Jones's ideas of envelopment even further than they do. Nephi describes the dynamic of the divine acting upon him thus: "He hath filled me with his love, even unto the consuming of my flesh" (2 Ne 4:21). Here, Nephi seems to describe a process of sanctification, in which his flesh, representative of the natural man, is consumed by Christ, who is "full of grace and truth" (2 Ne 2:6). In other words, his primary envelope is cauterized by divine love. Applying this image to women affords a vision of Christ's enveloping grace doing away with their original skin that proved too permeable—as well as with the pseudo-envelopes that women may adopt to mask the permeability of their original skin—offering in its stead a new, graced skin with the ability to properly delineate the self. Neither remaining in their "natural" porous and dissolute state nor assuming fabricated and inauthentic envelopes, women can instead implore the divine as did Nephi: "wilt thou encircle me around in the robe of thy righteousness!" (2 Ne 4:33). Even as he consumes the old, permeable, and unbounded skin and encircles women in divine grace, Christ strengthens women to delimit self from others even as they become more capacious and receptive to what matters most.

Atonement and the Development of Self

Within Latter-day Saint theology, being embraced by Christ and being enabled to reciprocate this embrace are only possible because of Christ's atonement. In the Book of Mormon, the personification of mercy overcoming justice through the atonement is depicted as embracing those who benefit from the atonement. Describing the intent of Christ's atoning sacrifice as bringing about the bowels of mercy (Alma 34:15), Amulek declares the accomplishment of this intent in fully embodied terms: "And thus mercy can satisfy the demands of justice, and encircles them in the arms of safety" (v.18). Being encircled is only possible on the condition that one exercises faith to the extent that one repents (v.18). This imagery is reinforced by Mormon, who near the end of the

Book of Mormon laments that his people, the Nephites, did not repent and make personally efficacious the atonement of Christ; he predicts that future generations will read the Book of Mormon and "sorrow that this people had not repented that they might have been *clasped* in the arms of Jesus" (Morm 5:11, emphasis added). Christ's atonement encircles, embraces, envelops, and clasps—it allows one to be protected from divine justice in the face of sin but also from social demands that keep a woman from fully becoming who she is divinely intended to be. Through the atonement, Christ makes possible a new self-relation for women as well as a reciprocal relation with the divine. Such love that makes possible this self-containment illustrates nicely why Irigaray describes the love of God as offering "a haven for women."[57] Although it may seem counterintuitive that Christ's *infinite* atonement would be offered in part to assist human beings to respect the bounds of their own finitude, spiritual truths are often paradoxical.[58]

The image of embrace further highlights that this grace is not irresistible—it must be received to prove efficacious. Women need not be passive in being divinely embraced since they can actively reciprocate. It is through this reciprocal relationship of love between a woman and God that she becomes a self.[59] Christ, who epitomizes selflessness and sacrifice, can hold each woman together as a cohesive self, so that she does not take the virtue of self-sacrifice to its extreme, effectively running faster than her strength can endure (see Mos 4:27), thereby making her sacrifice into a sin (see D&C 88:64–65). He can encircle and encapsulate her into a definite self, who can then, like he can, not only lay down her life for others (John 10:11–15), but also take it back up again (v. 18) and be engaged in her divinely-given vocation (Luke 2:49) to fulfill her own divine calling. As a woman allows Christ to contain and define the self that would otherwise remain soluble, she can find her life and develop herself into the individual she was foreordained to become. Then she can say like Paul, "by the grace of God I am what I am, and his grace toward me has not been in vain" (1 Cor 15:10, NRSV). Divine grace becomes operative in a woman's life as she embraces Christ and realizes her greatest potential. In so doing, she bolsters her own strengths, moving herself beyond an ethic of unilateral selflessness to become a self who can offer more toward the flourishing of her entire community than she could otherwise.

Irigaray's theoretical framework of a primary corporeal envelope and a secondary divinely gifted envelope parallels Gene Outka's concepts of creation and vocation. For ethicist Ruth E. Groenhout, these two concepts underlie Outka's account of self-love. The first concept is *creation*: all human persons are created by God and share in a basic sacredness. This sacredness means that one's own self should be valued as highly as other selves, although not more than others. The second concept is *vocation,* which can provide grounds to privilege the self based on a personal responsibility to God for one's own life. An individual is responsible to God for how she lives out her own life in a way that she is not—and cannot be—responsible for her neighbor. Because each individual has a singular obligation to become a particular person and carry out objectives that cannot be fulfilled in the same way by anyone else,[60] an individual must regard her manner of life as meaningfully hers, something for which she is "directly accountable." The debt of obedience she owes to God is hers alone;[61] she must "honor from first to last" both the space and time she is given.[62] In providing a particularly feminist reading of Outka's theory of agape, Groenhout emphasizes that his ethics not only affords but actually encourages the self-development that women need. She argues that the love commandment must be developed impartially, requiring self-love and other-love to similar degrees.[63] Receiving the grace that allows one to fulfill this vocation is crucial insofar as it is not just a possibility but a divinely appointed duty. A failure to become the particular individual that God intends a woman to be evinces faithlessness and sin—for only she can realize her unique set of traits and talents, not only for her own enjoyment but also for the benefit of others.

Taking up this line of thinking to address the issue of women's self-sacrifice, Groenhout elaborates that honoring one's own space and time limits the degree to which a woman can appropriately sacrifice for others. She writes, "If each individual has a unique vocation, or life's work to which she is called, her responsibility to give up the self is again placed within limiting brackets." Although one's vocation may require some specific forms of self-sacrifice, it will simultaneously preclude other self-sacrificial actions. One defaults on her own life responsibility if she fails to set and maintain appropriate boundaries between herself and others. "If an agent squanders her time and abilities in service to others' minor whims, her ability to carry out her true calling will be destroyed." For this reason, Christian vocation allows for "stringent limitations on when and under what circumstances self-sacrifice is morally acceptable."[64] That some self-sacrifice can be deemed morally unacceptable beyond merely being superfluous or undesirable intensifies the critical need for women to set and maintain boundaries that resist the tendency to abdicate responsibility for one's self-development in the name of selflessness. Women must claim the power that safeguards their unique place in creation and their personal vocations as sacrosanct and motivates them to eradicate the fear that would inhibit them from recognizing their shared standing with all other human beings (creation) and taking responsibility to bring their individual mission to fruition (vocation). Where this this self-understanding and commitment to act accordingly is lacking, Christ's redemptive embrace makes up for the natural woman's vitiated and porous original skin so that she can attain personal fulfillment.

The importance of regarding one's own unique place within creation and one's own individual calling with both respect and reverence is illustrated in a personal story shared by Dew. While a student at BYU, she planned to try out for the women's basketball team. The first day of tryouts, she walked into the gym, caught a glimpse of a group of intimidating players warming up, and turned around and walked out, never to return. Dew poignantly recollects, "I was completely disgusted with myself. I couldn't believe I hadn't at least had the courage to try! I could not believe that I had let my fear dash a childhood dream." Dew later shared with the BYU women's athletic director, Dr. Elaine Michaelis, who had been the coach of the women's basketball team the year Dew planned to try out, that she had almost gone out for the team forty years earlier. Michaelis related that her team had struggled that entire season because they could not fill their roster and always played their games short one player. Dew concludes that "*No one can take your place*."[65] Fear and self-effacement, rather than exaggerated self-regard, kept her from using, developing, enjoying, and sharing the talents that she had. What is more, it kept her from helping an entire team of women to perform at *their* best. This example elucidates that filling one's vocation is not selfish; rather, it is a matter of charity—true Christian love. Truly loving God, self, and others impels an individual to cast out fear (Moro 8:16) and become who she is meant to be to glorify God, find personal joy and fulfillment, and better serve others in ways that she alone is qualified to do. Conversely, having too little confidence and too little self-love costs not only oneself but also God and other people pain and disappointment.

In the nineteenth century, Eliza R. Snow worked to preempt this sort of disappointment by exhorting the women of the Relief Society to develop themselves to enhance the consecration of their talents: "My sisters, let us cultivate ourselves, that we may be capable of doing much good." For her, the impetus to develop oneself in a manner conducive to making greater contributions to the world derived from the single fact of being a daughter of God. She reasoned that self-cultivation would benefit both the individuals themselves and the wider society: "The organization of the Female Relief Society places the sisters in positions to bring into exercise and thus develop all of our faculties: thus in doing good to others, we benefit ourselves."[66] Snow's exhortation implies a notion of spiritual consecration,[67] which requires the potential dedication of every talent one possesses for the establishment of God's kingdom.[68] It is worth mentioning here that the commandment to consecrate remains binding upon the Latter-day Saint community; recent Church President Gordon B. Hinckley (1910–2008) asserts that the law of consecration was "not done away with" and is "still in effect."[69] Within Mormonism, consecration and sacrifice are closely intertwined, even inseparable.[70] According to apostle Bruce R. McConkie (1915–1985), the law of sacrifice requires that one be willing to sacrifice everything, including "character and reputation . . . honor and applause" for the truth's sake.[71] In the life of a woman who has so internalized the message of selflessness and being for others that she lacks a fully developed self, the sacrifice that may be required is the lauded public image of putting others first in myriad mundane and trivial ways in order to make room for the development of talents that enable her to make even greater contributions to God and God's kingdom.[72]

Accepting Divine Gifts

A reconceptualization of Christ's atonement and the resultant grace as that which allows women to set boundaries as beloved creatures with individual callings to protect, live out, and consecrate rather than to sacrifice too easily is aided when one regards Christ himself as a grace—as the very embodiment of God's unmerited favor and assistance. In the New Testament, this is exemplified in that Christ did not wait for human beings to qualify themselves for his redemptive power but made redemption available first, in order to qualify them. Paul teaches, "But God proves his love for us in that while we still were sinners Christ died for us" (Rom 5:8, NRSV). If Christ is viewed primarily as a gift—as that which is unmerited—his life can be reinterpreted without placing an undue stress on sacrifice and suffering that places pressure upon women to exacerbate their "natural" way of being in the world by following the example of martyrdom. One biblical interpreter reframes Jesus's existence thus: "the love that Jesus embodies is grace, not sacrifice. . . . Jesus' death in love, therefore, was not an act of self-denial, but an act of fullness, of living out his life and identity fully, even when that living out would ultimately lead to death."[73] Moreover, Christ himself was a recipient of grace in the sense that although he was the paradigm of self-sacrifice, he accepted care and meals from others. This model of relating ought to be at least as exemplary for women as the model of self-sacrifice.[74] True emulation of Christ requires balancing the sacrificial elements of Christ's life with those that demonstrate the ways in which he embodied and extended grace, and then seek to receive that grace, both embracing it and being embraced by it.

Beyond permitting self-definition and envelopment, the grace that encircles each individual also opens up within her a space for receptivity, a bounded capaciousness that affords her the power to receive and embrace divine gifts. Latter-day Saint scripture strengthens one who struggles with the compulsion to be overly selfless by depicting Christ as laying claim upon "all those who have faith in him" and defining those who have faith in Christ as those who will "cleave unto every good thing" (Moro 7:28). The grace that pours out of

Christ's life and atonement not only frees mortals from the consequences of falling short of the divine law, which they can never perfectly fulfill, it also enables them to receive all of the good that God intends for them. "If ye will lay hold upon every good thing, and condemn it not, ye certainly will be a child of Christ" (Moro 7:19). In this instance, faith is manifest not primarily through imitating the selflessness of Christ, but through receiving the abundant goods that life offers to human beings as gifts, recognizing them as forms of grace.

Because "every good gift cometh of Christ," one ought not to deny the gifts of God, but to "come unto Christ, and lay hold upon every good gift" (Moro 10:18, 8 and 30). These gifts are varied, which underscores the need for each to live up to their individual vocations, for the benefit of the entire body of Christ (vv. 8–17). The image of a woman with her own arms extended outward toward Christ, others, and the myriad opportunities present to her in the world, is a vision of a woman receiving and embracing a fullness of the divine will for her life—she both gives of herself and receives. Scripture enjoins Latter-day Saints to "live in thanksgiving daily, for the many mercies and blessings" that God bestows upon them (Alma 34:38) and pronounces that she "who receiveth all things with thankfulness shall be made glorious" (D&C 78:19). Coming unto Christ and becoming like Christ requires a gracious—and graced—receptivity to all that he offers rather than refusing the gift in the name of self-sacrifice.

Furthermore, the canon immediately segues from instruction to receive divine gifts to a discussion of grace: "Come unto Christ, and be perfected in him, and deny yourselves of all ungodliness; and if ye shall deny yourselves of all ungodliness, and love God with all your might, mind and strength, then is his grace sufficient for you, that by his grace ye may be perfect in Christ" (Moro 10:32). For a woman, denying herself of ungodliness may mean increasing both her sense of self and her receptivity to others, defining herself and realizing her own goals as well as being selfless and nurturing with others. Grace, redefined in a feminist context by Jones, enhances women's ability to feel worthy to receive divine gifts and magnify and multiply their talents without guilt over engaging in the joys of self-fulfillment. Divine grace works to amplify a woman's ability to receive Christ himself, the gift of his atonement and all that it effects, and every other good gift offered by God.

By demonstrating a willingness to receive the abundance of divine gifts that are extended, one manifests her faith in Christ and in his offer of salvation. The vastness that includes every good thing must go beyond opportunities to serve others to opportunities for personal growth, including education, career, and community involvement. Prophetic counsel includes the injunction given to young women to "become the woman of whom you dream."[75] Existing in faith must mean receiving the good that God intends for the individual in order that she may become most truly herself and thereby have greater gifts to offer others; in effect, she herself embodies grace and comes to be a conduit of grace for others as a direct result of being encircled by the grace of Christ.

As women employ grace both to cultivate a spiritual habit of receiving divine gifts and to set limits on the degree to which they sacrifice for others, they affect not only their own lives positively but also impact their entire communities in beneficial ways. Groenhout makes two key points on this score. First, she points out that women are not uniquely called to sacrifice for others—if women do an inordinate amount of sacrificing for others they actually preempt the possibility of other people experiencing the benefit of sacrificing their needs and desires for others. Second, she states that this imbalance is destructive to the moral community, as well as to those who sacrifice too much and those who are thereby kept from making sacrifices.[76] Moreover, these imbalances can adversely inflate the self-perception of those on whose behalf the sacrifice is performed. She asserts that self-sacrifice can be "destructive of others' ability to have a realistic conception of their own place in the universe." Offering children's relationship to their mother as an example, she writes that children who "believe that their mother's life should revolve around them ceaselessly are being trained to be selfish autocrats." In order to correct this unhealthy mode of relating, Groenhout insists that children be "raised to reciprocate the care they receive [so] that they can grow up into healthy adults, capable of fully ethical relationships with others."[77] The grace that allows women to maintain boundaries of selfhood and limit their own self-sacrifice also helps all others within their spheres of influence grow into more godly individuals, which in turn allows the Church to become more mature and better reflect the body of Christ.

Groenhout's insights are especially profound given Latter-day Saint depictions of the afterlife. Scripture avers that the same modes of relating in this existence carry over into the next life: "That same sociality which exists among us here will exist among us there, only it will be coupled with eternal glory, which glory we do not now enjoy" (D&C 130:2). Inviting God's grace to clothe and envelop a woman becomes necessary for maintaining a distinct self that can experience truly joyful relationships in both earthly and heavenly realms. Scripture further teaches that the "same spirit which doth possess your bodies at the time that ye go out of this life" will "have power to possess your body in the eternal world" (Alma 34:34). Given this reality, women urgently need to learn not only to serve and give of themselves but also to accept both gifts from God and service from other people rather than procrastinating the development of the Christlike trait of being willing to receive (Alma 34:32–33). To allow themselves to be enveloped by the divine in the here and now increases women's capacity to do so eternally. Further, the balanced sharing of sacrifice among all members of the ecclesiastical community facilitates the establishment of a Zion people who are by definition "of one heart and one mind" with "no poor among them" (Moses 7:18). Accomplishing this type of unity is ultimately only possible through the atonement, which must be appropriately incorporated into each individual life according to their personal needs. When the Latter-day Saint community recognizes the great cost of women's excessive self-sacrifice for others, then instead of praising women's self-effacement, the Latter-day Saint community will seek to be a grace to individual women by reordering cultural dynamics in ways that prove more conducive to the grace that helps them to become who they are meant to be and thereby fulfill their divinely appointed mission.

A more nuanced and balanced view of sin as I have been discussing it here requires as a corollary a more nuanced and balanced view of love as its corrective. As opposed to a one-sided understanding of love as self-sacrifice in the extreme, I propose a notion of love that does not manifest as deference or weakness, but as assertion and strength. For those prone to excessive selflessness, this love is necessarily a fruit of grace. Simone de Beauvoir offers a description of love that is not disempowering or endangering for a woman but vitalizing for herself and those to whom she relates. "The day when it will be possible for the woman to love in her strength and not in her weakness, not to escape from herself but to find herself, not out of resignation but to affirm herself, love will become for her as for man the source of life and not a mortal danger."[78] Divine grace fortifies the overly tenuous boundaries of self in a way that enables authentic selfhood and authentic loves, facilitating individual and communal flourishing and progression. Consecrated love manifests itself in the life of the graced individual as bounded love. These bounds are facilitated and reinforced through the atoning embrace of Christ, which sets women in a redeemed relation to God, themselves, and all others.

Becoming Whole through the Atonement

In conclusion, Latter-day Saint doctrine holds that all human beings, both women and men, must become new creatures through the atonement of Christ. Although it maintains that there are innumerably diverse ways to sin, contemporary discourse follows traditional Christian theology in defining sin according to typically male patterns and fails to recognize women's specific patterns of sinfulness. As a result, Latter-day Saints often erroneously conclude that women are men's moral superiors. To overlook a woman's sin is to deny a fundamental aspect of her personhood and to alienate her from the means to redemption and her divine potential. This is destructive for individual women, their families, and the Church. Feminist theologies complement Latter-day

Saint thought by naming unique forms of women's sin and their correspondingly unique need for grace. The very selflessness that may be laudable as virtuous in a man may prove to be a sinful surrender of responsibility to develop one's vocation in a woman. Therefore, the process of overcoming the natural woman can be a matter of her becoming more self-asserting, relying on the grace of Christ to redeem her original skin that renders her selfhood overly vulnerable to the demands of others.

Due to these considerations, women must come to experience grace as enveloping them, constituting them as independent selves who can then realize their unique and divinely gifted potentials. Latter-day Saint doctrine is clear that human beings are not saved *in* sin, but *from* sin (Alma 11:37) and that it is by grace that they are saved, after all they can do (2 Ne 25:23). When inordinate selflessness becomes a sin keeping one from fulfilling one's God-given vocation, one must both employ one's own efforts to forsake that sin and allow Christ's enveloping grace to remedy the problem. Conceiving of Christ's atonement as effecting the grace that envelops and contains an otherwise overly selfless and diffuse individual—that which bolsters and redeems an original skin with tenuous boundaries insufficient to protect and maintain independent selfhood—underscores that Christian atonement and the grace it affords are constitutive of and essential to authentic self-construction. Human beings are formed by grace and constituted in grace, yet due to cultural demands and learned patterns of sin, women must be ultimately clothed and contained by grace. To fulfill the measure of their creation and their personal vocation, they must be embraced, encircled, and entirely enveloped by grace to become whole and created anew. Latter-day Saint theology not only attests this reality but helpfully conceptualizes atonement itself as the very thing that envelops and contains an individual, making it possible to fully develop her divine potential.

Notes

1. For background on these theories, see Eric D. Huntsman's essay "Latter-day Saints and the Atonement in the New Testament" (chapter 2) and Ariel Bybee Laughton's essay, "'He Shall Find Satisfaction Through His Knowledge': Atonement in Early Christianity and the Middle Ages" (chapter 3) in this volume.

2. Kathryn Norlock, *Forgiveness from a Feminist Perspective* (Lanham, MD: Lexington Books, 2009, 2018), 90.

3. Norlock, *Forgiveness from a Feminist Perspective,* 10. Norlock draws on Alan Schrift's description of Cixous' thought. See also Alan Schrift, "On the Gynecology of Morals: Nietzsche and Cixous on the Logic of the Gift," in *Nietzsche and the Feminine,* edited by Peter J. Burgard (Charlottesville: University of Virginia Press, 1994), 218–219.

4. For further discussion of Valerie Saiving's work and how it is situated within Chris-

tian theology, see Deidre Nicole Green, "A Self That Is Not One: Kierkegaard, Niebuhr, and Saiving on the Sin of Selflessness," *Journal of Religion* 97.2 (Apr. 2017): 151–80.

5. Barbara Hilkert Andolsen, "Agape in Feminist Ethics," *The Journal of Religious Ethics* 9.1 (1981): 74.

6. Ezra Taft Benson, "Beware of Pride," *Ensign* (May 1989): 6.

7. Benson, "Beware of Pride," 10.

8. It is important to note that thinking of the variety of sin in terms of female/male disparities is a way of noting difference within a basic pattern; it is not to say that certain patterns of sin are *only* found within a particular gender. The "feminine" patterns I describe here need not be restricted to those who identify as female. Rather, the distinction along gender lines merely speaks to the ways socially prescribed roles are internalized and perpetuated. Manifestations of sin might be as varied as existing individuals.

9. Sheri L. Dew, *No One Can Take Your Place* (Salt Lake City: Deseret Book, 2004), 125.

10. Mary Daly, *Beyond God the Father* (Boston: Beacon, 1973), 100.

11. See Deidre Nicole Green, *Works of Love in a World of Violence: Kierkegaard, Feminism, and the Limits of Self-Sacrifice* (Tübingen: Mohr Siebeck, 2016), 32ff.

12. Serene Jones, *Feminist Theory and Christian Theology: Cartographies of Grace* (Minneapolis: Augsburg Fortress, 2000), 96–99.

13. Grace M. Jantzen, *Becoming Divine: Towards a Feminist Philosophy of Religion* (Bloomington: Indiana University Press, 1999), 6. For more discussion of Jantzen's work in conversation with Latter-day Saint perspectives on atonement, see Deidre N. Green, "Got Compassion? A Critique of Blake Ostler's Theory of Atonement," *Element: A Journal of Mormon Philosophy and Theology* 4.1 (Spring 2008): 1–21.

14. Jantzen, *Becoming Divine*, 12.

15. Rosemary Radford Ruether and Camille Williams, "A Dialogue on Feminist Theology: Can a Male Savior Save Women? Liberating Christology from Patriarchy," in *Mormonism in Dialogue with Contemporary Christian Theologies,* edited by David L. Paulsen and Donald W. Musser (Macon, GA: Mercer University Press, 2007), 262.

16. Rosemary Radford Ruether, *Sexism and God-Talk: Toward a Feminist Theology* (Boston: Beacon, 1993), 110.

17. Susan W. Tanner, "I Am the Light Which Ye Shall Hold Up," *Ensign* (May 2006): 104.

18. Neal A. Maxwell, "The Women of God," *Ensign* (May 1978): 11.

19. Margaret Merrill Toscano, "Are Boys More Important Than Girls? The Continuing Conflict of Gender Difference and Equality in Mormonism," *Sunstone* 146 (June 2007): 22.

20. Janice Allred, *God the Mother and Other Theological Essays* (Salt Lake City: Signature Books, 1997), 121.

21. Chieko N. Okazaki, *Lighten Up!* (Salt Lake City: Deseret Book, 1993), 159.

22. Ruether, *Sexism and God-Talk*, 181.

23. John A. Widtsoe, "Evidences and Reconciliations—XLVII—What Is the Place of Women in the Church?" *Improvement Era* (Mar. 1942): 161.

24. Ruether, *Sexism and God-Talk*, 181.

25. Ibid. For more discussion on the social nature of sin and redemption as it relates to Latter-day Saint thought, see Deidre Nicole Green, *Jacob: A Brief Theological Introduction* (Provo, UT: Neal A. Maxwell Institute for Religious Scholarship, 2020).

26. Judith Plaskow, *Standing Again at Sinai: Judaism from a Feminist Perspective* (San Francisco: HarperOne, 1991), 76–77.

27. Jones, *Feminist Theory and Christian Theology*, 131.

28. Joseph Smith, "To the Saints of God," *Times and Seasons* (Nauvoo, IL), Oct. 15, 1842, 951.

29. This point is underscored nicely within the Latter-day Saint canon, which asserts: "that same sociality which exists among us here will exist among us there, only it will be couple with eternal glory" (D&C 130:2).

30. Daphne Hampson, "Reinhold Niebuhr on Sin: A Critique," in *Reinhold Niebuhr and the Issues of our Time*, edited by Richard Harries (London: Mowbray, 1986), 49.

31. Mary Grey, *Redeeming the Dream: Feminism, Redemption and the Christian Tradition* (London: SPCK Publishing, 1989), 61.

32. Anne E. Carr, *Transforming Grace: Christian Tradition and Women's Experience* (San Francisco: Harper and Row, 1988), 8–9.

33. For more on this issue, see M. Sue Bergin, "A House Undivided," *BYU Magazine* (Summer 2017): 22–23.

34. A poem on the Mother of Heaven first appeared in *Times and Seasons*, November 15, 1845 (Jill Mulvay Derr, "The Significance of 'O My Father' in the Personal Journey of Eliza R. Snow," *BYU Studies* 36.1 [1996–97]: 86).

35. Wilford Woodruff, "Discourse by Wilford Woodruff, October 8, 1893 (in Salt Lake)," *Millennial Star* 56 (April 9, 1894): 229.

36. The First Presidency of The Church of Jesus Christ of Latter-day Saints, under the direction of Joseph F. Smith, states that "All men and women are in the similitude of the universal Father and Mother and are literally the sons and daughters of Deity" (First Presidency of the Church, "The Origin of Man," *Improvement Era* (Nov. 1909): 75–81.

37. See, for example, George Q. Cannon, "Mr. Cannon's Lecture," *Salt Lake Daily Herald*, Apr. 15, 1884, 8.

38. Maxwell, "The Women of God," 11.

39. See for example, Hoyt W. Brewster Jr. who claims that "the holy name of Deity is blasphemed when used in concert with gutter language and misused in everyday expressions.... Is it any wonder that our Father in Heaven has been so protective of the identity of our Mother in Heaven?" Hoyt W. Brewster Jr., *Behold, I Come Quickly: The Last Days and Beyond* (Salt Lake City: Deseret Book, 1994), 50. Brewster is a Latter-day Saint scholar and managing director of the Church's Priesthood Department (cited in David L. Paulsen and Martin Pulido, "'A Mother There': A Survey of Historical Teachings about Mother in Heaven"; both sources in *BYU Studies* 50.1 [2011], 73).

40. Susa Young Gates, "The Vision Beautiful," *Improvement Era* 23 (Apr. 1920), 542.

41. Erastus Snow, *Journal of Discourses* 19: 270–71.

42. Andolsen, "Agape in Feminist Ethics," 80–81.

43. Luce Irigaray, *Sexes and Genealogies*, translated by Gillian C. Gill (New York: Columbia University Press, 1993), 60–69.

44. Luce Irigaray, "Place, Interval: A Reading of Aristotle, *Physics* IV" in *An Ethics of Sexual Difference*, translated by Carolyn Burke and Gillian C. Gill (Ithaca, NY: Cornell University Press, 1993), 35.

45. Irigaray, "Place, Interval," 36.

46. Irigaray notes that in terms of the container that is a woman's body, there is competition among the container for the child, the container for the man, and the container for herself ("Place, Interval," 41).

47. Irigaray, "Place, Interval," 35.

48. Luce Irigaray, "Sexual Difference" in *The Irigaray Reader*, edited by Margaret Whitford (Oxford: Blackwell Publishers, 1991), 169–70.

49. Neal A. Maxwell, "Settle This in Your Hearts," *Ensign* (Nov. 1992): 66. Maxwell continues, "as Jesus begins to have a real place in our lives, we are much less concerned with losing our places in the world" (67).

50. Maxwell, "Settle This in Your Hearts," 67.

51. Jones, *Feminist Theory and Christian Theology*, 63.

52. Jones, *Feminist Theory and Christian Theology*, 62.

53. Jones, *Feminist Theory and Christian Theology*, 63.

54. Hampson, "Reinhold Niebuhr on Sin," 57–58.

55. Jones, *Feminist Theory and Christian Theology*, 121.

56. Jones, *Feminist Theory and Christian Theology*, 64.

57. Irigaray, *Sexes and Genealogies*, 63.

58. Jacob introduces the term "infinite atonement" to the Book of Mormon. See 2 Ne 9:7ff.

59. Hampson, "Reinhold Niebuhr on Sin," 53.

60. Hampson, "Reinhold Niebuhr on Sin," 166.

61. Gene Outka, *Agape: An Ethical Analysis* (New Haven: Yale University Press, 1972), 305.

62. Outka, *Agape*, 312.

63. Ruth E. Groenhout, "I Can't Say No: Self-Sacrifice and an Ethics of Care," in *Philosophy, Feminism, and Faith*, edited by Ruth E. Groenhout and Marya Bower (Bloomington: Indiana University Press, 2003), 166.

64. Groenhout, "I Can't Say No," 167.

65. Dew, *No One Can Take Your Place*, 197–99.

66. Eliza R. Snow, "Let Us Cultivate Ourselves," in *At the Pulpit: 185 Years of Discourses by Latter-day Saint Women*, edited by Jennifer Reeder and Kate Holbrook (Salt Lake City: The Church Historian's Press, 2017), 42.

67. In Mormonism, consecration is considered the highest and ultimate divine law: "The law of consecration and stewardship is the highest manifestation of gospel living." More than being "only a temporal economic program," this law is a "spiritual command as well (see D&C 29:35)" ("The Law of Consecration and Stewardship" in *Doctrine and Covenants Student Manual* [Salt Lake City: The Church of Jesus Christ of Latter-day Saints, 2002], 421).

68. Bruce R. McConkie, "Obedience, Consecration, and Sacrifice," *Ensign* (May 1975): 50–52.

69. Gordon B. Hinckley, *Teachings of Gordon B. Hinckley* (Salt Lake City: Deseret Book, 1997), 639; quoted in Steven C. Harper, "All Things Are the Lord's: The Law of Consecration in the Doctrine and Covenants," in *The Doctrine and Covenants: Revelations in Context*, edited by Andrew H. Hedges, J. Spencer Fluhman, and Alonzo L. Gaskill (Provo, UT: BYU Religious Studies Center; Salt Lake City: Deseret Book, 2008), 213.

70. McConkie, "Obedience, Consecration, and Sacrifice," 50; see also Harper, "All Things Are the Lord's," 213.

71. McConkie, "Obedience, Consecration, and Sacrifice," 50.

72. See Deidre Nicole Green, "Works of Love in a World of Violence: Feminism, Kierkegaard, and the Limits of Self-Sacrifice," *Hypatia: A Journal of Feminist Philosophy* 28.3 (Summer 2013): 568–83.

73. Gail O'Day, "The Gospel of John," in *The New Interpreter's Bible: Luke–John*, vol. 9, edited by Leander Keck (Nashville, TN: Abingdon, 1995), 734.

74. Groenhout, "I Can't Say No," 164.

75. Gordon B. Hinckley, "How Can I Become the Woman of Whom I Dream?" *Ensign* (May 2001): 95.

76. Groenhout, "I Can't Say No," 167–68.

77. Groenhout, "I Can't Say No," 168.

78. Simone de Beauvoir, *The Second Sex*, translated by Constance Borde and Sheila Malovany-Chevallier (London: Vintage Books, 2011), 724–25.

Selected Bibliography

Abelard, Peter. *Commentary on the Epistle to the Romans.* Translated by Stephen R. Cartwright. Volume 12 of *Fathers of the Church Medieval Continuations.* Washington, DC: The Catholic University of America Press, 2011.

———. *Commentary of the Epistle to the Romans.* Corpus Christianorum Continuatio Mediavalis. Volume 11.

Adams, Marilyn McCord. "Satisfying Mercy: St. Anselm's *Cur Deus Homo,* Reconsidered." *The Modern Schoolman* 62 (1995): 91–108.

Ahlstrom, Sydney E. *Theology in America: The Major Protestant Voices from Puritanism to Neo-Orthodoxy.* Indianapolis: Hackett Publishing Company, 1967.

Aliosi, John. "'His Flesh for Our Flesh': The Doctrine of the Atonement in the Second Century." *Detroit Baptist Seminary Journal* 14 (2009): 23–27.

Allen, David L. "Substitutionary Atonement and Cultic Terminology in Isaiah 53." In *The Gospel According to Isaiah 53: Encountering the Suffering Servant in Jewish and Christian Theology,* edited by Darrell L. Bock and Mitch Glasér, 171–90. Grand Rapids, MI: Kregel Academic & Professional, 2012.

Allred, Janice. *God the Mother and Other Theological Essays.* Salt Lake City: Signature Books, 1997.

Anderlonis, Joseph J. *The Soteriology of Gustaf Aulén: The Origins, Development, and Relevancy of the Christus Victor Atonement View.* Rome: Pontifica Università Gregoriana, 1988.

Andersen, Nancy J. "Mormon Hymnody: Kirtland Roots and Evolutionary Branches." *Journal of Mormon History* 32.1 (Spring 2006): 145–71.

Anderson, Devery S., ed. *The Development of LDS Temple Worship, 1846–2000: A Documentary History.* Salt Lake City: Signature Books, 2011.

Anderson, Garwood P. *Paul's New Perspective: Charting a Soteriological Journey.* Downers Grove, IL: InterVarsity Academic, 2016.

Andolsen, Barbara Hilkert. "Agape in Feminist Ethics." *The Journal of Religious Ethics* 9.1 (1981): 48–68.

Andrus, Hyrum L. *God, Man, and the Universe*. Salt Lake City: Bookcraft, 1968.

Anselm of Canterbury. *Why God Became Man (Cur Deus Homo)*. Patrilogia Graeca. Volume 158.

Aquinas, Thomas. *Summa Theologiae*. 61 volumes. Blackfriars critical edition. New York: McGraw-Hill, 1964–1981.

Arnold, Bill T. and H. G. M. Williamson. *Dictionary of the Old Testament: Historical Books*. Downers Grove, IL: InterVarsity, 2005.

Ashurst-McGee, Mark, David W. Grua, Elizabeth Kuehn, Alexander L. Baugh, and Brenden W. Rensink, eds. *Documents, Volume 6: February 1838–August 1839*. Vol. 6 of the Documents series of *The Joseph Smith Papers*, edited by Ronald K. Esplin, Matthew J. Grow, and Matthew C. Godfrey. Salt Lake City: Church Historian's Press, 2017.

Athanasius. *Against the Arians*. Patrilogia Graeca. Volume 25c.

———. *On the Incarnation of the Word*. Patrilogia Graeca. Volume 25g.

Augustine of Hippo. *On the Trinity*. Corpus Christianorum Series Latina. Volume 50.

Aulén, Gustaf. *Christus Victor: An Historical Study of the Three Main Types of the Idea of Atonement*. Translated by A. G. Herbert. New York: Macmillan, 1931, 1957. Reprint, Eugene, OR: Wipf & Stock, 2003.

———. *Den kristna försoningstanken*. Stockholm: Svenska Kyrkans Diakonistyrelses Bokförlag, 1930.

Austin, Michael. *Re-reading Job: Understanding the Ancient World's Greatest Poem*. Salt Lake City: Greg Kofford Books, 2014.

Baillie, Donald M. *God Was in Christ*. New York: Charles Scribner's Sons, 1948.

Bainbridge, William Sims. "Religious Insanity in America: The Official Nineteenth-Century Theory." *Sociological Analysis* 45.3 (1984): 223–40.

Baker, Denise N., ed. *The Showings of Julian of Norwich*. New York: Norton, 2005.

Baker, Mark D., and Joel B. Green. *Recovering the Scandal of the Cross: Atonement in New Testament and Contemporary Contexts*. 2nd edition. Downers Grove, IL: InterVarsity Academic, 2011.

Ball, Terry B. and Spencer S. Snyder. "Isaiah in the Doctrine and Covenants." In *You Shall Have My Word: Exploring the Text of the Doctrine and Covenants*, edited by Scott C. Esplin, Richard O. Cowan, and Rachel Cope, 108–33. Provo, UT: BYU Religious Studies Center; Salt Lake City: Deseret Book, 2012.

Balz, Horst. *Exegetical Dictionary of the New Testament*. 3 vols. Edited by Gerhard Schneider. Grand Rapids, MI: Eerdmans, 1990–93.

Banks, Robert, ed. *Reconciliation and Hope: New Testament Essays on Atonement and Eschatology, Presented to L. L. Morris on His 60th Birthday*. Milton Keynes, England: Paternoster, 1974.

Barbour, R. S. "Gethsemane in the Tradition of the Passion." *New Testament Studies* 16 (1969–70): 231–51.

Barker, Margaret. "Atonement: The Rite of Healing." *Scottish Journal of Theology* 49.1 (February 1996): 1–20.

Barlow, Philip. *Mormons and the Bible: The Place of the Latter-day Saints in American Religion*. Updated edition. New York: Oxford University Press, 2013.

———. "To Mend a Fractured Reality: Joseph Smith's Project." *Journal of Mormon History* 38.3 (Summer 2012): 28–50.

———. "Why the King James Version? From the Common to the Official Bible of Mormonism." *Dialogue* 22.2 (Summer 1986): 19–41.

Barnard, L. W. *Studies in the Apostolic Fathers and Their Background*. New York: Schocken, 1966.

Barth, Karl. *Church Dogmatics*. 14 Volumes. Edinburgh: T&T Clark, 1956.

Barton, John, and John Muddiman, eds. *The Oxford Bible Commentary*. Oxford: Oxford University Press, 2001.

Batty, J. Clair. "The Atonement: Do Traditional Explanations Make Sense?" *Sunstone* 8 (Nov./Dec. 1983): 11–16.

Bauer, Walter. *A Greek-English Lexicon of the New Testament and Other Early Christian Literature*. Edited by Frederick William Danker. Translated by William F. Arndt, F. Wilbur Gingrich, and F. W. Danker. 3d ed. Chicago: University of Chicago Press, 2000.

———. *Orthodoxy and Heresy in Earliest Christianity*. Philadelphia: Fortress, 1971.

Beaumont, Gustave de, and Alexis de Tocqueville. *On the Penitentiary System*. Paris: H. Fournier, 1833.

Beauvoir, Simone de. *The Second Sex*. Translated by Constance Borde and Sheila Maolvany-Chevallier. London: Vintage Books, 2011.

Bednar, David A. "The Atonement and the Journey of Mortality." *Ensign* (April 2012): 40–47.

Beecher, Maureen Ursenbach. "The Eliza Enigma." *Dialogue* 11.1 (Spring 1978): 30–43.

Behr, John. "Irenaeus of Lyons." In *T&T Clark Companion to Atonement*, edited by Adam J. Johnson, 569–70. London: Bloomsbury, 2017.

Beilby, James and Paul R. Eddy, eds. *The Nature of the Atonement: Four Views*. Downers Grove, IL: InterVarsity Academic, 2006.

Beisner, E. Calvin, Michael Cromartie, Thomas Sieger Derr, Diane Knippers, P. J. Hill, and Timothy Terrell. "A Biblical Perspective on Environmental Stewardship." Acton Institute. Accessed March 1, 2023. http://www.acton.org/public-policy/environ mental-stewardship/theology-e/biblical-perspective-environmental-stewardship.

Bell, Richard H. "Sacrifice and Christology in Paul." *Journal of Theological Studies* 53.1 (2002): 1–27.

Belnap, Daniel. "'And He Was Anti-Christ': The Significance of the Eighteenth Year of the Reign of the Judges, Part 2." *Journal of Book of Mormon Studies* 28 (2019): 91–136.

———. "'And It Came to Pass . . .': The Sociopolitical Events in the Book of Mormon Leading to the Eighteenth Year of the Reign of the Judges." *Journal of Book of Mormon Studies* 23 (2014): 101–39.

———. "'And Now My Son, I Have Somewhat More to Say': Corianton's Concerns, Alma's Theology, and Nephite Tradition." In *Give Ear to My Words*, edited by Kerry M. Hull et al., 203–33. Provo, UT: BYU Religious Studies Center, 2019.

Benson, Ezra Taft. "Beware of Pride." *Ensign* (May 1989): 4–7.

Benz, Ernst. *The Eastern Orthodox Church: Its Thought and Life*. Translated by Richard and Clara Winston. Garden City, NJ: Doubleday, 1963.

Berdyaev, Nikolai. *The Divine and the Human*. London, Geoffrey Bles, 2005.

———. *Truth and Revelation*. London: Geoffrey Bles, 1953.

Bergin, M. Sue. "A House Undivided." *BYU Magazine* (Summer 2017). Reprinted, *Y Magazine*. Accessed March 1, 2023. https://magazine.byu.edu/article/a-house-undivided/.

Berlin, Adele, and Marc Zvi Brettler, eds. *The Jewish Study Bible*. 1st edition. Oxford: Oxford University Press, 2004.

Bernard of Clairvaux. *Contra quaedam Capitula errorum Abaelardi*.

Bickmore, Barry R. "Of Simplicity, Oversimplification, and Monotheism." *The FARMS Review* 15:1 (2003): 215–58.

Big Cottonwood Ward, Granite Stake. Relief Society Minutes, vol. 1, July 7, 1869, 59–61. Salt Lake City: Church History Library, Church of Jesus Christ of Latter-day Saints.

Bihlmeyer, Karl. *Die apostolischen Väter: Neubearbeitung der Funkschen Ausgabe*. 3rd edition. Edited by W. Schneemelcher. Tübingen: Mohr Siebeck, 1956.

Bird, Michael F. "The Reception of Paul in the *Epistle to Diognetus*." In *Paul in the Second Century*, edited by M. F. Bird and J. R. Dodson, 70–90. London: T&T Clark, 2011.

Blass, F., and A. Debrunner. *A Greek Grammar of the New Testament and Other Early Christian Literature*. Translated and revised by Robert W. Funk. Chicago: University of Chicago Press, 1961.

Blumell, Lincoln H. "Luke 22:43–44: An Anti-Docetic Interpolation or an Apologetic Omission?" *A Journal of Biblical Textual Criticism* 19 (2014): 1–35.

Bock, Darrell L., and Mitch Glaser, eds. *The Gospel According to Isaiah 53: Encountering the Suffering Servant in Jewish and Christian Theology*. Grand Rapids: Kregel Academic & Professional, 2012.

Boer, Martinus C. de. "Paul's Use and Interpretation of a Justification Tradition in Galatians 2.15–21." *Journal for the Study of the New Testament* 28.2 (2005): 189–216.

Boersma, Hans. *Violence, Hospitality, and the Cross: Reappropriating the Atonement Tradition*. Grand Rapids, MI: Baker Academic, 2004.

Botner, Max, Justin Duff, and Simon Dürr, eds. *Atonement: Jewish and Christian Origins*. Grand Rapids, MI: William B. Eerdmans, 2020.

Botterweck, G. Johannes, Helmer Ringgren, and Heinz-Josef Fabry, eds. *Theological Dictionary of the Old Testament*. Compiled by Ronald E. Pitkin. 15 volumes. Grand Rapids, MI: William B. Eerdmans, 1995.

Bowman, Matthew. "The Profession of Nehor and the Holy Order of God: Theology and Society in Ammonihah." In *A Preparatory Redemption: Reading Alma 12–13*, edited by Matthew Bowman and Rosemary Demos, 1–12. Provo, UT: Neal A. Maxwell Institute for Religious Scholarship, 2018.

Boyd, Gregory A. "Christus Victor View." In *The Nature of the Atonement: Four Views*, edited by James Beilby and Paul R. Eddy, 23–53. Downers Grove, IL: InterVarsity Academic, 2006

Bradley, Don. *The Lost 116 Pages: Reconstructing the Book of Mormon's Missing Stories*. Salt Lake City: Greg Kofford Books, 2019.

Braude, Ann D. "Women's History *Is* American Religious History." In *Retelling U.S.

Religious History, edited by Thomas Tweed, 87–107. Berkeley: University of California Press, 1996.

Bray, Gerald Lewis. *Holiness and the Will of God: Perspectives on the Theology of Tertullian*. Atlanta: John Knox, 1979.

Brayford, Susan. *Genesis*. Leiden, Netherlands: Brill, 2007.

Breen, Jerry D. "The Ransom Saying (Matt 20:28): A Fresh Perspective." *Journal of Inductive Biblical Studies* 4.1 (Winter 2017): 32–60.

Brekus, Catherine. *Strangers and Pilgrims: Female Preaching in America, 1740–1845*. Chapel Hill: University of North Carolina Press, 2007.

Brewster, Hoyt W., Jr. *Behold, I Come Quickly: The Last Days and Beyond*. Salt Lake City: Deseret Book, 1994.

Briggman, Anthony. *God and Christ in Irenaeus*. Oxford: Oxford University Press, 2019.

Brock, Rita Nakashima. *Journeys by Heart: A Christology of Erotic Power*. New York: Crossroad, 1988.

Brock, Rita Nakashima and Rebecca Ann Parker. *Proverbs of Ashes: Violence, Redemptive Suffering, and the Search for What Saves Us*. Boston: Beacon, 2002.

Brodie, Thomas L. *Genesis as Dialogue: A Literary, Historical, and Theological Commentary*. New York: Oxford University Press, 2001.

Brown, Joanne Carlson, and Carole R. Bohn, eds. *Christianity, Patriarchy, and Abuse: A Feminist Critique*. New York: Pilgrim's Press, 1989.

Brown, Raymond E. *The Gospel according to John: A Literary and Theological Commentary*. New York: Oxford University Press, 1983.

———. *Introduction to the New Testament*. New York: Doubleday, 1997.

———. *An Introduction to New Testament Christology*. Mahwah, NJ: Paulist, 2004.

Brown, S. Kent. "Gethsemane." In Vol. 2 of *Encyclopedia of Mormonism*, edited by Daniel H. Ludlow, 542–43. New York: MacMillan, 1992.

Bruce, F. F. *The Epistle to the Hebrews*. Revised edition. Grand Rapids, MI: William B. Eerdmans, 1990.

Bruehl, R. G. "Countertransference," In *Dictionary of Pastoral Care and Counseling*, edited by Rodney J. Hunter, 239–41. Nashville, TN: Abingdon, 1990.

Buck, Charles. *Theological Dictionary*. Philadelphia: Joseph J. Woodward, 1829.

Bultmann, Rudolf. *The Gospel of John: A Commentary*. Translated by G. R. Beasley-Murray, R. W. N. Hoare, and J. K. Riches. Philadelphia: Westminster, 1971.

Burghardt, Walter J. "The Image of God in Man: Alexandrian Orientations." *Proceedings of the Catholic Theological Society of America* 16 (1961): 149–54.

Burns, J. Patout. "The Concept of Satisfaction in Medieval Redemption Theory." *Theological Studies* 36.2 (1975): 285–304.

Burton, Theodore M. "Blessed are the Peacemakers." *Ensign* 4 (Nov. 1974): 54–56.

Bushman, Richard Lyman. *Joseph Smith: Rough Stone Rolling*. New York: Alfred A. Knopf, 2005.

Bushnell, Horace. *Forgiveness and Law*. New York: Scribner, Armstrong and Co., 1874.

———. *The Vicarious Sacrifice*. New York: Charles Scribner and Co., 1868.

Caird, John. *The Fundamental Ideas of Christianity*. 2 volumes. Glasgow: James MacLehose and Sons, 1899.

———. *Institutes of the Christian Religion*. Translated by Henry Beveridge. Peabody, MA: Hendrickson, 2008.

———. "Reply to Sadoleto." In *A Reformation Debate*, edited by John C. Olin, 49–94. Grand Rapids, MI: Baker, 2002.

———. *Sermons on Genesis 1–11*. Translated by Rob Roy MacGregor. East Peoria, IL: Banner of Truth Trust, 2009.

Calvin, John. "Bible Commentaries: Genesis 9." In *Calvin's Commentary on the Bible*, StudyLight.org. Accessed March 29, 2023. https://www.studylight.org/commentaries/eng/cal/genesis-9.html.

Campbell, Alexander. *Delusions: An Analysis of the Book of Mormon*. Boston: Benjamin Greene, 1832.

Campbell, John McLeod. *The Nature of the Atonement*. London: Macmillan and Co., 1873.

Cannon, George Q. "Mr. Canon's Lecture." *Salt Lake Daily Herald*. Apr. 15, 1884.

Carey, George L. "The Lamb of God and Atonement Theories." *Tyndale Bulletin* 32 (1981): 97–122.

Carr, Anne E. *Transforming Grace: Christian Tradition and Women's Experience*. San Francisco: Harper and Row, 1988.

Carson, D. A. "Adumbrations of Atonement Theology in the Fourth Gospel." *Journal of the Evangelical Theological Society* 57.3 (2014): 513–22.

———. "The Root Fallacy." In *Exegetical Fallacies*, 28–33. 2nd edition. Grand Rapids, MI: Baker Academic, 1996.

Chan, Michael J., and Brent A. Strawn, eds. *What Kind of God: Collected Essays of Terence E. Fretheim*. Winona Lake, IN: Eisenbauns, 2015.

Charles, Melodie Moench. "Book of Mormon Christology." In *New Approaches to the Book of Mormon: Explorations in Critical Methodology*, edited by Brent Lee Metcalfe, 81–114. Salt Lake City: Signature Books, 1993.

Cherbonnier, Edmond L. "In Defense of Anthropomorphism." In *Reflections on Mormonism, Judaeo Christian Parallels*, edited by Truman G. Madsen, 155–74. Provo, UT: BYU Religious Studies Center, 1978.

———. "The Logic of Biblical Anthropomorphism." *Harvard Theological Review* 55.3 (1962): 187–206.

Chittester, Joan. *In Search of Belief*. Liguori, MO: Liguori, 1999.

Church of Jesus Christ of Latter-day Saints. "About the Temple Endowment." Accessed February 28, 2023. https://www.churchofjesuschrist.org/temples/what-is-temple-endowment.

———. "Inside Temples." Accessed March 2, 2023. https://www.churchofjesuschrist.org/temples/inside-temples.

Clark, Elizabeth A. *History, Theory, Text: Historians and the Linguistic Turn*. Cambridge, MA: Harvard University Press, 2004.

Clarke, Adam. *The New Testament of our Lord and Saviour Jesus Christ: A Commentary and Critical Notes*. 2 volumes. Nashville, TN: Abingdon, 1824.

Clement of Rome. *First Letter to the Corinthians*.

Clendenin, Daniel B. *Eastern Orthodox Christianity: A Western Perspective.* 2nd edition. Grand Rapids, MI: Baker Academic, 2003.

Cohen, Alexandra O., et al. "When Is an Adolescent an Adult? Assessing Cognitive Control in Emotional and Nonemotional Contexts." *Psychological Science* 27 (2016): 549–62.

Collins, Adela Yarbro. "Mark's Interpretation of the Death of Jesus." *Journal of Biblical Literature* 128.3 (2009): 545–54.

———. "The Signification of Mark 10:45 among Gentile Christians." *Harvard Theological Review* 90.4 (1997): 371–82.

Collins, Kenneth J. *The Theology of John Wesley: Holy Love and the Shape of Grace.* Nashville, TN: Abingdon, 2007.

Cope, Rachel. "A Sacred Space for Women: Hymnody in Emma Hale Smith's Theology." *Journal of Religious History* (2017): 242–64.

Cornaby, Hannah. *Autobiography and Poems.* Salt Lake City: J. C. Graham, 1882.

Cotter, David W. *Genesis.* Collegeville, MN: Liturgical Press, 2003.

Crawford, R. G. "Is the Penal Theory of the Atonement Scriptural?" *Scottish Journal of Theology* 23 (Aug. 1970): 257–72.

Creason, Stuart. "PQD Revisited." In *Studies in Semitic and Afroasiatic Linguistics Presented to Gene B. Gragg*, edited by Cynthia L. Miller, 27–42. Vol. 60 of *Studies in Ancient Oriental Civilization.* Chicago: Oriental Institute of the University of Chicago, 2007.

Crisp, Oliver D., and Fred E. Saunders. *Locating Atonement: Explorations in Constructive Dogmatics.* Grand Rapids, MI: Zondervan, 2015.

Cross, Frank Moore. *From Epic to Canon: History and Literature in Ancient Israel.* Baltimore, MD: Johns Hopkins University Press, 1998.

Culpepper, R. Alan. "An Introduction to the Johannine Writings." In *Johannine Literature.* Edited by John M. Court, Ruth Edwards, and Barnabas Lindars, 9–29. London: Bloomsbury T&T Clark, 2000.

———. *Mark.* Macon, GA: Smyth & Helwys, 2007.

Daly, Mary. *Beyond God the Father.* Boston: Beacon, 1973.

Daly, Robert J. *Christian Sacrifice.* Washington, DC: Catholic University of America Press, 1978.

Daniell, David. *William Tyndale: A Biography.* New Haven: Yale University Press, 2001.

Davids, Peter H. *The Epistle of James.* The New International Greek Testament Commentary. Grand Rapids, MI: Eerdmans, 1982.

Davidson, Karen Lynn, David J. Whittaker, Mark Ashurst-McGee, and Richard L. Jensen. *Histories, Volume 1: Joseph Smith Histories, 1832–1844.* The Histories series of *The Joseph Smith Papers*, vol. 1, edited by Ronald K. Esplin, Matthew J. Grow, and Matthew C. Godfrey. Salt Lake City: Church Historian's Press, 2012.

Davies, Brian. *The Thought of Thomas Aquinas.* Oxford: Oxford University Press, 1992.

Davies, Douglas J. *Joseph Smith, Jesus, and Satanic Opposition.* Farnham, Surrey: Ashgate Publishing Group, 2010.

———. *The Mormon Culture of Salvation: Force, Grace, and Glory.* Burlington, VT: Ashgate, 2000.

Davis, Ryan Conrad, and Paul Y. Hoskisson. "Usage of the Title Elohim." *Religious Educator* 14:1 (2013): 109–27.

Davis, S. T., D. Kendall, and G. O'Collins, eds. *The Redemption: An Interdisciplinary Symposium on Christ as Redeemer*. Oxford: Oxford University Press, 2004.

Deats, Paul, and Carol Robbs, eds. *The Boston Personalist Tradition in Philosophy, Social Ethics, and Theology*. Macon, GA: Mercer University Press, 1986.

Derr, Jill Mulvay. "Eliza R. Snow and The Woman Question." *BYU Studies* 16.2 (April 1976): 250–64.

———. *Mrs. Smith Goes to Washington: Eliza R. Snow Smith's Visit to Southern Utah*. Juanita Brooks Lecture Series. St. George, UT: Dixie State University Press, 2004.

———. "The Significance of 'O My Father' in the Personal Journey of Eliza R. Snow." *BYU Studies* 36.1 (1996–97): 85–126.

Derr, Jill Mulvay, Carol Cornwall Madsen, Kate Holbrook, and Matthew J. Grow, eds. *The First Fifty Years of Relief Society: Key Documents in Latter-day Saint Women's History*. Salt Lake City: Church Historian's Press, 2016.

Dew, Sheri L. *No One Can Take Your Place*. Salt Lake City: Deseret Book, 2004.

Dibelius, Martin. "Gethsemane." *Crozer Quarterly* 12 (1953): 254–65.

Dillistone, F. W. *The Christian Understanding of the Atonement*. Philadelphia: Westminster, 1968.

Doctrine and Covenants Student Manual. Salt Lake City: The Church of Jesus Christ of Latter-day Saints, 2002.

Douglas, Mary. "Atonement in Leviticus." *Jewish Studies Quarterly* 1 (1993–94): 109–130.

Dowd, Sharyn, and Elizabeth Struthers Malbon. "The Significance of Jesus' Death in Mark: Narrative Context and Authorial Audience." *Journal of Biblical Literature* 125 (2006): 271–97.

Downing, Don S. *Atonement and Psychotherapy*. Philadelphia: Westminster, 1966.

DuBose, Todd. "Lordship, Bondage, and the Formation of 'Homo Religiosus.'" *Journal of Religion and Health* 39:3 (2000): 217–26.

Dunn, Geoffrey D. "A Survey of Tertullian's Soteriology." *Sacris Erudiri* 42 (2003): 61–86.

Dunn, James D. G. *The Theology of Paul the Apostle*. Grand Rapids, MI: William B. Eerdmans, 1998.

Easton, Susan W. "The Book of Mormon Bears Witness of the Father through the Son." In *The Sixth Annual Church Educational System Religious Educator's Symposium on the Book of Mormon*, 20–23. Provo, UT: Brigham Young University, 1982.

Edwards, Christopher J. *The Ransom Logion in Mark and Matthew*. Tübingen: Mohr Siebeck, 2012.

Edwards, Jonathan. "Concerning the Necessity and Reasonableness of the Christian Doctrine of Satisfaction for Sin." In *The Works of President Edwards*. 10 vols. New York: G & C & H Corvill, 1830.

Ehat, Andrew F. "Joseph Smith's Introduction of Temple Ordinances and the 1844 Mormon Succession Question." Master's thesis, Brigham Young University, Provo, UT, 1982.

Ehat, Andrew F., and Lyndon W. Cook, eds. *Words of Joseph Smith*. Orem, UT: Grandin, 1991.

Ehrman, Bart D., ed. *The Apostolic Fathers*. Translated by Bart D. Ehrman. 2 volumes. Loeb Classical Library. Cambridge, MA: Harvard University Press, 2001.

Eisswen, Mitchell Alexander. "'Is He Going to Kill Himself?': The Willing Self-Sacrifice of Jesus and the Akedah in the Fourth Gospel." *Sacra Scripta* 11.2 (2013): 231–61.

Ellingworth, Paul. *The Epistle to the Hebrews*. The New International Greek Testament Commentary. Grand Rapids, MI: Eerdmans, 1993.

Ellison, Mark. "Beyond Justice: Reading Alma 42 in the Context of Atonement Theories." In *Give Ear to My Words*, edited by Kerry M. Hull et al., 20–49. Provo, UT: BYU Religious Studies Center, 2019.

England, Eugene. *Dialogues with Myself*. Salt Lake City: Orion Books, 1984.

———. "'Means unto Repentance': Unique Book of Mormon Insights into Christ's At-one-ment." In *Rediscovering the Book of Mormon*, edited by John L. Sorenson and Melvin J. Thorne, 153–67. Salt Lake City: Deseret Book Co., 1990.

———. *The Quality of Mercy*. Salt Lake City: Bookcraft, 1992.

———. "That They Might Not Suffer: The Gift of Atonement." *Dialogue* 1.3 (Fall 1966): 14–22.

Enns, Peter. *The Bible Tells Me So: Why Defending Scripture Has Made Us Unable to Read It*. San Francisco: HarperOne, 2015.

Ensor, Peter. "Justin Martyr and Penal Substitutionary Atonement." *Evangelical Quarterly* 83.3 (2011): 217–32.

———. "Tertullian and Penal Substitutionary Atonement." *Evangelical Quarterly* 86.2 (2014): 130–42.

Epistle of Barnabas.

Epistle to Diognetus.

Eskenazi, Tamara Cohen and Tikva Frymer-Kremsky. *The JPS Bible Commentary: Ruth*. Philadelphia: Jewish Publication Society, 2011.

Esther. "Celestial Marriage, Opening a New Era." *Woman's Exponent* 6.11 (Nov. 1, 1877), n.p.

Evans, Craig A. "Isaiah 53 in the Letters of Peter, Paul, Hebrews, and John." In *The Gospel According to Isaiah 53: Encountering the Suffering Servant in Jewish and Christian Theology*, edited by Darrell L. Bock and Mitch Glaser, 145–70. Grand Rapids, MI: Kregel Academic & Professional, 2012.

———. "Who Touched Me? Jesus and the Ritually Impure." In *Jesus in Context: Temple, Purity, and Restoration*, edited by Bruce David Chilton and Craig A. Evans, 353–76. Leiden, Netherlands: Brill, 1997.

Fenton, Elizabeth. "Open Canons: Sacred History and American History in *The Book of Mormon*." *J19: The Journal of Nineteenth-Century Americanists* 1.2 (Fall 2013): 339–61.

Fenton, Elizabeth, and Jared Hickman, eds. *Americanist Approaches to* The Book of Mormon. New York: Oxford University Press, 2019.

Fergusson, David. "Creation." *The Oxford Handbook of Systematic Theology*, edited by

John Webster, Kathryn Tanner, and Iain Torrance, 79–80. New York: Oxford University Press, 2007.

Fiddes, Paul S. *The Creative Suffering of God*. Oxford: Clarendon, 1988.

———. *Past Event and Present Salvation: The Christian Idea of Atonement*. Louisville, KY: Westminster/John Knox, 1989.

Finlan, Stephen. *Problems with Atonement: The Origins of, and Controversy about, the Atonement Doctrine*. Collegeville, MN: Liturgical Press, 2005.

First Presidency of the Church. "The Origin of Man." *Improvement Era* (Nov. 1909): 75–81. Reprinted in *Ensign* (Feb. 2002): 26–30.

Fitzmyer, Joseph A. "Reconciliation in Pauline Theology." In *No Famine in the Land: Essays in Honor of John L. McKenzie*, edited by J. W. Flanagan and A. W. Robinson, 155–77. Missoula, MT: Scholars Press, 1975.

Flanagan, J. W., and A. W. Robinson, eds. *No Famine in the Land: Essays in Honor of John L. McKenzie*. Missoula, MT: Scholars Press, 1975.

Flood, Derek. "Substitutionary Atonement and the Church Fathers: A Reply to the Authors of *Pierced for Our Transgressions*." *Evangelical Quarterly* 82.2 (2010): 142–59.

Fluhman, J. Spencer. "Atonement and Grace." Interview with Terryl Givens. Faith Matters Foundation. YouTube video, April 7, 2019. https://youtu.be/-YVgZH46kgg.

———. "The Triumph and the Glory of the Lamb: Doctrine and Covenants 76 in Historical Context." *Ensign* (Oct. 2017): 65–71.

Frederick, Nicholas J. *The Bible, Mormon Scripture, and the Rhetoric of Allusivity*. Madison, NJ: Fairleigh Dickinson University Press, 2016.

———. "The Paradoxical Lamb and the Christology of John's Apocalypse." In *Thou Art the Christ, the Son of the Living God: The Person and Work of Jesus in the New Testament*, Edited by Eric D. Huntsman, Lincoln Blumell, and Tyler J. Griffin, 260–74. Provo, UT: BYU Religious Studies Center, 2018; Salt Lake City: Deseret Book, 2018.

Fredriksen, Paula. "Vile Bodies: Paul and Augustine on the Resurrection of the Flesh." In *Biblical Hermeneutics in Historical Perspective*, edited by Mark S. Burrows and Paul Rorem, 75–87. Grand Rapids, MI: William B. Eerdmans, 1991.

Fretheim, Terence E. *Creation Untamed: The Bible, God, and Natural Disasters*. Theological Explorations for the Church Catholic series. Ada, MI: Baker Academic, 2010.

———. *God and World in the Old Testament: A Relational Theology of Creation*. Nashville, TN: Abingdon, 2005.

———. *God So Enters into Relationships That . . .: A Biblical View*. Minneapolis: Fortress, 2020.

———. "Preaching Creation: Genesis 1–2." *Word and World* 29 (2009): 75–83.

Gamble, Richard, ed. *Calvin's Work in Geneva*. 14 volumes. New York: Garland Publishing, Inc., 1992.

Gardner, Brant A. *The Gift and Power: Translating the Book of Mormon*. Salt Lake City: Greg Kofford Books, 2011.

———. *Second Witness: Analytical and Contextual Commentary on the Book of Mormon, Volume Three: Enos through Mosiah*. Salt Lake City: Greg Kofford Books, 2007.

Gardner, Martin R. "Mormonism and Capital Punishment: A Doctrinal Perspective, Past and Present." *Dialogue* 12.1 (Spring 1979): 9–26.

Gates, Susa Young. "The Vision Beautiful." *Improvement Era* 23 (Apr. 1920): 542–43.

Gerhardsson, Birger. "Sacrificial Service and Atonement in the Gospel of Matthew." In *Reconciliation and Hope: New Testament Essays on Atonement and Eschatlogy, Presented to L. L. Morris on His 60th Birthday*, edited by Robert Banks, 25–35. Milton Keynes, England: Paternoster, 1974.

Givens, Terryl. "Atonement and Grace." Interview by Spencer Fluhman. Faith Matters Foundation, YouTube video, April 7, 2019. https://www.youtube.com/watch?v=-YVgZH46kgg.

———. *By the Hand of Mormon: The American Scripture that Launched a New World Religion*. New York: Oxford University Press, 2002.

———. *Feeding the Flock. The Foundations of Mormon Thought*, vol. 2: *Church and Praxis*. New York: Oxford University Press, 2017.

———. *2nd Nephi: A Brief Theological Introduction*. Provo, UT: Neal A. Maxwell Institute for Religious Scholarship, Brigham Young University, 2020.

———. *Stretching the Heavens: The Life of Eugene England and the Crisis of Modern Mormonism*. Chapel Hill: University of North Carolina Press, 2021.

———. *Wrestling the Angel. The Foundations of Mormon Thought*, vol. 1: *Cosmos, God, Humanity*. New York: Oxford University Press, 2014.

Givens, Terryl L. and Fiona. *All Things New: Rethinking Sin to Salvation and Everything in Between*. Meridian, ID: Faith Matters Publishing, 2020.

———. *The Christ Who Heals: How God Restored the Truth that Saves Us*. Salt Lake City: Deseret Book, 2017.

Godfrey, Kenneth L. "The History of Intelligence in Latter-day Saint Thought." In *Pearl of Great Price: Revelations from God*, edited by H. Donl Peterson and Charles D. Tate Jr., 213–36. Provo, UT: BYU Religious Studies Center, 1989.

Goldingay, John. *The Theology of the Book Called Isaiah*. Downers Grove, IL: InterVarsity, 2014.

Gore, David Charles. *The Voice of the People: Political Rhetoric in the Book of Mormon*. Provo, UT: Neal A. Maxwell Institute for Religious Scholarship, 2019.

Gorringe, Timothy. *God's Just Vengeance: Crime, Violence, and the Rhetoric of Salvation*. Cambridge: Cambridge University Press, 1996.

Gottschalk, Marie. *The Prison and the Gallows: The Politics of Mass Incarceration in America*. Cambridge: Cambridge University Press, 2006.

———. *Caught: The Prison State and the Lockdown of American Politics*. Princeton: Princeton University Press, 2015.

Grant, Robert M. *The Early Christian Doctrine of God*. Charlottesville: University Press of Virginia, 1966.

Grayston, Kenneth, "*Hilaskesthai* and Related Words in the LXX." *New Testament Studies* 27 (1980/81): 640–56.

Green, Deidre Nicole. "Got Compassion? A Critique of Blake Ostler's Theory of Atonement." *Element: The Journal of the Society for Mormon Philosophy and Theology* 4.1 (Spring 2008): 1–21.

———. *Jacob: A Brief Theological Introduction*. Provo, UT: Neal A. Maxwell Institute for Religious Scholarship, 2020.

———. "A Self That Is Not One: Kierkegaard, Niebuhr, and Saiving on the Sin of Self-lessness." *Journal of Religion* 97.2 (April 2017): 151–80.

———. "Works of Love in a World of Violence: Feminism, Kierkegaard, and the Limits of Self-Sacrifice." *Hypatia: A Journal of Feminist Philosophy* 28.3 (Summer 2013): 568–83.

———. *Works of Love in a World of Violence: Kierkegaard, Feminism, and the Limits of Self-Sacrifice*. Tübingen, Germany: Mohr Siebeck, 2016.

Green, Joel B. "Healing View." In *The Nature of the Atonement: Four Views*, edited by James Beilby and Paul R. Eddy, 117–42. Downers Grove, IL: InterVarsity Academic, 2006.

Gregory of Nyssa. *Great Catechetical Oration*. Patrilogia Graeca. Volume 45.

Grensted, L. W. *A Short History of the Doctrine of the Atonement*. Manchester: Manchester University Press, 1920.

Grey, Mary. *Redeeming the Dream: Feminism, Redemption, and the Christian Tradition*. London: SPCK Publishing, 1989.

Grigsby, Bruce H. "The Cross as an Expiatory Sacrifice in the Fourth Gospel." *Journal for the Study of the New Testament* 15 (1982): 51–80.

Groenhout, Ruth E. "I Can't Say No: Self-Sacrifice and an Ethics of Care." In *Philosophy, Feminism, and Faith*, edited by Ruth E. Groenhout and Marya Bower, 152–74. Bloomington: Indiana University Press, 2003.

Grotius, Hugo. *A Defence of the Catholick Faith Concerning the Satisfaction of Christ. Written Originally by the Learned Hugo Grotius, and Now Translated by W. H.: A Work Very Necessary in These Times for the Preventing of the Growth of Socinianism*. London: Printed for Thomas Parkhurst and Jonathan Robinson, 1692, 84, 125.

Gruenler, Royce Gordon. "Atonement in the Synoptic Gospels and Acts: 'Poured Out for the Forgiveness of Sins.'" In *The Glory of the Atonement*, edited by Charles E. Hill and Frank A. James III, 90–105. Downers Grove, IL: InterVarsity, 2004.

Gunton, Colin E., ed. *The Doctrine of Creation: Essays in Dogmatics, History and Philosophy*. New York: T&T Clark, 2004.

Hahn, Scott. *Kinship by Covenant: A Canonical Approach to a Fulfillment of God's Saving Promises*. New Haven: Yale University Press, 2009.

Hampson, Daphne. "Reinhold Niebuhr on Sin: A Critique." In *Reinhold Niebuhr and the Issues of Our Time*, edited by Richard Harries. London: Mowbray, 1986.

Handley, George. *Home Waters: A Year of Recompense on the Provo River*. Salt Lake City: University of Utah Press, 2010.

Hansen, Lorin K. "The 'Moral' Atonement as a Mormon Interpretation." *Dialogue* 27.1 (1994): 195–227.

Hardy, Grant. *Understanding the Book of Mormon: A Reader's Guide*. Oxford: Oxford University Press, 2010.

Harper, Stephen C. "All Things Are the Lord's: The Law of Consecration in the Doctrine and Covenants." In *The Doctrine and Covenants: Revelations in Context*, edited by Andrew H. Hedges, J. Spencer Fluhman, and Alonzo L. Gaskill, 212–28. Provo, UT: BYU Religious Studies Center; Salt Lake City: Deseret Book, 2008.

Harrell, Charles R. *"This Is My Doctrine": The Development of Mormon Theology*. Salt Lake City: Greg Kofford Books, 2011.

Hart, David Bentley. *The New Testament: A Translation*. New Haven: Yale University Press, 2017.

———. *That All Shall Be Saved: Heaven, Hell, and Universal Salvation*. New Haven: Yale University Press, 2019.

Haws, J.B. "Doctrine and Covenants Theology, Eastern Orthodox Terminology: Seeking Clarity about Theosis/Deification." In *How and What You Worship: Christology and Praxis in Joseph Smith's Revelations*, edited by Rachel Cope, Carter Charles, and Jordan Watkins, 75–97. Provo, UT: BYU Religious Studies Center; Salt Lake City: Deseret Book, 2020.

Heal, Kristian S. "Joseph as a Type of Christ in Syriac Literature." *BYU Studies* 41.1 (2002): 29–49.

Hedges, Andrew H., Alex D. Smith, and Brent M. Rogers, eds. *The Joseph Smith Papers: Journals*. 3 volumes. Salt Lake City: Church Historian's Press, 2015.

Hedges, Andrew H., J. Spencer Fluhman, and Alonzo L. Gaskill, eds. *The Doctrine and Covenants: Revelations in Context*. Provo, UT: BYU Religious Studies Center; Salt Lake City: Deseret Book, 2008.

Heider, George C. "Atonement and the Gospels." *Journal of Theological Interpretation* 2.2 (2008): 259–73.

Hengel, Martin. *The Atonement: The Origins of the Doctrine in the New Testament*. Eugene, OR: Wipf and Stock, 2007.

———. "Der Kreuzestod Jesu Christi als Gottes souveräne Erlösungstat Exegese über 2 Kor 5,11–21." In *Theologie und Kirche. Reichenau-Gespräch der Evangelischen Landessynode Württemberg*, 60–89. Stuttgart: Caler Verlag, 1967.

Heschel, Abraham J. *The Prophets*. 2 volumes. New York: Harper and Row, 1962.

Hicks, Michael. *Mormonism and Music: A History*. Urbana, IL: University of Illinois Press, 1989.

Hill, Charles E. "Atonement in the Apocalypse of John: A Lamb Standing as if Slain." In *The Glory of the Atonement*, edited by Charles E. Hill and Frank A. James III, 190–208. Downers Grove, IL: InterVarsity, 2004.

Hill, Charles E. and Frank A. James III, eds. *The Glory of the Atonement*. Biblical, Historical and Practical Perspectives: Essays in Honor of Roger Nicole. Downers Grove, IL: InterVarsity, 2004.

Hilton, John, III, and Joshua P. Barringer. "The Use of 'Gethsemane' by Church Leaders: 1859–2018." *BYU Studies Quarterly* 58.4 (2019): 49–76.

Hinckley, Gordon B. "Don't Drop the Ball." *Ensign* (Nov. 1994): 46–49.

———. "Forgiveness." *Ensign* (Nov. 2005): 81–84.

———. "How Can I Become the Woman of Whom I Dream?" *Ensign* (May 2001): 93–96.

———. *Teachings of Gordon B. Hinckley*. Salt Lake City: Deseret Book, 1997.

———. "The Wondrous and True Story of Christmas." *Ensign* (Dec. 2000): 2–6.

Hinckley, Stuart W. "Capital Punishment." In volume 1 of the *Encyclopedia of Mormonism*, edited by Daniel H. Ludlow, 255. New York: MacMillan, 1992.

Hirstein, William, Katrina L. Sifferd, and Tyler K. Fagan. *Responsible Brains: Neuroscience, Law, and Human Culpability*. Cambridge, MA: MIT Press, 2018.

Holifield, E. Brooks. *Theology in America: Christian Thought from the Age of the Puritans to the Civil War.* New Haven: Yale University Press, 2003.

Holland, Jeffrey R. "Atonement of Jesus Christ." In volume 1 of the *Encyclopedia of Mormonism*, edited by Daniel H. Ludlow, 82–86. New York: Macmillan, 1992.

———. "A Saint through the Atonement of Christ the Lord." In *BYU Speeches*, 1–6. Provo, UT: Brigham Young University, January 18, 2022.

Holmes, Stephen R. "Penal Substitution." In *T&T Clark Companion to Atonement*, edited by Adam J. Johnson, 295–314. London: Bloomsbury, 2017.

Hoskisson, Paul Y. "The Fatherhood of Christ and the Atonement." *Religious Educator: Perspectives on the Restored Gospel* 1.1 (2000): 71–80.

Hough, Robert. "You Will Reap What You Sow." In *Curing Violence*, edited by Mark I. Wallace and Theophus H. Smith, 161–81. Sonoma, CA: Polebridge, 1994.

Hughes, Richard T., ed. *The American Quest for the Primitive Church.* Urbana, IL: University of Illinois Press, 1988.

Hughes, Virginia. "Science in Court: Head Case." *Nature* 464 (2010): 340–42.

Hugo, Victor. *Les Misérables: Fantine.* 30 Volumes. New York: The Century Co., 1906.

Hultgren, Stephen. "*Hilastērion* (Rom. 3:25) and the Union of Divine Justice and Mercy, Part II: Atonement in the Old Testament and in Romans 1–5." *Journal of Theological Studies* 70.2 (Oct. 2019): 536–99.

Humphreys, Fisher. *The Death of Christ.* Nashville, TN: Broadman, 1978.

Huntsman, Eric D. "After All We Can Do? Grace and the Book of Mormon." In *Mormons and Grace*, edited by Sheila Taylor. Salt Lake City: Greg Kofford Books, forthcoming.

———. *Becoming the Beloved Disciple: Coming unto Christ through the Gospel of John.* Springville, UT: Cedar Fort, 2018.

———. "The Lamb of God: Unique Aspects of the Passion Narrative in John." In *Behold the Lamb of God: The Fourth Annual BYU Religious Education Easter Conference*, edited by Richard Neitzel Holzapfel, Frank F. Judd Jr., and Thomas A. Wayment, 49–70. Provo, UT: BYU Religious Studies Center, 2008.

———. *The Miracles of Jesus.* Salt Lake City: Deseret Book, 2014.

———. "The Occasional Nature, Composition, and Structure of the Pauline Epistles." In *How the New Testament Came to Be: The 35th Annual Sidney B. Sperry Symposium*, edited by Kent P. Jackson, Frank F. Judd, and others, 190–207. Salt Lake City: Deseret Book, 2006.

———. "The Petrine *Kērygma* and the Gospel according to Mark." In *The Ministry of Peter, the Chief Apostle: The 43rd Annual Sidney B. Sperry Symposium*, edited by Frank F. Judd Jr., Eric D. Huntsman, and Shon D. Hopkin, 169–90. Provo, UT: BYU Religious Studies Center; Salt Lake City: Deseret Book, 2014.

———. "Preaching Jesus and Him Crucified." In *His Majesty and Mission*, edited by Nicholas J. Frederick and Keith J. Wilson, 55–76. Provo, UT: BYU Religious Studies Center; Salt Lake City: Deseret Book, 2017.

Huntsman, Eric D., Lincoln Blumell, and Tyler J. Griffin, eds. *Thou Art the Christ, the Son of the Living God: The Person and Work of Jesus in the New Testament; The 47th*

Annual Sidney B. Sperry Symposium. Provo, UT: BYU Religious Studies Center; Salt Lake City: Deseret Book, October 2018.

Hymns of The Church of Jesus Christ of Latter-day Saints. Salt Lake City: The Church of Jesus Christ of Latter-day Saints, 1985.

Ignatius, *To the Ephesians*.

Ignatius of Antioch. *Letter to the Magnesians*.

———. *Letter to the Smyrneans*.

Iovino, Joe. "God at Work Before We Know It: Prevenient Grace." The People of the United Methodist Church, March 2, 2018. https://www.umc.org/en/content/god-at-work-before-we-know-it-prevenient-grace.

Irenaeus. *Against Heresies*. Patrilogia Graeca. Volumes 7a and 7b. Translated by John Keble. London: James Parker & Co. and Rivingtons, 1872.

Irigaray, Luce. "Divine Women." In *Sexes and Genealogies*, 55–72. Translated by Gillian C. Gill. New York: Columbia University Press, 1993.

———. *Elemental Passions*. Translated by Joanne Collie and Judith Still. New York: Routledge, 1992.

———. "Equal to Whom?" *Differences* 1.2 (1989): 59–76.

———. "Place, Interval: A Reading of Aristotle, *Physics* IV." In *An Ethics of Sexual Difference*, 34–56. Translated by Carolyn Burke and Gillian C. Gill. Ithaca, NY: Cornell University Press, 1993.

———. *Sexes and Genealogies*. Translated by Gillian C. Gill. New York: Columbia University Press, 1993.

———. "Sexual Difference." In *The Irigaray Reader*, edited by Margaret Whitford, 165–77. Oxford: Blackwell Publishers, 1991.

Jantzen, Grace M. *Becoming Divine: Towards a Feminist Philosophy of Religion*. Bloomington: Indiana University Press, 1999.

Jefford, Clayton N. *Reading the Apostolic Fathers*. Peabody, MA: Hendrickson, 1996.

Jenson, Robert W. "Aspects of a Doctrine of Creation." In *The Doctrine of Creation: Essays in Dogmatics, History and Philosophy*, edited by Colin E. Gunton, 17–28. New York: T&T Clark, 2004.

Jersak, Brad. "Nonviolent Identification and the Victory of Christ." In *Stricken by God? Nonviolent Identification and the Victory of Christ*, edited by Brad Jersak and Michael Hardin, 18–53. Grand Rapids, MI: William B. Eerdmans, 2007.

Jersak, Brad and Michael Hardin, eds. *Stricken by God? Nonviolent Identification and the Victory of Christ*. Grand Rapids, MI: William B. Eerdmans, 2007.

Johnson, Adam J. "A Fuller Account: The Role of 'Fittingness' in Thomas Aquinas' Development of the Doctrine of Atonement." *International Journal of Systematic Theology* 12.3 (2010): 302–18.

———. "Peter Abelard." In *T&T Clark Companion to Atonement*, edited by Adam J. Johnson, 357–60. London: Bloomsbury, 2017.

Johnson, Adam J., ed. *T&T Clark Companion to Atonement*. London: Bloomsbury, 2017.

Johnson, Elizabeth A. *Consider Jesus: Waves of Renewal in Christology*. New York: Crossroad, 2000.

Johnson, Janiece Lyn. "'Give It All Up and Follow Your Lord': Mormon Female Religiosity, 1831–1843." Master's thesis, Brigham Young University, Provo, UT, 2001.

———. *"Give It All Up and Follow Your Lord": Mormon Female Religiosity, 1831–1843*. Provo, UT: BYU Studies, 2008.

Johnson, Janiece, and Jennifer Reeder. *Witness of Women: Firsthand Experiences and Testimonies of the Restoration*. Salt Lake City: Deseret Book, 2016.

Johnson, Junius. *Patristic and Medieval Atonement Theory*. Lanham, MD: Rowman & Littlefield, 2016.

Jones, Serene. *Feminist Theory and Christian Theology: Cartographies of Grace*. Minneapolis: Augsburg Fortress, 2000.

———. *Trauma and Grace: Theology in a Ruptured World*. Louisville, KY: Westminster John Knox, 2009.

Joslin, Barry C. "Christ Bore the Sins of Many: Substitution and the Atonement in Hebrews." *Southern Baptist Journal of Theology* 11.2 (Summer 2007): 74–103.

Justin Martyr. *Dialogue avec Tryphon, edition critique*. Vol. I. Translated by Philippe Bobichon. Fribourg: Academic Press Fribourg, 2003.

Kähler, Martin. *The So-Called Historical Jesus and the Historic Biblical Christ*. Translated by Carl E. Braaten. German original, 1896; Philadelphia: Fortress, 1964.

Kärkkäinen, Veli-Matti. *Christology: A Global Introduction*. Grand Rapids, MI: Baker Academic, 2016.

Keogh, Benjamin. "Lehi and His Dream: A Relational Reading." In *Re-Visioning the Dream: Interpreting 1 Nephi 8*, edited by Benjamin Keogh, Joseph M. Spencer, and Jennifer Champoux. Provo, UT: Neal A. Maxwell Institute for Religious Scholarship, forthcoming.

Kibbe, Michael. "Is it Finished? When did it Start? Hebrews, Priesthood, and Atonement in Biblical, Systematic, and Historical Perspective." *Journal of Theological Studies* 65.1 (April 2014): 25–61.

Kierkegaard, Søren. *The Concept of Anxiety*. Edited and translated by Reidar Thomte. Princeton: Princeton University Press, 1980.

Kim, Jintae. "The Concept of Atonement in the Gospel of John." *Journal of Greco-Roman Christianity and Judaism* 6 (2009): 9–27.

Kimball, Sarah M. "Early Relief Society Reminiscence, Mar. 17, 1882." Relief Society Record, 1880–1892. Church History Library, Church of Jesus Christ of Latter-day Saints, Salt Lake City.

King, Arthur Henry. "Atonement, The Only Wholeness." *Ensign* (April 1975): 12–18.

Kistemaker, Simon J. "Atonement in Hebrews: 'A Merciful and Faithful High Priest.'" In *The Glory of the Atonement, Biblical, Historical and Practical Perspectives: Essays in Honor of Roger Nicole*, edited by Charles E. Hill and Frank A. James III, 163–75. Downers Grove, IL: InterVarsity, 2004.

Kittel, Gerhard, ed. *Theological Dictionary of the New Testament*. 10 volumes. Grand Rapids, MI: William B. Eerdmans, 1977.

Kotsko, Adam. *The Politics of Redemption: The Social Logic of Salvation*. New York: Bloomsbury, 2010.

Kuster, Volker. *The Many Faces of Jesus Christ: Intercultural Christology.* New York: Orbis Books, 2001.

Lane, Jennifer C. "Redemption's Grand Design for Both the Living and the Dead." In *The Doctrine and Covenants: Revelations in Context*, edited by Andrew H. Hedges, J. Spencer Fluhman, and Alonzo L. Gaskill, 188–211. Provo, UT: BYU Religious Studies Center; Salt Lake City: Deseret Book, 2008.

Lane, William L. *The Gospel of Mark.* Grand Rapids, MI: William B. Eerdmans, 1974.

Lee, Dorothy A. *The Symbolic Narratives of the Fourth Gospel: The Interplay of Form and Meaning.* Sheffield: Sheffield Academic, 1994.

Lehi Ward, Alpine Stake. Relief Society Minutes, vol. 1, October 27, 1869, 26–29. Salt Lake City: Church History Library, Church of Jesus Christ of Latter-day Saints.

Levine, Baruch. *The JPS Torah Commentary: Leviticus.* Philadelphia: Jewish Publication Society, 1989.

Liddell, Henry George, and Robert Scott. *Greek-English Lexicon, with a Revised Supplement.* 9th Edition. Edited by Henry Stuart Jones. Oxford: Clarendon Press, 1996.

Lindemann, Andreas. "Paulinische Theologie im Brief an Diognet." In *Kerygma und Logos: Beiträge zu den geistesgeschichtlichen Beziehungen zwischen Antika und Christentum*, edited by A. M. Ritter, 337–50. Göttingen: Vandenhoeck & Ruprecht, 1979.

Lipka, Michael. "Some Major U.S. Religious Groups Differ from Their Members on the Death Penalty." Pew Research Center, July 13, 2015. https://www.pewresearch.org/fact-tank/2015/07/13/some-major-u-s-religious-groups-differ-from-their-members-on-the-death-penalty/.

Little, M. Elizabeth. "Kanab Relief Society." *Woman's Exponent* 9.21 (April 1, 1881): 165.

Longman, Tremper, III, and Peter Enns, eds. *Dictionary of the Old Testament: Wisdom, Poetry, and Writings.* Downers Grove, IL: InterVarsity Academic, 2008.

Ludlow, Daniel H., ed. *Encyclopedia of Mormonism.* 5 volumes. New York: Macmillan, 1992.

Lum, Kathryn Gin. *Damned Nation: Hell in America from the Revolution to Reconstruction.* Oxford: Oxford University Press, 2014.

Lunn, Nicholas P. "Jesus, the Ark, and the Day of Atonement: Intertextual Echoes in John 19:38–20:18." *Journal of the Evangelical Theological Society* 52.4 (December 2009): 731–46.

Lyman, Edward Leo, Susan Ward Payne, and S. George Elsworth, eds. *No Place to Call Home: The 1807–1857 Life Writings of Caroline Barnes Crosby, Chronicler of Outlying Mormon Communities.* Logan, UT: Utah State University Press, 2005.

Lyman, Eliza P. Journal. 142 pages. Church History Library, Church of Jesus Christ of Latter-day Saints, Salt Lake City.

MacCulloch, Diarmaid. *The Reformation: A History.* New York: Viking, 2004.

Mack, Temperance, to Harriett Whittemore, December 30, 1838. Whittemore Family Papers, Michigan Historical Collections. Ann Arbor: University of Michigan.

Mackintosh, H. R. *The Christian Experience of Forgiveness.* London: Nisbet and Co., 1927.

Madsen, Carol Cornwall. "Mormon Women and the Temple: Toward a New Understanding." In *Sisters in Spirit: Mormon Women in Historical and Cultural Perspec-*

tive, edited by Maureen Ursenbach Beecher and Lavina Fielding Anderson, 80–110. Urbana, IL: University of Illinois Press, 1987.

Madsen, Truman G. "B. H. Roberts: The Book of Mormon and the Atonement." In *The Book of Mormon: First Nephi, the Doctrinal Foundation*, edited by Monte S. Nyman and Charles D. Tate Jr., 297–314. Salt Lake City: Bookcraft, 1988.

Madsen, Truman G., ed. *Reflections on Mormonism: Judaeo Christian Parallels*. Provo, UT: BYU Religious Studies Center, 1978.

Maier, Harry O. "The Apostolic Fathers." In *T&T Clark Companion to Atonement*, edited by Adam J. Johnson, 371–76. London: Bloomsbury, 2017.

Marshall, Christopher D. *Beyond Retribution: A New Testament Vision for Justice, Crime, and Punishment*. Grand Rapids, MI: Eerdmans, 2001.

Martin, Ralph P. Martin, "Reconciliation and Forgiveness in the Letter to the Colossians." In *Reconciliation and Hope: New Testament Essays on Atonement and Eschatology, Presented to L. L. Morris on His 60th Birthday*, edited by Robert Banks, 104–24. Milton Keynes, England: Paternoster, 1974.

Martyr, Justin. *Dialogue with Trypho*.

Mason, Patrick Q., and J. David Pulsipher. *Weapons of Peace: Nonviolence and the Restoration*. Unpublished manuscript.

Matthews, Victor H., and Don C. Benjamin. *The Social World of Ancient Israel, 1250–587 BCE*. Grand Rapids, MI: Baker Academic, 1993.

Maxwell, Neal A. "The Doctrine and Covenants: The Voice of the Lord." *Ensign* (Dec. 1978): 4–7.

———. "Settle This in Your Hearts." *Ensign* (Nov. 1992): 65–67.

———. "The Women of God." *Ensign* (May 1978): 10–11.

McConkie, Bruce R. *Mormon Doctrine*. 2nd edition. Salt Lake City: Deseret Book, 1966.

———. "Obedience, Consecration, and Sacrifice." *Ensign* (May 1975): 50–52.

———. "The Purifying Power of Gethsemane." *Ensign* (May 1985): 9–11.

McConkie, Joseph Fielding, and Robert L. Millet. *Doctrinal Commentary on the Book of Mormon, Volume II—Jacob through Mosiah*. Salt Lake City: Bookcraft, 1988.

McCormack, Bruce L., ed. *Justification in Perspective: Historical Developments and Contemporary Applications*. Grand Rapids, MI: Baker Academic, 2006.

McFarland, Ian A. *Creation and Humanity: The Sources of Christian Theology*. Louisville, KY: Westminster John Knox, 2009.

———. "The Fall and Sin." In *The Oxford Handbook of Systematic Theology*, edited by John Webster, Kathryn Tanner, and Iain Torrance, 140–59. New York: Oxford University Press, 2007.

McGrath, Alister. "The Moral Theory of the Atonement: A Historical and Theological Critique." *Scottish Journal of Theology* 38 (1985): 205–20.

McGuckin, John A. "St. Gregory of Nyssa on the Dynamics of Salvation." In *T&T Clark Companion to Atonement*, edited by Adam J. Johnson, 155–74. London: Bloomsbury, 2017.

McMurrin, Sterling M. "Comments on the Theological and Philosophical Foundations of Christianity." *Dialogue* 25.1 (Spring 1992): 37–48.

———. *The Theological Foundations of the Mormon Religion*. Salt Lake City: University of Utah Press, 1965.
McWilliams, Warren. *The Passion of God*. Macon, GA: Mercer University Press, 1985.
Metzger, Bruce R. *A Textual Commentary on the Greek New Testament*. 2nd edition. Stuttgart: United Bible Societies, 1994.
Michaels, J. Ramsey. "Atonement in John's Gospel and Epistles: 'The Lamb of God Who Takes Away the Sin of the World.'" In *The Glory of the Atonement, Biblical, Historical and Practical Perspectives: Essays in Honor of Roger Nicole*, edited by Charles E. Hill and Frank A. James III, 106–18. Downers Grove, IL: InterVarsity, 2004.
Milad, Corine B. "Incarnation and Transfiguration: Origen's Theology of Descent." *Journal of Theological Interpretation* 12 (2018): 200–216.
Milgrom, Jacob. *Leviticus 1–16*. The Anchor Yale Bible Commentaries. New Haven: Yale University Press, 1998.
———. "The Temple in Biblical Israel: Kinships of Meaning." In *Reflections on Mormonism, Judaeo Christian Parallels*, edited by Truman G. Madsen, 57–66. Provo, UT: BYU Religious Studies Center, 1978.
Miller, Adam S. "A General Theory of Grace." In *Future Mormon: Essays in Mormon Theology*, 1–12. Salt Lake City: Greg Kofford Books, 2016.
———. *Original Grace*. Salt Lake and Provo, UT: Deseret Book and BYU Maxwell Institute, 2022.
Millet, Robert L. "Joseph Smith's Christology: After Two Hundred Years." In *The Worlds of Joseph Smith*, edited by John Welch, 231–50. Provo, UT: BYU Press, 2006.
Milton, John. *The Complete Poetry and Essential Prose of John Milton*. Edited by William Kerrigan, John Rumrich, and Stephen M. Fallon. New York: The Modern Library, 2007.
Moffitt, David M. *Atonement and the Logic of Resurrection in the Epistle to the Hebrews*. Leiden, Netherlands: Brill, 2011.
More, Thomas. *Workes*. London: London, John Cawood, John Walley, and Richard Tottle, 1557.
Morgan, Jacob. "The Divine Infusion Theory: Rethinking the Atonement." *Dialogue* 39.1 (Spring 2006): 57–81.
Morgan, Jonathan. "*Christus Victor* Motifs in the Soteriology of Thomas Aquinas." *Pro Ecclesia* 21.4 (2012): 409–21.
Motyer, Steve. "The Atonement in Hebrews." In *The Atonement Debate: Papers from the London Symposium on the Theology of Atonement*, edited by Derek Tidball, David Hilborn, and Justin Thacker, 136–53. Grand Rapids, MI: Zondervan, 2008.
Mozley, J. K. *The Impassibility of God*. London: Cambridge University Press, 1926.
Nauvoo Female Relief Society. Minutes, 1842–1844, March 17, 1842. Salt Lake City: Church History Library, Church of Jesus Christ of Latter-day Saints.
Nauvoo Female Relief Society. Minutes, 1842–1844, May 27, 1842, 57–58. Salt Lake City: Church History Library, Church of Jesus Christ of Latter-day Saints.
New International Dictionary of Old Testament Theology and Exegesis (*NIDOTTE*). Edited by Willem A. VanGemeren. 5 volumes. Grand Rapids, MI: Zondervan, 1997.

Newell, Linda King. "The Historical Relationship of Mormon Women and Priesthood." In *Women and Authority: Re-emerging Mormon Feminism*, edited by Maxine Hanks, 23–48. Salt Lake City: Signature Books, 1992.

Neyman, Jane. "Statements," November 29, 1854. Joseph Smith History Documents. Salt Lake City: Church History Library, Church of Jesus Christ of Latter-day Saints.

Nibley, Hugh W. *Approaching Zion*. Edited by Don E. Norton. Salt Lake City: Deseret Book, 1989.

———. "Assembly and Atonement." In *King Benjamin's Speech: "That Ye May Learn Wisdom,"* edited by John W. Welch and Stephen D. Ricks, 119–45. Provo, UT: FARMS, 1998.

———. "The Atonement of Jesus Christ." In 4 parts. *Ensign* (July 1990): 18–23; (Aug. 1990): 30–34; (Sept. 1990): 22–26; (Oct. 1990): 26–31.

———. "The Meaning of the Atonement." In *Approaching Zion*, edited by Don E. Norton, 554–614. Salt Lake City: Deseret Book, 1989.

Niebuhr, Reinhold. *Human Nature*. Volume 1 of *The Nature and Destiny of Man*. New York: Scribner's Sons, 1941.

Nietzsche, Friedrich. *The Genealogy of Morals*. Translated by Horace B. Samuel. Stilwell, KS: Digireads, 2007.

Noll, Mark. "New England Theology." *Evangelical Dictionary of Theology*. Edited by Walter A. Elwell. Grand Rapids, MI: Baker Books, 1984.

Norlock, Kathryn. *Forgiveness from a Feminist Perspective*. Lanham, Md.: Lexington Books, 2009, 2018.

Norman, Keith. "Toward a Mormon Christology." *Sunstone* 10 (Apr. 1985): 19–25.

Nyman, Monte S. *These Records Are True: A Teaching Commentary on Jacob through Mosiah*. Orem, UT: Granite Publishing, 2004.

O'Brien, Peter T. *The Epistle to the Philippians*. New International Greek New Testament Commentary. Grand Rapids, MI: Eerdmans, 1991.

O'Collins, Gerald. *Christology: A Biblical, Historical, and Systematic Study of Jesus*. New York: Oxford University Press, 2009.

O'Day, Gail. "The Gospel of John." *The New Interpreter's Bible: Luke–John*. Edited by Leander Keck. Nashville: Abingdon, 1995.

Oduyoye, Mercy Amba. "Jesus Christ." In *The Cambridge Companion to Feminist Theology*, edited by Susan F. Parsons, 151–70. Cambridge: Cambridge University Press, 2004.

Okazaki, Chieko N. *Lighten Up!* Salt Lake City: Deseret Book, 1993.

Olin, John C., ed. *A Reformation Debate*. Grand Rapids, MI: Baker, 2002.

Olson, Roger E. *The Story of Christian Theology*. Downers Grove, IL: Intervarsity, 1999.

Origen, *De principiis*.

———. *Homilies on Numbers*.

Ostler, Blake T. "The Book of Mormon as a Modern Expansion of an Ancient Source." *Dialogue* 20.1 (Spring 1987): 66–124.

———. "The Development of the Mormon Concept of Grace." *Dialogue* 24.1 (Spring 1991): 57–84.

———. *Exploring Mormon Thought, Volume 2: The Problems of Theism and the Love of God*. Salt Lake City: Greg Kofford Books, 2006.

Outka, Gene. *Agape: An Ethical Analysis*. New Haven: Yale University Press, 1972.

Packer, Boyd K. "The Mediator." *Ensign* (May 1977): 54–56.

———. "The Pattern of Our Parentage." *Ensign* (Nov. 1984): 66–69.

Paley, William. *Works*. 5 volumes. London: Longman, 1838.

Park, Benjamin E. "Salvation through a Tabernacle: Joseph Smith, Parley P. Pratt, and Early Mormon Theologies of Embodiment." *Dialogue* 43.2 (Summer 2010): 1–44.

Parry, Jay A. "'Called to Drink Deep of the Bitter Cup': Mary Fielding Smith." In *Women of Faith in the Latter Days: Volume One, 1775–1820*, edited by Richard E. Turley Jr. and Brittany A. Chapman, 376—88. Salt Lake City: Deseret Book, 2011.

Paul, Robert S. *The Atonement and the Sacraments*. New York: Abingdon, 1960.

Paulsen, David L., and Martin Pulido. "'A Mother There': A Survey of Historical Teachings about Mother in Heaven." *BYU Studies* 50.1 (2011): 71–97.

Payson Ward, Utah Stake. Volume 1, September 9, 1871, 110. Salt Lake City: Church History Library, Church of Jesus Christ of Latter-day Saints.

Pelikan, Jaroslav. *Jesus Through the Centuries: His Place in the History of Culture*. New Haven: Yale University Press, 1999.

Perry, Michael F. "The Supremacy of the Word: Alma's Mission to the Zoramites and the Conversion of the Lamanites." *Journal of Book of Mormon Studies* 24 (2015): 119–37.

Petersen, Boyd Jay. "'Redeemed from the Curse Placed Upon Her': Dialogic Discourse on Eve in the *Woman's Exponent*." *Journal of Mormon History* 40.1 (Winter 2014): 135–74.

Peterson, David. "Atonement in the New Testament." In *Where Wrath and Mercy Meet: Proclaiming the Atonement Today*, edited by David Peterson, 26–67. Milton Keynes, England: Paternoster, 2001.

———. "Atonement Theology in Luke–Acts: Some Methodological Reflections." In *The New Testament in Its First Century Setting: Essays on Context and Background in Honour of B. W. Winter on His 65th Birthday*, edited by P. J. Williams, Andrew D. Clarke, Peter M. Head, and David Instone-Brewer, 56–71. Grand Rapids, MI: William B. Eerdmans, 2004.

Peterson, David, ed. *Where Wrath and Mercy Meet: Proclaiming the Atonement Today*. Oak Hill College Annual School of Theology Series. Milton Keynes, England: Paternoster, 2001.

Pittenger, W. Norman. *The Christian Understanding of Human Nature*. Philadelphia: Westminster, 1964.

Plaskow, Judith. *Sex, Sin, and Grace: Women's Experience and the Theologies of Reinhold Niebuhr and Paul Tillich*. Lanham, MD: University Press of America, 1980.

———. *Standing Again at Sinai: Judaism from a Feminist Perspective*. San Francisco: HarperOne, 1991.

Polycarp of Smyrna. *Epistle to the Philippians*.

Porter, Stanley E. *The Apostle Paul: His Life, Thought, and Letters*. Grand Rapids, MI: William B. Eerdmans, 2016.

Porter, Stanley E., and Bryan R. Dyer, eds. *The Synoptic Problem: Four Views*. Grand Rapids, MI: Baker Academic, 2016.

Potter, R. Dennis. "Did Christ Pay for Our Sins?" *Dialogue* 32.4 (Winter 1999): 73–86.

Pratt, Parley P. *The World Turned Upside Down, or Heaven on Earth*. Liverpool: James and Woodburn, 1842.

Prothro, James B. "The Strange Case of Δικαιόω in the Septuagint and Paul: The Oddity and Origins of Paul's Talk of 'Justification.'" *Zeitschrift für die neutestamentliche Wissenschaft und die Kunde der älteren Kirche* 107.1 (2016): 48–69.

Pugh, Ben. *Atonement Theories: A Way Through the Maze*. Eugene, OR: Cascade Books, 2014.

"Questions and Answers, 8 May 1838." *Elders' Journal* (July 1838): 42–44. The Joseph Smith Papers. https://www.josephsmithpapers.org/paper-summary/questions-and-answers-8-may-1838/3.

Quinn, Philip L. "Abelard on Atonement: 'Nothing Unintelligible, Arbitrary, Illogical, or Immoral about It.'" In *Reasoned Faith: Essays in Philosophical Theology in Honor of Norman Kretzmann*, edited by Eleonore Stump, 281–300. Ithaca, NY: Cornell University Press, 1993.

Rahner, Karl. *Theological Investigations, Volume I: God, Christ, Mary and Grace*. Translated by Cornelius Ernst. Baltimore: Helicon, 1963.

Rainbow, Paul A. *Johannine Theology: The Gospel, the Epistles, and the Apocalypse*. Downers Grove, IL: IVP Academic, 2014.

Rambo, Shelly. "How Christian Theology and Practice Are Being Shaped by Trauma Studies: Talking about God in the Face of Wounds that Won't Go Away." *The Christian Century* 136.24 (Nov. 1, 2019): 1–7.

———. *Spirit and Trauma: A Theology of Remaining*. Louisville: Westminster John Knox, 2010.

Rashdall, Hastings. *The Idea of Atonement in Christian Theology*. London: MacMillan and Co., 1925.

Rausch, Thomas P. *Who Is Jesus? An Introduction to Christology*. Collegeville, MN: Liturgical Press, 2003.

Rees, B. R. *Pelagius: Life and Letters*. Woodbridge, UK: Boydell Press, 1991.

Reichenbach, Bruce R. "Healing View." In *The Nature of the Atonement: Four Views*, edited by James Beilby and Paul R. Eddy, 117–42. Downers Grove, IL: InterVarsity Academic, 2006.

Renlund, Dale G. "Our Good Shepherd." *Ensign* (May 2017): 29–32.

Ribbens, Benjamin J. "Ascension and Atonement: The Significance of Post-Reformation, Reformed Responses to Socinians for Contemporary Atonement Debates in Hebrews." *Westminster Theological Journal* 80.1 (Spring 2018): 1–23.

Richards, Jane Snyder. *Reminiscences of Mrs. F. D. Richards*. Holograph. 1880.

Ricks, Stephen D. "Kingship, Coronation, and Covenant in Mosiah 1–6." In *King Benjamin's Speech: "That Ye May Learn Wisdom,"* edited by John W. Welch and Stephen D. Ricks, 233–76. Provo, UT: FARMS, 1998.

Ricoeur, Paul. *Figuring the Sacred: Religion, Narrative, and Imagination*. Translated by David Pellauer. Edited by Mark I. Wallace. Minneapolis: Fortress, 1995

Ridderbos, Herman. "The Earliest Confession of the Atonement in Paul." In *Reconciliation and Hope: New Testament Essays on Atonement and Eschatology, Presented to L. L. Morris on His 60th Birthday*, edited by Robert Banks, 76–89. Milton Keynes, England: Paternoster, 1974.

———. *Gospel of John: A Theological Commentary*. Translated by John Vriend. Grand Rapids, MI: William B. Eerdmans, 1997.

Rieger, Nathan. "Good News for the Postmodern Man: Christus Victor in the Lucan Kerygma." In *Stricken by God? Nonviolent Identification and the Victory of Christ*, edited by Brad Jersak and Michael Hardin, 378–403. Grand Rapids, MI: William B. Eerdmans, 2007.

Ripley, Jason. "Atonement and Martyrdom in the Gospel of John." *Horizons in Biblical Theology* 42.1 (2020): 58–89.

Roberts, Alexander and James Donaldson, eds. *The Ante-Nicene Fathers*. 10 Volumes. Grand Rapids, MI: William B. Eerdmans, 1977.

Roberts, B. H. *Seventies Course in Theology*. 2 volumes. Dallas: S. K. Taylor Publ. Co., 1976.

———. *The Truth, the Way, the Life: An Elementary Treatise on Theology: The Masterwork of B. H. Roberts*. Edited by Stan Larson. San Francisco: Smith Research Associates, 1994.

Roberts, J. J. M. *First Isaiah: A Commentary*. Minneapolis: Fortress, 2015.

Robinson, Stephen E. "Believing Christ." *Ensign* (Apr. 1992): 5–9.

———. *Believing Christ: The Parable of the Bicycle and Other Good News*. Salt Lake City: Deseret Book, 1994.

Rohr, Richard. *The Universal Christ: How a Forgotten Reality Can Change Everything We See, Hope For, and Believe*. New York: Convergent, 2019.

Roth, Martha T., editor in charge. *The Assyrian Dictionary of the Oriental Institute of the University of Chicago* (*The Chicago Assyrian Dictionary*). 21 volumes. Chicago: University of Chicago Press, 1921–2011. Reprinted, Oriental Institute of the University of Chicago. Accessed March 1, 2023. https://oi.uchicago.edu/research/publications/assyrian-dictionary-oriental-institute-university-chicago-cad.

Ruether, Rosemary Radford. *Sexism and God-Talk: Toward a Feminist Theology*. Boston: Beacon, 1993.

Ruether, Rosemary Radford, and Camille Williams. "A Dialogue on Feminist Theology: Can a Male Savior Save Women? Liberating Christology from Patriarchy." In *Mormonism in Dialogue with Contemporary Christian Theologies*, edited by David L. Paulsen and Donald W. Musser, 251–64. Macon, GA: Mercer University Press, 2007.

Saiving, Valerie. "The Human Situation: A Feminine View." *Journal of Religion* 40.2 (Apr. 1960): 100–112.

Santaquin Ward, Utah Stake. Relief Society Minutes, vol. 3, July 1, 1875. Salt Lake City: Church History Library, Church of Jesus Christ of Latter-day Saints.

Sawyer, John F. A. *Isaiah through the Centuries*. Hoboken, NJ: Wiley Blackwell, 2018.

Scaer, Peter J. "The Atonement in Mark's Sacramental Theology." *Concordia Theological Quarterly* 72.3 (2008): 227–42.

Schaff, Philip. *History of the Christian Church*. 8 volumes. 3rd edition. Peabody, MA: Hendrickson, 2006.

Schmiechen, Peter. *Saving Power: Theories of Atonement and Forms of the Church*. Grand Rapids, MI: William B. Eerdmans, 2005.

Schreiner, Thomas R. "Penal Substitution View." In *The Nature of the Atonement: Four Views*, edited by James Beilby and Paul R. Eddy, 67–98. Downers Grove, IL: InterVarsity Academic, 2006.

Schrift, Alan. "On the Gynecology of Morals: Nietzsche and Cixous on the Logic of the Gift." In *Nietzsche and the Feminine*, edited by Peter J. Burgard, 210–29. Charlottesville: University of Virginia Press, 1994.

Schwöbel, Christoph. "God, Creation, and the Christian Community: The Dogmatic Basis of a Christian Ethic of Createdness." In *The Doctrine of Creation: Essays in Dogmatics, History and Philosophy*, edited by Colin E. Gunton, 149–76. New York: T&T Clark, 2004.

Seely, David Rolph. "William Tyndale and the Language of At-one-ment." In *The King James Bible and the Restoration*, edited by Kent P. Jackson, 25–42. Provo, UT: BYU Religious Studies Center, 2011.

Seibert, Eric A. *The Violence of Scripture: Overcoming the Old Testament's Troubling Legacy*. Minneapolis: Fortress, 2012.

Shanks, Hershel. "God as Divine Kinsman: What Covenant Meant in Ancient Israel." *Biblical Archaeology Review* 25.4 (July/Aug. 1999): 32–33, 60.

Shannon, Avram R. "Law of God/God of Law: The Law of Moses in Alma's Teachings to Corianton." In *Give Ear to My Words*, edited by Kerry M. Hull et al., 129–54. Provo, UT: BYU Religious Studies Center, 2019.

Shipps, Jan. *Mormonism: The Story of a New Religious Tradition*. Urbana: University of Illinois Press, 1985.

Skousen, Royal. *Analysis of Textual Variants in the Book of Mormon: Part One 1, Nephi 1–2, Nephi 10*. Provo, UT: FARMS, 2004.

Skousen, Royal, ed. *The Book of Mormon: The Earliest Text*. New Haven: Yale University Press, 2009.

Skousen, W. Cleon. *A Personal Search for the Meaning of the Atonement*. Sound recording on CD. Provo, UT: Ensign Productions, Sounds of Zion, 2002.

Smith, Alex. D., Adam H. Petty, Jessica M. Nelson, and Spencer W. McBride, eds. *Documents, Volume 14: 1 January–15 May 1844*. Volume 14 in the Documents series of *The Joseph Smith Papers*, edited by Ronald K. Esplin, Matthew J. Grow, and Matthew C. Godfrey. Salt Lake City: Church Historian's Press, 2023.

Smith, Bathsheba W. *Autobiography*. Holograph Manuscript, circa 1875–1906. MS 8606. Salt Lake City: Church History Library, Church of Jesus Christ of Latter-day Saints.

———. Bathsheba W. Smith, Deposition, 8th Circuit Court Testimony, 1892. Salt Lake City: Church History Library, Church of Jesus Christ of Latter-day Saints.

———. "Pioneer Stake." *Woman's Exponent* 34.2–3 (July/Aug. 1905): 14.

Smith, Emma, ed. *A Collection of Sacred Hymns for the Church of the Latter Day Saints*. Kirtland, OH: F. G. Williams, 1835.

Smith, Joseph. Discourse, March 27, 1842. Nauvoo, Illinois, the Joseph Smith Papers. https://www.josephsmithpapers.org/paper-summary/discourse-27-march-1842/1.

Smith, Joseph, Jr. *History of the Church of Jesus Christ of Latter-day Saints*. Edited by B.

H. Roberts. 7 volumes. Salt Lake City: Church of Jesus Christ of Latter-day Saints, 1932–51.

———. "King Follett Sermon." *Ensign* (Apr. 1971): 13–17. Republished at the website of The Church of Jesus Christ of Latter-day Saints, https://churchofjesuschrist.org/study/ensign/1971/04/the-king-follett-sermon.

———. *Lectures on Faith*. Salt Lake City: Deseret Book, 1985.

———. "To the Saints of God." *Times and Seasons* (Nauvoo, IL), Oct. 15, 1842.

Smith, Joseph Fielding. *Church History and Modern Revelation*. 4 volumes. Salt Lake City: Council of the Twelve Apostles of the Church of Jesus Christ of Latter-day Saints, 1946–1949.

———. *Doctrines of Salvation*. 3 volumes. Edited by Bruce R. McConkie. Salt Lake City: Bookcraft, 1954–56.

———. *Life of Joseph F. Smith*. Salt Lake City: Deseret News Press, 1938.

Smith, Joseph Fielding, ed. and comp. *Teachings of the Prophet Joseph Smith*. Salt Lake City: Deseret Book, 1976.

Smith, Julie M. "Huldah's Long Shadow." In *A Dream, a Rock, and a Pillar of Fire: Reading 1 Nephi 1*, edited by Adam S. Miller, 1–16. Provo, UT: Neal A. Maxwell Institute for Religious Scholarship, 2017.

———. "Narrative Atonement Theology in the Gospel of Mark." *BYU Studies Quarterly* 54.1 (2015): 29–41.

Smith, Mark S. *The Early History of God: Yahweh and Other Deities in Ancient Israel*. 2nd edition. Grand Rapids, MI: William B. Eerdmans, 2002.

Smith, Mary Fielding, to Joseph Fielding, June 1839. In *The Women of Mormondom* by Edward W. Tullidge, 255–56. New York: Tullidge and Crandall, 1877.

Snow, Eliza R. "An Address." *Woman's Exponent* 2.8 (Sept. 15, 1873): 62–63.

———. "Female Relief Society." *Deseret Evening News* (Apr. 18, 1868), 2.

———. "Female Relief Society." *Deseret Evening News* (Apr. 22, 1868), 2.

———. "Let Us Cultivate Ourselves." In *At the Pulpit: 185 Years of Discourses by Latter-day Saint Women*, edited by Jennifer Reeder and Kate Holbrook, 41–45. Salt Lake City: The Church Historian's Press, 2017.

———. "Sacramental Hymn [How Great the Wisdom and the Love]." In *Sacred Hymns and Spiritual Songs for the Church of Jesus Christ of Latter-day Saints*, 401–2. Salt Lake City: Deseret News, 1871.

———. "Sketch of My Life." *The Personal Writings of Eliza Roxcy Snow*, edited by Maureen Ursenbach Beecher, 6–46. Logan, UT: Utah State University Press, 2000.

Snow, Erastus. *Journal of Discourses*.

Sorenson, John L. "Religious Groups and Movements among the Nephites, 200–1 B.C." In *The Disciple as Scholar: Essays on Scripture and the Ancient World in Honor of Richard Lloyd Anderson*, edited by Stephen D. Ricks, Donald W. Parry, and Andrew H. Hedges, 163–208. Provo, UT: FARMS, 2000.

Souga, Thérèsa. "The Christ-Event from the Viewpoint of African Women: A Catholic Perspective." In *With Passion and Compassion: Third World Women Doing Theology*, edited by Virginia Fabella and Mercy Amba Oduyoye, 22–29. Maryknoll, NY: Orbis Books, 1990.

Spackman, T. Benjamin. "The Israelite Roots of Atonement Terminology." *BYU Studies Quarterly* 55.1 (2016): 47–48.

Sparks, Kenton. *Sacred Word, Broken Word: Biblical Authority and the Dark Side of Scripture*. Grand Rapids, MI: William B. Eerdmans, 2012.

Spencer, Joseph M. *1st Nephi: A Brief Theological Introduction*. Provo, UT: Neal A. Maxwell Institute for Religious Scholarship, 2020.

———. "Is Not This Real?" *BYU Studies Quarterly* 58.2 (2019): 87–104.

———. "Notes on Novelty," *SquareTwo* 6.1 (Spring 2013). Republished online. http://squaretwo.org/Sq2ArticleMillerSymposiumSpencer.html.

———. *An Other Testament*. 2nd edition. Provo, UT: Neal A. Maxwell Institute for Religious Scholarship, 2016.

———. *The Vision of All: Twenty-Five Lectures on Isaiah in Nephi's Record*. Salt Lake City: Greg Kofford Books, 2016.

Spjuth, Roland. "Gustaf Aulén." In *T&T Clark Companion to Atonement*, edited by Adam J. Johnson, 389–92. London: Bloomsbury, 2017.

Stapley, Jonathan. *The Power of Godliness: Mormon Liturgy and Cosmology*. New York: Oxford University Press, 2018.

Stavropoulos, Cristoforos. "Partakers of Divine Nature." In *Eastern Orthodox Theology: A Contemporary Reader*, edited by Daniel B. Clendenin, 183–92. Grand Rapids, MI: Baker Academic, 1995.

Stendahl, Krister. *Paul Among Jews and Gentiles*. Philadelphia: Fortress, 1979.

———. "The Sermon on the Mount and Third Nephi." In *Reflections on Mormonism: Judaeo-Christian Parallels*, edited by Truman G. Madsen, 139–54. Provo, UT: BYU Religious Studies Center, 1978.

Stevens, George. *The Christian Doctrine of Salvation*. Edinburgh: T&T Clark, 1905.

Stevenson, Angus, ed. *Oxford Dictionary of English*. 3rd edition. Oxford: Oxford University Press, 2010.

Stevenson, Bryan. *Just Mercy: A Story of Justice and Redemption*. New York: Spiegel & Grau, 2014.

Suggit, John N. "The Raising of Lazarus." *The Expository Times* 95:4 (1984): 106–8.

Szink, Terrence L., and John W. Welch. "King Benjamin's Speech in the Context of Ancient Israelite Festivals." *King Benjamin's Speech: "That Ye May Learn Wisdom,"* edited by John W. Welch and Stephen D. Ricks, 147–223. Provo, UT: FARMS, 1998.

Talmage, James E. Conference Report, April 1930.

———. *Jesus the Christ*. 17th edition. Salt Lake City: Deseret Book, 1948.

Tanner, Susan W. "I Am the Light Which Ye Shall Hold Up." *Ensign* (May 2006): 103–5.

Taves, Ann. *Fits, Trances, and Visions: Experiencing Religion and Explaining Experience from Wesley to James*. Princeton: Princeton University Press, 1999.

Taylor, Elmina S. *Biographical Sketch*. January 1881. Salt Lake City: Church History Library, Church of Jesus Christ of Latter-day Saints.

Taylor, John. *Mediation and Atonement*. Salt Lake City: Stevens & Wallis, Inc., 1950.

Taylor, Vincent. *Jesus and His Sacrifice*. New York: St. Martin's, 1965.

Tertullian. *Against Marcion*. Corpus Christianorum Series Latina (CCL). Volume 1.

———. *On Running Away from Persecution*. Corpus Scriptorum Ecclesiasticorum Latinorum (CSEL). Volume 25.

Thiessen, Matthew. "The Many for One or One for the Many? Reading Mark 10:45 in the Roman Empire." *Harvard Theological Review* 109.3 (2016): 447–66.

Thomas, John Christopher. *A Pentecostal Reads the Book of Mormon: A Literary and Theological Introduction*. Cleveland, TN: Center for Pentecostal Theology, 2016.

Thomas, Mark. "Revival Language in the Book of Mormon." *Sunstone* 8 (May/June 1983): 19–25.

Thomasson, Gordon C. "Mosiah: The Complex Symbolism and Symbolic Complex of Kingship in the Book of Mormon." *Journal of Book of Mormon Studies* 2.1 (1993): 21–38.

Thompson, Deanna A. "Faith in a Traumatized World." Lecture given at Brigham Young University on February 13, 2020.

Thompson, Mercy Fielding. "Recollections of the Prophet Joseph Smith." *Juvenile Instructor* 27.13 (July 1, 1892): 398–40.

Tidball, Derek, David Hilborn, and Justin Thacker, eds. *The Atonement Debate: Papers from the London Symposium on the Theology of Atonement*. Grand Rapids, MI: Zondervan, 2008.

Tillich, Paul. *Systematic Theology*. 3 Volumes. Chicago: University of Chicago Press, 1957.

Tobler, Ryan G. "'Saviors on Mount Zion': Mormon Sacramentalism, Mortality, and the Baptism for the Dead." *Journal of Mormon History* 39.4 (Fall 2013): 182–238.

Toscano, Margaret Merrill. "Are Boys More Important Than Girls? The Continuing Conflict of Gender Difference and Equality in Mormonism." *Sunstone* 146 (June 2007): 19–29.

Tracy, Nancy N. "Life History of Nancy Naomi Alexander Tracy, Written by Herself." Typescript. L. Tom Perry Special Collections. Provo, UT: Brigham Young University.

Traherne, Thomas. *Selected Writings*. Edited by Dick Davis. Manchester, England: Carcanet, 1980.

Travis, Stephen H. *Christ and the Judgement of God: The Limits of Divine Retribution in New Testament Thought*. Peabody, MA: Hendrickson, 2008.

Trible, Phyllis. *God and the Rhetoric of Sexuality*. Philadelphia: Fortress, 1986.

Tripolitis, Antonia. *Doctrine of the Soul in the Thought of Plotinus and Origen*. Roslyn Heights, NY: Libra, 1977.

Tugwell, Simon. *The Apostolic Fathers*. Harrisburg, PA: Morehouse, 1989.

Tullidge, Edward W. *The Women of Mormondom*. New York: Tullidge and Crandall, 1877.

Turley, Kylie Nielson. *Alma 1–29: A Brief Theological Introduction*. Provo, UT: Neal A. Maxwell Institute for Religious Scholarship, 2020.

Turner, H. E. W. *The Patristic Doctrine of Redemption*. London: A. R. Mowbray & Co., 1952.

Uchtdorf, Dieter F. "The Gift of Grace." *Ensign* (May 2015): 107–10.

Ulansey, David. "The Heavenly Veil Torn: Mark's Cosmic *Inclusio*." *Journal of Biblical Literature* 110.1 (1991): 123–25.

Ulrich, Michaël. "King Mosiah's Address." *Journal of Book of Mormon Studies* 28 (2019): 301–9.

Vail, Eric M. *Atonement and Salvation: The Extravagance of God's Love*. Kansas City, MO: Beacon Hill Press, 2016.

Vajda, Jordan. *Partakers of the Divine Nature: A Comparative Analysis of Patristic and Mormon Doctrines of Divinization*. Provo, UT: FARMS, 2002.

Van der Kolk, Bessel. *The Body Keeps the Score: Brain, Mind, and Body in the Healing of Trauma*. New York: Penguin Books, 2015.

Vidu, Adonis. *Atonement, Law, and Justice: The Cross in Historical and Cultural Contexts*. Grand Rapids, MI: Baker Academic, 2014.

Volluz, Corbin. "Jesus Christ as Elder Brother." *BYU Studies* 45:2 (2006): 141–58.

Wallace, Daniel B. *Greek Grammar beyond the Basics: An Exegetical Syntax of the New Testament*. Grand Rapids, MI: Zondervan, 1996.

Washington, H. A., ed. *Thomas Jefferson: Inaugural Addresses*. Washington, DC: Taylor & Maury, 1854.

Wayment, Thomas A. "The Hebrew Text of Alma 7:11." *Journal of Book of Mormon Studies* 14.1 (2005): 101–3

Weaver, J. Denny. *The Nonviolent Atonement*. 2nd Edition. Grand Rapids, MI: William B. Eerdmans, 2011.

———. "The Nonviolent Atonement: Human Violence, Discipleship and God." In *Stricken by God? Nonviolent Identification and the Victory of Christ*, edited by Brad Jersak and Michael Hardin, 316–55. Grand Rapids, MI: William B. Eerdmans, 2007.

Webb, C. C. J. *God and Personality*. London: George Allen & Unwin Ltd., 1919.

Webb, Stephen H. *Mormon Christianity: What Other Christians Can Learn from the Latter-day Saints*. New York: Oxford University Press, 2013.

Weber Stake. Relief Society Minutes, vol. 1, May 9, 1879, 55–56. Salt Lake City: Church History Library, Church of Jesus Christ of Latter-day Saints, Salt Lake City.

———. Young Women Minutes, June 9, 1881. Salt Lake City: Church History Library, Church of Jesus Christ of Latter-day Saints, Salt Lake City.

———. Young Women Minutes, Sept. 9, 1881. Salt Lake City: Church History Library, Church of Jesus Christ of Latter-day Saints, Salt Lake City.

———. Young Women Minutes, Mar. 14, 1884. Salt Lake City: Church History Library, Church of Jesus Christ of Latter-day Saints, Salt Lake City.

Webster, John. *The Domain of the Word: Scripture and Theological Reason*. New York: T&T Clark, 2012.

Webster, John, Kathryn Tanner, and Iain Torrance, eds. *The Oxford Handbook of Systematic Theology*. New York: Oxford University Press, 2007.

Webster, Noah, ed. *An American Dictionary of the English Language*. New York: S. Converse, 1828.

Weinandy, Thomas G. "Athanasius's Incarnational Soteriology." In *T&T Clark Companion to Atonement*, edited by Adam J. Johnson, 135–54. London: Bloomsbury, 2017.

Welch, John W. "What Was a 'Mosiah'?" In *Reexploring the Book of Mormon*, edited by John W. Welch, 105–7. Provo, UT: FARMS, 1992.

Wells, Emmeline B. "'Eliza Roxie Snow Smith': A Tribute of Affection." *Woman's Exponent* 16 (Dec. 15, 1887): 108–10.

———. "General Conference Relief Society." *Woman's Exponent* 32.12 (May 1904): 93–95.

———. "General Relief Society Conference." *Woman's Exponent* 21.1–2 (June 1 and 15, 1898): 290.

———. "Relief Society Conference." *Woman's Exponent* 19.20 (Apr. 15, 1891): 156.

———. "Relief Society Conference." *Woman's Exponent* 20.20 (May 1, 1892): 156–57.

———. "Weber Stake." *Woman's Exponent* 13.23 (May 1, 1885): 182–83.

Wells, Lydia Ann. *Papers.* March 28, 1881. Embedded in the 1880 Memorial Jubilee Box that Lydia Ann Wells wrote that is found in the John McCleve Young Family History Collection (1869–1975). Salt Lake City: Church History Library, Church of Jesus Christ of Latter-day Saints.

Westermann, Claus. *Genesis 1–11: A Commentary.* Translated by John J. Scullion. Minneapolis: Augsburg, 1984.

Weston, Paul. "Proclaiming Christ Crucified Today: Some Reflections on John's Gospel." In *Where Wrath and Mercy Meet: Proclaiming the Atonement Today*, edited by David Peterson, 136–62. Milton Keynes, England: Paternoster, 2001.

Wheeler, David L. *A Relational View of the Atonement.* New York: Peter Lang, 1989.

White, O. Kendall, Jr. *Mormon Neo-Orthodoxy: A Crisis Theology.* Salt Lake City, Signature Books, 1987.

White, Vernon. *Atonement and Incarnation.* Cambridge: Cambridge University Press, 1991.

Whitney, Elizabeth Ann. "A Leaf from an Autobiography." *Woman's Exponent* 7.7 (Sept. 1, 1885): 51.

Widtsoe, John A. "Evidences and Reconciliations—XLVII—What Is the Place of Women in the Church?" *Improvement Era* 45.3 (Mar. 1942): 161, 188.

———. *Rational Theology as Taught by The Church of Jesus Christ of Latter-day Saints.* Signature Mormon Classics edition. Salt Lake City: Signature Books, 1997.

Wilkins, Michael J. "Isaiah 53 and the Message of Salvation in the Four Gospels." In *The Gospel According to Isaiah 53: Encountering the Suffering Servant in Jewish and Christian Theology*, edited by Darrell L. Bock and Mitch Glaser, 109–32. Grand Rapids, MI: Kregel Academic & Professional, 2012.

Williams, Delores. *Sisters in the Wilderness: The Challenge of Womanist God-Talk.* Maryknoll, NY: Orbis, 1993.

Williams, Garry J. "Penal Substitutionary Atonement in the Church Fathers." *Evangelical Quarterly* 83.3 (2011): 195–216.

Williams, Jarvis. "Violent Atonement in Romans: The Foundation of Paul's Soteriology." *Journal of the Evangelical Theological Society* 53.3 (Sept. 2010): 579–99.

Williams, P. J., Andrew D. Clarke, Peter M. Head, and David Instone-Brewer, eds. *The New Testament in Its First Century Setting: Essays on Context and Background in Honour Of B. W. Winter On His 65th Birthday.* Grand Rapids, MI: William B. Eerdmans, 2004.

Winter, Michael. *The Atonement: Problems in Theology.* Collegeville, MN: Liturgical Press, 1995.

Wood, Allen, and George di Giovanni, eds. *Religion within the Boundaries of Mere Reason and Other Writings*. Cambridge: Cambridge University Press, 2016.

Woodbury, Joyce N. "Christ's Atoning Sacrifice: The Role of the Crucifixion." *Sunstone* 8 (Nov./Dec. 1983): 17–21.

Woodruff, Wilford. "Discourse by Wilford Woodruff, October 8, 1893 (in Salt Lake)." *Millennial Star* 56 (Apr. 9, 1894): 228–29.

———. Journal, 1833–1898. Entry of December 23, 1843. Salt Lake City: Church History Library, Church of Jesus Christ of Latter-day Saints.

Wright, N. T. "New Perspectives on Paul." In *Pauline Perspectives: Essays on Paul 1878–2013*, 273–91. Minneapolis: Fortress, 2013. Also in *Justification in Perspective: Historical Developments and Contemporary Applications*, edited by Bruce L. McCormack, 243–64. Grand Rapids: Baker Academic, 2006, 243–64.

———. "Redemption from the New Perspective? Towards a Multilayered Pauline Theology of the Cross." In *Pauline Perspectives: Essays on Paul 1878–2013*, 292–331. Minneapolis: Fortress, 2013. Also in *The Redemption: An Interdisciplinary Symposium on Christ as Redeemer*, edited by S. T. Davis, D. Kendall, and G. O'Collins, 69–100. Oxford: Oxford University Press, 2004.

Young, Brigham. *Complete Discourses*. 5 volumes. Edited by Richard S. Van Wagoner. Salt Lake City: Smith-Petit Foundation, 2009.

Zornberg, Avivah Gottlieb. *The Beginning of Desire: Reflections on Genesis*. New York: Schocken Books, 2011.

Contributors

NICHOLAS J. FREDERICK received his BA in Classics and his MA in Comparative Studies from Brigham Young University before completing a PhD in the History of Christianity from Claremont Graduate University. He is currently an Associate Professor in the department of Ancient Scripture at Brigham Young University. His research focuses primarily on the Book of Mormon, in particular the intertextuality between the Book of Mormon and the Bible.

FIONA GIVENS graduated from the University of Richmond with degrees in French, German, and European history. She is an independent scholar who has published articles with *Routledge*, *Dialogue*, and *Exponent II*, and is the co-author with Terryl Givens of *The God Who Weeps: How Mormonism Makes Sense of Life* (2012); *The Crucible of Doubt: Reflections on the Quest for Faith* (2014); *The Christ Who Heals: Re-Visioning the Savior* (2017); and *All Things New: Rethinking Sin, Salvation and Everything Between* (2020).

DEIDRE NICOLE GREEN is assistant professor of Latter-day Saint/Mormon Studies at the Graduate Theological Union. She earned her PhD in Religion from Claremont Graduate University and her Master of Arts in Religion from Yale Divinity School. She is the author of *Works of Love in a World of Violence* and *Jacob: A Brief Theological Introduction*.

SHARON J. HARRIS is assistant professor of English at Brigham Young University. She studies the intersections of literature and music in the early modern period and holds degrees in music, humanities, and literature from BYU, University of Chicago, and Fordham University. Her research in literary studies has been published in various journals and funded by the Folger Shakespeare Library, Yale Beinecke Library, and UCLA Clark Library. She is the author of *Enos, Jarom, Omni: A Brief Theological Introduction*.

J.B. HAWS is an associate professor of Church History, a former associate dean of Religious Education, and the current chair of Church History and Doctrine at Brigham Young University. His PhD is from the University of Utah in American History. He has published on changes in American perceptions of Latter-day Saints; on theosis in contemporary Latter-day Saint and Eastern Orthodox theology; and on interfaith dialogue.

ERIC D. HUNTSMAN received his BA in Classical Greek and Latin from Brigham Young University in 1990 and his MA and PhD in Ancient History from the University of Pennsylvania in 1992 and 1997. He is a professor of Ancient Scripture at Brigham Young University, where he is also affiliated with the Ancient Near Eastern Studies, Classics, and Global Women's Studies programs. Having served as the coordinator of the Ancient Near Eastern Studies program from 2012–2020, he began a two-and-a-half-year appointment as the academic director of the BYU Jerusalem Center program in 2022. His publications focus on the infancy and passion narratives, the miracles of Jesus, and the Gospel of John.

BENJAMIN KEOGH is a PhD candidate in historical and systematic theology at the University of St Andrews with a project focused on relation and atonement in conversation with John Calvin and Friedrich Schleiermacher. A native of Scotland, he lives in St Andrews with his wife and three children.

ARIEL BYBEE LAUGHTON received her PhD in Religion from Duke University in 2010. Her areas of study include the history of late antique Christianity, the writings of the early Latin and Greek Church Fathers, and women, gender, and sexuality in the ancient world. She is currently an independent scholar and writer in Houston, Texas.

ADAM S. MILLER is a professor of philosophy at Collin College in McKinney, Texas. He earned a BA in comparative literature from Brigham Young University and an MA and PhD in philosophy from Villanova University. He is the author of ten books, including *Speculative Grace, The Gospel According to David Foster Wallace, An Early Resurrection,* and *Mormon: A Brief Theological Introduction.* He also directs the Latter-day Saint Theology Seminar.

JENNIFER REEDER is the nineteenth-century women's history specialist at the Church History Department for the Church of Jesus Christ of Latter-day Saints. She earned her PhD in American History from George Mason University and an MA in history, archival management, and documentary editing from New York University. Reeder has focused her work on making women's words and biographies accessible and utilized in both academic and devotional ways. She wrote a biography of Emma Hale Smith and currently leads a project collecting Eliza R. Snow's discourses digitally with a future print volume of selected sermons for the Church Historian's Press, the print imprimatur of the Church History Department. She coauthored two books: *At the Pulpit: 185 Years of Discourses by Latter-day Saint Women* and *The Witness of Women: Firsthand Experiences and Testimonies of the Restoration.*

T. BENJAMIN SPACKMAN is a PhD Candidate in History of Christianity and Religions of North America at Claremont Graduate University. He received an MA with further doctoral work in Semitics at the University of Chicago. His dissertation examines the intersection of religion, science, epistemology, and hermeneutics in twentieth-century Latter-day Saint creationist/evolution conflict.

JOSEPH M. SPENCER is a philosopher and assistant professor of ancient scripture at Brigham Young University. He is the author of dozens of articles and four books, most recently *1st Nephi: A Brief Theological Introduction*. Professor Spencer serves as the editor of the *Journal of Book of Mormon Studies*, the associate director of the Latter-day Saint Theology Seminar, and a vice president of the Book of Mormon Studies Association.

General Index

Abbott, Ann Marsh, 163–64
Abelard, Peter, 8, 32, 58–59, 81–83
Abinadi: and covenant, 120–21; and divine incarnation, 77, 95, 107–9; and eternal/divine atonement, 102–4, 112; and nonviolent atonement, 9, 237–39, 243–45; prophecies of Christ, 126
Abish, 125
Adam: Calvin on, 196, 198; and death, 98, 202; dispensation of, 25, 191; and escape, 222; and original sin, 40, 70–80, 105–7, 168, 185, 242, 263
agency: and alternative substitution model of atonement, 138–47; and creation, 217; divine endowment, 260, 263; and the image of God, 78; and the law, 97; moral, 257, 259; and neuroscience, 204; and Satan, 76; and theosis, 150–53; and women, 257
Alma the Younger, 44, 99, 108–9, 123
Amulek, 95, 99, 102–4, 107, 112, 227, 264
angels: announces eschaton, 151; of death, 36, 45; and Latter-day Saint women, 167; visitation to Adam and Eve, 70; visitation to Benjamin, 237–45; visitation to Alma, 120; visitation to Jesus Christ, 166; visitation to Mary, 43
Anselm of Canterbury, 4, 32, 57, 81–84, 104, 136, 195, 197, 202
Anti-Nephi-Lehies, 110, 120
apostasy, 124, 194, 201

Aquinas, Thomas, 6, 83–86
Athanasius of Alexandria, 74–79, 85, 150
atonement: Christian fellowship as, 162–63, 167; collective, 6, 9, 115–29, 134; and debt, 2, 7, 24, 37, 49, 75, 81–84, 136, 138, 140, 152, 195–96, 200, 266; divine and eternal, 102–4; and ecology, 22; facts of, 31; and individual development, 264–68; infinite, 9, 81, 84, 98–99, 104, 107, 117, 128, 192, 227–28, 265; Latter-day Saints acceptance of both objective and subjective models, 8; Lucan, 44; neologism, 3; 1995 survey on, 136; nonviolent, 32–33, 38, 40, 44, 57; objective model, 4–8, 32, 43, 49, 57; participatory, 7, 70, 73; perfect, 133–36, 154; quasi-universalism, 131, 151–54; recapitulation, 47, 72–73; subjective model, 4–8, 32, 44, 49, 58–59, 137; sufficient and superabundant, 84; three key theological points in the Book of Mormon, 95; universal, 2, 6, 107, 140, 151, 194, 202, 229; as verb, 10n12, 16, 94, 103, 105, 108; and wholeness, 254–55, 261, 271–72. *See list of theories of atonement by name*
atonement, conditions of: and justification, 34, 139–40; in Latter-day Saint thought, 7, 139–40; to prevent penalty, 72; and sequence, 182–92
atonement, relational: and creation, 217–22; defined, 213–14; and the fall, 222–24; and Lazarus, 214–17; relation matters to

atonement, relational (*continued*)
   God, 225–29; relations key to atonement, 9, 224–30
Augustine of Hippo, 6, 78–81, 205, 207, 253
Aulén, Gustaf, 4–6, 32–33, 43, 46, 56, 68–69, 135; three categories, 5, 68

baptism, 208, 240; as adoption, 208; Aquinas on, 85; children and, 111, 169; and church membership, 240; covenant, of, 25; of fire, 192; for the dead, 24, 169, 191; and inheritance of the Celestial Kingdom, 153; of Jesus Christ, 97; of Mary Fielding Smith, 169; in 3 Nephi, 121; Paul on, 40, 47; rebaptism, 198; requirements for, 23–24
Baptists, 162, 164
Benson, Ezra Taft, 94, 253
Bigler Smith, Bathsheba W., 163
blood: Abinadi does not mention, 244–46; atonement, 201; bloodless atonement, 32–33, 244, 246; bloodshed, 227–28, 237; blood transfusion metaphor, 148; in the Book of Mormon, 103–12; Christ's atonement, 6, 98, 133, 197; covenant (blood poured out), 42–47, 79, 165; from every pore, 72, 95, 105–12, 137, 206, 241–43; justification through Christ's, 35, 38–39, 82; material image of, 242; precious, 71; ransom, 82; sprinkling of, 39, 70
Book of Mormon: Law of Moses in, 96, 102–6, 120, 123–27, 227–28, 238, 242, 244; and political theology, 236; pre- and post-Christian split, 96–97; pre-Christian Christianity, 96–99, 238; resource for theological reflection, 235; subtitle, 115; visions of Christian atonement, 236
Buell, Presendia, 167
Burton, Theodore M., 208
Bushman, Richard L., 139

Calvin, John, 57, 86, 197–99, 255, 262
Campbell, Alexander, 1
canon: extracanonical Christian texts, 69; and grace, 269; Latter-day Saint, 2, 5, 7, 94, 96, 131–32, 152, 201, 217, 221, 253–56, 260, 263–64
celestial kingdom, 139, 144, 153

Christianity: early, 5, 38, 49, 69, 87, 94, 194, 196, 202; Eastern, 5, 202; Western, 5, 23, 78, 195–98, 202, 246
Christology, 44–45, 120, 122, 124, 228
Christus Victor, 4–6, 32, 36, 46–49, 56, 58, 68, 95; Narrative Christus Victor, 44, 46
Church of Sweden, 4
Congregationalists, 164
Consecrate (consecration), 267–68, 271
covenants: and baptism, 161, 208; in the Book of Mormon, 110, 238–40, 243, 245; Christians as covenant people, 69; of Christ's blood, 38, 42–43, 165; and communal salvation, 6, 115–29, 215; and kinship, 15, 20–25; and Latter-day Saint temple worship, 48, 162, 168–71; relationship, 57; universal, 35
creation: atonement central to, 72–73, 103, 188, 213–14, 217–26, 229–30; Christ as Creator, 107, 241; and divine potential, 252; God's absolute control over, 218; humans as incomplete, 196; in Latter-day Saint temple liturgy, 168; new creatures, 40, 226, 253–54, 257, 271; re-creation in God's image, 75, 77, 79; rejection of *ex nihilo*, 139; and vocation, 265–67, 272
cross: in the Book of Mormon, 106, 108, 110, 112; centrality, 197, 203; in the Doctrine and Covenants, 153; in early Christianity, 69–71, 74–75, 79–85; as metaphor, 135, 143; in New Testament, 36–40, 45, 47
crucifixion: Augustine on, 79, 81; in the Book of Mormon, 100, 105, 108, 112, 116, 244; crucified with Christ, 39–40; of Jesus, 41, 77, 82, 85, 188, 196; in Latter-day Saint hymnody, 3; and modern atonement theory, 202–3

Day of Atonement, 16, 39, 42, 48, 69. See also Yom Kippur
devils: Christ saves from, 6, 42, 47, 99, 142; in early Christianity, 76–80; Jesus Christ accused of having been possessed by, 105, 241; Jesus Christ triumphs over, 4, 32, 46, 56–67, 68, 149; in medieval Christianity, 81–86; Satan identified in New Testament, 46

Dew, Sheri L., 254, 267
divine empathy theory, 134–35, 155n15
double death, 78–80, 100
Dutch (Netherlands), 2, 225

ecclesiology, 86, 122, 163, 253, 271
Edwards, Jonathan, 140, 198
Egypt, 18, 20, 35–38, 47, 96, 116, 126–27
England, G. Eugene, 4, 8, 83, 147, 195
English: King James Version (KJV) as official English-language Bible for Latter-day Saints, 18, 31; origins of at-one-ment, 3–4; Protestantism, 195; translation from other languages, 15–21, 39, 45, 50–55, 96, 179
Episcopalians, 164
Epistle of Barnabas, 69–70
Epistle to Diognetus, 69
eschatology: in the Doctrine and Covenants, 151; incarnation and, 226; Latter-day Saint ideas of, 15, 21, 24, 194, 207; in the New Testament, 36, 49, 113n10
eternal life, 40, 45, 73, 103, 111–12, 221
Eve, 70, 72, 77, 80, 168–69, 196, 198, 222–23
expiation: and collective atonement, 115; in early Christianity, 71; in the Greek New Testament, 32, 39–40, 46–55, 58, 60n8; Hebrew roots of term, 3, 16, 22

Fall, the: in the Book of Mormon, 104, 107–9, 242, 253–54; and death, 98; and incarnation, 74–78; and Latter-day Saint temple liturgy, 168–70; and legalism, 80–81, 84; and the natural man, 185; and recapitulation, 72–73; and relationality, 213–14, 222–27; and satisfaction, 196–97
female deity, 260–61
feminist theology, 5, 32, 203, 224, 251–62, 266, 269, 271
Fielding, Joseph, 161
Fretheim, Terence E., 214, 217–19, 222, 225
Fundamentalism (Christian), 2, 199

Gates, Susa Young, 261
genealogy, 24, 122
Gentiles, 34–35, 38, 41–42, 115, 181
Gethsemane, 147, 161, 166, 168, 208; absent in John's gospel, 45; Christ's suffering in, 188, 208, 242; in Latter-day Saint atonement theology, 2, 8, 48, 77, 95–98, 105–12, 147; and Latter-day Saint women, 161, 166
givenness, 180–90, 193
Givens, Terryl: on atonement, 44, 138–44, 147, 235; on Eugene England, 8, 83
God: fish hook of, 76; Fretheim's five characteristics of God-human relation, 214; as Great Spirit, 125; image of, 74–80, 203, 219–21, 255; kingdom of, 100, 135, 139–41, 144–45, 148, 153, 168, 181, 185, 225–26, 267–68; speech acts in Genesis, 218–19, 231n21; weeping, 118, 187, 208, 214–16; wrathful, 35, 38, 46, 57, 140, 151, 197–200
Godhead/godhead, 194, 196, 208, 215
Golgotha, 77, 208
government, 162, 201, 236–41
governmental theory of atonement, 2, 95, 140–41
grace: accepting of, 268–72; and atonement, 9, 180–93; in the Book of Mormon, 96–97, 100; cheap grace, 17; and Christ's example, 82; growth from grace to grace, 139, 142, 151; infusion of, 85; and justice, 205; justification by, 135; Latter-day Saint women and, 161–62, 166–67; prevenient, 151; and resurrection, 74–75, 112; and salvation, 46, 49; and sin, 253–58; and theosis, 150–53; and women, 258–66
Greek (language): patristics, 72, 196–97, 202; theological vocabulary, 16, 34–42, 45–48, 58, 182, 188, 206. *See also* Greek New Testament; *hilastērion*; *katallagē*
Greek New Testament, 3–5, 31–93, 96, 206
Greek Orthodox, 150
Gregory of Nyssa, 74–79, 196, 219
Groenhout, Ruth E., 265–66, 270
Grotius, Hugo, 2, 140, 149

Hampson, Daphne, 259, 262–63
Handley, George, 22
Hansen, Lorin K., 7–8
Harris, Martin, 136–37, 146
Hart, David Bentley, 202–6, 219
healing: in the Book of Mormon, 95,

healing (*continued*)
228–29; in the Doctrine and Covenants, 146–49; in Israelite theology, 17; and Latter-day Saint atonement theology, 4–9, 194–95, 202–9; in Lazarus narrative, 216; in the New Testament, 32, 44, 47, 49–55, 59; Satan healed, 76

Heavenly Mother, 260–61

Hebrew (language), 3, 15–22, 206

Hebrew Bible, 15–30, 69–70, 85; and atonement, 3 5, 7, 19–23; and Book of Mormon peoples, 96, 100, 126; in early Christianity, 69–70; healer motif in, 44; and Latter-day Saint, 5, 15; in medieval Christianity, 85; Septuagint, 34, 39; synonymous parallelism, 100

Hegel, G. W. F., 222, 224

hell, 6, 36, 76, 80, 99, 125, 152, 165, 198–99, 203

hilastērion (place of atonement; mercy seat), 32, 39, 45, 47, 60n8

Hinckley, Gordon B., 7, 267–68

Holifield, E. Brooks, 2, 140

Holy Spirit (Holy Ghost): and atonement, 44; Comforter, 166, 209; discernment, 220; divine life of, 75; and early Latter-day Saint women, 167, 170–71; and the Eucharist, 202; God as, 125, 225; knowledge gained through, 102, 192, 226; and light, 141, 151; loss of, 146; and the natural man, 106, 185, 252; and resurrection, 97; and Zion, 194

hope: in Book of Mormon, 118, 125, 127, 242–43; in the Doctrine and Covenants, 131–34, 145, 152–53; for early Latter-day Saint women, 162, 170–71; false, 192; of glory, 101, 109–11; in moral exemplar theory, 82–83

humiliation, 35, 71, 189, 227

hymns, 3, 45, 135, 144, 164–66

Ignatius of Antioch, 70, 202

incarnation: of Christ, 72; compassion view of atonement, 235; in early Christian soteriology, 74–79; in governmental theory of atonement, 149; Jesus as Incarnate Word, 45, 73; in medieval Christianity, 85–86; and punitive theory of atonement, 202; and relationality, 214–15, 224–30; as reorienting event, 226

intelligences, 139–42, 149

Irenaeus of Lyons, 6, 49, 56, 58, 72–77, 196

Irigaray, Luce, 261–65

Isaac, 46, 69–70, 126, 163

Israel (Israelites): atonement terminology, 16–21; in the Book of Mormon, 97, 99, 115–22, 126–29; Christ as King of, 241; and collective atonement, 115; conceptions of atonement, 15; in early Christian thought, 70; exodus from Egypt, 35–36; and Isaiah, 134; Latter-day Saint application of Israelite ideas, 21–25; in New Testament language, 35–36, 39, 43, 45; and Restorationism, 162

Jacobs, Zina, 167

Jefferson, Thomas, 199

Jerome, 47

Jesus Christ: angelic visitation, 166; baptism of, 97; clasped in the arms of, 265; crucifixion, 41, 77, 82, 85, 188, 196; death required, 43; faithfulness of, 35; as Father and Son, 77, 102–3, 114n16, 149; as Holy One of Israel, 99; as Incarnate Word, 45, 73; intercessor, 43, 77, 81, 97–98, 145, 197; as king, 243; and the Law of Moses, 102, 244; Lehi preaches on, 123–24; Logos hymn, 45; mighty shoulders, 143; mighty to save, 143, 146–49; and Nicodemus, 225; and obedience, 45, 48, 80, 83; as paschal lamb, 38, 45–47; passion, 41, 45, 82–86, 116, 214, 225–27; politicized, 125–28; as prophet, 243–44; and resurrection, 96–99, 105–6; sacrifice and sacrificer, 45; spoke Aramaic, 41; and submission, 48, 71, 77, 226, 244–45; visitation to Nephites, 206, 229

Jews (Jewish): Book of Mormon addresses, 94, 101, 115, 117; Christian interpretation of texts, 5, 122; in early Christianity, 69–70; ideas of atonement, 97; Jewish Christians, 35–38, 42; law, 22; in Lazarus narrative, 215–16; legal authorities, 41, 45; scripture in Book of Mormon, 122–24, 127. *See also* Hebrew Bible; Yom Kippur

Johannine, 33, 44–49, 56–59

Jones, Serene, 205, 255, 262–64, 269
Joseph of Egypt, 127
justice: in an alternative substitution model, 138, 140; in early Christianity, 76–81; in Latter-day Saint thought, 235; in medieval Christianity, 81–86; and mercy, 39, 49, 95, 109, 145, 264–65; and penal substitution, 7, 72, 99, 136; retributive, 195–209
justification: and Augustine, 78–81; in the Book of Mormon, 97; and Calvin, 198, 262; in the Doctrine and Covenants, 140; in early Christianity, 82, 85–86; and grace, 135; in the New Testament, 32–40, 46, 49–58; not described in Christ's ministry, 207
Justin Martyr, 70–72, 86, 197

Kant, Immanuel, 223–24
katallagē, 3, 31–32, 37, 50–55, 96, 179–80
Kimball, Sarah M., 162, 170
kinship: with Christ, 149; in Israelite religion, 15, 19–25; levirate marriage, 19, 24
kippēr, 16–17

Lamanites, 94–95, 110, 116–17, 120–29, 237, 241, 248
Last Cornaby, Hannah, 162
Law of Moses (Mosaic Law): in Book of Mormon, 96, 102–6, 120, 123–27, 227–28, 238, 242, 244; covenant, 38, 42–43; and creation, 220–21; deliverance of Israel, 35; observation in New Testament era, 34, 38–39; ritual, 35, 104, 111, 243, 245; symbol of Christ, 69
Lazarus, 54, 214–17, 224, 229
legalism, 9, 80, 136, 195, 197, 200
liberalism, 2, 8
liberation, 41–42, 191, 202, 258, 262
Lord's Supper, sacrament of (Eucharist), 38, 42–43, 104, 164–66, 202
love: and atonement, 77, 82–83, 118, 147, 171; of Christ, 263–65, 268–71; Christlike attribute, 106, 185, 245; and community, 200, 208; and debt, 136; of God, 36, 38, 40, 49, 225; great commandment, 228; in hymns, 164–65; and kinship, 19–23; and mercy, 98; and mortality, 145; and relation, 213; self-love, 265–67; and self-sacrifice, 253–56, 259–60
Luther, Martin, 34, 46, 58, 86, 262
Lutherans, 4, 32, 34, 253, 262

Mack, Temperance Bond, 164
Macrina, 196
Marcion, 71
Martha, 214–17
Mary (Mother of Jesus), 43, 159, 161–65, 226, 241
Mary Magdalene, 166, 214–16, 241
Maxwell, Neal A., 132, 262
McConkie, Bruce R., 201, 267
mediation: in Boyd K. Packer's sermon, 7, 38, 81; Christ as, 37, 133, 153
mercy: and the American penal system, 199; and atonement, 107–9, 136–37, 140, 144–47, 207; Christ's work of, 72, 77, 82, 84, 97, 132, 165, 243; and grace, 24; and innocence of little children, 111; and justice, 7, 49, 95, 97, 264; mercy seat, 39, 47–48; plan of, 80–81, 98–99
metaphor: of atonement, 7, 25, 36, 39, 43, 135, 141, 143, 148–50, 246; blood discussed as, 242; of criminality, 198; and gender, 251; and the indescribable, 49; of kinship, 20–22; two-edged, 32
Methodists, 2, 140, 161, 164
Millet, Robert, 183
Milton, John, 197, 200
modernism, 7
moral exemplar theory, 2, 59, 82, 86
moral influence theory, 7–8, 32, 59, 96, 134–35
More, Thomas, 3
Morgan, Jacob, 137, 146, 151
mythology, 182–83, 187

natural man, 106, 185, 189, 242, 252, 257, 264, 268
Nephites: in Book of Mormon narrative, 94–95; and covenant, 116–17, 120–29; Jesus visits, 206, 229; and political theology, 236–41; prophets, 95–96, 105; and self-relation, 265; and the sword of Laban, 245
New Testament. *See* Greek New Testament

General Index   315

Neyman, Jane, 169
Noah (Book of Mormon monarch), 102, 126, 237–45

obedience: and atonement, 81, 133, 143; communal, 217; debt of, 266; Jesus and, 45, 48, 80, 83; and kinship, 20–21; and the law, 71–73, 140, 150, 153; and salvation, 1
Okazaki, Chieko N., 258
Old Testament. *See* Hebrew Bible
olive tree, allegory of, 117–22
opposition, 8, 97, 122, 161, 217, 222–23
Origen of Alexandria, 57, 77, 196
orthodoxy: Book of Mormon as, 132; Eastern Orthodox Church, 49, 58, 150; and fundamentalism, 2; Greek Orthodox Church, 150; Laman and Lemuel as, 123; neo-orthodoxy, 7; and plurality's necessity, 220; and theology, 8

Packer, Boyd K., 7, 38, 81
Paley, William, 196
parable of the bicycle, 183, 190
Passover, 38, 42, 45–46, 56–59
Pauline Epistles, 33–41, 56
penal substitution theory: agency-consequence-substitution model, 138–47; and American prisons, 199–200, 203; in ancient Israel, 16; in the Book of Mormon, 2, 95, 108, 235; in the Doctrine and Covenants, 132; in early Christianity, 70–72; and feminist scholarship, 251; Latter-day Saint understandings of, 5–8, 57, 200–201; in medieval Christianity, 85–86; in Pauline epistles, 37–38; Protestant conceptions of, 32, 49, 197–98. *See also* satisfaction theory of atonement
Potter, Dennis, 136, 147
Pratt, Orson, 3
Pratt, Parley, 3, 192
pre-earth life, 6, 131, 149
Presbyterian, 164
pride, 76, 78, 251–58, 262–63
priesthood (priest): Christ as, 85; in the Doctrine and Covenants, 153; Dominican, 215; gendered, 254–55; high priest, 24, 39, 42; Israelite terminology, 15–16, 22; of Noah, 102, 126, 237–39, 243–44; and pride, 253; symbolism in New Testament, 47–49; women (priestesses), 162, 167–70
prophecy (prophesy): in Book of Mormon, 102; of Christ, 41, 71, 77, 123–24; concerning Lamanites, 117, 127–28; and covenant, 116–28; in Hebrew Bible, 43–44, 169; Judahite, 120, 123–24
propitiation, 39, 45, 50, 91n65. *See also* expiation
Protestantism, 48–49, 150, 165, 195, 207; evangelical, 7, 17, 199, 201, 235; and God's Otherness, 150; hymns, 165; and Latter-day Saint intellectual milieu, 7, 31, 49, 207; reformers, 4–5, 32–34; and retributive justice, 195–96, 201; vocabulary, 17, 25, 48
punishment: alternative substitution model, 138, 144; in the Book of Mormon, 97, 99, 108; in early Christianity, 69–71, 78–80; in medieval Christianity, 84; and penal substitution, 7, 32, 37, 40, 136, 149. *See also* justice, retributive

ransom: in early Christianity, 69–71, 76–81; Hebrew etymology, 3; Israelite usage of, 16, 31; in Latter-day Saint theology, 135, 142, 251; in medieval Christianity, 81–86; in New Testament, 31, 37, 41–43, 47, 50–57
reconciliation (reconcile): in ancient Israelite terminology, 16; and atonement, 3–4, 73, 79, 82–85; in the Book of Mormon, 96, 101, 124; and grace, 179–80, 192; and healing, 194, 200, 205; in the New Testament, 31–32, 37–40, 47–58; and relationality, 213–14, 229; and Restoration, 162; and sealing, 8. *See also katallagē*
Redeemer. *See* Jesus Christ
redemption (redeem): in the Book of Mormon, 96, 98, 103, 108–11, 237–38, 243–44; and Christ's suffering for more than sin, 4; and covenant (communal salvation), 116, 120–22, 125–28, 228–30; in the Doctrine and Covenants, 133–34, 140, 145, 148, 153; in early Christianity, 71–80; familial, 191; in governmental theory of atonement, 2; in Hebrew ety-

mology, 3; in hymnody, 164–65; of Israel, 43; in Israelite religion, 5, 15, 18–24; in medieval Christianity, 82, 85; in the New Testament, 31–33, 37, 40, 44–57; and relations, 224, 226; and retributive justice, 199, 201, 203, 207, 209; and self-sacrifice, 9, 251–63, 266–72; violence cannot redeem violence, 227

relational atonement. *See* atonement, relational

relationships: after death, 270; in ancient Israelite religion, 17, 21–24, 70; and Aquinas, 83; community, 116–19, 122, 125, 258–62; of God and women, 9, 262–65, 271; and grace, 180, 183, 187, 190–91; Latter-day Saint, 25, 87; in the New Testament, 32, 37–38, 57; of religion and politics, 236, 241; and self-sacrifice, 253–58. *See also* atonement, relational

Relief Society, 162–70, 254, 258, 267

Renlund, Dale G., 207

repentance: and agency, 144; Augustine on, 78–80; in the Book of Mormon, 109–12, 120–21, 129, 254; and catalyzation of atonement, 180, 193; change of heart, 78, 142; collective, 120–21, 129, 137; of the dead, 153; in early Christianity, 79–80; and ecological restoration, 22; England on, 83; to escape suffering, 72, 145–46; godliness, 78; God's joy over repentant sinners, 225; and grace, 264–65; and healing, 206, 229; and the law, 242; Latter-day Saint emphasis on, 3; in medieval Christianity, 83; orientation to God, 142, 144; to prevent suffering, 72, 137, 145–46; and satisfaction, 7; stereotypically defined as male, 254; and women, 254

Restoration, the: atonement theologies, 5, 33, 48–49, 194–95; and healing, 208; and reconciliation, 37; Restorationism, 162–64; scripture, 3, 6, 8, 129; and vicarious work for the dead, 169; women and, 166, 170–71

resurrection: and ascension, 226; and baptism, 47; central to atonement, 1, 180, 188, 193, 228–29; and the Christus Victor model, 6, 32, 36, 40; disbelief in, 240; in early Christianity, 71–75, 79; and healing,
148, 152; and incarnation, 202; Jesus as the resurrection, 214; and Latter-day Saint temple theology, 169–70; in the New Testament, 31, 34, 43–44, 47; salvation through, 6, 57, 80–81, 95–112

revelation: in the Book of Mormon, 102, 112, 223; and the Doctrine of Covenants, 24–25, 35, 131–39, 142, 145–46, 151–52, 180, 207, 263; to Eliza R. Snow, 260; to Emma Smith, 166; Latter-day Saint, 49, 86; Pearl of Great Price as, 3, 220–21

Richards, Jane Snyder, 163

ritual: in the Doctrine and Covenants, 153; in the Hebrew Bible, 15–17, 22, 69–70, 85, 228; and Latter-day Saint women, 168–69; pollution, 15–17, 22

Roberts, B. H., 140–41

Robinson, Stephen, 183

Roman Catholicism, 20, 150, 201, 215, 228

Ruether, Rosemary Radford, 255–58

sacramentalism, 152–54

sacrifice: and atonement in the Book of Mormon, 95–99, 102, 104, 108, 111–12; and atonement in early Christianity, 69–71, 75, 80; and atonement in medieval Christianity, 81–86; and early Latter-day Saint women, 163–65, 170; and God's honor, 197; God's self-sacrifice, 23; of Isaac as type of Jesus, 69–70; Jesus' incomprehensible, 142; and Latter-day Saint priesthood, 153; and the Law of Moses, 3, 17, 227, 238, 242–45; and mercy, 264; in the New Testament, 31–34, 38–48, 57; and relationship, 214; in Valerie Saiving's scholarship, 252, 272n4; and violence, 236; women's self-sacrifice, 251, 255–59, 265–71

Satan. *See* devils (Satan)

satisfaction theory of atonement: in the Book of Mormon, 77, 95–99, 108–9, 264; Latter-day Saint views of, 6–8, 251; in medieval Christianity, 81–86; and Methodists, 2; in New Testament, 32, 37, 49, 57; objective atonement model, 4, 6, 8; and penal substitution, 5, 142; and retributive justice, 195–98, 202; vicarious, 134–36. *See also* penal substitution

Savior. *See* Jesus Christ
science, 68, 195, 202–5
sealing (ritual), 8, 169–70, 180, 193
selflessness, 251–59, 262–72
Semitic languages, 20
Septuagint, 34–35, 39, 42
Shakers, 164
Sherem, 102, 126
slavery (enslaved people): and atonement metaphor, 32, 36–37, 76–77; debt, 24; and Israelite kinship, 18–21; Satan as, 80; to sin, 40, 42, 82
Smith, Amanda Barnes, 165
Smith, Emma Hale, 164–69; Elect Lady, 163, 166, 169
Smith, Hyrum, 161
Smith, Joseph: defines fundamental Latter-day Saint principles, 1, 153; and Doctrine and Covenants, 3, 131, 139, 154, 191, 207–8, 245; and friendship, 259; and justification, 34–35; and the New Testament, 31, 49; and the Old Testament, 15, 24–25, 133–34; and theosis, 74, 141–42, 152; understanding of atonement, 96, 180, 200; and women, 162–63, 166–69
Smith, Joseph F., 152, 171
Smith, Joseph Fielding, 98
Smith, Lucy Mack, 167–68
Smith, Mary Fielding, 161, 166, 168, 171
Smith, Mercy Fielding, 161, 168
Snow, Eliza R., 162, 165–69, 260–61, 267
Snow, Erastus, 261
Snow, Lorenzo, 74
Socinus, 59
sola fide, 1
soteriology: in the Doctrine and Covenants, 131, 151; early Christians on, 4, 6–7, 57, 68–81, 196–97, 201–2; and Jewish scriptures, 5; medieval Christians on, 81–87; and the New Testament, 31–32, 42–46, 50
submission (submissive), 48, 71, 77, 81, 106, 185–88, 226, 244–45, 253; Christlike attribute, 106, 185–88, 253; and God's sovereignty, 81; of Jesus, 48, 71, 77, 226, 244–45
subordination, 183, 253
suffering (suffer): Abelard on, 82–83; Aquinas on, 84–86; in the Book of Mormon, 71–72, 101, 105–12, 241–45; cannot undo other violence, 227; Christ's compassion in, 8, 105–12, 163–64, 207, 226, 263; communal, 115, 149, 259; in the Doctrine and Covenants, 135–38, 142, 145–46, 149, 200; and grace, 185–91; in hymnody, 165; in the New Testament, 31, 33, 40, 45–48, 166; *paschō*, 48; and penal substitution, 69–71, 196; salvific nature of, 1; and self-sacrifice, 268; solidarity in, 7; Suffering Servant, 43, 46, 244; and trauma, 195, 203–5
Synoptic Gospels, 33, 41–45

Tanner, Susan W., 256
Taylor, Elmina S., 170
Taylor, John, 166
telos, 118, 150–52
temple: and atonement, 22; in the Book of Mormon, 237; Holy of Holies, 42, 48; imagery, 47–48; Jerusalem, 48; Kirtland, 164; modern Latter-day Saint temple worship, 24, 162, 166–70, 191, 208; Second Temple, 17; veil rendered, 42
Tertullian, 70–72, 86, 195–97
theology, sequential, 9, 182–84, 187–88; nonsequential, 9, 182–84, 187
theosis (exaltation), 6, 44, 48–49, 57–58, 72–77, 86, 131, 150–52, 168, 202, 226; light, 150–51
Tracy, Nancy, 166
tree of life, 223–24, 228
Trinity, 75, 78–80. *See also* Godhead
Tyndale, William, 3, 206

Uchtdorf, Dieter F., 147
Unitarians, 164

violence: atonement models, 5, 9; cannot redeem violence, 213, 227; death of Jesus, 82; divine, 21, 23; gendered, 251; and Latter-day Saint history in Missouri, 134; and Narrative Christus Victor, 46; and retributive justice, 209; sacrifice imagery, 236, 244–46; sword of Laban, 250n29; and trauma, 204–5. *See also* atonement, nonviolent

Watts, Isaac, 165
Weaver, J. Denny, 44, 46, 195
Wells, Lydia Ann, 170
Whitney, Elizabeth Ann, 162, 167–68
Whitney, Newel K., 162, 168, 170
Widtsoe, John A., 258
Womanism, 5, 32, 203
women: and accepting divine gifts, 268–71; divine potential, 260–62; early Latter-day Saint women and atonement, 6, 161–71; and enveloping grace, 262–64; and individual development, 264–68; and kinship, 19, 22; and pride, 251–58; and self-relation, 9, 258–60; and vocation, 265–69, 272; and wholeness, 271–72
worthiness, 22, 269; unworthiness, 22, 71, 207
woundedness, 195, 202–3, 207

Yahweh (YHWH) *or* Jehovah, 18, 20, 27n26, 37, 106, 220
yasha (*yāšaʾ*), 17–18
Yom Kippur (*yôm hakkippûrîm*), 16–17, 48
Young, Brigham, 3, 200–201

Scriptural Index

Old Testament/
Hebrew Bible

Gen 1:3, 218–19
Gen 1:3, 6, 11, 14, 20, 24, 26, 218
Gen 1:3, 6, 14, 218
Gen 1:4, 219
Gen 1:5, 219
Gen 1:8, 219
Gen 1:9, 219
Gen 1:10, 219
Gen 1:11, 24, 218
Gen 1:14, 218
Gen 1:16, 218
Gen 1:20, 218
Gen 1:26, 219
Gen 2:24, 169, 223
Gen 3:15, 56
Gen 3:16, 223
Gen 4:8, 223

Exod 3:8, 35
Exod 6:6, 20
Exod 12:3–14, 21–29, 45
Exod 14:30, 18
Exod 15:3, 23
Exod 15:26, 59
Exod 24:6–8, 42
Exod 24:8, 38
Exod 29:12, 42

Lev 4:7, 18, 25, 30, 34, 42
Lev 4:20, 26, 31, 35, 16
Lev 7:13, 42
Lev 8:15, 42
Lev 9:9, 42
Lev 16, 39
Lev 19:17–18, 19
Lev 19:18, 23
Lev 25:25–34, 19
Lev 25:47–50, 19

Num 35:6, 19

Deut 6:4, 23
Deut 12:16, 42
Deut 21:22–23, 71

Ps 20:6, 18
Ps 44:6–7, 18
Ps 103:2–3, 59
Ps 103:4, 57
Ps 110:1, 56
Ps 118:15, 18
Ps 144:10, 18

Isa 9:6, 241, 248
Isa 53:3–5, 57
Isa 53:3–6, 47
Isa 53:4, 43, 85
Isa 53:5, 136

Isa 53:5b, 59, 65n79
Isa 53:7, 244
Isa 53:10–12, 43
Isa 58:12, 169
Isa 63:3, 149

Jer 31:31–33, 43

Ezek 45:15, 46
Ezek 45:18–22, 38

Hos 6:1–2, 59

Obad 1:21, 169

Mal 4:6, 24, 169

New Testament

Matt 1:19, 53
Matt 1:21, 18, 43, 53, 56
Matt 3:15, 53
Matt 5:6, 10, 20, 53
Matt 5:45, 53
Matt 6:1, 33, 53
Matt 6:13, 53
Matt 6:25–34, 181
Matt 6:34, 187–88
Matt 7:1, 187
Matt 8:8, 13, 53

Matt 8:17, 59
Matt 8:25, 53
Matt 9:5–6, 35, 59
Matt 9:13, 53
Matt 9:21, 22c, 53
Matt 10:22, 53
Matt 10:41, 53
Matt 11:19, 53
Matt 12:37, 53
Matt 13:7, 43, 49, 53
Matt 13:15, 53
Matt 14:30, 53, 66n82
Matt 15:28, 53
Matt 16:19, 53
Matt 16:25, 53
Matt 18:18, 53
Matt 19:25, 53
Matt 20:4, 53
Matt 20:28, 43, 53, 57
Matt 21:9, 17
Matt 21:32, 53
Matt 22:37, 39, 228
Matt 22:39, 253
Matt 23:28–29, 35, 53
Matt 23:35, 42
Matt 24:13, 22, 53
Matt 25:37, 46, 53
Matt 26:26–29, 38, 57
Matt 26:28, 38, 43, 104
Matt 26:39, 188
Matt 27:19, 53
Matt 27:40, 42, 49, 53
Matt 27:43, 53
Matt 27:51, 42, 48

Mark 2:1–2, 42
Mark 2:9–11, 59
Mark 2:17, 53
Mark 3:4, 53
Mark 5:23b, 28b, 34c, 53
Mark 5:29, 53
Mark 6:20, 53
Mark 6:56b, 53
Mark 8:31, 41
Mark 8:35, 53
Mark 9:30–31, 41
Mark 10:26, 52c, 53
Mark 10:32–34, 41

Mark 10:45, 41, 53, 57
Mark 13:13, 20, 53
Mark 14:22–24, 57
Mark 14:22–26, 38
Mark 14:24, 38, 42, 104
Mark 15:30–31, 53
Mark 15:39, 42, 48
Mark 16:16, 53

Luke 1:6, 54
Luke 1:6, 17, 54
Luke 1:47, 69, 54
Luke 1:69, 71, 77, 54
Luke 1:75, 54
Luke 2:11, 54
Luke 2:25, 54
Luke 2:30, 54
Luke 2:38, 54
Luke 2:49, 265
Luke 3:6, 54
Luke 4:18, 56
Luke 4:18–19, 44, 65n75
Luke 4:18–19, 32, 59
Luke 5:17, 54
Luke 5:32, 54
Luke 6:9, 54
Luke 6:18, 19, 54
Luke 7:7, 54
Luke 7:29, 35, 54
Luke 7:50, 54, 59
Luke 8:12, 36, 48c, 50c, 54
Luke 8:47, 54
Luke 8:48, 59
Luke 9:2, 11, 42, 54
Luke 9:24, 54
Luke 10:29, 54
Luke 11:21–22, 56
Luke 11:4, 54
Luke 11:50, 42
Luke 12:57, 54
Luke 13:16, 54
Luke 13:23, 54
Luke 13:32, 54
Luke 14:4, 54
Luke 14:14, 54
Luke 15:7, 54
Luke 16:15, 54
Luke 17:15, 54

Luke 17:19c, 54
Luke 18:9, 54
Luke 18:13, 54
Luke 18:14, 54
Luke 18:26, 42c, 54
Luke 19:9, 54
Luke 19:10, 54, 56
Luke 20:20, 54
Luke 21:28, 54
Luke 22:19–20, 38, 57
Luke 22:20, 38, 43
Luke 22:35, 54
Luke 22:37, 57
Luke 22:39–44, 48
Luke 22:42, 161
Luke 22:43, 166
Luke 22:44, 105, 242
Luke 22:51, 54
Luke 23:35, 37, 39, 54
Luke 23:45, 42, 48
Luke 23:47, 50, 54
Luke 24:21, 54
Luke 24:25–27, 59
Luke 24:26, 43, 57

John 1:1–18, 45
John 1:12, 45
John 1:28, 56
John 1:29, 45, 57
John 1:36, 45
John 1:38–39, 46, 215
John 1:41, 49, 215
John 3:3, 5, 225, 233n53
John 3:6, 225
John 3:13, 226
John 3:14, 226
John 3:15–16, 36, 45
John 3:16, 225
John 3:17, 54
John 3:36, 57
John 4:14, 45
John 4:22, 54
John 4:42, 54
John 4:47, 54
John 5:13, 54
John 5:21, 45
John 5:30, 54
John 5:34, 54

John 6:33–58, 45
John 7:24, 54
John 8:44, 46
John 10:9, 54
John 10:10, 46, 56, 180
John 10:10, 28, 45
John 10:11–15, 265
John 10:17–18, 45
John 10:40, 215
John 11:1–46, 214
John 11:3, 215–16
John 11:3, 34, 215
John 11:11, 216
John 11:12, 54
John 11:14, 54
John 11:19, 215
John 11:25, 215
John 11:25–26, 45
John 11:33, 216
John 11:33, 35, 215
John 11:34, 215
John 11:37, 215
John 11:39, 216–17, 231n10
John 11:42, 216–17
John 11:43–44, 217, 231n10
John 11:45–46, 216
John 12:27, 47, 54
John 12:31, 46, 56
John 12:40, 54
John 14:6, 45
John 14:18, 166
John 14:26–27, 209
John 14:30, 46
John 16:8–10, 54
John 16:11, 46, 56
John 17:1–3, 45
John 17:3, 9–11, 21, 45, 49
John 17:25, 54
John 19:14, 56
John 19:30, 45
John 19:34–35, 45

Acts 2:21, 40, 47, 54
Acts 2:24, 54
Acts 2:32–36, 57
Acts 3:14, 54
Acts 4:9b, 12, 54
Acts 4:12, 54
Acts 4:19, 54
Acts 4:22, 30, 54
Acts 5:30–31, 57
Acts 5:31, 54
Acts 7:25, 54
Acts 7:34, 35, 54
Acts 7:52, 54
Acts 9:34, 54
Acts 10:22, 54
Acts 10:35, 54
Acts 10:36–43, 41
Acts 10:38, 54
Acts 10:38–43, 57
Acts 11:14, 54
Acts 13:10, 54
Acts 13:23, 54
Acts 13:26, 47, 54
Acts 13:39, 54
Acts 14:9b, 54
Acts 15:1, 11, 54
Acts 16:17, 54
Acts 16:30–31, 54
Acts 17:26, 208
Acts 17:31, 54
Acts 20:28, 56
Acts 22:14, 54
Acts 22:20, 42
Acts 24:15, 54
Acts 24:25, 54
Acts 27:20, 31, 54
Acts 27:34, 54
Acts 28:8, 27, 54
Acts 28:28, 54

Rom 1:16, 51
Rom 1:17, 51
Rom 1:32, 51
Rom 2:13, 51
Rom 3:4, 20, 24, 26, 28, 30, 51
Rom 3:5, 21, 22, 25–26, 51
Rom 3:7, 48, 72, 105–6, 112, 159n48, 241–42, 249n22
Rom 3:9, 36, 45, 56
Rom 3:10, 51
Rom 3:22–26, 57
Rom 3:23, 258
Rom 3:23–25, 57, 258
Rom 3:24, 37, 51, 58
Rom 3:24–25, 35
Rom 3:24–25, 28, 30, 35
Rom 3:25, 39, 45, 47, 51, 63n40
Rom 4:2, 5, 51
Rom 4:3, 5, 6, 9, 11, 13, 22, 51
Rom 4:5, 22–25, 35
Rom 4:12, 54, 119
Rom 4:17, 51
Rom 4:22–25, 58
Rom 5:1, 35
Rom 5:1, 9, 51
Rom 5:6–8, 34, 41
Rom 5:6–10, 38, 58
Rom 5:7, 51
Rom 5:8, 268
Rom 5:9, 35, 51, 58
Rom 5:9–10, 51
Rom 5:10, 51
Rom 5:11, 3, 16, 31, 51, 94, 113n7, 179
Rom 5:14–15, 40, 58
Rom 5:16, 51
Rom 5:17, 21, 51
Rom 5:21, 36, 45
Rom 5:26, 47
Rom 6:3–11, 40, 58
Rom 6:4–5, 47
Rom 6:6 (7–12), 56
Rom 6:7, 35, 51, 58
Rom 6:12–14, 36, 45
Rom 6:13, 16, 18–20, 51
Rom 7:10, 53
Rom 7:14–25, 56
Rom 7:14, 36, 45
Rom 7:24, 51
Rom 8:3, 36, 39, 45, 56
Rom 8:3, 14–17, 58
Rom 8:10, 51
Rom 8:16–17, 49
Rom 8:19–22, 56
Rom 8:23, 37, 51
Rom 8:24, 51
Rom 8:30, 33, 35, 51
Rom 8:38–39, 36

Rom 9:27, 51
Rom 9:30–31, 51
Rom 10:3–6, 10, 51
Rom 10:9, 13, 51
Rom 10:10, 51
Rom 11:11, 51
Rom 11:14, 26, 51
Rom 11:15, 51, 58
Rom 11:26, 51
Rom 13:11, 51
Rom 14:17, 51
Rom 15:31, 51

1 Cor 1:18, 36
1 Cor 1:18, 21, 51
1 Cor 1:30, 37, 51
1 Cor 3:15, 51
1 Cor 4:4, 51
1 Cor 5:5, 51
1 Cor 5:7, 38
1 Cor 5:7–8, 56
1 Cor 6:11, 35, 51, 58
1 Cor 6:20, 37, 51
1 Cor 7:11, 37, 51
1 Cor 7:16, 51
1 Cor 7:23, 37, 51
1 Cor 8:11, 34, 41
1 Cor 9:22, 51
1 Cor 10:33, 51
1 Cor 11:20–26, 38
1 Cor 11:23–25, 57
1 Cor 11:25, 38
1 Cor 11:25a, 57
1 Cor 15:2, 36, 51
1 Cor 15:3, 57–58
1 Cor 15:3–4, 34, 41
1 Cor 15:10, 265
1 Cor 15:19–26, 169
1 Cor 15:23, 56
1 Cor 15:26, 36
1 Cor 15:54–56, 36

2 Cor 1:6, 51
2 Cor 1:10, 51
2 Cor 2:15, 36, 51
2 Cor 3:9, 51
2 Cor 5:14–15, 17, 21, 58
2 Cor 5:17, 226

2 Cor 5:18–19, 51
2 Cor 5:18–20, 37, 51, 58
2 Cor 5:21, 39, 51
2 Cor 6:2, 51
2 Cor 6:7, 14, 51
2 Cor 7:10, 51
2 Cor 9:9, 10, 51
2 Cor 10:3–4, 56
2 Cor 11:15, 51

Gal 1:4, 34–35, 41, 50, 56
Gal 2:16, 46, 50
Gal 2:16–17, 34, 58
Gal 2:17, 36, 50
Gal 2:19–21, 58
Gal 2:19b, 39
Gal 2:21, 50
Gal 3:6, 21, 50
Gal 3:8, 58
Gal 3:10–14, 57
Gal 3:11, 50
Gal 3:13, 37, 50, 57
Gal 3:22, 36, 45
Gal 3:8, 11, 24, 50
Gal 3:8, 24, 34, 58
Gal 4:3, 9, 56
Gal 4:4–5, 37, 57
Gal 4:5, 50
Gal 5:4, 50
Gal 5:5, 50

Eph 1:7, 14, 37, 52
Eph 1:13, 52
Eph 1:20–22, 56
Eph 2:2, 5, 56
Eph 2:3–5, 56
Eph 2:5, 8, 52
Eph 2:16, 52, 58
Eph 4:8, 56
Eph 4:24, 52
Eph 4:30, 37, 52
Eph 5:9, 52
Eph 5:16, 52
Eph 5:23, 52
Eph 6:1, 52
Eph 6:12, 56
Eph 6:14, 52
Eph 6:17, 52

Phil 1:7, 50
Phil 1:11, 50
Phil 1:19, 28, 50
Phil 2:12, 50
Phil 3:6, 50
Phil 3:6, 9, 50
Phil 3:10, 163
Phil 3:20, 50
Phil 3:20–21, 36
Phil 4:8, 50

Col 1:13, 51
Col 1:14, 37, 51, 57
Col 1:20a, 57–58
Col 1:20–22, 51
Col 2:10, 15, 20, 56
Col 2:15, 56
Col 4:1, 51
Col 4:5, 51

1 Thess 1:10, 50
1 Thess 2:16, 50
1 Thess 5:8, 9, 50
1 Thess 5:9–10, 34, 41

2 Thess 2:10, 50
2 Thess 2:13, 50
2 Thess 3:2, 50

1 Tim 1:1, 52
1 Tim 1:9, 52
1 Tim 1:15, 52
1 Tim 2:3, 52
1 Tim 2:4, 15, 52
1 Tim 3:16, 52
1 Tim 4:10, 52
1 Tim 4:16, 52
1 Tim 6:11, 52

2 Tim 1:9, 52
2 Tim 1:10, 52
2 Tim 2:10, 52
2 Tim 2:10–12, 49
2 Tim 2:12, 58
2 Tim 2:22, 52
2 Tim 3:11, 52
2 Tim 3:15, 52
2 Tim 3:16, 52

2 Tim 4:8, 52
2 Tim 4:17–18, 52
2 Tim 4:18, 52

Titus 1:3, 52
Titus 1:3–4, 52
Titus 1:8, 52
Titus 2:10, 13, 52
Titus 2:11, 52
Titus 2:14, 37, 52, 57
Titus 3:4, 6, 52
Titus 3:5, 52
Titus 3:7, 52, 58

Heb 1:9, 54
Heb 1:14, 54
Heb 2:3, 10, 54
Heb 2:14–15, 56, 58
Heb 2:14–18, 47
Heb 2:17, 54
Heb 4:15–16, 24
Heb 5:7, 54
Heb 5:7–9, 48
Heb 5:9, 54, 58
Heb 5:13, 54
Heb 6:9, 54
Heb 7:2, 54
Heb 7:22, 57
Heb 7:25, 54
Heb 8:6, 57
Heb 9:1–14, 48
Heb 9:1–10:18, 57
Heb 9:5, 39, 47, 54
Heb 9:12, 15, 54
Heb 9:15a, 57
Heb 9:15b, 57
Heb 9:28, 54
Heb 10:38, 54
Heb 11:4, 54
Heb 11:7, 54
Heb 11:7, 33, 54
Heb 12:11, 54
Heb 12:13, 54
Heb 12:23, 54

Jas 1:1, 46
Jas 1:20, 51
Jas 1:21, 51

Jas 2:1, 45
Jas 2:10, 57
Jas 2:14, 51
Jas 2:17, 46
Jas 2:23, 51
Jas 3:18, 51
Jas 4:12, 51
Jas 5:6, 16, 51
Jas 5:15, 20, 51
Jas 5:16, 51

1 Pet 1:5, 9–10, 53
1 Pet 1:18, 53
1 Pet 1:18–19, 47
1 Pet 2:1, 53
1 Pet 2:2, 53
1 Pet 2:19–21, 59
1 Pet 2:20, 59
1 Pet 2:24, 53
1 Pet 2:24–25, 47, 59
1 Pet 3:3–5, 166
1 Pet 3:12, 18, 53
1 Pet 3:16–17, 59
1 Pet 3:21, 53
1 Pet 3:21–22, 47
1 Pet 4:1–2, 13–16, 59
1 Pet 4:13–14, 59
1 Pet 4:13–16, 58
1 Pet 4:18, 53
1 Pet 5:10, 59

2 Pet 1:1, 53
2 Pet 1:1, 11, 20, 53
2 Pet 1:13, 53
2 Pet 2:5, 21, 53
2 Pet 2:7, 9, 53
2 Pet 2:7–8, 53
2 Pet 3:2, 18, 53
2 Pet 3:13, 53
2 Pet 3:15, 53

1 John 1:9, 54, 59
1 John 2:1, 29, 54
1 John 2:2, 31, 45, 54
1 John 2:29, 54
1 John 3:2, 49
1 John 3:7, 54
1 John 3:7, 10, 54

1 John 3:8, 46, 56
1 John 3:12, 54
1 John 4:10, 54
1 John 4:10, 31, 45, 54
1 John 4:14, 54

Jude 1:3, 52
Jude 1:5, 23, 52
Jude 1:25, 52

Rev 1:1, 4, 9, 46
Rev 1:5, 53
Rev 1:5b–6, 49
Rev 5:6, 46
Rev 5:9, 53
Rev 5:10, 58
Rev 7:10, 53
Rev 7:17, 46
Rev 12:10, 53
Rev 14:3–4, 53
Rev 15:3, 46, 53
Rev 16:5, 7, 53
Rev 19:1, 53
Rev 19:2, 53
Rev 19:9, 46
Rev 19:11, 53
Rev 21:23, 46
Rev 22:1, 46
Rev 22:3, 46
Rev 22:8, 46
Rev 22:11, 53

Book of Mormon

1 Ne 1:9, 122
1 Ne 1:19, 123
1 Ne 1:19–20, 123
1 Ne 2:4, 223
1 Ne 2:6, 223
1 Ne 2:11–13, 123, 223
1 Ne 2:13, 123
1 Ne 2:16, 123, 260
1 Ne 2:16–17, 223
1 Ne 2:18, 223
1 Ne 5:14, 116
1 Ne 6:2, 116
1 Ne 8:14, 223
1 Ne 8:18, 223

1 Ne 8:37, 224
1 Ne 10:9, 97
1 Ne 10:21, 22
1 Ne 12:6, 228
1 Ne 12:11, 228
1 Ne 13:41, 34–35, 39–41, 117
1 Ne 15:34, 22
1 Ne 17:20–22, 123
1 Ne 17:22, 123
1 Ne 19:5, 123
1 Ne 19:23, 120

2 Ne 1:15, 263
2 Ne 2:3, 97
2 Ne 2:6, 264
2 Ne 2:6–10, 95
2 Ne 2:7, 70, 97
2 Ne 2:8, 97
2 Ne 2:9, 98
2 Ne 2:10–12, 49
2 Ne 2:16, 260
2 Ne 2:26–27, 260
2 Ne 3:4, 116
2 Ne 4:21, 264
2 Ne 4:33, 264
2 Ne 9:7, 98–99, 101
2 Ne 9:7–12, 95
2 Ne 9:8–10, 80
2 Ne 9:10, 36
2 Ne 9:10, 19, 6
2 Ne 9:18, 23, 80
2 Ne 9:21, 263
2 Ne 9:25–26, 99
2 Ne 10:24, 38
2 Ne 10:25, 99, 101–2
2 Ne 25:1, 123
2 Ne 25:1–2, 5, 123
2 Ne 25:2, 124
2 Ne 25:16, 101, 117
2 Ne 25:18, 124
2 Ne 25:20, 124
2 Ne 25:23, 38, 272
2 Ne 25:23–27, 124
2 Ne 25:24, 124
2 Ne 28:28, 192
2 Ne 33:9, 38

Jacob 1:8, 80
Jacob 2:21–31, 252
Jacob 2:22, 252
Jacob 3:11, 80
Jacob 4:5, 70
Jacob 4:11, 38, 101, 129
Jacob 4:11–12, 101
Jacob 4:12, 101, 112, 119
Jacob 4:17, 119
Jacob 5:3, 118
Jacob 5:7, 11–13, 18, 118
Jacob 5:20, 24, 118
Jacob 5:20, 24, 14, 21–26, 118
Jacob 5:27, 119
Jacob 5:41, 47, 118
Jacob 5:50, 119
Jacob 5:52, 54, 65, 119
Jacob 5:61, 119
Jacob 7:6–7, 126
Jacob 7:9, 102
Jacob 7:12, 102

Enos 1:13, 117
Enos 1:14–17, 117

W of M, 1:13, 245

Mos 2:3, 238, 242
Mos 2:8, 238
Mos 2:12, 237
Mos 2:14, 18, 237
Mos 2:19, 241
Mos 2:32, 237
Mos 3:5, 241, 243, 247n12
Mos 3:7, 58, 72, 105, 112, 159, 241–42, 249n22
Mos 3:7, 11, 106
Mos 3:8, 241
Mos 3:9, 241
Mos 3:9–10, 105
Mos 3:11, 72, 105, 242
Mos 3:14, 245
Mos 3:15, 106, 242
Mos 3:16, 106, 242
Mos 3:18, 106, 242
Mos 3:19, 106, 185, 242, 253
Mos 4:2, 107, 243

Mos 4:6–4:7, 106–7
Mos 4:11, 240
Mos 4:27, 265
Mos 4:28, 259
Mos 4:29, 252
Mos 5:8–10, 161
Mos 6:2, 238
Mos 6:3, 239
Mos 7:19, 126
Mos 7:20, 126
Mos 7:25, 237
Mos 7:27, 126
Mos 7:28, 126
Mos 11:3, 237
Mos 11:6, 237
Mos 11:12, 237
Mos 12:20–24, 126
Mos 12:27–28, 126
Mos 12:28, 244
Mos 12:29, 259
Mos 12:32, 244
Mos 13:27, 244
Mos 13:27–35, 126
Mos 13:28, 102–3
Mos 13:29–30, 244
Mos 13:31–32, 245
Mos 15:1, 237, 243
Mos 15:6–7, 244
Mos 15:7, 243–44
Mos 15:9, 49
Mos 15:10, 243
Mos 15:13–14, 243
Mos 15:18, 103, 243
Mos 15:19, 103
Mos 15:20, 103, 249n24
Mos 15:21–26, 101
Mos 15:24, 103
Mos 16:14, 244
Mos 17:10, 103, 249n25
Mos 18:1, 238
Mos 18:3–4, 238
Mos 18:8, 236
Mos 18:8–9, 208
Mos 18:8–10, 24, 230n8
Mos 18:16, 238
Mos 18:17, 238
Mos 18:35, 238
Mos 23:7, 248

Mos 26:1, 239
Mos 26:1–2, 240
Mos 26:4, 240
Mos 26:5, 240, 248n18
Mos 27:1, 239
Mos 27:25, 253
Mos 28:2, 125
Mos 29:13, 240
Mos 29:16–17, 240
Mos 29:38, 237

Alma 1:19, 127
Alma 5:13–14, 78
Alma 5:15–19, 78, 80
Alma 5:21, 108–9
Alma 5:27, 108
Alma 7:10, 226
Alma 7:11, 226
Alma 7:11–12, 7, 44, 96, 207
Alma 7:11–13, 7
Alma 7:13, 226
Alma 7:21, 22
Alma 11:37, 22, 272
Alma 12:16, 32, 80
Alma 13:5, 108
Alma 13:30, 80
Alma 15:1–2. 77
Alma 15:2, 5, 77
Alma 15:3–4, 77
Alma 15:5, 77
Alma 15:7, 77
Alma 15:8–9, 77
Alma 18:24–29, 125
Alma 19:12–13, 125
Alma 19:16, 125
Alma 19:29, 125
Alma 21:9, 109–10
Alma 21:9–11, 125
Alma 22:6, 125
Alma 22:7, 18, 125
Alma 22:14, 109–10
Alma 24:10, 9
Alma 24:13, 110
Alma 25:15, 125
Alma 25:16, 101, 125
Alma 26:15, 264
Alma 31:10, 127

Alma 31:16, 127
Alma 31:5, 245
Alma 33:22, 108–9
Alma 34:8, 103–4
Alma 34:9, 104, 227
Alma 34:9–13, 7
Alma 34:9–13, 7
Alma 34:9–16, 99
Alma 34:10–11, 104
Alma 34:10–15, 70
Alma 34:11, 104, 227
Alma 34:12, 104, 227
Alma 34:13, 7, 70, 104, 227–28
Alma 34:14, 228
Alma 34:15, 264
Alma 34:15–41, 96
Alma 34:16, 7
Alma 34:18, 264
Alma 34:32–33, 270
Alma 34:34, 270
Alma 34:38, 269
Alma 39:9, 80
Alma 40:26, 22
Alma 42:13–25, 49
Alma 42:14–26, 95
Alma 42:15, 80, 109
Alma 42:22–24, 99
Alma 42:23, 81, 109
Alma 42:25, 81
Alma 42:7–9, 11, 80
Alma 42:7, 12–15, 72
Alma 42:7, 12, 14, 80
Alma 45:10–11, 128
Alma 46:13–15, 127
Alma 46:18, 127
Alma 46:21–24, 127
Alma 46:24, 27, 127

Hel 5:9, 110
Hel 14:16–18, 80

3 Ne 8–10, 23
3 Ne 9:13, 206
3 Ne 11:11, 161, 188
3 Ne 12:30, 80
3 Ne 21:26, 116

3 Ne 23:1–2, 121
3 Ne 23:1–5, 121
3 Ne 23:2, 122
3 Ne 23:9, 11, 122
3 Ne 23:13, 122, 130n8

Morm 5:11, 265
Morm 9:32–33, 96

Moro 7:19, 269
Moro 7:28, 268
Moro 7:41, 111
Moro 8:8–17, 269
Moro 8:16, 267
Moro 8:20, 111
Moro 10:8, 18, 30, 269
Moro 10:32, 269

Doctrine and Covenants

D&C 1:31, 146
D&C 2:1–3, 24
D&C 6:9, 145
D&C 6:20, 263
D&C 6:36–37, 135
D&C 8:1, 133
D&C 18:11, 145
D&C 19:2, 3, 11, 149
D&C 19:16–17, 146
D&C 19:18, 149, 161, 249n22
D&C 19:20, 146
D&C 25:1, 168
D&C 25:3, 166
D&C 25:5, 166
D&C 25:7, 164
D&C 25:10, 13, 15, 168
D&C 25:11–12, 164–65
D&C 25:14, 170–71
D&C 25:15, 169
D&C 29:1, 133
D&C 29:34, 132
D&C 29:39–40, 145
D&C 29:44–45, 145
D&C 37:3, 163
D&C 45:3, 149

D&C 45:3–5, 135, 200
D&C 45:4, 149
D&C 50:24, 151
D&C 50:40–42, 143
D&C 57:3, 163
D&C 61:1–2, 132
D&C 62:1, 135
D&C 63:17–18, 80
D&C 74:7, 133
D&C 76:50–70, 74
D&C 76:51, 153
D&C 76:54, 153
D&C 76:58–59, 152
D&C 76:69, 133, 153
D&C 76:102, 145
D&C 76:107, 149
D&C 78:19, 269
D&C 84:20–22, 153
D&C 84:44–45, 141
D&C 84:46, 151
D&C 88:6, 146
D&C 88:12–13, 141
D&C 88:17, 148
D&C 88:21, 144
D&C 88:32, 145, 152, 207
D&C 88:35, 145
D&C 88:38–39, 140
D&C 88:38–40, 141
D&C 88:40, 140
D&C 88:41, 151
D&C 88:64–65, 265
D&C 88:67, 151

D&C 88:106, 149
D&C 88:107, 151
D&C 93:20, 139
D&C 93:4, 16, 149
D&C 93:21, 149
D&C 93:24, 141
D&C 93:29, 141
D&C 93:29–30, 139
D&C 93:31, 142, 145, 149
D&C 93:32, 142
D&C 93:36, 141
D&C 101:78, 260
D&C 107:19, 153
D&C 109:4, 144
D&C 110:4, 147
D&C 112:13, 148
D&C 121:37, 146, 253
D&C 121:41, 255
D&C 128:18, 25, 191
D&C 130:2, 67n103, 208, 270
D&C 132:19–20, 24, 74
D&C 132:20, 151
D&C 132:32, 163
D&C 133:50, 149
D&C 138:12–13, 70
D&C 138:2, 133
D&C 138:29–35, 24
D&C 138:32, 152
D&C 138:35, 153
D&C 138:4, 133
D&C 138:58, 153

Pearl of Great Price

Moses 1:1, 220
Moses 1:3, 220
Moses 1:4, 220
Moses 1:26, 220
Moses 1:28, 220
Moses 1:39, 73, 221
Moses 2:1, 221
Moses 2:30, 221
Moses 4:3, 159n48, 260
Moses 5:5–7, 70
Moses 5:7, 226
Moses 6:54, 207
Moses 7:18, 163, 230, 271
Moses 7:63–64, 194

Abr 1:4, 220
Abr 1:16, 220
Abr 1:19, 220–21
Abr 3:1–2, 220
Abr 3:3, 12, 221
Abr 3:3, 16, 221
Abr 3:12, 221
Abr 3:14, 221
Abr 3:15, 23–26, 221
Abr 3:22–26, 73
Abr 3:25–26, 221
Abr 3:26, 221

A of F 2, 207

The University of Illinois Press
is a founding member of the
Association of University Presses.
_____

University of Illinois Press
1325 South Oak Street
Champaign, IL 61820-6903
www.press.uillinois.edu